Robyn Ness

Sams **Teach Yourself**

Adobe®

Dreamweaver® CS5

in **24** Hours

SAMS   800 East 96th Street, Indianapolis, Indiana, 46240 USA

Sams Teach Yourself Adobe® Dreamweaver® CS5 in 24 Hours

Copyright © 2011 by Pearson Education

ISBN-13: 978-0-672-33330-9

ISBN-10: 0-672-33330-9

Library of Congress Cataloging-in-Publication Data:

Bruce, Betsy.

Sams teach yourself Adobe Dreamweaver CS5 in 24 hours / Betsy Bruce, John Ray, and Robyn Ness.

p. cm.

ISBN 978-0-672-33330-9 (pbk.)

1. Dreamweaver (Computer file) 2. Web sites—Authoring programs. 3. Web sites—Design. I. Ray, John, 1971- II. Ness, Robyn. III. Title. IV. Title: Teach yourself Adobe Dreamweaver CS5 in 24 hours.

TK5105.8885.D74B782157 2011

006.7'8—dc22

2010045974

Printed in the United States of America

First Printing December 2010

Trademarks

Warning and Disclaimer

Bulk Sales

Sams Publishing offers excellent discounts on this book when ordered in quantity for bulk purchases or special sales. For more information, please contact

**U.S. Corporate and Government Sales
1-800-382-3419
corpsales@pearsontechgroup.com**

For sales outside of the U.S., please contact

**International Sales
international@pearson.com**

Acquisitions Editor
Mark Taber

Development Editor
Songlin Qiu

Managing Editor
Kristy Hart

Project Editor
Andy Beaster

Indexer
Erika Millen

Proofreader
Dan Knott

Technical Editor
Scott Antall

Publishing Coordinator
Vanessa Evans

Cover Designer
Gary Adair

Compositor
Nonie Ratcliff

Table of Contents

About the Authors

Betsy Bruce is a developer and consultant who specializes in creating eLearning applications using Dreamweaver, Authorware, Captivate, and Flash. She was lead developer at the Cobalt Group in Seattle and was Manager of Technical Services at MediaPro, Inc. She is an Adobe-certified trainer for Dreamweaver, Contribute, Flash, Captivate, and Authorware.

John Ray is a Senior Business Analyst and leads the enterprise application development team for The Ohio State University Research Foundation. In his spare time, he has written a number of books, on topics ranging from IT security to operating systems and iPhone development—including *Sams Teach Yourself iPhone Application Development in 24 Hours*, *Sams Teach Yourself iPad Application Development in 24 Hours*, *Mac OS X Unleashed*, and *Maximum Linux Security*. He can be found on the web at http://www.johneray.com.

Robyn Ness is a web developer at The Ohio State University, focusing on issues of usability, information design, and content development. She has contributed to books on Dreamweaver, Adobe CS3, digital media production, and digital photography. In her spare time she takes a ridiculous number of digital photographs, some of which can be seen at floraphotographs.com.

Dedication

This book is dedicated to people who love their pets, who are nice to others, and who are excited by the prospect of learning new things. You're a rare and special group.

Acknowledgments

Many thanks to the group at Sams Publishing—Songlin Qiu, Mark Taber, and Scott Antall—for keeping the project under control and making sure that my words make sense!

Most of all, thanks to you, the reader, for being interested in taking up web development in Dreamweaver! You're about to venture into one of the most exciting, rewarding, and creative fields available to technology professionals today.

We Want to Hear from You!

As the reader of this book, *you* are our most important critic and commentator. We value your opinion and want to know what we're doing right, what we could do better, what areas you'd like to see us publish in, and any other words of wisdom you're willing to pass our way.

You can email or write me to let me know what you did or didn't like about this book—as well as what we can do to make our books stronger.

Please note that I cannot help you with technical problems related to the topic of this book, and that due to the high volume of mail I receive, I might not be able to reply to every message.

When you write, please be sure to include this book's title and author as well as your name and phone or email address. I will carefully review your comments and share them with the author and editors who worked on the book.

E-mail: feedback@samspublishing.com

Mail: Mark Taber
            Associate Publisher
            Sams Publishing
            800 East 96th Street
            Indianapolis, IN 46240 USA

Reader Services

Visit our website and register this book at informit.com/register for convenient access to any updates, downloads, or errata that might be available for this book.

Introduction

There was a time, not long ago, when the idea of using an application to develop websites was considered a travesty! The idea that an application could create code that would be clean, would be efficient, and would display properly in virtually any web browser seemed like pure fantasy.

Dreamweaver has forever changed how we think about web development. It is no longer the realm of the professional programmer. It is no longer a tangled mess of complicated codes and files. With the help of Dreamweaver, web development has become both a structured and a creative process. As a website development environment, it keeps your pages nice and neat and your links in working order. As a visual design tool, it frees you from the complexities of coding and allows you to focus on the content and look and feel of your site.

What is truly unique about Dreamweaver is that it can author virtually any type of website with any appearance. You may have heard someone say, "That site was made with such and such a tool." In Dreamweaver, the application helps you create your designs as you envision them, rather than trying to force you into a mold.

What Is Dreamweaver CS5?

Dreamweaver CS5 is the latest release of Adobe's award-winning HTML editor and web application development tool. Dreamweaver offers tools that can be adapted to a very design-centric environment, or a code-centric programming focus. The depth and maturity of the tools ensure that everyone, regardless of their skill level or needs, will be able to use Dreamweaver effectively.

Dreamweaver, like most Adobe products, is fully cross-platform. The Mac OS X and Windows versions of the software offer the same features, with very slight variations in look and feel. Projects that you create in Dreamweaver can easily be shared among Windows and Mac users alike.

Dreamweaver's openness doesn't end at the desktop—it extends to the servers it supports, as well. Using the built-in tools, you can create websites that are ready for almost any modern web server—and transfer them to your remote host without ever leaving the application.

Making use of the latest web technologies, Dreamweaver makes it simple to add design elements using Cascading Style Sheets, and dynamic interfaces with Spry AJAX components. These features can help you create a new, modern website, or transform an existing site into a compelling online experience featuring animation, drag-and-drop elements, drop-down menus, and much, much more!

What's New In Dreamweaver CS5?

In Dreamweaver CS5, Adobe has adapted to recent advancements in web technology. They have continued their work to make Dreamweaver's code more streamlined and easy to apply so beginners and experts alike can design a high-quality website. They've also cleaned up some rough edges and made site management in Dreamweaver even simpler. A few of the changes you'll find in this version are listed here:

▶ Streamlined site setup for getting into page design faster and easier

▶ Fireworks and the basics of creating site graphics

▶ Cleaner implementation of cascading stylesheets in Dreamweaver's array of pre-set layouts

▶ Integration with Adobe BrowserLab, which shows you what your designs look like on different browsers you may not have access to personally

▶ Content Management Support for WordPress and other widely used CMS systems

▶ The HTML5 features to leverage one of the latest (and coolest) web technologies

Dreamweaver never ceases to amaze with the range of features it provides. As you work through the 24 hours in this book, you'll find information on everything from the basics of site file structures all the way to content management systems and version control.

Who Should Use Dreamweaver CS5?

One word: everyone. First-time web developers will love the ability to visually develop a site using tools that feel natural and provide instant feedback. Experienced developers may choose to start a layout visually and then switch to a code view to finish it off by hand. Dreamweaver gives you the flexibility to work the way you want, without getting in the way.

Who Should Use This Book?

This book is for anyone new to Dreamweaver CS5 and anyone already using the application who wants to take it to the next level. Beginners will quickly learn how to create new pages, create and manage CSS, and deploy websites. More experienced readers will find the tips and tricks they need in order to use the application to its fullest.

Conventions Used in This Book

This book uses several design elements and conventions to help you prioritize and reference the information it contains:

- ▶ New terms appear in a **semibold typeface**.

- ▶ When you are asked to type or enter text, that text appears in **bold**.

- ▶ Menu options are separated by a comma. For example, when you should open the File menu and choose the New Project menu option, the text says "Select File, New Project."

- ▶ A special `monospace` font is used on programming-related terms and language, and code.

- ▶ Placeholders—words or characters that represent the real words or characters you would type in code—appear in *`italic monospace`*.

- ▶ Some code statements presented in this book are too long to appear on a single line. In these cases, a line-continuation character is used to indicate that the following line is a continuation of the current statement.

NOTE

Items of Interest

Notes offer interesting information related to the current topic.

TIP

Useful Tidbits

Tips offer advice or show you an easier way to perform a task.

CAUTION

Potential Pitfalls

Cautions alert you to a possible problem and suggest ways to avoid it.

HOUR 1
A World Wide Web of Dreamweaver Possibilities

The World Wide Web is a collection of interconnected documents created by people like you and me. This enormous network of information serves people all over the world. Today, researchers and students can find and share information with peers around the world without setting foot outside their homes, offices, and schools. Services like InformIT's Safari take traditional printed media (like this book) and make it available online. The World Wide Web is the world's new digital library, and you can contribute to it!

Maybe you dream of sharing information over the Web. For instance, you can share your portfolio, family pictures, creative writing, or genealogical research with friends, family, or the entire world! Or maybe you want to sell T-shirts, photos, cookie mixes, books, or note cards online. Perhaps you have to create a website for the company or public agency that employs you. These are all excellent applications for Adobe Dreamweaver.

I've received hundreds of emails from readers around the world who, like you, purchased this book to learn Dreamweaver. Some of these readers send me links to the websites they created using this book, and I'm thrilled to view them. Other readers are students who use this book in a course on HTML and web development. Please keep those links coming!

WHAT YOU'LL LEARN IN THIS HOUR:

▶ Types of web pages you can create with Dreamweaver

▶ Examples of text, images, hyperlinks, forms, multi-media, interactivity, and page layout design created in Dreamweaver

▶ How Dreamweaver can create reusable, updatable web pages and web page elements

▶ What the built-in file transfer tool can do

NOTE

Can Information on the Web Be Trusted?

The Web allows anyone to present information online—*anyone*. This openness means that as an information consumer, you need to be wary of what you read. Wikipedia, for example (http://www.wikipedia.org), provides a reader-contributed encyclopedia. Wikipedia articles are written and edited by the visitors themselves, people who may or may not be experts. Although Wikipedia provides some level of review, other sites may actively present information that is patently false. You need to be careful that you get information from a trusted and credible source. When in doubt, look for other sources to confirm or refute what you read online.

What Can You Do with Dreamweaver?

Dreamweaver is the most popular professional web creation tool, and you are in excellent company as a user of this exceptional software. Dreamweaver is integrated into the industry-standard Adobe Creative Suite. This makes Dreamweaver adoption a clean and effective addition into a content publishing workflow. Many large corporations standardize on Dreamweaver as their web development tool of choice. Dreamweaver is also a popular tool for independent web developers who work on websites for their clients. As a cross-platform tool, Dreamweaver works virtually identically on Macintosh and Windows-based computers and is popular on both platforms.

Defining the Technology

The foundation of Dreamweaver, and web development as a whole, is the Hypertext Markup Language (HTML), a language used to describe the structure of content so that it can be viewed over the Web in a web browser. In this book, we'll use the most modern version of HTML called XHTML (Extensible Hypertext Markup Language). Dreamweaver writes the XHTML for you, so you don't need to know how to write XHTML to get started using Dreamweaver. I suggest to all of my students and to you, the reader of this book, that learning some XHTML will help you become a more professional and flexible web page author. Hour 7, "Looking Under the Hood: Exploring HTML," introduces you to viewing and editing code in Dreamweaver.

If you are new to web development, you might not know some of the possibilities available to you in Dreamweaver. This hour explores examples of the types of elements you can add to your web pages no matter what its topic or purpose. Most people who are interested in creating web pages have spent some time looking at websites. Many of you are experts at navigating around and getting information on the Web! Now that you are learning web development, you'll begin to look at web pages differently: Instead of reading a column of text, you'll now think, *How can I create a column of text in Dreamweaver?*

One of the best ways to learn is by examining examples of web pages you find while browsing the Web. Most browser software has a Source or Page

Source command (usually under the View menu) that enables you to view the HTML code of a web page. Even better, you can actually save a web page to your hard drive by selecting the Save Page As or the Save As command under the browser's File menu. After you save the web page, you can open the files in Dreamweaver and examine the page's structure. This is a great way to figure out how a web page author created an effect. If you are a beginner, you probably won't understand everything in the web page, but this is still a great way to learn by emulating others.

If you don't perfectly understand everything in this hour, don't worry; later hours cover all the concepts with step-by-step instructions so that you can follow along. This hour gives you an overview of the types of web pages you can create with Dreamweaver.

Dissecting Website Examples

FloraPhotographs.com—a site specializing in macro photography of flowers—serves as a point of reference for many examples throughout this book. FloraPhotographs.com uses a modern web design using the latest web technologies, such as a full CSS layout and dynamic AJAX elements. Don't know what that means? Don't worry—you'll be a web acronym expert by the end of the book! Best of all, FloraPhotographs.com was designed in Dreamweaver, so it is an example of the types of designs you can create yourself!

Basic Web Page Elements: Text, Images, and Hyperlinks

Most web pages have at least these three minimal elements:

► Text

► Images

► Hyperlinks

Figure 1.1 shows that the Flora Photographs **home page**, the web page that is the entry point for the website, contains only those elements, plus a search box in the upper-right corner of the page. Those three elements are the foundation of most websites, providing information (text) along with graphical support (images), plus a method to navigate to other pages (hyperlinks). Although Flora Photographs is a graphics-heavy site, it still

NOTE
Should I Learn Dreamweaver or XHTML First?

This is the-chicken-or-the-egg question that comes up often when I speak with people who want to learn about web design and development. I think that it's best to learn a tool such as Dreamweaver first and then expand your knowledge of XHTML as you complete real-world projects. You will have more context for the XHTML you are learning after you have a basic understanding of Dreamweaver.

CAUTION
Copyright Laws and Content

Remember that there are copyright laws protecting the intellectual property of companies and individuals, including websites. You cannot copy the content (text, HTML, or images) from copyright-protected websites. It's also bad form to outright steal other people's page design.

includes obvious text and hyperlink elements so that users can find their bearings.

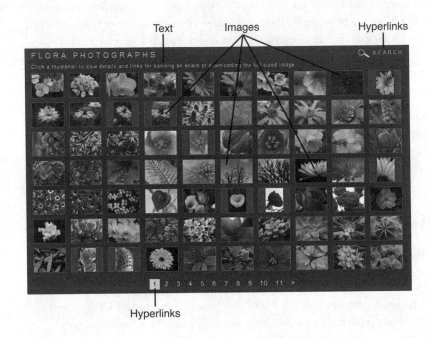

FIGURE 1.1 Flora Photographs contain text, image, and hyperlink elements.

NOTE

Choosing Fonts

Fonts were traditionally developed for print, but several new fonts have been developed to be easy to read on a computer screen. Arial, Verdana, and Trebuchet are three popular screen fonts. You can find out more about web typography at http://www.webstyleguide.com/wsg3/8-typography/.

Notice that there are several styles of text in Figure 1.1. The site title is larger and presented in a different color than the instructions and link text. Controlling the size and coloring of text is an effective way to guide your users' eyes where you want them on the page. Less important elements are smaller, whereas more significant navigation is frequently larger and highlighted.

Obviously, there are also many images in Figure 1.1. In web pages, images are always external image files. The XHTML tells the browser where the image should appear in the web page. In the Flora Photographs example, there are dozens of images onscreen. These are all separate references to image files within the site. The web browser must request and display each image separately when the page loads. Sometimes a single large image is broken into smaller pieces to improve page loading times and to give the designer additional flexibility in the layout. Dividing an image into smaller pieces is called slicing and is discussed in Hour 9, "Making Web Graphics in Fireworks CS5." Images can also have transparent elements—such as the "lens" of the search magnifying glass in Figure 1.1. In this small icon, the lens portion is transparent, allowing the background color of the site to show through.

There are numerous hyperlinks in Figure 1.1. Clicking these hyperlinks takes you to different pages of flowers, a search screen, or other parts of the Flora Photographs site. By default, hyperlinks appear in blue text and are underlined, but you can change this using CSS. Flora Photographs, for example, removes the underline from links but adds a rollover effect so that the links highlight when your mouse cursor is over them. You'll learn about creating hyperlinks in Hour 5, "Making Hyperlinks, Anchors, and Mailto Links," and formatting them using CSS is covered in Hour 11, "Formatting Web Pages with Cascading Style Sheets."

Dreamweaver can add a hyperlink to an image as well as text, as with the magnifying glass in Figure 1.1. You can even define just a small section of an image as a hyperlink by creating an imagemap. Hour 8, "Displaying Images," introduces you to image properties and the different types of images you can display in a web page, and shows you how to add image maps to web pages.

Page Layout

When creating web pages, you need to keep in mind that people will be viewing your design at different screen resolutions (for example, 800×600, 1024×768, 1280×1024) and might not have the browser window maximized to take up the whole screen. **Page layout**, the design and positioning of text and images on the web page, often requires a lot of thought, time, and experimentation.

The Flora Photographs website has a clean page style that makes it easy to view in browser windows of various sizes. The page layout for this website uses CSS, covered in Hour 11 and Hour 12, "Using CSS for Positioning." Figure 1.2 shows a page from Flora Photographs open in the Dreamweaver editor. The CSS Styles panel is open on the right side of the screen, displaying a list of the CSS rules applied to this website. The Dreamweaver interface and other items visible in Figure 1.2 are covered in depth throughout this book.

CSS enables you to format the way text appears, how various XHTML tags appear, and the positioning of various layout elements on the web page. Figure 1.2 displays the CSS Styles panel on the right side. All the CSS definitions are listed under the external style sheet name nav.css. An external

TIP

Exporting from Page Layout Software

You can export web pages from most software programs, including Word, and then use Dreamweaver to clean up and edit the results. Test a representative page before you decide whether this method works for the content with which you are working.

style sheet enables all the pages in the site to share the same styles. And, best of all, the external style sheet enables the website developers to make a change to a single file to update the entire website.

CSS layout   CSS styles

CSS is the standard for designing page layouts for web pages, though it is still an evolving technology. The positioning and page layouts subset of the CSS language is sometimes called **CSS-P**. This subset defines page design essentials such as the widths and heights of elements, whether they float beside adjoining elements or break to a new line, and whether the elements stack on top of other elements.

As more devices large and small incorporate web browsers, people might be viewing your web pages on a mobile phone or even in a flat-panel screen embedded in the refrigerator door! Figure 1.3 shows Adobe Device Central CS5, which installs with Dreamweaver CS5. You launch this application to emulate how different devices display a web page. It's important to test your page layout so that viewers using different devices have a pleasant viewing experience on your website. You'll further explore the emulator and mobile devices in Hour 13, "Creating CSS for Mobile Devices and Printing."

Forms: Collecting Data for E-Commerce, Newsletters, or Anything Else

Some websites have a business purpose for exchanging information with visitors, whether it be selling automobiles (http://www.acura.com),

FIGURE 1.3
The Adobe Device Central CS5 emulator enables you to test your websites on various mobile and small-screen devices.

auctioning movie memorabilia (http://www.ebay.com), planning a healthier diet (http://www.mypyramid.gov), or selling a design on a T-shirt, coffee mug, or mouse pad (http://www.cafepress.com). All these websites offer visitors the option of entering information into **forms** in order to purchase goods or receive information. Forms enable websites to become a two-way conduit as a visitor not only views information on the website but also can send information back.

The Flora Photographs site uses web forms to collect user feedback and to provide an interactive search feature for users. The search form shown in Figure 1.4 consists of radio buttons, a drop-down menu, and a submit button, three of the form elements that are discussed in Hour 21, "Creating a Form and Collecting Data."

Creating scripts is an advanced topic that is beyond the scope of this book on Dreamweaver, but examples of scripting languages and locations to download scripts are discussed in Hour 22, "Sending and Reacting to Form Data." The Flora Photographs website uses PHP, a popular and widely supported free scripting language. You can tell that the script is written for PHP because the file extension is .php. Creating a script to search a website is the tiny tip of the iceberg of what PHP can do.

FIGURE 1.4
A search form enables the viewer to enter information and then submit it to a script that returns results.

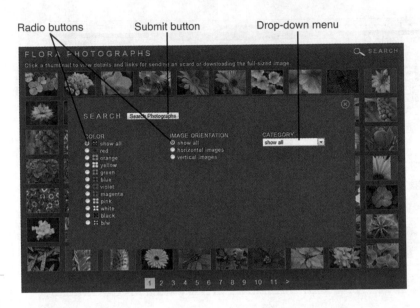

Scripting for Forms

Although creating forms is easy, creating the scripts to make those forms function can be complicated. Don't assume that web design is the most difficult part of a web development project—sometimes the scripting work is an arduous process.

Easy Online Sales

As you grow your web presence and begin to consider possible online sales, sites like Café Press can help! This online service allows you to create a wide variety of branded products and sell them with very little overhead and no additional programming for your website!

FloraPhotographs.com uses PHP to maintain its catalog of images and to generate e-cards that can be sent to other people. These **dynamic web pages**, in which the page content changes depending on the user's actions, can also be created in Dreamweaver. After you master the 24 hours in this book, you might decide to advance to learning a server application language such as PHP. It's perfectly realistic, however, to continue creating **static web pages** (the opposite of dynamic web pages), such as the ones described in this book, and be a successful web page author.

In an e-commerce site, such as the Flora Photograph's CafePress.com site, an HTML form collects information about the purchaser.

Figure 1.5 displays a form that includes text fields and drop-down menus to collect address information. An asterisk (*) is a common way to signify that a text field must be filled out in order to submit the form. When you're creating your own forms, Dreamweaver provides a Validate Form behavior, scripted in JavaScript, to make sure that the visitor enters the correct type of information (see Hour 21).

Multimedia

Many websites include movies, audio, music, animations, 3D renderings, and other multimedia elements. These elements require that you download

FIGURE 1.5
This form collects information about the purchaser, and a script validates the form, making sure that all required information is entered before the form is processed.

and install a player application, such as Flash (http://www.adobe.com/flash), QuickTime (http://apple.com/quicktime), Windows Media (http://microsoft.com/windows/windowsmedia), or RealPlayer (http://www.real.com/), to see or hear the multimedia files. Web pages created in Dreamweaver can automatically trigger the download of the appropriate player, making it easy for the website visitor. As more and more people have access to higher-bandwidth connections, a greater number of websites include multimedia files that require more transfer capacity.

Many pages, such as YouTube (youtube.com) shown in Figure 1.6, have turned to Flash for creating completely cross-platform video and animation fields. In these cases, an Adobe Flash file containing video, audio, and animation effects plays when you initially load the web page...if you have the Flash player installed, that is! But the large majority of computers have the ever-present Flash player, so most viewers are capable of seeing Flash movies. Although Adobe Flash software is required to create Flash movies from scratch, Dreamweaver is capable of inserting, configuring, and previewing Flash movies. Hour 10, "Adding Flash and Other Multimedia to a Web Page," explains how to add Flash and other types of multimedia to a web page.

NOTE

Installed Player Applications

Often an operating system (such as Macintosh OS X or Windows Vista) comes with several popular multimedia player applications already installed. For instance, the Adobe Flash player comes installed on most computers. And players are included when you install the major browsers. Sometimes, however, computers in a corporate environment have players stripped out.

FIGURE 1.6
Flash movies have gained in popularity and offer full cross-platform compatibility.

Interactivity

Dreamweaver can add JavaScript to a web page even if you don't know how to write JavaScript. Dreamweaver Behaviors add JavaScript to the page, enabling it to capture the user clicking on an image, rolling the cursor over an element, or many other events that the browser can detect, all using a point-and-click interface, as shown in Figure 1.7.

Dreamweaver behaviors can add interactivity without any programming experience! Hour 18, "Adding Interactivity with Behaviors," discusses and demonstrates behaviors. You might not have a need for some of the interactive capabilities of Dreamweaver, but others, such as the Swap Image behavior to create a rollover effect on an image, in which the image changes when the user rolls the cursor over it, can be helpful in creating a modern and attractive web design.

TIP

Creating Rollover Effects

You can use Dreamweaver's Swap Image behavior to create the effect in which an image changes when the user rolls the mouse over the image. You can also add the behavior by using Dreamweaver's Rollover Image object—it adds the behavior for you. There are often multiple ways to accomplish your goal in Dreamweaver.

Dreamweaver also makes it possible to easily include JavaScript code that others have written. Let's take a look at a popular interactive behavior called a "lightbox":

Testing an Interactive Behavior

1. Open the live Flora Photographs site in your browser: http://www.floraphotographs.com/.

2. Click the Search link.

A "window" appears within the web page and the background dims in a smooth animation.

This animated effect, as shown in Figure 1.4, is called a lightbox and is preferred over creating pop-up windows. With Dreamweaver, you can download and use this same lightbox effect (called "lightview") without writing a line of code!

Available browser events

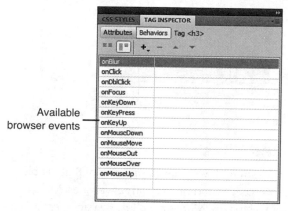

FIGURE 1.7
Dreamweaver makes it simple to react to browser events.

Uploading a Website to the Web

You can create web pages for days, weeks, months, or even years, but eventually you'll either want or need to put them on a web server somewhere and share them with other people. You don't need another piece of software to accomplish this task: Dreamweaver has fully functional file transfer protocol (FTP) software built in, enabling you to connect to a remote web server and upload your files from Dreamweaver. Figure 1.8 shows Dreamweaver's expanded Files panel connected to a remote web server. The remote site files on the server are visible on the left, and the local files are visible on the right

TIP

Finding Web Hosting

If you don't yet have a home for your remote, public website, you can find many websites rating the thousands of hosting companies vying for your business. You can type "web hosting reviews" into a search engine such as Google (http://www.google.com) or check out http://www.web-hosting-reviews.org. You need to specify the features you want on your website and what type of server you'd prefer (usually a choice of Windows or UNIX). You might want to wait to make your choice until you've finished this book so that you understand more of the possibilities of the Web.

side of the screen. Hour 23, "Uploading, Sharing, and Managing Web Projects," explains the details.

FIGURE 1.8
Dreamweaver has built-in FTP software that enables the transfer of web pages to a web server.

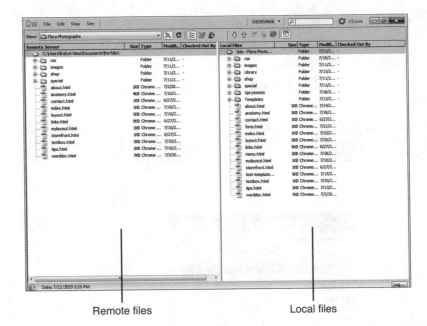

Remote files   Local files

Reusable Code and Files

Dreamweaver is an industrial-strength web development tool that enables you to work on individual web pages and on very large websites. Many websites have thousands of web pages. Managing all those pages, especially when a change is required, can be a daunting task. Dreamweaver has reusable and updatable pages, called **templates**, which you can use as the basis for a web page. Web pages created from a template maintain a link to the original template, so when the original is updated, the changes can be propagated to all the web pages based on the template. Dreamweaver templates are covered in Hour14, "Using Site Assets, Library Items, and Templates."

Dreamweaver also offers another type of reusable element, called a **library item**, which inserts only a portion of a web page. Like templates, library items maintain a link to the parent library item and can be updated throughout an entire website. In the FloraPhotographs.com website, the header and footer on each page are library items (shown in Figure 1.9).

This enables the web developers to add additional information to the footer in the future, save the library item, and automatically update every page in the website without opening each web page.

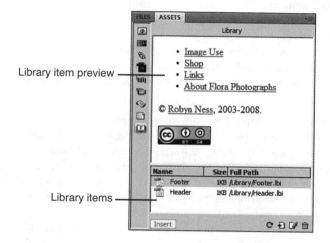

Library item preview

Library items

FIGURE 1.9
You can insert Dreamweaver library items into web pages and update them later without opening each web page.

Summary

In this hour, you saw examples of both basic and advanced functionalities of Dreamweaver. You examined a photography web page, identifying text, images, and hyperlinks. You saw examples of forms and were introduced to how scripts work in the background to process what users enter into forms. You saw examples of multimedia either launched from a hyperlink on a web page or embedded directly into the web page. Examples of interactivity demonstrated what you can accomplish with Dreamweaver behaviors. And you were introduced to Dreamweaver file transfer capabilities and using reusable elements to help manage large websites.

Q&A

Q. Do I have to understand how to accomplish everything that Dreamweaver can do before I start working on a website?

A. You have to understand only the basics of Dreamweaver—that is, its interface and how to work with text, images, and hyperlinks. You'll also want to understand how to design a page layout for your web pages. Then you can learn some of the specialized functions that are necessary for the website you want to create. For instance, if you are creating an e-commerce website, you'll want to learn about forms (Hours 21 and 22). If you are interested in creating an interactive website, you'll want to understand Dreamweaver behaviors (Hour 18).

The best way to learn is by doing, so don't be afraid to dig in and create web pages in Dreamweaver. You can always improve or edit the pages later.

Q. **I work with several programmers who say that Dreamweaver is a waste of money, and that I should just learn HTML and create web pages by typing HTML tags into a text editor. Is that really a better way to create web pages?**

A. That might be the ideal way to create web pages for your programmer friends, but it takes a long time to learn HTML and even longer to learn how to program and write the JavaScript that Dreamweaver behaviors contain. (Not to mention the file management and site upload features built into Dreamweaver to help you stay organized!) I always recommend that after you master Dreamweaver, you take a look behind the scenes (which we'll do in this book!). There are always some things that will be easier to do in Dreamweaver, and some things that will be easier to do by hand.

Workshop

Quiz

1. What is the name of the web page element that a user clicks to navigate to another web page?

2. What is the name of the language used to style text and create web page layouts in Dreamweaver?

3. What is the Dreamweaver feature that enables you to add JavaScript and interactivity to your web pages?

Quiz Answers

1. A hyperlink is the web page element that navigates the user to another web page.

2. Cascading Style Sheets is an important style sheet language used to define both the structure and the presentation of web pages.

3. Dreamweaver behaviors enable you to add JavaScript and interactivity to your web pages.

Exercises

1. Visit a few of your favorite websites (stores, news sites, and so on). Look at the elements on each page and identify their functionality. Begin to consider how you would go about designing a similar page and what features of Dreamweaver you might need.

2. Go to Web Pages That Suck (http://www.webpagesthatsuck.com) and read some of the articles and critiques of other web pages so that you know what to avoid!

3. Go to CSS Zen Garden (http://www.csszengarden.com) and click some of the design links on the right side of the home page. Do you notice that the content in each design's web page is the same? Only the CSS changes for each design. Pretty amazing!

HOUR 2
A Tour of Dreamweaver

I'm sure you are itching to begin creating dazzling and fun websites, the type that you'll show off to your friends, family members, and co-workers. Or maybe you've been assigned the task of creating a website in Dreamweaver for your job. First, however, you have to understand the Dreamweaver interface and the numerous functions that are going to help you be successful as a web developer. Understanding the Dreamweaver user interface enables you to understand the instructions in the rest of this book.

If you have used other Adobe tools, you'll recognize the standard Adobe user interface elements, such as Tab groups and inspectors. If you have used previous versions of Dreamweaver, you should quickly skim this hour to see what exciting changes and updates Adobe has made to the new version of Dreamweaver. This hour provides an important orientation to the concepts you'll use to create web pages in later hours.

Acquainting Yourself with Dreamweaver

Dreamweaver is a complete web development environment and Hypertext Markup Language (HTML) editor, an authoring tool, a dynamic web page development tool, and a website management tool, all rolled into one. Web pages are created using HTML, but you can do many things without ever laying your eyes on any HTML. If you want to produce professional-quality web pages, including scripting, Dreamweaver makes it easy to do so.

HTML is the language of web pages. It consists mainly of paired tags contained in angle brackets (<>). The tags surround objects on a web page, such as text, or stand on their own. For instance, the HTML code to make text

WHAT YOU'LL LEARN IN THIS HOUR:

▶ How to use the Dreamweaver user interface

▶ How to access commands

▶ How to manage panels, inspectors, and windows

▶ How to get help in Dreamweaver

bold looks like this: bold text; notice how the tags are paired, one before and one after the text they affect. The ending tag of the paired tag always begins with a forward slash. HTML also allows you to use single tags: <img src="smile.gif">. By default, Dreamweaver uses a stricter version of HTML called **XHTML** (Extensible Hypertext Markup Language), and all the examples in this book are in XHTML. XHTML requires the use of paired tags, so the earlier image tag example could look like this: <img src="smile.gif"></img>. The shortcut XHTML would look like this: <img src="smile.gif" />, where the closing slash is added to the end of the tag.

Dreamweaver is a **WYSIWYG** (what you see is what you get) web page editor that is extremely powerful while also being easy to use. You can create new websites by using Dreamweaver, and you can import and edit existing websites, too. Dreamweaver does not change or rearrange your code. One of Dreamweaver's most popular features has always been that it leaves existing sites intact; the folks at Adobe, the company that creates Dreamweaver, call this feature **Roundtrip HTML**. No conversion or importation process is necessary to work on any standard HTML, XHTML, or XML file in Dreamweaver. All you need to do is open the files and make your edits.

Dreamweaver is also an authoring tool. What do I mean by *authoring tool*? **Authoring tools** enable you to create a complete application that includes interactivity. Dreamweaver can be used as simply an HTML editor, but it can also be used to create multimedia applications. You can author an experience complete with audio, animation, video, and interactions for your viewers.

The Welcome Screen

Before opening any files, Dreamweaver displays a box with a green bar across the top; this is the Welcome screen (shown in Figure 2.1). The Welcome screen lists common Dreamweaver tasks, such as Open a Recent Item, Create New, and Top Features. At the bottom of the Welcome screen are links to the Getting Started, New Features, and Resources pages on the Adobe website. Whenever you don't have web pages open in Dreamweaver, it displays the Welcome screen. My Welcome screen shown in Figure 2.1 probably looks different from yours because I have a list of files I've recently opened in the Open a Recent Item column. After you have opened files in Dreamweaver, this list offers a quick way to open them again.

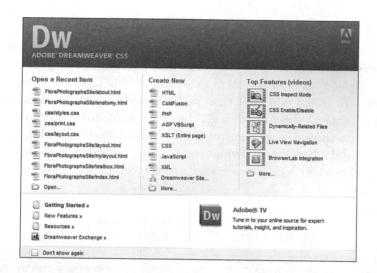

FIGURE 2.1
The Dreamweaver Welcome screen.

You can configure Dreamweaver not to display this Welcome screen by clicking Don't Show Again in the lower-left corner of the window (as shown in Figure 2.1). You can also toggle this preference by choosing Edit, Preferences, and then clicking the General category to display the Show Welcome Screen setting, as shown in Figure 2.2. You explore many other Dreamweaver preferences throughout this book.

NOTE

Macintosh Preferences Under the Dreamweaver Menu

Dreamweaver's Macintosh version presents the Preferences command under the Dreamweaver menu, the first menu in the menu bar after the Apple menu, instead of under the Edit menu.

FIGURE 2.2
Turn on and off the Welcome screen in the General category of Dreamweaver preferences.

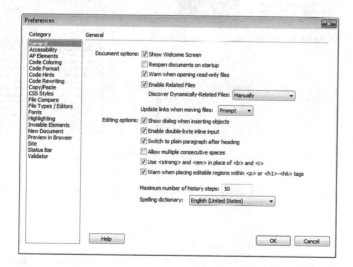

Workspace Modes

Dreamweaver recognizes that different people have different web development roles and different uses for their software. Designers, for example, are mostly interested in the visual elements of a web page. Programmers, on the other hand, want to get their hands on the underlying code. To make life easy for everyone, in Dreamweaver, Adobe has created a handful of different workspaces that can accommodate almost every need.

By default, Dreamweaver places you in the "Designer" workspace mode, which is what we used when writing this book. To switch workspace modes, use the drop-down menu on the right side of the Dreamweaver Menu bar, labeled in Figure 2.3. Alternatively, use the Workspace Layout menu under the Window menu.

The Workspace

The Welcome screen appears in an important part of Dreamweaver called the **Document window**. The Document window displays a web page approximately as it will appear in a web browser. The Document window is bordered on the right by Tab groups, as shown in Figure 2.3. These Tab groups contain the commands and lists you use to modify and organize web pages and web page elements. The Document window, the Tab groups, and other elements, which you explore in a few minutes, are grouped into an integrated interface if you are working in the Windows operating system.

FIGURE 2.3
The Dreamweaver workspace contains the Document window along with integrated panels.

The Macintosh version of Dreamweaver CS5, as shown in Figure 2.4, has panels that float on top of the Document window. You can move floating panels, launched from the Window menu, to any location on the desktop. The Mac and Windows versions of Dreamweaver look slightly different from each other but have the same features and functionality and produce fully compatible files.

FIGURE 2.4
The Macintosh workspace includes the Document window with panels that float on top.

The Menu Bar

Some people prefer to use menu commands and some people prefer to click icons (I like keyboard shortcuts). For the menu-liking crowd, this section describes the organization of Dreamweaver's menus that make up the menu bar, visible at the top of the screen in Figures 2.3 and 2.4.

The File and Edit menus are standard in most programs. The File menu contains commands for opening, closing, saving, importing, exporting, and printing files. The Edit menu contains the Cut, Copy, and Paste commands, along with the Find and Replace command and the Preferences command (in Windows). You can configure many elements of the Dreamweaver user interface and its operation with the Preferences options.

The View menu turns on and off the display of the head content; invisible elements; layer, table, and frame borders; image maps; and various toolbars. A check mark signals that a feature is currently turned on.

The Insert menu is roughly equivalent to the Insert panel that you explore in a few minutes because you can add all the items available on the Insert

TIP

Open Panels from the Window Menu

You don't have to worry about finding a specific panel and remembering which Tab group contains it because you can simply select the name of the panel from the Window menu. This Window menu enables you to quickly find and open all of Dreamweaver's panels. You see a check mark next to the name of the panel if it is already open. You can even open and close the Insert panel (the Insert command) and the Property inspector (the Properties command) in the Window menu.

TIP

The Dreamweaver Application Menu

The Macintosh version of Dreamweaver includes the Dreamweaver menu in addition to the menus previously described. This menu contains the About Adobe Dreamweaver command that is available from the Help menu in the Windows version. It also gives you access to the Preferences command. The Keyboard Shortcuts command is in this menu instead of the Edit menu, as in the Windows version of Dreamweaver.

panel by using this menu. If you prefer to click visual icons, use the Insert panel instead of the text commands in the Insert menu. The Modify menu enables you to modify properties of the currently selected object. After you've added an object to your web page, use the commands under the Modify menu to make it look and act the way you'd like.

The Format menu gives you access to multiple ways of fine-tuning the appearance of the text in a web page. The Format menu mirrors many of the properties available in the Property inspector (you learn about that in a few minutes) when text is selected. You can use this menu to indent text, create a list, and modify font properties. The Commands menu offers useful commands such as Clean Up XHTML and Clean Up Word HTML. Most important to those of you who are questionable spellers, the Commands menu contains the Check Spelling command. You can also use this menu to format and sort a table, create a photo album, and optimize an image for the Web.

The Site menu presents the commands that have to do with an entire website. You explore Dreamweaver website management in Hour 3, "Setting Up a Website," Hour 23, "Uploading, Sharing, and Managing Web Projects," and Hour 24, "Maintaining a Website." The Window menu is important because it opens and closes all the Dreamweaver panels and inspectors that you learn about later in this hour. There's also a list of all the open files at the bottom of the menu.

You learn about the help system later this hour. Along with providing links to the HTML-based help files, the Help menu contains the command to launch the Extension Manager (the Manage Extensions command). There are numerous links to Adobe resources, including the Dreamweaver Support Center on the Adobe website. Selecting the About Dreamweaver command is useful if you need to find out which version of Dreamweaver you are running. You want to keep an eye on the Adobe website in case the company releases an update for Dreamweaver later. It's always a good idea to keep your software as up-to-date as possible.

The Insert Panel

The Insert panel is located on the top right of the screen, as shown in Figure 2.5. It contains buttons for inserting web page elements, such as images, tables, forms, and hyperlinks. You can either click or drag a button's icon to insert that object into a web page. All the commands in the Insert panel are also accessible from the Insert menu.

FIGURE 2.5
The Insert panel displays a list of
the categories for inserting web
page elements.

The Insert panel has the following categories:

- ▶ Common
- ▶ Layout
- ▶ Forms
- ▶ Data
- ▶ Spry
- ▶ InContext Editing
- ▶ Text
- ▶ Favorites

The Insert panel has a drop-down menu at its top, shown in Figure 2.6, which enables you to choose from the eight available categories. To display a category, drop down the menu and then select the category. By default, the Common category displays, but if you are working on forms, you might want to display the Forms category, and if you are working with text, you might want to display the Text category.

Some of the objects in the Insert panel are drop-down menus that organize a group of related objects. For instance, in the Common category, the Images object drops down a menu displaying Image, Image Placeholder, Rollover Image, Fireworks HTML, Navigation Bar, and other image-related commands. All these objects have to do with images, so they are grouped together in a single drop-down menu in the Insert panel.

FIGURE 2.6
The Insert panel drop-down menu displays a list of the categories and Color Icons option to replace the black-and-white interface icons with color versions.

Table 2.1 lists all the objects available in the Insert panel, with descriptions. The table briefly describes each of the objects in the Insert panel except those found in the Data tab because those objects are used for creating dynamic web pages and sites. While you read through this table, familiarize yourself with the types of objects and content you can add to a web page in Dreamweaver.

TABLE 2.1   Insert Panel Objects

Icon	Icon Name	Description
Common Category		
	Hyperlink	Inserts a hyperlink, including the text and the link location.
	Email Link	Adds a hyperlink that launches an empty email message to a specific email address when clicked.
	Named Anchor	Places a named anchor at the insertion point. Named anchors create hyperlinks within a file.
	Horizontal Rule	Adds a horizontal bar at the insertion point; used to separate different pieces of content.
	Table	Creates a table at the insertion point.
	Insert Div Tag	Adds a <div> tag, a common container tag used to store text and graphics. (Also in the Layout category.)

TABLE 2.1   Insert Panel Objects

Icon	Icon Name	Description
	Image	Places an image at the insertion point. (In the Images drop-down menu.)
	Image Placeholder	Inserts a placeholder for an image. (In the Images drop-down menu.)
	Rollover Image	Prompts you for two images: the regular image and the image that appears when the user puts the cursor over the image. (In the Images drop-down menu.)
	Fireworks HTML	Places HTML exported from Adobe Fireworks at the insertion point. (In the Images drop-down menu.)
	Draw Rectangle Hotspot	Enables you to draw a rectangle over a specific region of an image and link it to a specific URL. (In the Images drop-down menu.)
	Draw Oval Hotspot	Enables you to draw an oval over a specific region of an image and link it to a specific URL. (In the Images drop-down menu.)
	Draw Polygon Hotspot	Enables you to draw a polygon over a specific region of an image and link it to a specific URL. (In the Images drop-down menu.)
	Flash (SWF)	Places an Adobe Flash movie at the insertion point. (In the Media drop-down menu.)
	Flash Video (FLV)	Places and configures a Flash Video object at the insertion point. (In the Media drop-down menu.)
	Shockwave	Places a Shockwave movie (that is, an Adobe Director movie prepared for the Web) at the insertion point. (In the Media drop-down menu.)
	Applet	Places a Java applet at the insertion point. (In the Media drop-down menu.)
	param	Inserts a tag that enables you to enter parameters and their values to pass to an applet or an ActiveX control. (In the Media drop-down menu.)
	ActiveX	Places an ActiveX control at the insertion point. (In the Media drop-down menu.)

TABLE 2.1   Insert Panel Objects

Icon	Icon Name	Description
	Plugin	Places any file requiring a browser plug-in at the insertion point. (In the Media drop-down menu.)
	Widget	Inserts a widget.
	Date	Inserts the current date at the insertion point.
	Server-Side Include	Includes SSI code and simulates a server-side include at the insertion point.
	Comment	Inserts a comment at the insertion point.
	Meta	Inserts a meta tag into the head section of a web page. This object can insert a name type meta tag, aiding search engines, or an http-equiv type meta tag that can redirect the user to a different URL or give additional information about the web page, such as assigning parental control information to a page. (In the Head drop-down menu.)
	Keywords	Inserts a keywords meta tag into the head section, adding keywords to the web page to help search engines properly index it. (In the Head drop-down menu.)
	Description	Inserts a description meta tag into the head section, adding a description to the web page to help search engines properly index it. (In the Head drop-down menu.)
	Refresh	Inserts a refresh meta tag into the head section. This tag sets the number of seconds before the page automatically jumps to another web page or reloads itself. (In the Head drop-down menu.)
	Base	Inserts a base tag into the head section. This enables you to set a base URL or a base target window affecting all the paths on the web page. (In the Head drop-down menu.)
	Link	Inserts the address of an external file, usually a script or style sheet file. (In the Head drop-down menu.)

TABLE 2.1   Insert Panel Objects

Icon	Icon Name	Description
	Script	Inserts scripted code at the insertion point. (In the Script drop-down menu.)
	No Script	Inserts the `noscript` tag surrounding HTML code that is displayed by browsers that do not support scripts. (In the Script drop-down menu.)
	Make Template	Creates a Dreamweaver template from the current web page. (In the Templates drop-down menu.)
	Make Nested Template	Creates a nested Dreamweaver template from the current template. (In the Templates drop-down menu.)
	Editable Region	Adds an editable region to a template. (In the Templates drop-down menu.)
	Optional Region	Adds an optional region to a template; this region can be set to either show or hide. (In the Templates drop-down menu.)
	Repeating Region	Adds a repeating region to a template. (In the Templates drop-down menu.)
	Editable Optional Region	Adds an editable optional region to a template. (In the Templates drop-down menu.)
	Repeating Table	Adds a repeating table to a template and defines which cells can be edited. (In the Templates drop-down menu.)
	Tag Chooser	Enables you to choose a tag to insert from a hierarchical menu of all available tags.

Layout Category

Icon	Icon Name	Description
Standard	Standard mode	Turns on Dreamweaver's Standard mode, and at the same time turns off either Expanded Tables mode or Layout mode.
Expanded	Expanded Tables mode	Turns on Dreamweaver's Expanded Tables mode, temporarily adding cell padding and borders to all tables.
	Insert Div Tag	Adds a `<div>` tag, a common container tag used to store text and graphics. (Also in the Common category.)

TABLE 2.1   Insert Panel Objects

Icon	Icon Name	Description
	Draw AP Div	Draws an AP Div container in a web page.
	Spry Menu Bar	A widget that creates a menu bar using the Spry framework. (Also in the Spry category.)
	Spry Tabbed Panels	A widget that creates a set of tabbed panels using the Spry framework. (Also in the Spry category.)
	Spry Accordion	A widget that creates a set of collapsible panels using the Spry framework. (Also in the Spry category.)
	Spry Collapsible Panel	A widget that creates a single collapsible panel using the Spry framework. (Also in the Spry category.)
	Table	Creates a table at the insertion point. (Also in the Common category.)
	Insert Row Above	Adds a row above the currently selected row of a table.
	Insert Row Below	Adds a row beneath the currently selected row of a table.
	Insert Column to the Left	Adds a column to the left of the currently selected column in a table.
	Insert Column to the Right	Adds a column to the right of a currently selected column in a table.
	IFrame	Inserts an inline frame that contains another HTML document.
	Left Frame	Creates a frame to the left of the current frame. (In the Frames drop-down menu.)
	Right Frame	Creates a frame to the right of the current frame. (In the Frames drop-down menu.)
	Top Frame	Creates a frame above the current frame. (In the Frames drop-down menu.)
	Bottom Frame	Creates a frame below the current frame. (In the Frames drop-down menu.)
	Bottom and Nested Left Frame	Creates a frame to the left of the current frame and then adds a frame below. (In the Frames drop-down menu.)
	Bottom and Nested Right Frame	Creates a frame to the right of the current frame and then adds a frame below. (In the Frames drop-down menu.)

TABLE 2.1   Insert Panel Objects

Icon	Icon Name	Description
	Left and Nested Bottom Frame	Creates a frame below the current frame and then adds a frame to the left. (In the Frames drop-down menu.)
	Right and Nested Bottom Frames	Creates a frame below the current frame and then adds a frame to the right. (In the Frames drop-down menu.)
	Top and Bottom Frame	Creates a frame below the current frame and then adds a frame above. (In the Frames drop-down menu.)
	Left and Nested Top Frames	Creates a frame above the current frame and then adds a frame to the left. (In the Frames drop-down menu.)
	Right and Nested Top Frame	Creates a frame above the current frame and then adds a frame to the right. (In the Frames drop-down menu.)
	Top and Nested Left Frames	Creates a frame to the left of the current frame and then adds a frame above. (In the Frames drop-down menu.)
	Top and Nested Right Frame	Creates a frame to the right of the current frame and then adds a frame above. (In the Frames drop-down menu.)
Forms Category		
	Form	Places a form at the insertion point.
	Text Field	Inserts a text field.
	Hidden Field	Inserts a hidden field.
	Textarea	Inserts a **textarea**, which is a multiline text field.
	Checkbox	Inserts a check box.
	Checkbox Group	Inserts a group of related check boxes.
	Radio Button	Inserts a radio button.
	Radio Group	Inserts a group of related radio buttons.

TABLE 2.1   Insert Panel Objects

Icon	Icon Name	Description
	Select(List/Menu)	Inserts a list or a drop-down menu.
	Jump Menu	Creates a jump menu that allows users to select a website from a menu and go to that site.
	Image Field	Inserts an image field, which enables an image to act as a button.
	File Field	Inserts a file field, which enables the user to upload a file.
	Button	Inserts a button.
	Label	Assigns a label to a form element, enabling browsers for people with visual impairments to access extra information about the form elements nested within the label.
	Fieldset	Groups related form fields to make the form accessible to browsers for people with visual impairments. Fieldset wraps around a group of form elements and appears to sighted people as a box drawn around the group, with the fieldset title at the top.
	Spry Validation Text Field	A text field that includes validation logic using the Spry framework. (Also in the Spry category.)
	Spry Validation Textarea	A textarea that includes validation logic using the Spry framework. (Also in the Spry category.)
	Spry Validation Checkbox	A check box that includes validation logic using the Spry framework. (Also in the Spry category.)
	Spry Validation Select	A select object (called a list/menu in Dreamweaver) that includes validation logic using the Spry framework. (Also in the Spry category.)
	Spry Validation Password	A password field that includes validation logic using the Spry framework. (Also in the Spry category.)

TABLE 2.1   Insert Panel Objects

Icon	Icon Name	Description
	Spry Validation Confirm	A second password field whose value is compared to the Spry Validation password field to ensure that they match. (Also in the Spry category.)
	Spry Validation Radio Group	A group of radio buttons that include validation logic using the Spry framework. (Also in the Spry category.)

Spry Category

Icon	Icon Name	Description
	Spry Data Set	Defines an XML or HTML data source.
	Spry Region	Defines a container to receive data via the Spry framework.
	Spry Repeat	Defines a container to receive repeating data via the Spry framework.
	Spry Repeat List	Defines a list to receive repeating data via the Spry framework.
	Spry Validation Text Field	A text field that includes validation logic using the Spry framework. (Also in the Forms category.)
	Spry Validation Textarea	A textarea that includes validation logic using the Spry framework. (Also in the Forms category.)
	Spry Validation Checkbox	A check box that includes validation logic using the Spry framework. (Also in the Forms category.)
	Spry Validation Select	A select object (called a list/menu in Dreamweaver) that includes validation logic using the Spry framework. (Also in the Forms category.)
	Spry Validation Password	A password field that includes validation logic using the Spry framework. (Also in the Forms category.)
	Spry Validation Confirm	A second password field whose value is compared to the Spry Validation password field to ensure that they match. (Also in the Forms category.)

TABLE 2.1   Insert Panel Objects

Icon	Icon Name	Description
	Spry Validation Radio Group	A group of radio buttons that include validation logic using the Spry framework. (Also in the Forms category.)
	Spry Menu Bar	A widget that creates a menu bar using the Spry framework. (Also in the Layout category.)
	Spry Tabbed Panels	A widget that creates a set of tabbed panels using the Spry framework. (Also in the Layout category.)
	Spry Accordion	A widget that creates a set of collapsible panels using the Spry framework. (Also in the Layout category.)
	Spry Collapsible Panel	A widget that creates a single collapsible panel using the Spry framework. (Also in the Layout category.)
	Spry Tooltip	Displays a helpful tip on mouseover using the Spry framework. (Also in the Forms category.)

InContext Editing Category

Icon	Icon Name	Description
	Create Repeating Region	Adds a repeating region to an InContext site template.
	Create Editable Region	Adds an editable region to an InContext site template.

Text Category

Icon	Icon Name	Description
B	Bold	Makes the selected text bold by using the strong tag.
I	Italic	Makes the selected text italic by using the em tag.
S	Strong	Makes the selected text bold by using the strong tag.
em	Emphasis	Makes the selected text italic by using the emphasis tag.
¶	Paragraph	Makes the selected text into a paragraph.
[""]	Block Quote	Makes the selected text into a block quote, indented from the right and the left, by using the blockquote tag.

TABLE 2.1   Insert Panel Objects

Icon	Icon Name	Description
PRE	Preformatted Text	Makes the selected text preformatted (using the pre tag, displaying the text in a monospaced font and with the ability to enter spaces).
h1	Heading 1	Makes the selected text a heading size 1 (largest) by using the h1 tag.
h2	Heading 2	Makes the selected text a heading size 2 by using the h2 tag.
h3	Heading 3	Makes the selected text a heading size 3 by using the h3 tag.
ul	Unordered List	Makes the selected text into an unordered (bulleted) list.
ol	Ordered List	Makes the selected text into an ordered (numbered) list.
li	List Item	Makes the selected text into a **list item** (by using the li tag), a single item in an ordered or unordered list.
dl	Definition List	Creates a definition list. A **definition list** consists of definition terms and definition descriptions.
dt	Definition Term	Creates a definition term within a definition list.
dd	Definition Description	Creates a definition description within a definition list.
abbr.	Abbreviation	Wraps the abbr tag around text, adding a full-text definition to an abbreviation. This aids search engines in indexing a web page properly.
W3C	Acronym	Wraps the acronym tag around text, adding a full-text definition to an acronym. This aids search engines in indexing a web page properly.
BR↵	Line Break	Places a line break, the br tag, at the insertion point. (In the Characters drop-down menu.)

TABLE 2.1   Insert Panel Objects

Icon	Icon Name	Description
	Non-Breaking Space	Inserts a special character ( ) that creates a space. The nonbreaking space character also prevents a line break from occurring between two words. (In the Characters drop-down menu.)
	Left Quote	Inserts the special character for a left quote. (In the Characters drop-down menu.)
	Right Quote	Inserts the special character for a right quote. (In the Characters drop-down menu.)
	Em Dash	Inserts the special character for an em dash (—). (In the Characters drop-down menu.)
	En Dash	Inserts the special character for an en dash (—). (In the Characters drop-down menu.)
	Pound	Inserts the special character for the pound currency symbol. (In the Characters drop-down menu.)
	Euro	Inserts the special character for the Euro currency symbol. (In the Characters drop-down menu.)
	Yen	Inserts the special character for the yen currency symbol. (In the Characters drop-down menu.)
	Copyright	Inserts the special character for the copyright symbol. (In the Characters drop-down menu.)
	Registered Trademark	Inserts the special character for the registered trademark symbol. (In the Characters drop-down menu.)
	Trademark	Inserts the special character for the trademark symbol. (In the Characters drop-down menu.)
	Other Characters	Opens a menu that displays many additional special characters. (In the Characters drop-down menu.)

The Favorites category enables you to add objects that you use frequently to a single Insert panel category. By the end of this book, you will have a better idea of the types of objects you want to place in the Favorites category to help you work more quickly in Dreamweaver. These are your personal favorites, the objects you use most often, collected in one handy Insert panel category.

The Document Window

The Document window is the part of the Dreamweaver interface you will be using most often in your work. By default, the Document window is maximized, and its title and filename appear under the menu bar/Application bar at the top of the screen. You explore saving a file, giving it a filename, and giving it a title in Hour 4, "Adding Text and Lists." The Document toolbar appears at the top of the Document window.

The Document Toolbar

The Document toolbar, shown in Figure 2.7, gives you quick access to important commands. The three buttons on the left of the Document toolbar enable you to toggle among Code view, Design view, and a Split view with both Code view and Design view visible. The Live View option toggles the Design view into a read-only mode that presents your site as if it were being viewed in a real web browser. The Live View makes it possible to preview advanced effects (such as rollovers or other JavaScript behaviors) without launching a web browser. The Live View drop-down menu allows you to disable JavaScript and other plug-ins to see the effect on your design.

FIGURE 2.7
The Document toolbar contains commands you commonly apply to web pages when editing in Dreamweaver.

NOTE

Viewing Live Code

For advanced developers, two other view options—Live Code and Inspect—can be clicked when Live View is enabled. Live Code allows the developer to see the source code of the page as the Live View browser is interpreting it. Inspect allows you to click on objects to see properties applied to them, which is especially helpful when using CSS (Cascading Style Sheets) for layout and styling your page elements; Hours 11 through 13 cover CSS in depth.

I probably use Design view 60% of the time and divide the other 40% of my Dreamweaver time between Code view and Split view—jumping into Live View mode as needed to preview the page. The Split view showing both the Design view and the Code view is useful when you're learning HTML because it enables you to see the tags that Dreamweaver adds while you create a web page.

The Title text box in the Document toolbar is where you give a web page a title (the default title, Untitled Document, isn't very interesting!). This appears in the visitor's browser title bar when the visitor views the page. The web page title is saved in the browser's Favorites or Bookmarks list as the name of the web page, so it should be meaningful. The web page title is also important because it affects the ranking of your page in many search engines such as Google.

Four drop-down menus are on the Document toolbar:

▶ **Check Browser Compatibility**—This menu includes options to look for code known to display inconsistently in different web browsers, as well as the option to check for newly reported problems or report a problem. Lumped in with these features is Check Spelling, which appears under the Commands menu.

▶ **Preview/Debug in the Browser**—This gives you quick access to the list of browsers you'll use to preview web pages.

▶ **Visual Aids**—The Visual Aids menu is active only in Design mode and only when Live View is not activated. The menu gives you access to turn on and off all the visual aids for viewing page elements that are invisible in a rendered webpage. These options are also available in View, Visual Aids.

NOTE

Where's My Document Toolbar?

If the Document toolbar isn't visible, select View, Toolbars, Document.

▶ **File Management**—This menu lists commands such as those for getting files to and from a web server. You explore these commands in Hours 23 and 24, when you upload and manage a website.

The Document toolbar also contains the Refresh Design View button. This button refreshes the Design view when you are editing the code (in Code view or the Split view) so that you can instantly see the changes you make to the code. This button is active only when you are viewing the Document window in Code view or the Split view.

The Status Bar

The Dreamweaver Document window has a status bar along its bottom. It contains the tag selector, the Window Size drop-down menu, the magnification and selection tools, download statistics, and character encodings, as shown in Figure 2.8. These convenient tools are just some of the nice touches that Dreamweaver CS5 offers to help you have a productive and fun experience designing for the Web.

FIGURE 2.8
The status bar contains tools that help you get information about a web page.

The tag selector in the lower-left corner of the Document window provides easy access to the HTML tags involved in any object on the screen. If, for example, the cursor is located in a table cell, the tag selector enables selection of any of the HTML tags which control that object. The currently selected tag appears furthest to the right and looks button-like. The tags to the left of the selected tag are the tags wrapped around the selected tag.

On the right side of the status bar, you find three icons that control how the cursor appears and functions in the Document window. By default, the Select tool (arrow cursor) is selected. You can also select the Hand tool, enabling you to drag the cursor to scroll across the web page in the Document window. The Zoom tool turns the cursor into a magnifying glass and enables you to zoom in on the web page. Next to the Zoom tool is the Set Magnification menu, from which you can select a certain magnification level from 6% to 6400%.

The Window Size drop-down menu helps you re-create a target screen resolution by resizing the Document window. You always want to make sure that your design looks good at a low (800×600) and high screen resolution. You can use the Window Size drop-down menu to quickly resize the Document window to view the approximate amount of screen real estate you have at a particular resolution. The Window Size drop-down menu works only when you do not have the Document window maximized.

TIP

The Tag Selector Is Your Friend

The tag selector will be important later, when you start using behaviors in Hour 18, "Adding Interactivity with Behaviors." You apply behaviors to specific tags, and sometimes the tags are difficult to select—especially the <body> tag, which contains the entire web page content. The tag selector makes it very easy to select the entire body of a web page by clicking the <body> tag.

Define Special Window Sizes

Create your own custom settings for the Window Size menu by selecting the last choice in the Window Size pop-up menu, the Edit Sizes command. This command takes you to the Status Bar category in the Dreamweaver Preferences dialog box, where you can add your custom window size. For instance, do you want to create a web page that is readable on your wireless phone? My Apple iPhone has the capability to display 320×480 pixels, so I could create a custom size to create a web page for my phone.

Toggle All Panels On and Off

Pressing F4 on your keyboard triggers the Hide Panels/Show Panels command (Window, Hide Panels). This command is a great way to get more screen real estate temporarily in order to see the entire web page. When the panels are visible, F4 hides them; when they are hidden, F4 shows them. This toggle button is a quick way to hide and then show the Dreamweaver panels.

Notice the sizes available in the Window Size menu:

▶ The dimensions listed on the right (in parentheses) represent the screen resolutions.

▶ The numbers listed on the left are the estimated browser window dimensions. They are smaller than the screen resolutions because the browser interface (buttons and menus, for instance) takes up space. For example, when the viewer's monitor is set to 640×480, the viewable area is only 536×196 pixels.

Because bandwidth might be an issue when you're developing for the Web, it's nice to know the estimated file size and download time of a web page. The estimated download time shown in the status bar is based on the modem setting in the Status Bar category in the Dreamweaver Preferences dialog box. The default modem setting is 128Kbps; you might want to change this setting to whatever the bandwidth speed is for the targeted viewer of your web page. (Most people in the United States browse the Web at a speed of at least 56Kbps or better; 128Kbps is the slowest speed of most DSL Internet connections.) Dreamweaver takes into account images and other assets contained in the web page when calculating the file size and download time.

Panels and Inspectors

You set properties of objects and add functionality to web pages through Dreamweaver's panels and inspectors. Most commands in Dreamweaver are available in several places, usually as menu commands, Document toolbar commands, and panel commands. Dreamweaver's panels are grouped into Tab groups beside the Document window.

You can open every panel from the Window menu, and by default Dreamweaver has all the important panels and the Property inspector open. If a panel or an inspector is open, its menu selection has a check mark beside it in the Window menu. To close a panel or an inspector, deselect the command in the Window menu. The panel doesn't actually go away, but the group collapses so that you see only its title tab.

Panels and Tab Groups

Dreamweaver includes many specialized panels. We'll explore nearly all of them in upcoming chapters, but to give you a taste of their usefulness, let's quickly summarize the four panels that are provided by default in the Designer view mode:

▶ **Insert**—As discussed earlier, the Insert panel lets you insert nearly any HTML object into your document.

▶ **CSS Styles**—The CSS Styles panel helps you manage styling rules you've applied to your document. We'll discuss CSS further in Hours 11 through 13.

▶ **Files**—The Files panel displays all the files connected with your web site so you can easily work with them. Hours 3 and 23 focus on using the Files panel to manage your site.

▶ **Assets**—The Assets panel collects an organized listing of the different properties and elements you add to your site to help you better manage them and use them consistently. It contains sections for images, colors, links, different types of media files, scripts, and templates. Hour 14, "Using Site Assets, Library Items, and Templates," delves into it in greater detail.

The Files and Assets panels are combined into one Tab group which means you can switch between them, but not view both together. Also, the Properties Panel is open at the bottom of the screen.

You can expand or collapse a Tab group or an inspector by double-clicking a panel title in the group, or the Tab group's gray title bar, as shown in Figure 2.9. You can undock a panel or Tab group by dragging its title (or the gray title bar itself for a Tab group) from where it currently docks. To dock a panel or group, drag and drop it from its title to another Tab group or the Document window. When it docks, you see an outline around the group or panel. Because the Macintosh version of Dreamweaver has floating panels, you can move them wherever you want anytime!

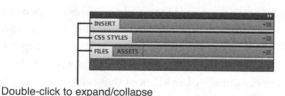

Double-click to expand/collapse

FIGURE 2.9
Expand and collapse Tab groups by double-licking their titles.

TIP

Save Your Workspace

You might have different panel configurations that are handy for different projects. Dreamweaver enables you to save individual configurations to use later by selecting Window, Workspace Layout, New Workspace, and then giving the configuration a name. For instance, you might have a configuration when a site requires creating Cascading Style Sheets (CSS) that has the CSS Styles panel, the AP Elements panel, and the Files panel visible. You could save that with the name *CSS Site*.

TIP

Advanced Panel Maintenance

You can completely close a Tab group, removing it from display on the screen, by selecting the Close Tab group command from the contextual menu that appears when you right-click the Tab group title bar.

You can also choose Collapse to Icons, which displays the panels in Tab groups as single icons, which, when clicked, open for quick access. This is shown in Figure 2.10.

To resize panels or Tab groups, simply position your cursor on the side or bottom of the panel or group, where it turns into a double arrow. Click and drag to expand or collapse the element.

Insert panel icon

CSS Styles panel icon

Files panel icon

Assets panel icon

FIGURE 2.10
Panels can be collapsed to individual icons that take up much less space.

The Property Inspector

The Property inspector displays all the properties of the currently selected object. The Property inspector is like a chameleon that changes depending on the environment; it looks different and displays appropriate properties for whichever object is selected in the Document window. For example, when an image is selected, the Property inspector presents image properties, as shown in Figure 2.11.

FIGURE 2.11
The Property inspector displays image properties when an image is selected.

Sometimes you will notice an HTML and CSS button appear in the Property inspector. These buttons toggle between attributes that you can apply to an object in HTML and those that require CSS, as shown in Figure 2.12. This example shows how the Property inspector looks when text is selected, which is a perfect example of an element that can be changed both through HTML and CSS. We make sure you know which should be selected as we work through the book!

FIGURE 2.12
The Property inspector displays text properties when text is selected, but you can choose whether to focus on HTML or CSS properties.

Context Menus

You can access and modify object properties in multiple ways in Dreamweaver. I'm sure you'll find your favorite ways very quickly. Context menus are one of the choices available. These menus pop up when you right-click an object in the Document window. The contents of the menu are dependent on which object you clicked. For instance, Figure 2.13 shows the context menu that pops up when you right-click a table.

FIGURE 2.13
The context menu for tables gives you quick access to many table commands.

Getting Help

You select Help, Dreamweaver Help (or use the standard help shortcut key, F1) to launch the Dreamweaver help files. The left side of the help page contains the Search box where you can enter a topic. The right side of the page is where the help content files appear. The Next and Previous arrow buttons enable you to page through all the help topics.

One of the easiest ways to get help on your current task is to launch context-sensitive help. When you have an object selected (and you can see its properties in the Property inspector), click the Help icon in the Property inspector, shown in Figure 2.14, to go directly to information about that object.

TIP

Using Help to Learn About Dreamweaver

While you are getting familiar with Dreamweaver, you might want to use the Next and Previous arrow buttons to navigate through the topics. The topics are grouped, so you might get more information on your current topic on the next page. If you keep clicking either of these arrows, you will eventually go on to another topic. This is a good way to expand your knowledge on the topic you are currently researching.

Help

FIGURE 2.14
Clicking the Property inspector Help
icon takes you directly to
information about the properties of
the object currently selected. In this
instance, you go directly to help
information about tables.

Summary

In this hour, you learned about the Dreamweaver Document window and other elements of the Dreamweaver user interface, such as the Insert panel, the menus, the status bar, and the panels. You explored expanding Tab groups. You saw the commands available in Dreamweaver's menus, Insert panel, and status bar. This hour introduced you to the Property inspector and showed you how to access Dreamweaver help.

Q&A

Q. How do I get as much room in the Document window as I possibly can?

A. You could collapse the groups and expand the document window manually, but there's a much easier way! Press F4 (the shortcut for the Hide Panels command in the Window menu). The F4 command works in most of Adobe's products to hide much of the user interface so that you see only your project. The F4 command also toggles the panels back on.

Q. There's something wrong with my Dreamweaver installation because it looks very different from the examples in your book. All the panels appear out of place, and I don't know how to move them. Help!

A. When Dreamweaver was set up, someone changed the default workspace from Designer, which is used in this book. You can switch it back by selecting Window, Workspace Layout, Designer.

Workshop

Quiz

1. Which menu do you use to open a Dreamweaver panel that isn't currently visible in the Tab groups?

2. What icon in the status bar enables you to magnify web pages in the Document window?

3. Is Dreamweaver an HTML editor, an authoring tool, or a website management tool?

Quiz Answers

1. The Window menu enables you to turn on and off all the panels and inspectors. There is a check mark beside a command if the panel is currently visible.

2. The Zoom tool enables you to magnify web pages in the Document window.

3. Sorry, this is a trick question! Dreamweaver is all these things.

Exercises

1. Open the Dreamweaver Preferences dialog box from the Edit menu (the Dreamweaver menu for Mac users). Select the General category and examine each of the available settings. Experiment with changing any of these settings. Click the Help button and read about each of the settings. Don't change settings randomly, especially if you don't understand what the settings do.

2. Experiment with expanding and collapsing Tab groups. Resize the Tab groups. Explore some of the panel drop-down menus found in the upper-right corner of the panel. Use the F4 key (Hide Panels/Show Panels command) to toggle the options. Remember, you can reset to a default layout by choosing Window, Workspace Layout, Designer from the menu.

3. Launch the New Features tour (the link that says New Features) from the Welcome screen that appears when you open Dreamweaver CS5. You must be connected to the Internet to take this tour.

4. Click HTML under the Create New column in the middle of the Welcome screen. This creates a blank HTML document in the Document window.

HOUR 3
Setting Up a Website

Dreamweaver makes it very easy to open and edit single web pages—much like you would a word processing document. If you're planning to create multiple pages, however, the very first thing you should do is define a site. That's what you'll do this hour. Defining a site gives you a home base to work from. Without a site definition, Dreamweaver may run into difficulties linking or organizing your files.

You use Dreamweaver's Files panel to plan, create, and manage projects. Eventually you'll have lots of files: web pages (HTML, or hypertext markup language, files), image files, CSS (Cascading Style Sheets) files, and other types of files. It's important that you define your website to start off on the right foot.

Defining a New Website

This hour introduces creating a home directory for your website and then telling Dreamweaver about it. This directory will store files for your site, and you'll build a logical structure beneath it with directories for supporting files such as images, scripts, and style sheets (more about this in later hours). Many beginning web developers simply start making web pages, skipping the site definition step—this is not recommended. You'll make your web development life easier by completing this important step before any development takes place.

Every website has a root directory. The **root** of a website is the main directory that contains files and other directories. When you define a website, Dreamweaver considers that directory and all the files (or other directories) within it to be the entire universe of that particular website. If you attempt to insert an image from outside that universe, Dreamweaver prompts you to save the file inside the website.

WHAT YOU'LL LEARN IN THIS HOUR:

▶ How to define a website by using the Site Definition Wizard

▶ How to modify a website definition

▶ How to organize a website

TIP

Directories or Folders?

I (and many other people) use the terms *directory* and *folder* interchangeably. Both terms refer to a named container for files and other directories or folders. If you create a reference to a file in another directory, you must provide the name of the directory (also called a "path") that contains the file.

Dreamweaver needs you to define your website so that it knows how to find files. For instance, if an image is located in an `images` directory within the site, Dreamweaver knows how to properly reference the image within a web page. If, however, the image is somewhere outside the defined site, Dreamweaver might not be able to reference it properly, and you might end up with bad links in your website. You learn more about how Dreamweaver links to files in Hour 5, "Making Hyperlinks, Anchors, and Mailto Links."

You have to define a new website for every project you create. Even when projects are related, you might decide to break them down into smaller sites so that the number of files isn't unwieldy in a single site. For instance, I created websites for a college within a major university. Rather than trying to create a single site for the entire college, I found it easier to break down the information into different sites by department. This created more manageable chunks of information than lumping everything together. Regardless of the size of your site, you can have only a single site open in Dreamweaver at once.

To begin defining a website, open the Manage Sites dialog box by selecting Site, Manage Sites, as shown in Figure 3.1.

The Manage Sites dialog box, shown in Figure 3.1, is where you can create, edit, duplicate, remove, export, and import Dreamweaver site definitions. The title says it all: This is where you manage your websites! To begin defining a new site, click the New button in the Manage Sites dialog box and choose Site. The Site Setup dialog box appears, as shown in Figure 3.2.

FIGURE 3.1
The Manage Sites dialog box lists all the websites you have defined and enables you to manage them.

FIGURE 3.2
The Site Setup dialog allows you to name your site and create or select your web directory.

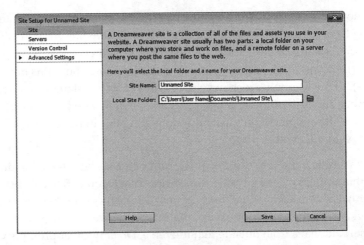

At minimum, you must fill in a name for the site and point Dreamweaver to where the files are stored on your computer. You can define a site even if you don't have any files; you simply define the site and create an empty directory that is ready to hold all the web files you create.

Fill in the Site section of the wizard using the following steps:

Filling In the Site Section

1. In the Site Setup dialog (refer to Figure 3.2), fill in a site name. This name is used only inside Dreamweaver, so it can be anything you want. The site name should be meaningful—it should identify the purpose of the website when you drop down the Site menu to change sites.

2. As shown in Figure 3.2, the text box at the bottom of the dialog box asks you to enter the location of the site directory. Click the folder icon to the right of the text box to navigate to the directory where you will store your local site, the files you will work on in Dreamweaver. Either use an existing directory on your hard drive or create a new directory for your site.

3. Click the Save button.

Building the Site Cache

After you click the Save button, Dreamweaver displays a message, telling you that it will now create the initial site cache. When you click OK, a progress bar appears (and disappears very quickly if you have nothing in your site). The initial site cache is created each time you create a new site. The **site cache** stores information about the links in your site so that they can be quickly updated if they change. Dreamweaver continues to update the cache as you work.

Using the Files Panel

After you've defined your site, the site title you specified appears in the Site drop-down menu at the top of the Files panel (shown in Figure 3.3). As you create web pages and save them to your site, they appear in the Files panel. You use the Files panel to open web pages to edit in Dreamweaver. Right now you might not have any web pages in your site, but eventually you'll want to use the Files panel to create folders to organize the many web pages you've created.

TIP

Open Manage Sites from the Site Menu

You can open the Manage Sites dialog box from the Files panel or from the Site menu. Many of the commands available in the Site menu are repeated in the Files panel so that you can access the commands from either location.

FIGURE 3.3
The Files panel enables you to
change sites and open web pages.

Site drop-down menu

Expand/Collapse button

The Site drop-down menu is where you access the websites you have defined. If you work on multiple projects, you have multiple sites to choose from. For instance, you might have your own personal website defined, plus a site for your child's school or a site for a client whose website you are creating.

There is no special procedure for importing an existing website into Dreamweaver. If a copy of the existing website exists in a folder on your hard drive, simply define a site in Dreamweaver which points to that folder. That is all you need to do. All the files are available to edit in Dreamweaver, and you can easily modify web pages and then save them. Open a web page by double-clicking the filename listed in the Files panel.

So far you've used the collapsed version of the Files panel, but the next section introduces the expanded version of the Files panel.

Expanding the Files Panel

There is a larger version of the Files panel, available to use when you need to work with files in your site and need access to more site-oriented commands. To open the expanded Files panel, perform the following actions:

1. Click the Expand/Collapse button in the Files panel, shown earlier in Figure 3.3.

   The Expanded Files panel, shown in Figure 3.4, is a larger representation of the Files panel and has two panes: Local Files (on the right, by default) and Remote Site (on the left), which you set up in Hour 23,

"Uploading, Sharing, and Managing Web Projects." Because you have not yet defined a remote site, you should not have any files in the Remote Site pane at this point.

Expand/Collapse button

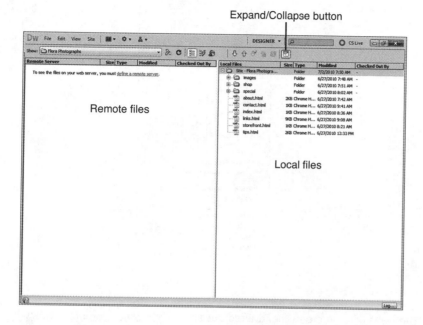

Remote files

Local files

FIGURE 3.4
The Expanded Files panel has two panes: Local Files and Remote Site.

When you click the Files Expand/Collapse button on the Macintosh, the Expanded Files panel opens in a new window. On Windows, it expands to fill the majority of the screen.

2. Click the Expand/Collapse button again to return to the smaller version of the Files panel.

Creating New Files in the Files Panel

You can create new files and new folders right in the Dreamweaver Files panel. Right-click in the Files panel to open the Files panel menu. This context menu, shown in Figure 3.5, has two commands of interest at the top: New File and New Folder. You use those commands to create files and olders (also called **directories**) in the Files panel.

FIGURE 3.5
The Files panel context menu
contains commands to create new
folders and files in a website.

Create new files
and folders

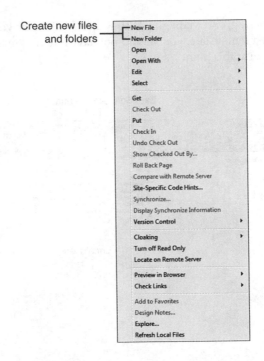

New File
New Folder
Open
Open With   ▶
Edit   ▶
Select   ▶

Get
Check Out
Put
Check In
Undo Check Out
Show Checked Out By...
Roll Back Page
Compare with Remote Server
Site-Specific Code Hints...
Synchronize...
Display Synchronize Information
Version Control   ▶

Cloaking   ▶
Turn off Read Only
Locate on Remote Server

Preview in Browser   ▶
Check Links   ▶

Add to Favorites
Design Notes...
Explore...
Refresh Local Files

▼ TRY IT YOURSELF

Creating an Images Directory

The websites you create need directories for organization; probably every site will at least have an images directory for all the images in the site. To create an images directory, follow these steps:

1. Right-click in the Files panel.

   You need to be careful about what is selected when you select the New Folder command so that you do not nest the folder within another folder. To add a folder at the site root, select the top line in the Files panel, which begins with the word *Site*.

2. Select the New Folder command. An untitled folder is added to your site.

3. Name the new folder **images**.

4. Repeat steps 1 and 2 and create a folder called **css**.

Now try adding a new file to your site with these steps:

1. Right-click on the root folder and select the New File command.

2. A new untitled web page is created in the website. Name the web page index.html, which is one of the popular default page names for many servers.

Using the **default page name** enables users to find your page more easily by just entering a basic web page address without the specific page appended. Another common default page name is default.htm. Both the .htm and the .html file extensions are acceptable. The .htm file extension became popular because the older versions of Microsoft Windows could handle only three-character file extensions; this is no longer a limitation in newer versions of Windows.

Editing Site Settings

So far in this hour, you have used the Site Setup dialog box to define a website. Now let's edit those settings and along the way explore the Advanced Settings tab to complete additional site settings.

To edit the site definition, follow these steps:

1. Open the Manage Sites dialog box again by selecting the Manage Sites command from the Site menu, or by choosing Manage Sites from the File panel's Site drop-down menu.

2. Select the site you just created from the list and then click the Edit button. The Site Setup dialog box opens again.

3. Click Advanced Settings option from the list, as shown in Figure 3.6.

TIP

Name Files Consistently

I think it's a good idea to name everything with lowercase letters. Some servers and scripting languages are case-sensitive. When you name everything with lowercase letters, you don't need to remember whether you used uppercase letters. Also, never use spaces in file names. When displayed in a web browser address bar, spaces are encoded as %20, making URLs hard to read.

TIP

A Quick Way to Edit Site Definitions

A fast way to open the Site Setup dialog box is by simply double-clicking the name of the site in the Files panel's Site drop-down menu.

TRY IT YOURSELF ▼

Editing the Advanced Settings

Editing the Advanced Settings
continued

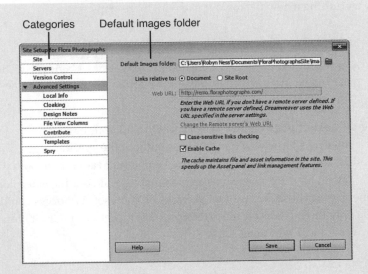

FIGURE 3.6
The Advanced Settings section contains additional site properties.

Advanced Settings include:

▶ **Local Info**—Set a default images folder and other options to help Dreamweaver write links to them. We'll explore this further in the next section.

▶ **Cloaking**—Select files types to exclude from all operations in Dreamweaver, a useful feature if you keep non-site project files (such as meeting notes or original graphic files) in the project folder you designate as your site folder.

▶ **Design Notes**—Choose options for sharing Design Notes. We'll explore these setting further in Hour 24, "Maintaining a Website."

▶ **File View Columns**—Change the order of the information columns that appear in the Files panel associated with each file, such as size, type, notes, and modified date.

▶ **Contribute**—Configure Dreamweaver to use rollback and event logging supported by Contribute, a web editing package that complements Dreamweaver. See Hour 14, "Using Site Assets, Library Items, and Templates," for additional information about working with Contribute.

▶ **Templates**—Set how Dreamweaver manages file reference paths when you use templates. Hour 14 covers templates in details.

▶ **Spry**—If using the Spry framework for interactivity, select the folder in which the widgets are stored. Hour 19, "Using Spry, the Widget Browser, and Extensions," discusses Spry and related technologies.

Set up a default images folder in the Local Info category in this way:

1. Select the folder icon next to the Default Images Folder text box.

2. Navigate to the images folder you just created. Now Dreamweaver knows where you keep your images for the site.

3. Click the Save button.

4. Click the Close button to close the Site Setup dialog box.

You learn about other advanced options later in this book. In Hour 23, you set up the Remote Info category in order to upload your files to a remote website. In Hour 24, you explore the Cloaking and the Design Notes categories.

Considering Site Organization

There are many opinions about the proper way to organize a website. Some people like to compartmentalize all the files into directories and subdirectories. Some people like to have a very shallow structure, with many files in a single directory. As you get more experienced at web development, you'll find your ideal method of organization. It's nice to exchange ideas with other web developers or hobbyists so that you can learn from the successes and failures of others and they can learn from yours.

I have a `Projects` directory on my hard drive, represented in Figure 3.7. The `Projects` directory contains a directory for each project on which I'm working. Within each project directory is a `Web` directory. This is the directory where I keep all the development files for the site and the directory that I set as the root in Dreamweaver.

TIP

Check Case Sensitivity

In the Local Info tab of the Advanced Settings dialog box is the Use Case-Sensitive Link Checking check box. If you select this setting, Dreamweaver checks that the links in your site use the same case (uppercase or lowercase) as the filenames. This is very useful if you are eventually uploading your website to a case-sensitive UNIX server.

FIGURE 3.7
An example of a directory structure
in which the website is housed in
the Web directory.

Plan Now, Benefit Later

It's a good idea to set up a common directory structure even if you aren't anticipating an extensive site. Web sites have a way of growing over time. As developers come and go, a standardized structure helps ensure that all of the components of the site can be located and maintained.

This directory structure enables me to put other files, such as correspondence, contracts, invoices, and spreadsheets, in the client's folder without making them part of the website. It's good practice to keep other files separate from those you plan to transfer to the Web. You might prefer to have one directory that contains all your websites. Do whatever works best for you.

Put some thought into how you'll organize the files in your website before you start a project. You probably want to create a separate images folder to hold your images. If you have other types of assets, such as sound or video, you might want to create separate folders for those too. I always create a styles directory to hold external Cascading Style Sheets files; you explore these in the later hours of this book.

I try to logically break up sections of websites into separate directories. If your website has obvious divisions (departments, lessons, products, and so on), you can create directories to hold the web pages for each division. You'll be surprised at how even a small website becomes quickly unmanageable when all the files are dumped into one directory.

Most websites use many image files. If you have different sections in your website, do you want to have separate images directories in each section? It might be a good way to organize your site. Then again, if images are used across multiple sections, it might make the images hard to find. Make sure that your organizational logic isn't going to break down as you add files to your site.

Luckily, if you do have to rearrange assets, Dreamweaver updates any links for you. When you move a file, Dreamweaver asks you whether you want to search and update links to that file. That's what the site cache is created for. However, it is still best to make wise design decisions at the beginning of a big project .

Summary

In this hour, you learned how to define a website and determine its root. You learned how to quickly add files and folders to a site. In addition, you learned how to use the Files panel and expand it into the Expanded Files panel. And you explored ideas about how to organize a site.

Q&A

Q. How do I import a website into Dreamweaver?

A. There is no set procedure for importing a site. You simply define a site exactly as you did this hour, pointing to the root directory of the folder you'd like to import. Dreamweaver presents all the files in the Files panel, enabling you to open and edit them. If the site you need to import is on a web server, you first need to read Hour 23 and set up remote site settings pointing to the server.

Q. If I need to move files within my site, is it okay to do it within Dreamweaver?

A. If you need to do some housekeeping or rearranging, it's best to do it within Dreamweaver. Dreamweaver automatically updates links to files and warns you if deleting a file will affect other files within your site. Be sure to take care of these tasks within Dreamweaver and not elsewhere; otherwise, you might break links or other dependencies between files in the site.

Workshop

Quiz

1. Why do you need to define a website?

2. What is the purpose of the Files panel?

3. True or false: You must go through a conversion process to import an existing website into Dreamweaver.

Quiz Answers

1. You define a website so that Dreamweaver knows where the root of the site is and what your site management preferences are.

2. The Files panel can be used to create new files and folders, edit existing files, and access site management features.

3. False. No conversion process is necessary to import an existing website into Dreamweaver.

Exercises

1. Try defining a new website. Add some files and folders to the new site. Name one of the files index.htm.

2. Search for *Site Map* in Google (http://www.google.com) and look at the organization of other sites on the Web. The folders used to store web pages might or might not reflect the same structure outlined in the site map. Click some of the pages and look at the folder structure in the URLs.

3. Open up the Site Setup dialog box and explore the other categories in the Advanced Settings tab (Design Notes or Cloaking, for instance). We cover the other categories in upcoming hours.

HOUR 4
Adding Text and Lists

Content is king on the web. Without compelling content, you won't get visitors, and without visitors, you won't have a site! In this hour, we start dealing with the most common type of content: text. You get started creating web pages with Dreamweaver by becoming familiar with adding text and setting text properties. You learn how Dreamweaver formats the appearance of text using Cascading Style Sheets (CSS). This hour introduces the role of CSS, and Hour 11, "Formatting Web Pages with Cascading Style Sheets," gives more in-depth information on using CSS.

Creating a New Page

The New Document dialog box enables you to select the type of document you want to create. This dialog box is organized into several categories:

- ▶ Blank Page
- ▶ Blank Template
- ▶ Page from Template
- ▶ Page from Sample
- ▶ Other

Each category lists different types of documents and layouts you can create. You are going to start with a completely blank HTML document. In other hours, you explore selecting document types from other categories in the New Document dialog box.

WHAT YOU'LL LEARN IN
THIS HOUR:

- ▶ How to create a new web page and set up properties for the whole page
- ▶ How to use the Property inspector to change text fonts and font sizes
- ▶ How Dreamweaver creates CSS styles and how to rename and apply styles
- ▶ How to align text and add unordered and ordered lists
- ▶ How to preview a web page in different browsers

**Creating a Blank
HTML Page**

To create a new blank HTML web page, do the following:

1. Select File, New.

2. Select the Blank Page category.

3. Select HTML from the Page Type column, as shown in Figure 4.1.

4. Select <none> from the Layout column.

5. Ensure that XHTML 1.0 Transitional is selected in the DocType drop-down menu.

6. Click the Create button.

   A new document is created, and you can add text, images, and other objects to it.

FIGURE 4.1
The New Document dialog box enables you to select the type of document you want to create.

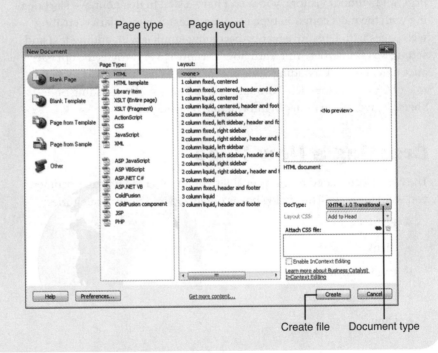

Page type   Page layout

Create file   Document type

The keyboard shortcut to open the New Document dialog box is Ctrl+N (Command+N on the Macintosh). You can also create a new page from Dreamweaver's Welcome page (remember the screen that is visible in the Document window when you first open Dreamweaver?). The middle column in the Welcome page is titled Create New, and you can select HTML from that column to quickly create a blank web page.

Saving a File

Even if you haven't added anything to a new page, it's always a good idea to save and name it right away. The insertion of images, movies, links, and other objects requires that you save the web page first. Remember to save the file in the directory you've previously defined as the site root as discussed in Hour 3, "Setting Up a Website."

The .htm and .html file extensions are interchangeable. Traditionally, the .html extension has been more popular with developers working on the Mac or UNIX platforms because those operating systems have always supported longer file extensions. The .htm file extension reflected the older Windows version three-character file extension limit. Windows no longer has a character limit for file extensions, so using the universal .html extension is a good choice.

To save a web page, perform the following steps:

1. Select File, Save As or File, Save to save changes to an existing file.

2. Navigate to the correct directory, either the root of the defined site or a subdirectory within the root of the defined site.

3. Enter a filename. Dreamweaver automatically adds an .html extension.

4. Click the Save button.

TRY IT YOURSELF ▼

Saving a Web Page

CAUTION

Servers Might Be Case-Sensitive

Filenames are case-sensitive on many web servers. Servers running the various flavors of the UNIX or LINUX operating systems enable you to create files named mydog.gif, Mydog.gif, and MYDOG.gif in the same directory because the capitalization differs. Microsoft operating systems, such as Windows, are not case-sensitive. So, if you are developing in Windows, your links might work perfectly and then cease to work when you upload them to a case-sensitive server!

Adding Text to a Web Page

To enter text into the new web page you just created, you can simply type into the Document window. Type some text to serve as a heading at the top of the page, press the Enter key, and type a couple of sentences. This is the best way to add text to the web page if you are writing it as you create the page. If the text exists elsewhere, however, such as in a Microsoft Word document, an email, or another type of text file, you want to look at the next section on copying and pasting text into Dreamweaver.

Copying and Pasting Text from a File

Often you need to transfer text that exists as a word processing document into a web page. You can easily copy text from another application, such as Microsoft Word or even the spreadsheet application Microsoft Excel, and paste it into Dreamweaver. Dreamweaver can paste text two ways: with and without text formatting.

TIP

Spelling and Grammar Are Important!

I like to create text for web pages in a robust word processing application such as Microsoft Word so that I have the automatic spell check and grammar check. I can then copy and paste the text into a web page in Dreamweaver. You can, of course, use Dreamweaver's spell-checker, but there is no grammar-checker in Dreamweaver.

▼ TRY IT YOURSELF

Copying and Pasting Text from Another Program

To copy and paste text from a word processing program or another program, follow these steps:

1. Open a Word document (.doc) or another word processing document.

2. Select at least a couple of paragraphs.

3. Copy the text by selecting Edit, Copy or using the keyboard command (Ctrl+C for Windows or Command+C on the Mac).

4. Go to Dreamweaver and place the insertion point where you want to paste the text.

5. Select Edit, Paste or use the keyboard shortcut (Ctrl+V in Windows or Command+V on a Mac). The text is pasted into Dreamweaver, and it retains much of its formatting, including fonts, paragraphs, color, and other attributes.

Copying and Pasting Structural Formatting

I often want to reformat the text in the web page, so I usually paste into Dreamweaver without font formatting.

The following text details how to copy and paste text from a word processing program with only structural formatting (paragraphs, lists, tables) and no font formatting (bold, colored text, font sizes):

Copying and Pasting Structural Formatting

1. Open a Word document (.doc) or another word processing document.

2. Select at least a couple of paragraphs.

3. Copy the text by selecting Edit, Copy or using the keyboard command (Ctrl+C for Windows or Command+C on the Mac).

4. Go to Dreamweaver and place the insertion point where you want to paste the text.

5. Select Edit, Paste Special.

6. Select Text with Structure (Paragraphs, Lists, Tables, Etc.), as shown in Figure 4.2.

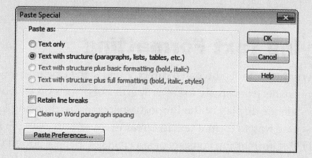

FIGURE 4.2
The Paste Special dialog box enables you to choose exactly what formatting properties get pasted along with your text into Dreamweaver.

Formatted Text and the Web

Even though you can copy and paste formatted text into Dreamweaver, this doesn't necessarily mean that all the formatting will transfer, nor does it mean that the text styles will look identical in a web browser. There are formatting and style constraints on the web that just can't be accounted for in the copy and paste process.

If you have a preferred way to paste text from other applications, you can set that preference as Dreamweaver's default. You can then simply use the Paste command or the keyboard shortcut (Ctrl+V for Windows or Command+V on the Mac). Change the default Paste command in Dreamweaver Preferences' (Edit, Preferences) Copy/Paste category, as shown in Figure 4.3. If you use Microsoft Word, be sure that you also check the Clean Up Word Paragraph Spacing option so that you don't get extra spaces between your paragraphs. This is a nice feature that saves you from cleaning up the extra spaces by hand.

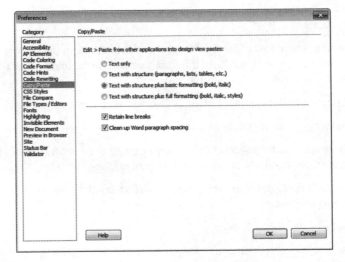

FIGURE 4.3
The Copy/Paste preferences enable you to change the default formatting that Dreamweaver uses when it pastes content from other applications.

Applying Text Formatting

The Property inspector is the panel directly under the Document window. You use this panel extensively to set properties of objects on a web page. You can toggle the display of the Property inspector by choosing Window, Properties. One way to format text in Dreamweaver is by using HTML formatting. HTML formatting consists of special tags that are added to stylize the text in a document. To use HTML formatting, click the HTML button in the Properties inspector, then select the Format drop-down menu in the Property inspector. There are four basic formatting options:

- ▶ **None**—This option removes any formatting styles currently applied to the selection.

- ▶ **Paragraph**—This option applies paragraph tags (<p></p>) to the selection. This adds two carriage returns after the selection.

- ▶ **Heading 1 through Heading 6**—These options apply heading tags to the selection. Heading 1 is the largest heading and Heading 6 is the smallest. Applying a heading tag makes everything on the line that heading size.

- ▶ **Preformatted**—This option displays text in a fixed-width, or mono-spaced, font (on most systems, 10-point Courier). The text resembles typewriter text. You probably won't use this format option too often.

Select the top line heading in your web page and apply Heading 1 formatting, as shown in Figure 4.4.

Property inspector

Text formats

FIGURE 4.4
The Format drop-down menu in the Property inspector applies heading, paragraph, and preformatted formatting to text.

Understanding Paragraph and Break Tags

While you are creating web pages, you use the different heading and paragraph formats to mark different types of text. These formatting options wrap the text you've selected with HTML tags. The Heading 1 format used above adds the <h1> tag before the selection and the closing tag </h1> after the selection. Likewise, the Paragraph format wraps a paragraph of text in the <p> and </p> tags.

Paragraph tags surround a block of text, placing two carriage returns after the block. You create a new paragraph by pressing the Enter or Return key. Think of paragraph tags as creating a container for the block of text. This container is a square box that contains text. In Hour 11, you understand how to modify this container with CSS.

It's important to understand the difference between the paragraph (<p>) and break (<br>) tags.

The break tag inserts a single carriage return into text and is best used for creating a new line within a paragraph such as when formatting an address on different lines. You can insert a break into a web page by using the keyboard shortcut Shift+Enter or by selecting the Line Break object from the Characters drop-down menu in the Text category of the Insert panel.

Pressing Shift+Enter twice to insert two line breaks and pressing Enter to create a paragraph look visually identical on a web page. However, the break tag does not create a container as the paragraph format does, and any formatting applies to the entire container that contains a break. This distinction becomes more important as you begin formatting portions of web pages in different ways with CSS as introduced in Hour 11.

Setting Page Properties

You can set global page properties, such as the default font and font size for all the text on the page and a page title. These can be added in the Page Properties dialog box. To get started, select Modify, Page Properties to open this dialog box. .

The Page Properties dialog box, shown in Figure 4.5, has six property categories listed in the left column: Appearance (CSS), Appearance (HTML), Links (CSS), Headings (CSS), Title/Encoding, and Tracing Image. Next you learn about the property settings in the Appearance (CSS and HTML), Headings, and Title/Encoding categories; the Links category settings is covered in Hour 5, "Making Hyperlinks, Anchors, and Mailto Links." You simply click one of the categories to modify its property settings.

Setting Global Page Appearance

You use the settings in the Appearance category of the Page Properties dialog box to set the text font, size, and color, along with several other settings, for the entire web page. For instance, the text on a web page is black by default. You can change the default text color on the web page by changing this setting in Page Properties.

You might notice, however, that there are *two* Appearance categories in Page Properties window—Appearance (HTML) and Appearance (CSS)—and both have almost the same exact settings!

The Appearance (HTML) settings are provided for legacy purposes—these options use HTML to control the appearance. The Appearance (CSS)

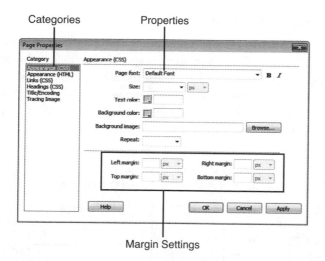
Categories   Properties

Margin Settings

FIGURE 4.5
The Page Properties dialog box
enables you to set properties for
the entire web page.

settings, on the other hand, use Cascading Style Sheets to set the appearance. Cascading Style Sheets are the recommended way of applying visual styling to web pages and should be used whenever possible.

Setting the Global Page Font and Font Size

Select the Appearance (CSS) category in the Page Properties dialog box by clicking the category name on the left side of the dialog box. You can select the default page font for the entire page along with the default text size and color. These settings may be overridden by any local text setting, such as the settings you apply later this hour.

TRY IT YOURSELF ▼

Setting the Page Font Properties

To set the page font properties, follow these steps:

1. In the Page Properties dialog box, select the font family you want from the Page Font drop-down menu.

2. You can also set the default text to be bold, italic, or both. I don't suggest selecting either!

3. Select the font size in the Size drop-down menu. If you select a numeric font size, you also have to select a unit type, such as points or pixels.

4. Click the Apply button at the bottom of the Page Properties dialog box to view the font changes you've made so far. You might have to adjust the position of the Page Properties dialog box so that it isn't blocking your view. The Apply button enables you to view your changes without closing the Page Properties dialog box.

Setting the Global Text Color

In a number of areas in Dreamweaver, you can change the color of an object or text. In HTML and CSS files, colors are specified by using a hexadecimal numbering system, but if you don't know the hexadecimal translation of the color you'd like to use, you can use Dreamweaver's color picker. You access the Dreamweaver color picker by clicking on the color picker box, shown in Figure 4.6. Dreamweaver's color palette appears.

FIGURE 4.6
Select the color picker to open
Dreamweaver's color palette.

You can experiment with picking a color by using the color picker in a number of ways:

▶ Pick one of the available color swatches by clicking it with the eyedropper.

▶ By default, the Color Cubes palette displays. You can switch to one of the five other panels: Color Cubes, Continuous Tone, Windows OS, Mac OS, and Grayscale.

▶ Use the eyedropper to pick up any color onscreen by simply clicking the eyedropper on it. You can pick up any color on the computer screen, not just colors in Dreamweaver. Try selecting a color from one of the icons in the Insert panel. You need to arrange Dreamweaver so that you can see other Windows and click the eyedropper on the colors.

▶ Click the System Color Picker button to create a custom color as shown in Figure 4.7. This opens the system color picker, where you can either pick one of the basic colors or click anywhere in the color spectrum to mix your own color. Click the Add to Custom Colors button and then click the OK button to use the color.

Windows System Color Picker   Macintosh System Color Picker

FIGURE 4.7
The system color picker enables you to mix your own custom colors on either a Windows (left) or Macintosh OS X (right) computer.

You can also type the color information directly into the color text box in the Property inspector:

▶ Colors are represented in HTML by three hexadecimal numbers preceded by the pound (#) sign. For instance, the hexadecimal RGB (red, green, blue) value for a light blue hue is represented as #0099FF, where the value for R is 00, the value for G is 99, and the value for B is FF. If you know the hexadecimal value for a color, you can simply type it in. CS5 also understands the color shortcuts (removing repeated values) so #0099FF could also be entered as #09F.

▶ Browsers also support a wide range of color names in addition to hexadecimal values. For instance, you could type in **red** instead of **#FF0000**.

To clear the current color without picking another color, click the Default Color button in the color picker.

Setting the Background Color and Background Image of a Web Page

You can set the background color of an entire page in the Appearance (CSS) category of the Page Properties dialog box. For example, if you'd like to set the web page background color to white, you can enter the hexadecimal

Eight to Ten Percent of People Are Colorblind!

You should check that your color combination is visible to the many people who are colorblind. Use the Colorblind Web Page Filter at http://colorfilter. wickline.org/ to check your design. The filter returns a version of your web page displayed as it would look to someone who is colorblind.

color code (#FFFFFF) into the Background Color text box, type **white** into the box, or use the color picker. Of course, you can pick any color that you want as the background color, but make sure that the combination of the background color and the text color doesn't make your web page difficult to read. If you apply a dark background color, you should use a light text color for contrast so that the viewer can easily read the text.

You can also set a background image for a web page. For the web page background to look nice, you should find or create an image especially designed as a web page background. You can find these specially designed background images on the Web or in image galleries that you purchase. A background image should never interfere with the readability of a page.

To add a background image, click the Browse button and navigate to an image file saved on your hard drive. The image has to be saved in the GIF, JPEG, or PNG format. (You learn more about image formats in Hour 8, "Displaying Images.") Click the OK button. You might receive a message from Dreamweaver that a `file://` path will be used until you save your document. Just click OK; Dreamweaver automatically corrects that path after you save the web page.

When an image is smaller than the browser window, you can choose whether it repeats horizontally, vertically, or both. Use the Repeat drop-down menu to choose whether the image won't repeat at all (No Repeat), will repeat in horizontal and vertical directions (Repeat), or will repeat horizontally or vertically (Repeat-x and Repeat-y, respectively).

Setting the Page Margins

Margins set the amount of space between the contents of the web page and the edges of the browser window. You set the margins for a page in the Page Properties Appearance (CSS) dialog box. The default setting for page margins varies from browser to browser, so it's impossible to predict the amount of whitespace that will be visible around the border of your web page design. You might want to change the margins if you notice that there are gaps at the top and on the left side of your web pages.

You can change the page margins by entering values into the margin boxes, as shown in Figure 4.5 above. There are four page margin settings: Left Margin, Top Margin, Right Margin, and Bottom Margin. Many web designers set the Left and Top Margin settings to 0 pixels so that the design is snug to the upper-left corner of the browser window.

Setting Global Heading Properties

You create a heading by selecting one of the heading formats, Heading 1 through Heading 6, in the Format drop-down menu in Dreamweaver's HTML Property inspector. In the Headings (CSS) category of the Page Properties dialog box, you can set global properties for these headings, as shown in Figure 4.8. You can select a Heading Font for all six heading sizes. You can also set a unique font size and color for each size.

FIGURE 4.8
Set the font, font size, and color for headings in the Headings category of the Page Properties dialog box.

TRY IT YOURSELF ▼

Setting a Heading Style

To set how Heading 1 will appear, follow these steps:

1. Select Modify, Page Properties if you don't already have the Page Properties dialog box open. You should already have some text set to Heading 1 on the page.

2. Select a default font for all the headings by selecting one of the fonts beside the Heading font setting. You can also click the Bold or Italic button if you'd like.

3. Enter a large font size beside Heading 1. A good size to try is 36 pixels. You can also change the color by clicking on the color picker in the Heading 1 settings.

4. Click the Apply button (refer to Figure 4.8) to apply your changes without closing the Page Properties dialog box.

Heading Sizes

Remember that headings become smaller as the heading number increases. So, Heading 1 is logically meant to be larger than Heading 2. You can override these sizes, but it isn't a good idea to do so.

Adding a Page Title

The Title/Encoding category of the Page Properties dialog box enables you to set the document title of your web page along with the document and encoding types. The title of your web page is important because it appears in the title bar of the browser when someone views the page. This same title is saved to a user's browser Bookmarks or Favorites list when the address of your site is saved; therefore, you should make it meaningful and memorable.

▼ TRY IT YOURSELF

Adding a Title to a Document

To add a title to a document, follow these steps:

1. Select Modify, Page Properties if you don't already have the Page Properties dialog box open.

2. Select the Title/Encoding category.

3. Type a descriptive title in the Title box at the top of the Page Properties dialog box as shown in Figure 4.9.

FIGURE 4.9
The document title can be entered in the Page Properties or in the Title text field.

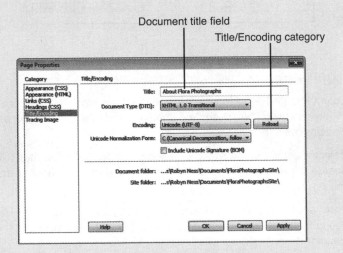

Document title field

Title/Encoding category

4. Click the OK button to save the settings. The current page title also appears in the Title text box in the Document toolbar. You can always add the title in this text box instead of opening the Page Properties dialog box. By default, all pages are titled "Untitled Document" before a title is added.

The Title/Encoding category houses the Document Type setting, which you first encountered earlier this hour when you created a new HTML file. By default, Dreamweaver applies the XHTML 1.0 Transitional document type, which provides a good balance of older HTML functionality and new XML structure. This tag tells the browser the flavor of HTML that your web page is written in and helps the browser interpret the page.

There are various alphabets in the world, and using the Encoding command is how you tell a web browser which one you are using for your web page. By default, Dreamweaver lists the Unicode (UTF-8) encoding type that has become the standard for computer code creation in all languages. Creating pages using Unicode encoding ensures that your web pages will be standards-based and viewable all over the world.

Introducing Cascading Style Sheets

As I mentioned earlier, you were creating CSS styles while you were modifying settings in the Page Properties dialog box. Dreamweaver automatically adds CSS to your web page, and the styles created are visible in the CSS Styles panel (Window, CSS Styles), as shown in Figure 4.10. To view the styles in a web page, make sure that the All button is selected at the top of the CSS Styles panel and expand the list of styles by clicking the Expand/Collapse (+) button next to <style>.

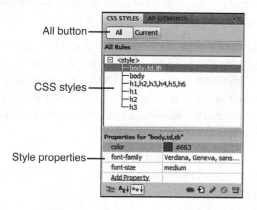

FIGURE 4.10
The CSS Styles panel displays a list of styles created by Dreamweaver when you set properties in the Page Properties dialog box.

The styles created by the Dreamweaver Page Properties dialog box are **redefined** tag styles. These styles add formatting properties and alter the default appearance of various tags. For instance, when you change the background color of the page, Dreamweaver redefines the <body> tag,

NOTE

Goodbye, `<font>` Tag

Note that older browsers—pre-1997 browsers older than Internet Explorer 4 or Netscape Navigator 4—don't support CSS. The older method of formatting text is to use the `<font>` tag. This tag has been deprecated by the World Wide Web Consortium (W3C), the Web standards organization. **Deprecated** means that the W3C is removing it from the approved tag list and eventually it might not be supported by browsers. Dreamweaver CS5 does not insert any `<font>` tags into your code. If you have existing web pages in your website that use this tag, you should plan to update them by replacing the `<font>` tags with CSS.

CAUTION

Choose Your Fonts Wisely

Remember, just because you can see the font and it looks great on your machine doesn't mean that everyone has that font. If a font isn't available, the browser uses the default font—usually Times New Roman—instead. The fonts in the predefined font combinations in Dreamweaver are commonly available fonts in popular operating systems.

which is the tag that contains everything on the web page. These styles are defined in the web page you are working in, but in Hour 11, you learn how to place these styles in an external style sheet that can be shared by multiple web pages.

Changing Text Attributes in the Property Inspector

In the first part of this hour, you learned about the global page settings that affect text. In the next section, you explore setting properties of sections of text on the page using Dreamweaver's Property inspector. The Property inspector enables you to change the font, font size, and color for sections of text using either HTML or CSS—by clicking the HTML or CSS buttons at the left of the panel. Again, CSS is the modern standard for styling pages, so that's what we'll focus on.

When referring to the two modes of the Property inspector, I call them simply CSS or HTML modes. Just click the appropriate button to switch to the correct mode.

Selecting a Text Font

To apply a specific font to a selection of text, select some text and then click the CSS button in the Property inspector. Next, select the Font drop-down menu in the Property inspector, as shown in Figure 4.11.

The fonts in the Font drop-down menu are defined in groups. Specifying a group instead of an individual font increases the odds that your viewers will have at least one of the fonts in the group. The browser attempts to display text with the first font listed, but if that font isn't available, the browser continues through the list. Dreamweaver has predefined groups to choose from, and you can create your own groups.

After choosing your font, Dreamweaver opens a New CSS Rule dialog. We get into this window in depth in Hour 11, but, for now, just enter a unique name for your style in the Selector Name field and then click OK, as shown in Figure 4.12.

FIGURE 4.11
The Font drop-down menu has several font groups from which to choose.

Text font

Text size   Text color

FIGURE 4.12
Choose a selector name for your style.

The selector name is a unique identifier that refers to a CSS style. By changing a font setting, you're creating a new CSS style for your document, and you must provide a name. You can reuse a style that you've already created by choosing the selector name from the Targeted Rule pop-up menu in the CSS mode of the Property inspector or the "Class" popup menu in the HTML mode.

Changing Text Size

As with the font settings, you change text size by selecting one of the size settings in the Property inspector Size drop-down menu shown in Figure 4.13, or by typing a number in the text box. If you select one of the numbers at the top of the list, the Units drop-down menu becomes active so

TIP

Use Ems Instead of Points

Many web designers use relative measurement units such as ems or percent for font measurement. **Ems** are a measurement based on the height of the capital letter "M"; 1em is equal to the height of M in the default font size. **Points** are used for designing type for print but are often unpredictable for displaying text on a computer screen. The great thing about using a relative measurement like ems is that you are respecting your user's font-size choices. If they have set the browser font size to a higher setting, if they have problems seeing, for instance, then your font measurements will be relative to those choices. If you set the font size to 1.25ems for a heading, the text will be a quarter size bigger than the default font that the user has set.

that you can select the unit type. Point and pixel are the most common unit types. You can also select one of the relative sizes (xx-small, medium, large, ems, and so on). These text size settings enable the text to appear relative to the size settings that the user configures in his browser. This is particularly helpful for users who have vision impairment, but it makes it difficult for you to strictly control how your web page appears to the user.

FIGURE 4.13
The Size drop-down menu in the Property inspector enables you to set the size of the selected text.

As with choosing a font, if you haven't defined any other styles, you are asked to create a new CSS selector name for the font size. If you've already set a style (and it is selected in the Targeted Rule menu), the size attribute is added onto your existing CSS selector—creating a compound style.

Selecting a Text Color

You change the text color by either selecting a color using the color picker or by entering a hexadecimal color value, such as #0000FF for blue, into the Text Color text box.

Once again, the same CSS process is enforced. If the color is the only attribute you're setting, Dreamweaver forces you to define a new CSS Selector name. If another style has already been defined and is selected in the Targeted Rule menu, the color becomes an additional attribute of that style.

Viewing and Changing CSS Styles

As you create new styles, you may want to review them to see what effects they apply, and what their names are, and maybe even change a selector name to better match its use in your document. To do this, we can open the CSS Styles panel, by choosing Window, CSS Styles.

Click the All button to show all the defined styles in the active document. Styles created as described above are represented by the name you provided, preceded by a "." (period). To see what effects the style applies to your page, highlight the style name, and then view the properties at the bottom of the CSS Style panel, as shown in Figure 4.14.

NOTE

CSS Styles in HTML Mode

If you happen to be in the HTML mode of the Property inspector, you can still apply CSS styles by selecting your text, then choosing the style name from the Class drop-down menu.

User-defined CSS style —

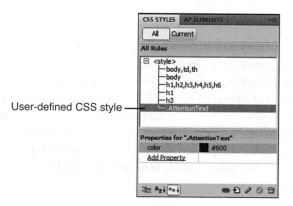

FIGURE 4.14
The name of the CSS style that Dreamweaver created is displayed in the CSS Style drop-down menu.

TRY IT YOURSELF ▼

Deleting an Existing Style

To delete an existing style (if, for example, you've defined a given style under more than one name:

1. Select the style in the CSS Styles panel.

2. Right-click on the style name.

3. Choose delete.

TRY IT YOURSELF ▼

Editing a Style Name

To edit the name of a style to make it more meaningful, do the following:

1. Double-click the style name in the CSS Styles panel.

2. Give the style a name that describes the function of the style in the page.

3. Click OK.

You should never re-create the same formatting by creating additional, identical CSS styles. Instead, you should reapply an existing CSS style.

Applying a CSS Style

Follow these steps to apply a CSS style:

1. Select the appropriate text on the web page.

2. With the CSS button highlighted in the Property inspector, select a style from the Apply portion of the Targeted Rule drop-down menu in the Property inspector.

3. Repeat this process until you have styled all the text you'd like restyled.

You learn how to edit the style definition in Hour 11.

NOTE
No Guarantees in Website Design

There is no way to guarantee that a web page will look the same on a viewer's computer as it does on your computer. Browser preferences enable the user to override font settings, size settings, background colors, and hyperlink colors. Don't expect the page fonts and colors to be exact. If it makes you feel better, though, keep in mind that most users don't change the browser defaults.

You might have noticed that not all the styles listed in your CSS Styles panel appear in the Targeted Rule or Class drop-down menus in Dreamweaver's Property inspector. For instance, the h1 style and the body, td, and th styles don't appear. That's because you apply these redefined tag styles by simply applying the HTML tag to text. In the case of the h1 style, you simply select Heading 1 from the Property inspector's Format drop-down menu in HTML mode. The styles you defined begin with a period, and are known steps to apply a CSS style: as **class selectors**, a special type of style that you apply individually to selections of text.

Aligning Text

You can align text to the left, center, or right just as you can in a word processing program. You can also justify the text so that the left and right margins are evenly set down the page.

Setting Text Alignment

To align some text in the center of the page, follow these steps:

1. Select the text.

2. Click the Align Center icon (see Figure 4.15) in the Property inspector (CSS mode). These icons are very similar to icons in popular word processing programs.

3. Enter a new CSS selector name, if you're prompted. If you're not, the alignment will be added to the currently selected CSS selector.

FIGURE 4.15
The alignment icons in the Property inspector look and act like the alignment commands in word processing software.

Alternatively, with the text selected, select Format, Align, Center. The Text menu also contains all the text formatting commands used in this hour.

Creating Lists and Indenting Text

By using Dreamweaver, you can create bulleted lists, called **unordered lists** in HTML, and numbered lists, called **ordered lists** in HTML. The Unordered List and Ordered List buttons appear in the Property inspector (HTML mode) when you select text.

Create an unordered list by following these steps:

1. Type three items for the list, pressing the Enter (or Return) key after each item so that each item is on its own line.

2. Drag the cursor over all three items to select them.

3. Click the Unordered List button in the Property inspector (HTML mode), as shown in Figure 4.16.

Creating an Unordered List

FIGURE 4.16
The Property inspector has buttons to create ordered and unordered lists. You can click the Indent and Outdent buttons to nest lists and to indent and outdent text.

A bullet precedes each line in an unordered list. Now let's see how we can add a second list within that list:

1. Place the insertion point after the last item.

2. Press the Enter key to make a new line. The new line should be preceded by a bullet.

3. Type three items, as you did in the previous list.

4. Drag the cursor over these new items and click the Indent button in the Property inspector.

Now the second list nests within the third item of the first list. You can tell because it is indented and preceded by a different style of bullet. Use the Outdent button to place the nested list back in line with the main list.

TIP

Customize Your Bullets and Numbers

You can change the bullet or number style by clicking the List Item button in the Property inspector (refer to Figure 4.16) when your cursor is located within the list. Oddly, the List Item button does not appear if you select the entire list. Pick the bullet style (either bullet or square) for an unordered list or pick a number style for an ordered list. You can also start the number count at a number other than 1 by entering the initial number in the Start Count box.

To turn the nested unordered list into an ordered list, select the three items in the nested list again and click the Ordered List button in the Property inspector. To bring the nested list back in line with the main list, click the Outdent button.

With regular text, you use the Indent and Outdent buttons to modify the margins of a block of text. In HTML there is no easy way to tab or indent text, so Dreamweaver uses the `<blockquote>` tag to indent passages of text. This tag actually indents both the left and the right sides of the text, so it might look strange if you indent multiple times.

Adding a Separator to a Page: The Horizontal Rule

A graphical item that has been around since the Stone Age of the Web (almost 20 years ago!) is the horizontal rule. That little divider line is still useful. A horizontal rule is a shaded line that divides a web page into sections. Note that you can't place anything else on the same line with a horizontal rule.

Add a horizontal rule to your web page by selecting the Horizontal Rule object from the Common category of the Insert panel. If you're a menu kind of person, you can do this by selecting Insert, HTML, Horizontal Rule. The Property inspector presents the properties of a horizontal rule. You can set width and height values in either pixels or percentages of the screen. You can also set the alignment and turn shading on and off.

Many objects in HTML have width and height values either in absolute pixel values or as a percentage of the size of the container they are in. If a horizontal rule in the body of a web page is set to a percentage value and the user changes the size of the browser window, the horizontal rule resizes to the new window size. If the horizontal rule is set to an absolute pixel size, it does not resize, and the user sees horizontal scrollbars if the horizontal rule is wider than the screen.

Previewing in a Browser

Even though Dreamweaver is a WYSIWYG (what you see is what you get) tool, you need to see how your page really looks in particular browsers. You should save your work before you preview it in a browser. Saving your work lets Dreamweaver correctly set the paths to linked files, such as images. Dreamweaver prompts you to save the web page before it launches the page in a browser.

Adobe says you can define up to 20 browsers for previewing. Good luck finding 20 browsers! I generally have the following browsers installed for testing: Mozilla Firefox, Microsoft Internet Explorer, Safari, Chrome, and Opera on my Windows machine and Safari, Firefox, and sometimes Opera on my Mac. You must have these programs installed on your computer before you can use them to preview your web pages. All the browsers mentioned have free versions and are available for download over the Internet.

TRY IT YOURSELF ▼

Setting Up a Browser for Previewing

To set up a browser, follow these steps:

1. Select the File, Preview in Browser, Edit Browser List command. Dreamweaver's Preferences dialog box opens to the Preview in Browser category. Dreamweaver might have already located browser(s) and entered them here during the installation process, so the list might not be empty.

2. Click the plus button to add a browser, as shown in Figure 4.17.

3. Leave the Name text box empty for now; Dreamweaver automatically picks up the name of the browser.

Setting Up a Browser for Previewing
Continued

FIGURE 4.17
Set the browsers you will use to preview your web pages in the Preview in Browser category in the Preferences dialog box.

4. Click the Browse button next to the Application text box and navigate to the browser program. For computers running Windows, the default installation location for most browsers is in the `Program Files` directory. For the Mac, look in your `Applications` folder.

5. Click either the Primary Browser check box or the Secondary Browser check box. This determines which keyboard shortcut you use to launch the browser. The keyboard shortcut for one primary browser is F12, and the shortcut for one secondary browser is Ctrl+F12.

6. Repeat steps 2–5 until all browsers have been added.

7. Make sure that the Preview Using Temporary Files option is not selected. Click the OK button when you are done.

Below the browser list is a single check box option that controls whether you directly view your web page in the browser or whether you want Dreamweaver to create a temporary file to display in the browser. When the box is checked, you won't need to save your web page before previewing in a browser because Dreamweaver creates a temporary file for you to display in the browser. If you uncheck this box, you have to save your web page before previewing it in the browser. I prefer to uncheck this box and know that I'm viewing the actual web page instead of a temporary file. Even after you've saved your page in Dreamweaver and previewed it in the browser, you can still undo changes that you made before closing the page.

Select File, Preview in Browser or select Preview/Debug in Browser on the Document toolbar to view the current web page. Select the browser you want to use from the menu. If the browser is already open, you might have to switch to the application to see your page. If the browser isn't already open, Dreamweaver opens it and loads the requested page so that you can preview it.

Summary

Congratulations! You've created your first web page in Dreamweaver and learned a lot about formatting the page and text on the page. Many of the tasks described in this hour will become habitual to you with every web page you create, and you will be able to quickly move through the steps you've practiced here.

In this hour, you learned how to enter and import text into a web page. You set text properties, including headings, fonts, lists, and alignment. You were introduced to CSS, the language of presentation on the Web. You used a horizontal rule to separate the page into sections, and previewed your work in a browser.

Q&A

Q. Where can I learn more about CSS styles? They seem important.

A. CSS styles are important, and they are part of the movement in web development toward separating content (the words and images on the web page) from the presentation (font size, colors, and positioning). This separation is important because it is becoming more and more common to deliver content to various devices, such as PDAs (personal digital assistants), and to people with disabilities, such as impaired sight.

You learn much more about CSS styles in Hour 11.

Q. I indented a line of text by clicking the Indent button. I wanted it to act as a tab acts in my word processing program, but it seems to indent both the beginning and the end of the line. What's going on?

A. There is no easy way in HTML to tab as you do in your word processing program. The Indent button applies the `<blockquote>` tag to the text. This tag, as you noticed, actually indents both the left and the right of the text. The block quote tag was originally designed for quotes in research-type documents. One way to indent text is to use CSS-Positioning techniques that you learn about in Hour 12, "Using CSS for Positioning."

Workshop

Quiz

1. What button in the Property inspector do you select to nest a list?

2. By default, which heading size is largest on the screen: Heading 1 or Heading 6?

3. How do you change global settings, such as the default font and font size for all the text on the page?

Quiz Answers

1. The Indent button nests one list within another.

2. Heading 1 is the largest size and Heading 6 is the smallest.

3. The Page Properties dialog box, under Modify, Page Properties, controls page-level properties.

Exercises

1. Experiment with creating lists. Create an ordered list, an unordered list, a definition list (see the Text tab of the Insert panel), and some nested lists. As you do this, look at the tag selector in the status bar and see which HTML tags are used. What do you think the <li> tag is for?

2. Select one of the color boxes in the Page Properties dialog box and set up a custom color. Use the eyedropper to pick a color from anywhere onscreen. You can even pick a color from another application you have open.

HOUR 5
Making Hyperlinks, Anchors, and Mailto Links

Clicking a **hyperlink** allows the viewer to jump to another web page, jump to another section of the current web page, or launch an email message. A website is made up of a group of web pages, and hyperlinks enable viewers to navigate from page to page. Hyperlinks, in the simplest form, are the familiar underlined and colored (usually blue) text that you click. You can also make an image a hyperlink.

Hyperlinks help make the Web a powerful source of information. If you've surfed the Web at all, I'm sure you've clicked many, many hyperlinks. But hyperlinks can also make the Web confusing. Sometimes it is difficult to remember the exact path you took to find information, and that can make it difficult to get back to the information when you want to see it again.

A web address is called a **uniform resource locator (URL)**. You can link many types of files over the Web, but a browser displays only a few file types. A browser can display the supported image formats, HTML, player applications (such as Flash), and a few other specialized types of files. If a link leads to a file that the browser can't display (a `.zip` file, for example), the browser usually asks you whether you'd like to save the file to your hard drive.

WHAT YOU'LL LEARN IN THIS HOUR:

▶ When to use relative and absolute paths
▶ How to create a hyperlink to another page within a website and a hyperlink to a page outside a website
▶ How to create hyperlinks within a page
▶ How to add a link that opens a preaddressed email message

Exploring Relative and Absolute Paths

Whenever you create a hyperlink to another web page in a web page, you have to enter a path to the file. You must also enter a path when you add an image to a web page. Dreamweaver helps make sure that these paths are correct, but it's important that you understand the difference between the three types of paths:

▶ An **absolute path** (also called a **full path**) is the full URL to a web page. The path points to the exact same file regardless of where the path is referenced from. This type of path always begins with the transfer protocol (HTTP, HTTPS, FTP, File, and so on).

▶ A **document-relative path** points to the location of a file in relationship to the page being viewed. The path points to the file relative to the file location of the file that contains the reference.

▶ A **site root–relative path** points to the location of a file in relationship to the root of the site. This type of path always begins with a forward slash (/).

You explore each of these types of paths in order to understand how to correctly reference files in hyperlinks.

Understanding Absolute Paths

An absolute path is a like a house address. If I gave the address of my house to someone who lives in another town, I would say, "I live at 123 Spruce Street, Columbus, Ohio 43210, USA." This is all the information that anyone would need to get to my exact location or to send me a letter (this isn't my real address, so if you really want to send me a letter, send it in care of the publisher!).

The link to Flora Photographs shown in Figure 5.1 is an absolute path. It contains the entire path to a file on the Internet. Because you have no control over this site, linking to it means that you need to check to see that the link remains valid. If the site moves in the future, you have to update the link.

A URL consists of up to five sections, as shown in Figure 5.2 and listed here:

▶ **Protocol**—The first part of the URL is the protocol. It is http for web pages to indicate Hypertext Transfer Protocol (HTTP). Sometimes you might want to link to a file on a File Transfer Protocol (FTP) server (another method of communicating over the Internet to move files to and from a server), using ftp instead of http as the protocol in the URL.

▶ **Domain**—The second part of the address is the domain name. This is the web server where the web page is located; for example, in Figure 5.2, the domain name is floraphotographs.com. A colon and two forward slashes (://) separate the protocol and the domain name.

Link text

FIGURE 5.1
Entering an absolute path links to a
specific web page.

Absolute path

▶ **Port**—An optional third part of a URL is the port. The default port for
a web server is port 80. When you enter http as the protocol, port 80
is implied and doesn't usually need to be included. You might need
to enter port information when entering addresses to specialized web
applications that listen on a port other than port 80.

▶ **Path to file**—The fourth part of the address is the path to the filename. The path includes all directories and the filename. Most web
pages end in .htm or .html. Other common file endings are .cgi for
Common Gateway Interface; .asp for Active Server Pages; .jsp for
JavaServer Pages; .aspx for ASP.NET files; .php for PHP pages; and
.cfm for ColdFusion Markup Language.

▶ **Query string**—The filenames might be followed by an optional fifth
part of a URL: a query string. A query string is added to a URL to
send data to a script for processing. We explore query strings in Hour
22, "Sending and Reacting to Form Data."

You might see a URL that does not have a filename referenced at the end,
such as http://www.adobe.com/devnet/mx/dreamweaver/. No specific
file is referenced in this URL, but only the final directory is included

FIGURE 5.2
A URL consists of multiple
sections. Every URL must contain a
protocol, a domain name, and the
complete path to a file.

| Protocol | Domain | Port | Path to file | Query string |

`http://floraphotographs.com:80/ecards/index.php?photoID=324`

(/dreamweaver/ in this case). This type of address works because the web server looks for a default page in the directory. Most web servers have a default page name that doesn't need to be explicitly entered at the end of the URL. Usually the default page name is `index.html`, `index.htm`, `default.htm`, `default.html`, or `welcome.htm`. On some servers, any of these names work. This functionality can be configured in web server software.

Default pages in the root of a site are often referred to as **home pages**. To create a home page for a website, ask your webmaster or web hosting service for the default page name for your web server. If you don't have a default page on your website and a visitor doesn't enter a filename at the end of the URL, that person might see all the contents of your directories instead of a web page. Or the user might get an error message!

Most browsers don't require that you enter the protocol into the browser's address box to go to a web page. The browsers assume that you want to use the HTTP protocol to access a web page. However, if you are surfing to an FTP file, you have to enter **ftp** as the protocol at the beginning of the URL. Even though browsers assume HTTP, you still need to preface absolute links entered into Dreamweaver with http://.

TIP

Browsing Directories

You can set whether browsing of directories and files is enabled on most web servers. If you use a hosting service and you cannot turn off directory browsing, make sure that you have a default web page in each directory. You don't want people to be able to browse around the file structure of your website.

Understanding Document-Relative Paths

Remember the house-address analogy I used in my absolute path discussion earlier? If I gave directions to my house to someone who knows my mom, I might tell them, "I live next door to my mom and always will." (I love my mom but I do not actually live next door to her!) The directions in this case are relative to my mom's location and assume that if my mom moves, I will move, too, so as to continue living next door to her. This is analogous to a document-relative path.

Within your own website, you usually use document-relative paths so that you can move your site anywhere and your links still work. While developing in Dreamweaver, you create a website on your local hard drive but eventually move the site to a web server. Document-relative paths work the same in both locations.

It's important to use document-relative paths instead of absolute paths in your website. If you have an absolute path to a file on your local drive, the link looks like the following:

```
file:///C¦/My Documents/first_page.html
```

This file, `first_page.html`, is on the C: drive in a directory called `My Documents`. If the creator of this web page previews this page in his browser, it works fine for him. So what's the problem? The reason it works fine for him is that he has the page available on his hard drive. But other people don't have access to his hard drive and will not be able to access the page.

Document-relative paths don't require a complete URL. The path to the linked file is expressed relative to the current document. You use this type of path when inserting images into a web page. You also use a document-relative path when creating a hyperlink to a web page within your website. Luckily, Dreamweaver saves the correct document-relative path after you save a web page.

The following are some examples of document-relative paths:

- ► When linking to a file that is in the same directory as your current file, you enter only the filename as the path. For instance, if the file `collections.html` in Figure 5.3 has a link to `joy.html`, the path would simply be the filename because both files are in the same directory.

- ► To link to a file in a directory nested within the current file's directory, you enter the directory name and the filename as a path. For instance, if the `storefront.html` file in Figure 5.3 has a link to the `clothing.html` file in the `shop` directory, the path is `shop/clothing.html`.

- ► When linking to a file in a directory above the current directory (called the **parent directory**), you enter `../` plus the filename as a path. The `../` means go up to the next parent directory. For instance, if the `clothing.html` file in Figure 5.3 has a link to the `storefront.html` file in the site root, the path is `../storefront.html`.

If you add links before first saving your web page, Dreamweaver inserts them as absolute links; you might receive an error message warning you of this when you add a link. It does this because it cannot calculate a relative link until the file has been saved. After saving the file, Dreamweaver can tell where your document is relative to all linked files and changes the links

NOTE

Links Work with Other Files, Too

You don't have to limit your links to web pages. You can link to movies, word processing files (.doc files, for instance), PDF files, and audio files. The URLs work the same regardless of the content. Of course, the browser you use has to recognize the content type to display it properly. You learn more about the players necessary to play audio files and how to view PDF documents in Hour 10, "Adding Flash and Other Multimedia to a Web Page."

FIGURE 5.3
Document-relative paths depend on the relative position of the files in the directory structure.

Document-relative path from storefront.html: shop/clothing.html

Document-relative path from collections.html: joy.html

Document-relative path from clothing: ../storefront.html

to document-relative addresses. Accidentally using absolute paths is an easy mistake to make. Dreamweaver looks out for you, however, and attempts to correct these problems for you.

Understanding Site Root–Relative Paths

There is a third type of path, called **site root–relative**. Sticking with the house analogy (and I might be stretching the boundaries of this analogy), a site root–relative link is like two people living in the same city. As long as they live in the same city, they can give directions to each house via a famous landmark in the middle of the city. Creating site root–relative links is similar because each link references the site root.

In a site root–relative link, the path is relative to the root of the entire website. The **root** of the website is defined as the top level of a website, usually where the site's main home page is located. Site root–relative linking is used when many different sections of the website need to access a common group of files, such as a corporate logo.

Site root–relative paths are not the best choice for beginning web development workers. The main difficulty occurs when you preview pages: You might have references to site root–relative links that aren't available on your local hard drive. In that case, you won't be able to preview your work properly in a browser without loading it onto the server.

Adding a Hyperlink Within a Website

In this section, you create several new web pages and save them to your website. You can use these pages to practice linking by using document-relative paths.

TIP

Click Here...

It's generally bad form to explicitly reference a hyperlink by saying, "Click *here* to see our statistics." It's better to incorporate a hyperlink into a natural sentence, such as, "The *Q4 2009 statistics* show that sales increased by 32%." This hyperlink would open another web page showing the detail of the Q4 statistics. Ideally, hyperlinks seamlessly blend into the text of your documents.

Do the following to create a simple multipage structured website:

1. Create a new website that holds your files. Make sure that the site is selected. You will be creating "home," "store," "links," and "contact us" pages.

2. Select File, New to open the New Document dialog box.

3. Choose Blank Page, HTML, Layout <none>, as shown in Figure 5.4. We're interested only in creating links, so blank pages work just fine for this example.

FIGURE 5.4
Create a new blank page for your links.

▼ TRY IT YOURSELF

Linking a Multipage Website

Continued

4. Select XHTML 1.0 Transitional from the DocType drop-down list.

5. Click the Create button.

6. Immediately save and name the page `index.html`. This is the home page for the site.

7. Repeat steps 1–6 and create the following pages:

  ▶ `storefront.html`

  ▶ `links.html`

  ▶ `contact.html`

Now you add hyperlinks so that you can navigate among the Products, Links, and Contact Us pages, as well as return to the Home page.

▼ TRY IT YOURSELF

Adding Hyperlinks

To add hyperlinks, follow these steps:

1. Open the home page (`index.html`).

2. Enter the text you need for navigation, styling it as an unordered list. (Unordered lists are commonly used for navigation structures. CSS can be used to remove bullets and even switch to a horizontal list, but for now we'll focus on linking.)

3. Select the text *Store* by either dragging your cursor over the letters or simply clicking within the text.

4. Select the Browse to File tool (which looks like a folder) next to the Link drop-down menu in the Property inspector (HTML mode). Select the filename `storefront.html`.

5. In the Select File dialog box, make sure that the Relative To drop-down menu at the bottom shows Document, making the link document-relative, as shown in Figure 5.5.

6. Click OK. Dreamweaver enters a relative address into the Link drop-down menu, as shown in Figure 5.6.

7. Repeat steps 1–6, linking each of the links to the other pages (`links.html` and `contact.html`).

Adding Hyperlinks
Continued

Document-relative

FIGURE 5.5
Set the Relative to: dropdown
menu to Document.

Browse to File
Point to File

Document-relative link

FIGURE 5.6
When linking to a relative file
within the same website,
Dreamweaver enters the path to
the file in the Property inspector's
Link box.

8. Your home page is now linked to the other pages in your site. You must now establish the links from the other content pages to the home page.

9. Open each of the linked pages (`links.html`, `contact.html`, and `storefront.html`) and create breadcrumb text (see the following Note to learn about breadcrumbs) at the top of the page that resembles "Home > Store" (in `storefront.html`) and "Home > Contact Us" (in `contact.html`) and so on.

10. Finally, revisit each of the pages (`storefront.html`, `contact.html`, `links.html`), select the label Home, and click the Point to File tool next to the Link drop-down menu and point the arrow that appears to the home page (`index.html`). This tool lets you link a site file within the Files panel rather than navigating to it.

▼ TRY IT YOURSELF

Adding Hyperlinks
Continued

Each hyperlink appears as an underlined blue hyperlink in the Dreamweaver Document window. Preview the web page in the browser and click a link. You should jump to another page! When you click the HOME link, you should return to the home page.

NOTE

Breadcrumbs

Breadcrumbs are a navigation technique commonly used in web design. The term refers to a trail of links displayed horizontally across the top of the web page. The rightmost link displays the page that you are currently viewing, whereas the links to the left display the pages you used to get there. For instance, HOME > ABOUT US > JOBS shows a web page listing jobs that is in the About Us section of a website. The term *breadcrumbs* refers to the technique used by Hansel and Gretel to return home by leaving a trail of breadcrumbs to follow.

Setting Link Color Preferences

You set the link colors in the Page Properties dialog box just as you set the default text color in Hour 4, "Adding Text and Lists." Open the Page Properties dialog box (Modify, Page Properties) and select the Links (CSS) category, as shown in Figure 5.7. You set the link font and font size for all the links on the page at the top of the dialog box. You can set the following four options here:

▶ **Link Color**---The default color of all the links on the page.

▶ **Visited Links**---The color of a link after it has been visited by the browser.

▶ **Rollover Links**---The color of a link when the cursor is over the link.

▶ **Active Links**---The color of the link when the user is actively clicking the link (while the mouse button is down).

FIGURE 5.7
You set the appearance attributes of links in the Page Properties dialog box's Links (CSS) category.

Use the color picker to add a link color, visited link color, rollover link color, and active link color. When you apply the changes to your web page, you should see all your links in the link color. When the viewer's browser has visited one of your links, the link appears in the visited link color. The viewer sees the active link color while the mouse is actively clicking the link. The link colors are defined for the entire page, so all your links will be the color you specify.

Dreamweaver sets the link colors by using CSS styles. You can also turn off the hyperlink underline by setting the Underline style. There are four choices: Always Underline, Never Underline, Show Underline Only on Rollover, and Hide Underline on Rollover. After you click the OK button, Dreamweaver saves the CSS describing how the links appear on the web page in the code of the page.

TIP

The Hyperlink Underline

Many usability experts advise against removing the underline because it makes links on the page more difficult to identify. That said, this practice is becoming more acceptable and can look very nice when properly applied.

Organizing a Long Page by Using Named Anchors

Have you ever visited a web page on which you clicked a link and it took you to another part of the same web page? For instance, frequently asked questions (FAQs) often have hyperlinks at the top of the page listing the questions; when you click one of the hyperlinks, you jump farther down the page to the question's answer. That type of web page is created with **named anchors**. You use named anchors because sometimes it's less confusing to jump within the same web page than to jump to another web page.

To create a long page with named anchors, first add a named anchor to the location on the page where the user jumps. Then create a hyperlink that links to the named anchor. You can start creating a named anchor with a page that has multiple sections, such as the one shown in Figure 5.8.

FIGURE 5.8
A website can have multiple sections, with a menu at the top of the page linking to the sections.

Links to named anchors

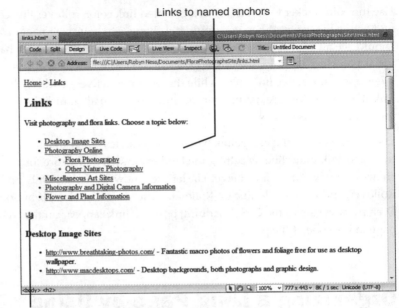

Named Anchor icon

▼ TRY IT YOURSELF

Using Named Anchors

To create a page for this example, follow these steps:

1. Create a new blank web page by selecting File, New, Blank Page, HTML, <none> or open the Links page you created earlier. At the top of the page add several categories that will link to other parts of the page. Save your page.

2. Create headings related to the categories. My example organizes links to related sites, but you can enter dummy text.

3. Place the insertion point in front of one of the headings. This is the area of the page to which users jump when they click the link to the named anchor.

4. Select Insert, Named Anchor or select Named Anchor in the Common category of the Insert panel. The Named Anchor dialog box, shown in Figure 5.9, appears.

FIGURE 5.9
After you select the Named Anchor command, give the anchor

TRY IT YOURSELF ▼

Using Named Anchors
Continued

5. Name the anchor and then click OK.

6. Repeat steps 1–5, creating a named anchor and then creating a link to that anchor, until the web page is complete.

Understanding Invisible Elements

You might have received a message stating that you will not see a named anchor because it is invisible. After inserting a named anchor a small yellow symbol appears in the Document window at the location where you inserted the named anchor; it is the visual representation of a named anchor, which is an invisible element.

Some objects that you insert into a web page aren't designed to be viewable within a website. Because Dreamweaver is a WYSIWYG (what you see is what you get) design tool, Adobe designed a way to show objects that are invisible on the web page. You can turn on or off invisible elements using the Visual Aids drop-down menu (it looks like an eye on top of a dotted rectangle) in the Document toolbar. When the Invisible Elements feature is enabled, Dreamweaver displays the invisible elements so you can select the markers to view or edit the properties for the objects that they represent in the Property inspector.

Linking to a Named Anchor

You've created a named anchor, but that really isn't very useful unless you link something to it. Add a text link at the top of the page. It might not be obvious that your web page is jumping to the named anchor location unless you have enough content to scroll in the browser, so add some extra text or simply some blank space so that you can see the jumping effect when you test your page in the browser. To link to the new named anchor, follow these steps:

1. Select the text tolink to the named anchor.

2. Enter the name of the named anchor, preceded by a pound sign (for example, `#desktop`) in the Link box labeled in Figure 5.8.

You can link to a named anchor in another file. To do so, you simply append the name of the named anchor to the filename, as demonstrated in the following line:

http://www.floraphotographs.com/links.html#desktop

You also can drag the Point-to-File icon, shown in Figure 5.6, to a named anchor. When the Point-to-File icon is dragged over a named anchor, the name of the anchor appears in the Link box of the Property inspector. To select the named anchor, simply release the mouse button while the Point-to-File icon is over the named anchor.

Adding a Mailto Link

It's nice to put a link in a web page to allow a viewer to send email. This type of link is called a **mailto link**. The Dreamweaver Email Link object helps you implement a mailto link. The user must have an email application set up to work with the browser for these links to work.

To create a mailto link, select some text to be the link. Click the Email Link object (in the Common panel of the Insert panel), and the Email Link dialog box appears (see Figure 5.10). Enter the email address and click OK. The text looks like a hyperlink, but instead of linking to another page, it opens a preaddressed email message.

FIGURE 5.10
Use Dreamweaver's Email Link object to insert an email link.

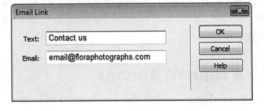

TIP

Avoiding Inviting Spam?

Here are some additional tips on avoiding inviting spam:

▶ Don't enter your email address into guest books.

▶ Don't respond to spam asking to be removed from a list.

▶ Create a throwaway email address that you change every so often and use only for your website.

Spammers troll the Internet for mailto links. If you use mailto links in your web pages, expect to get a lot of **spam**, or junk email, sent to the email address used in the mailto links.

An effective way to cut back on the spam is to use an email link obfuscator, such as the ASCII Email Obfuscator (http://digitalcolony.com/lab/maskemail/maskemailascii.aspx). These tools generate mailto links that work in your browser, but are very difficult for spammers to harvest. All you do is provide the email information you want to obfuscate, and the tool generates a piece of HTML code that you can paste into your page.

Summary

In this hour, you learned the difference between absolute, document-relative, and site root–relative paths. You created links to external websites and relative links to pages within a website. You learned how to insert a named anchor and then link to it, and you created a mailto link to allow a viewer to launch an email message directly from a web page.

Q&A

Q. The named anchor that I want to link to is low enough on the page that I can't see it onscreen. How can I use the Point-to-File tool to reach it?

A. If you drag the Point-to-File tool to either the top or the bottom of the Document window, the window scrolls. Hold the tool near the edge of the window until it has scrolled to the point where the named anchor is visible on the screen. Alternatively, first select the text that will be the hyperlink and then scroll down the page (carefully so as not to click on the window anywhere and deselect the text). When you see the named anchor, grab the Point-to-File icon and drag the tool to the anchor.

Q. I found a page on another site that I want to link to, but the URL is long. Do I have to retype it in Dreamweaver?

A. The easiest way to enter a lengthy URL is to copy the URL from the browser's address text box (by pressing Ctrl+C in Windows or Command+C on the Mac). You can then paste the URL into Dreamweaver's Link drop-down menu.

Q. Is there any way to add a subject line into an email link?

A. Yes! In the Dreamweaver Email Link dialog box, add a question mark immediately after the email address (no space) and then type **subject=** and the subject that you want to appear. You can also add some text for the body of the email message by typing **&body=**. You can also simply edit the link in the Property inspector's Link drop-down menu. The link looks like this:

```
mailto:jray@jraymail.com?subject=Sams Teach Yourself
➥Adobe Dreamweaver in 24 Hours&body=I'm interested in discussing
➥this book.
```

Workshop

Quiz

1. How can you view a named anchor if it isn't currently visible onscreen?

2. What is the difference between a document-relative path and a site root–relative path?

3. When does a web page viewer see the active link color?

Quiz Answers

1. Select View, Visual Aids, Invisible Elements to see invisible element items.

2. A site root-relative path begins with a forward slash, whereas a document-relative path does not.

3. A web page viewer sees the active link color while actively clicking a hyperlink.

Exercises

1. Surf the Web for 10–15 minutes with your new awareness of the different types of links. When you place the cursor over a link, you can usually see the address of the link in the status bar at the bottom of the browser. Look for links to named anchors, too.

2. Create a favorite links page, including links to all your favorite websites. You can either use the URL of the link as the text that displays or create a hyperlink out of a descriptive word or phrase. Hint: The major browsers have methods of exporting all your bookmarks or favorites. These methods can give you a huge head start on this exercise.

3. Create a frequently asked questions web page about a topic you understand well. List the questions at the top of the page as an unordered list. Repeat the question and add the answer at the bottom of the page, and then add a named anchor. Make the questions at the top of the page link to the appropriate named anchor below.

Displaying Data in Tables

Tables provide the capability to logically present data in columns and rows. This hour introduces you to creating tables.

Using tables can be a powerful way to organize and display data. You use tables in HTML just as you use them in a word processing application. Tables consist of rows, columns, and cells. Dreamweaver presents many ways to format tables the way you would like them to appear to your viewer.

Creating a Table for Data

Let's begin exploring tables by adding a table that holds some data. Examples of this type of table are a phone list of people in your company or class at school, a list of wedding gifts and prices, or a monthly budget with items and dollar amounts. If you've ever used Microsoft Excel to keep track of a list, you'll feel right at home with HTML tables.

> NOTE
>
> **Other Uses for Tables**
>
> In the past, tables had been heavily used for page layout—in fact, this was originally the only way to create complex page designs. Since the advent of CSS, however, using tables for layout has become a no-no. Although you may still find sites that use tables in this way, CSS is cleaner and provides a more flexible, updatable, and accessible means of defining a page's look and feel. Hour 12, "Using CSS for Positioning," introduces you to using CSS for page layout.

WHAT YOU'LL LEARN IN THIS HOUR:

- ▶ How to create and format a table
- ▶ How to add and sort data in a table
- ▶ How to export data from a table
- ▶ How to align the contents of table cells
- ▶ How to nest a table within a table cell

Inserting a Table into Your Web Page

To insert a table into your web page, follow these steps:

1. Place the insertion point in your web page where you want to insert the table.

2. Select Insert, Table. The Table dialog box appears, as shown in Figure 6.1.

FIGURE 6.1
The Table dialog box enables you to set the initial values of the table. You can always edit these values in the Property inspector later.

3. Accept the default values or enter your own values into the Rows and Columns text boxes.

4. Set the width of the table (for example, 500 pixels) and the border size (for example, 2 pixels) in this dialog box. You learn about all these parameters, including the accessibility settings at the bottom of the dialog box, later in this hour.

5. When you finish setting values in this dialog box, click OK.

Tables (`<table>` and `</table>`) are made up of table rows (`<tr>` and `</tr>`) that contain either table cells (`<td>` and `</td>`) and (`</th>`) for row or column headings. In HTML, tables are structured by their rows; you do not need to define columns, and no tag in HTML creates columns. In the rest of this hour, you modify the attributes of tables, table rows, and table cells.

When you select a table or when the insertion point is within a table, Dreamweaver displays the width of the table and the width of each of the columns in the table header menu, which appears either above or below the table. The Table Selector menu, shown in Figure 6.2, is the green menu that is visible only in Dreamweaver and doesn't appear in the web browser. To turn off the display of the Table Selector menu in Dreamweaver, select View, Visual Aids, Table Widths. You explore the Table Selector menu a bit more later this hour.

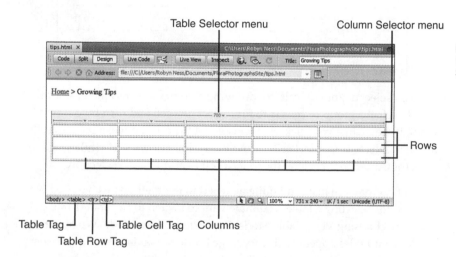

FIGURE 6.2
Dreamweaver displays the Table Selector menu below a table.

Selecting Table Elements

You can select a table in a couple ways. I think the easiest way to select the table is to click the little arrow in the Table Selector menu, shown in Figure 6.2. Choose the Select Table command from the Table Selector menu to select the table. You can also use the tag selector in Dreamweaver's status bar by clicking the table tag to select a table. Click inside one of the cells in your table. The status bar displays the tag hierarchy, including the table tag that you can click on to select the entire table.

To select a cell, simply click inside it. To select an entire row, position your cursor slightly to the left of the table row until the cursor turns into a solid black arrow. Click while the cursor is the solid black right-pointing arrow and the row turns red to select the row. Use the same procedure, positioning your cursor slightly above the column, to select an entire column, as shown in Figure 6.3. Or click the little arrow below the column to open the column selector menu, and then choose Select Column.

Arrow cursor

FIGURE 6.3
The cursor, positioned slightly
above a table column, turns into a
solid black arrow. Select an entire
column by clicking with this cursor.

You can select a group of cells by dragging the cursor across them. Another
way to select a group of cells is to first select one cell and then hold down
the Shift key while you click another cell. All the cells between the two cells
are then selected. To select cells individually, hold down Ctrl while you
click (or Command+click on the Mac) a cell to add it to the selection.

If you find that you just can't quite get used to the methods we've already
covered for selecting a table, you may want to switch to Expanded Tables
mode by choosing View, Table Mode, Expanded Tables Mode. When in this
mode, your tables appear with very large borders, making them quite easy
to select. One word of caution: Although this doesn't alter the appearance
of the table in your browser, it means that Dreamweaver's Design mode
isn't showing an accurate representation of your page. You'll want to
switch back to Standard mode after completing your table manipulations.

Regardless of how you select tables and table elements, the Property
inspector shows different attributes depending on what is selected. There
are two basic ways that the Property inspector appears while you're working with tables:

CAUTION

Drag over Cells Carefully

When a table is empty, it's easy
to drag the cursor across the
group of cells you want to
select. Start dragging while your
cursor is inside the first cell.
When the cells contain assets,
however, it's too easy to accidentally move objects from their
cells when you use this procedure.

  ▶ When you select an entire table, the Property inspector looks as
    shown in Figure 6.4, displaying properties of the entire table.

  ▶ When you select an individual cell, entire row, or entire column, the
    Property inspector looks as shown in Figure 6.5, displaying proper-
    ties that affect the selected cells.

Table properties   Rows   Columns   Width

Clear buttons
Convert buttons

FIGURE 6.4
The Property inspector displays properties that apply to the entire table when you select the entire table.

Row, column, or cell properties

FIGURE 6.5
The Property inspector displays properties of selected cells when you select an individual cell, entire row, or entire column.

Setting Cell Padding, Cell Spacing, and Header Options

Let's add a new table to explore the setting for cell padding, cell spacing, and header in the Table dialog box (see Figure 6.6). Click the Table icon in the Common category of the Insert panel (or select Insert, Table).

▶ **Cell padding**—This is where you set the amount of space between an object contained in a cell and the border of the cell. The cell padding sits between the contents of the cell and the inside cell border.

▶ **Cell spacing**—This is where you set the amount of space between table cells. The cell spacing sits between the outer cell borders of adjacent cells.

▶ **Header**—The header settings enable you to add a header row at the top of the table, along the left, or along both edges. By default, the text in header cells appears bold and centered.

The Table dialog box displays illustrations next to each of these settings, highlighting the area of the cell that the setting affects.

TIP

Dreamweaver Keeps Your Table Settings

Did you notice that when you inserted another table, Dreamweaver kept the row and column settings you entered earlier? That makes it easy to create multiple tables that have similar settings.

FIGURE 6.6
Set the Cell Padding, Cell Spacing, and Header settings in the Table dialog box.

Making a Table Accessible to People with Disabilities

Users who are visually impaired and using text-to-speech synthesizer software to read your web page will have the most trouble reading large tables full of data. These users will greatly appreciate your small effort to design a table that is easier for people to navigate and extract data from. Dreamweaver has made this easy for you by placing the accessibility settings at the bottom of the Table dialog box.

You can add a caption for a table that appears in the browser and is visible to everyone. You should always add a summary for your table, as shown in Figure 6.7. Only text-to-speech browsers read the summary, and it helps the user evaluate whether to progress through the table data or skip the information.

After you've entered all the settings into the Table dialog box, click the OK button to create the table.

Modifying a Table and Adding Content

When you have your table structure determined, you can start adding text or images to the table. You can also fine-tune the structure as you work in Dreamweaver by using the Property inspector and selecting table cells or

TIP

Layout Tables Are Not Accessibility Friendly

Accessibility is one of the main reasons it's not a good idea to use tables for layout. Although pages that use tables for layout look good visually, they are difficult to navigate for people using text-to-speech browsers—regardless of whether you completed the accessibility settings.

FIGURE 6.7
The Accessibility settings are
important for people who have
visual impairments.

Accessibility settings ——

entire tables. Later in this hour, you use some of the built-in table color
schemes available in Dreamweaver.

Adding and Sorting Data

To enter data, you click in a table cell, type, and then tab to the next cell.
You can press Shift+Tab to move backward through the table cells. When
you reach the rightmost cell in the bottom row, pressing Tab creates a new
row. Add data to your table until you have enough data to make it interesting to sort.

NOTE

Creating New Table Rows

When you press the Tab key to
create a new table row,
Dreamweaver gives the new row
the attributes of the previous
row. This might be what you
want. But if you use the Tab key
to create a new row from a
header cell row, your row will be
more header cells!

TRY IT YOURSELF ▼

**Sorting a Table Using
the Sort Table
Command**

Dreamweaver makes it easy to sort the data in your table by using
Commands, Sort Table. To sort a table by using the Sort Table command, follow these steps:

1. Select the table and then select Commands, Sort Table. The Sort Table
   dialog box, shown in Figure 6.8, appears. It contains several drop-down
   menus to help you sort the table.

2. Select the column to sort in the Sort By drop-down menu.

3. Select whether you want to sort the column alphabetically or numerically
   in the Order drop-down menu.

4. Select whether you want to sort in ascending or descending order in the
   drop-down list directly to the right of the Order drop-down menu.

▼ TRY IT YOURSELF

5. Below this first set of sorting options, you can set up a secondary search, if necessary. If you do this, Dreamweaver first sorts by the primary column and then sorts by the secondary column.

6. If the first row of the table is a header row, leave the Sort Includes the First Row box unchecked. If you don't have header cells, you should include the first row in the sort.

7. If you'd like the header and footer rows of the table to be sorted, select Sort Header Rows or Sort Footer Rows, respectively.

8. The Keep All Row Colors the Same After the Sort Has Been Completed check box allows you to keep table row attributes with the row after the sort. If you have formatted your table in a certain way, you should check this box so that your formatting isn't lost.

9. Click OK to start the sort.

FIGURE 6.8
The Sort Table dialog box contains drop-down menus with sorting options.

NOTE

Modifying the Number of Rows and Columns

When you use the Property inspector to adjust the number of rows and columns, Dreamweaver inserts a new column to the far right of the table. It inserts a new row at the bottom of the table. If you remove columns or rows in the Property inspector, Dreamweaver removes the columns from the right side and the rows from the bottom. You lose any data that is in the removed columns or rows.

Adding and Removing Rows and Columns

To insert or remove a row or column from a table, use the context menu that pops up when you right-click a table cell. Right-click a table cell and select the Table submenu; another menu appears, with a number of commands to add and remove rows, columns, or both, as shown in Figure 6.9. Select one of these commands to make a change to the table.

You can use the icons in the Layout category of the Insert panel to add rows either above or below the current row or to add columns to the left or the right of the current column. You can also add or remove rows and columns by editing the table properties in the Property inspector. Adjust the number of rows and columns in the Property inspector with an entire table selected to add or remove groups of cells.

FIGURE 6.9
The context menu has a Table submenu that contains many commands to add, remove, or change the rows and columns of a table.

It's fine to nest tables within tables within tables. Placing a table within a table cell creates a nested table. The dimensions of the table cell limit the nested table's width and height. To nest a table, place the insertion point inside a table cell and insert a new table (Insert, Table). However, if you nest too much, the browser might display the tables slowly.

Changing Column Width and Row Height

You can change column width and row height by dragging the cell borders or by entering values in the Property inspector. If you prefer to eyeball the size, position the cursor over a cell border until the cursor turns into the double-line cursor. Drag the double-line cursor to change the column width or row height.

Use the W (width) and H (height) boxes in the Property inspector to give exact values to widths and heights. Values are expressed in either pixels or percentages. A percentage value changes your table size as the size of the browser window changes, whereas a pixel value always displays the table at a constant size.

Resizing and Coloring Tables

Just as you can change the size of cells, rows, and columns, you can change the size of an entire table. With the entire table selected, drag the resizing handles to make the table a different size. If you have not given width and height values to cells, rows, and columns, the cells distribute themselves proportionally when the entire table size is changed. Or use the W and H boxes in the Property inspector, with the entire table selected, to give the table either pixel or percentage size values.

To clear all the width and height values from a table, select the Table Selector menu when the table is selected in the Document window. This menu contains commands to clear the cell heights and widths. It also contains commands to convert all the values to pixel or percentage values. These commands are handy if you set table attributes to pixel values and want to change them to percentage values and vice versa. Buttons for these commands are available in the lower half of the Property inspector when you select the table.

Merging and Splitting Table Cells

You might want some rows in your table to have fewer cells than other rows. For example, you might want the top row of a table to have a title centered over all the columns. How do you accomplish that?

You can increase or decrease the column span and row span by either **splitting** or **merging** cells. To merge an entire row so that it appears as one cell, select the row and click the Merge button (see Figure 6.10) or right-click anywhere on the row and select the Merge Cells command from the Table submenu of the context menu. Now you can position the content of the entire row over all the columns.

FIGURE 6.10
The Merge button appears in the Property inspector when you select an entire row. This button causes all the selected cells to appear as one cell.

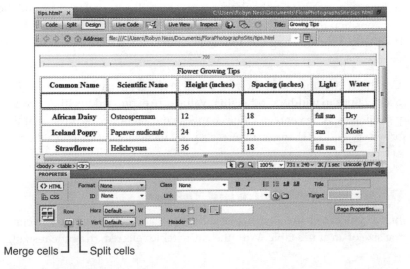

Merge cells ⎯⏋ ⎿⎯ Split cells

Use the Split Cell command to add additional rows or columns to a cell. The Split button is beside the Merge button in the Property inspector. Click the Split button or right-click in the cell and select the Split Cell command from the Table submenu of the context menu, and the Split Cell dialog box appears. Enter the number of rows or columns you would like to split the cell into and click OK. Now a single cell splits into multiple cells.

Aligning Table Cell Contents

You can align the contents of a cell or a group of cells vertically—from top to bottom—or horizontally—from left to right.

When setting the vertical alignment, you have the following options in the Vertical Alignment drop-down menu:

- ▶ **Default**—This is usually the same as middle alignment of the cell contents.

- ▶ **Top**—This aligns the cell contents at the top of the cell.

- ▶ **Middle**—This aligns the cell contents in the middle of the cell.

- ▶ **Bottom**—This aligns the cell contents at the bottom of the cell.

- ▶ **Baseline**—This is applied to multiple cells in a row, aligning the bottom of the objects across all cells. For instance, if you have very large text in the first cell and small text in the second cell, the bottom of each line of text aligns with baseline vertical alignment.

Align the contents of a cell or a group of cells horizontally with the Horizontal Alignment drop-down menu. When setting the horizontal alignment, you have the following options:

- ▶ **Default**—This is usually the same as Left for cell content and Center for header cell content.

- ▶ **Left**—This aligns the cell contents on the left of the cell.

- ▶ **Center**—This aligns the cell contents in the center of the cell.

- ▶ **Right**—This aligns the cell contents on the right of the cell.

Adding Color to a Table

You can add color to a table in several places:

- ▶ A background color for a table cell
- ▶ A background color for a table row
- ▶ A background color for a table column

Figure 6.11 shows where the color settings are located in the Property inspector. Cell properties always have priority over the same properties in the row or column. For instance, I applied green as the column background color and then applied pink to an individual cell, the single cell would be pink and all the other cells in the column would be green.

FIGURE 6.11
Adding colors in the Property inspector controls the background color attributes of table cells.

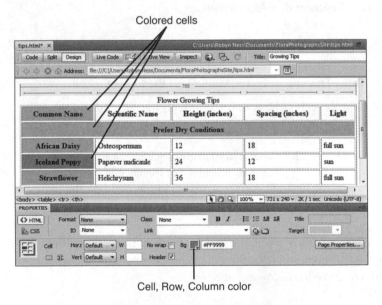

Colored cells

Cell, Row, Column color

Exporting Data from a Table

You can export table data from an HTML table. You can then import the data into a spreadsheet, a database, or another application that has the capability to process delimited data—that is, data separated by a delimiter. A **delimiter** is the character used between the individual data fields. Commonly used delimiters are tabs, spaces, commas, semicolons, and colons. When you are exporting a data file, you need to pick a delimiter that does not appear in the data.

To export table data from Dreamweaver, follow these steps:

1. Select a table or place your cursor in any cell of a table.

2. Select File, Export, Table. The Export Table dialog box appears, as shown in Figure 6.12.

FIGURE 6.12
Open the Export Table dialog box by selecting File, Export. You use this dialog box to export delimited data that can be imported by other applications.

3. Select the data delimiter from the Delimiter drop-down menu.

4. Select the line break style from the Line Breaks drop-down menu. The line break style is dependent on the operating system, so select the operating system that will be running when the data file is imported. For example, if you are sending the data file to someone who will be running a spreadsheet on a Macintosh computer, select Macintosh.

5. Click the Export button and save the file. Give the file a title. Usually comma-delimited files end with .csv and tab-delimited files end with .txt.

Summary

In this hour, you learned how to add a table to a web page. You also learned how to add and remove table cells and rows and how to set the column width and row height of a table. You entered data into a table and then sorted that data by using the Sort Table command. You also learned how to export table data for an external application to use.

Q&A

Q. **When I set a column width to a certain value, such as 50 pixels, why doesn't the column display at that value in the browser?**

A. Have you set the width of the entire table to a value that is the sum of all the column values? If not, the table might be stretching the columns to make up for the extra width that the table has in its width attribute.

Q. **Are pixel values or percentage values better to use with tables?**

A. It depends. If you want your table always to appear the same size, use pixel values. However, if the browser window is narrower than the table, the viewer has to scroll horizontally to view the entire table. Horizontal scrolling is not desirable. If you use percentage values in your table, it's much harder to predict what the final table is going to look like in the viewer's browser. If you use tables with pixel values, you might need to mandate a certain screen resolution to view the table. Be aware that some people disapprove of this type of mandate on the Web.

Workshop

Quiz

1. What are the HTML tags, as displayed in the Dreamweaver tag selector, for a table, a table row, and a table cell? Extra credit: What's the tag for a table header?

2. If you apply a background color to an entire table and a background color to a cell, which color shows up in the cell?

3. What's the name of the character that separates cell data held in a data text file that you can import into Dreamweaver?

Quiz Answers

1. The tag for a table is <table>, the tag for a table row is <tr>, and the tag for a table cell is <td>. The tag for a table header is <th>.

2. The cell attributes take precedence over the table attributes, so the color you applied to the cell shows up.

3. The character that separates cell data held in a text file is a delimiter.

Exercises

1. Create a table with text in column 1 and numbers in column 2. Try both ascending and descending sorts on both the alphabetic (text) data in column 1 and the numeric data in column 2.

2. Create a table in Dreamweaver, enter some data, and export the table data by using the Table Export command. Remember where you saved the file and then open it with a text editor, such as Notepad (Windows) or TextEditor (Mac). What does the file look like? Add another record in the text file, making sure that you use the same delimiter, and then import that data back into Dreamweaver.

3. Insert a table and experiment with merging and splitting cells. Insert a nested table into one of the cells in Standard mode.

Looking Under the Hood: Exploring HTML

Even though Dreamweaver handles HTML (Hypertext Markup Language) behind the scenes, you might occasionally want to look at the code. Dreamweaver also makes the transition easier for those stoic HTML hand-coders who are making a move to a visual HTML development tool such as Dreamweaver. You won'wt be sorry! I'm a very competent HTML hand-coder, but I can get some aspects of my work done much quicker by using Dreamweaver.

Dreamweaver offers several ways to access HTML code. During this hour, you explore the HTML-editing capabilities of Dreamweaver. You'll use Dreamweaver's capability to clean up the code produced when saving a Word document as HTML. You'll explore the numerous reference "books" available within Dreamweaver to look up tags and tag attributes. If you don't already know HTML, you'll find that viewing HTML while Dreamweaver creates it for you is a great way to learn.

By default, Dreamweaver creates a type of HTML called **XHTML**. This stands for *Extensible HTML*, which is a slightly stricter form of HTML based on XML. The code you see in Dreamweaver and in this book is XHTML, but I (and most other people) usually just call it HTML. In HTML, the code can have mistakes in it and still work, whereas XHTML has very specific rules that must be followed in order to work in all browsers:

- ▶ **XHTML elements (tags) must be lowercase**—Tags must be written in lowercase (`<p>Paragraph here</p>`) and not uppercase (`<P>Paragraph here</P>`).

- ▶ **XHTML elements must always be closed**—In HTML, some tags have a closing tag, such as `<p>` and `</p>`, while others you can use by themselves, like the break tag`<br>`. In XHTML, all tags must be closed, so the break tag is written as, `<br />` and is considered "self-closing."

WHAT YOU'LL LEARN IN THIS HOUR:

- ▶ How to structure the code in a web page
- ▶ How to use the Quick Tag Editor
- ▶ How to view and edit HTML code
- ▶ How to clean the HTML that Microsoft Word creates
- ▶ Which code reference books are available in Dreamweaver

NOTE

The Future of HTML

There have been many variations on HTML over the years,
which have added and removed
tags and changed the way page
elements and their attributes
are presented in the code. The
default XHTML that
Dreamweaver CS5 creates is
still current, but there is a
newer, extended version of
HTML called HTML5 that
includes support for video playback and interactive screen elements, such as drag and drop
and drawing tools. In Hour 20,
"Using the Dreamweaver HTML5
Features," we'll take a closer
look.

TIP

Toggle the Panels Off

You can toggle all the panels on
and off by pressing the F4 key
(or Window, Hide Panels).
Pressing F4 again toggles the
panels back on (or select
Window, Show Panels). This is
especially useful for Mac users
whose floating panel version of
Dreamweaver might cause the
panels to block the view of the
web page design or code.

▶ **XHTML elements must be properly nested**—In HTML, the browser renders the following code: `<strong><em>Bold and italic text</strong></em>`. But this code is not properly nested, and XHTML requires it to look like this: `<strong><em>Bold and italic text</em></strong>`.

Exploring Code View

The Dreamweaver Document window enables you to view a web page in either Design view or Code view. You can see the Design and Code views at the same time by clicking the Split Code View button in the Document toolbar (or choose View, Code and Design). When you do this, it's easy to pop back and forth between the views with just the click of a button. You'll probably do the majority of your web page development in Design view while occasionally looking at Code or Split Code view to tweak the code or troubleshoot a problem.

Create a new HTML page in Dreamweaver. Then click the Code View button in the toolbar to view the page's HTML code, as shown in Figure 7.1. The first line in the code is the **document type declaration**, which uses the doctype tag. In Hour 4, "Adding Text and Lists," you selected the document type in the Page Properties (Modify, Page Properties) dialog box. The document type declaration announces which version of HTML the page uses. Dreamweaver adds this line automatically, so you shouldn't have to worry about it. After the document type declaration, HTML tags enclose the entire web page.

By default, Dreamweaver creates web pages by adding XHTML tags. When you select an object from Dreamweaver's Insert panel, Dreamweaver inserts the appropriate tag or tags into your web pages. Tags have properties called **attributes** that Dreamweaver uses to fine-tune the way the object displays on the page. For instance, an image tag (`<img>`) has the `src` (source) attribute, which sets the files that the image tag displays. Most image tags also have height and width attributes that tell the browser the size of the image. These are just a few of the many attributes of an image tag. Here is an example of an image tag with standard attributes:

```
<img src="market.jpg" height="156" width="124"/>
```

Document type declaration

Head

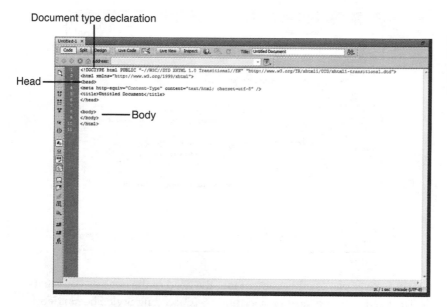

Body

FIGURE 7.1
Code view displays the basic code
of a new web page, including the
document type declaration, head,
and body.

Exploring the Head and Body of a Web Page

There are two main sections to a web page: the head and the body. You'll
see these sections in the code. Head tags surround the head, and body tags
surround the body. All the content visible in a web page is in the body. The
head of the document contains code that supports the web page. In the
head of the document, Dreamweaver automatically adds the `<title>` tag
because the document title is part of the head.

Right under the title, Dreamweaver inserts a meta tag, like this:

```
<meta http-equiv="Content-Type" content="text/html; charset=utf-8" />
```

This meta tag specifies the character set that the browser should use to display the page. The preceding example shows the Unicode (UTF-8) encoding that safely represents all character sets. This encoding setting should
work well for all languages, but you can set a different default character in
the New Document category of Preferences (select Edit, Preferences), as
shown in Figure 7.2. You can also set the default file extension in this
Preferences category.

FIGURE 7.2
You set the default character set
and the default file extension in
the New Document category of
the Dreamweaver Preferences
dialog box.

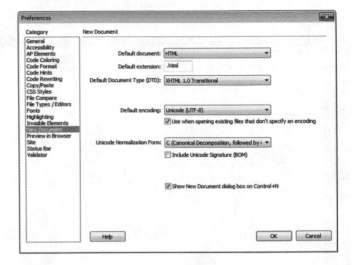

Dreamweaver places other content into the head of the page as you create
it. The head is where most JavaScript, CSS (Cascading Style Sheets) definitions, and other code reside. While in Design mode, if you'd like to see a
visual representation of the head content, select View, Head Content. You
then see icons at the top of the Document window representing the elements in the head. When you click one of the icons, its properties appear in
the Property inspector, as shown in Figure 7.3.

FIGURE 7.3
The elements in the head are
represented by icons when you view
the head content.

You display both Design view and Code view by clicking the Split Code View button. While in Split Code view, place your cursor over the divider between the Design and Code views to modify the window sizes. Type some text into the Design view pane. The text is inserted into the body of the document. If you select an object in the Document window, the code for that object is highlighted in Code view. This is a quick way to get to the code of a selected object. If your web page is large, there might be a lot of HTML to go through, and it might not be easy to find the code for which you are looking. Try displaying only Design view. Highlight a single word that you typed. When you select Code view, the word is highlighted.

If you make changes to the code in Split Code view, Dreamweaver doesn't display the changes in the design portion of the window until you click the Refresh button in the Property inspector or click into the Design view.

TIP

Coding by Hand? Use Live View!

If you find yourself frequently coding by hand in Split Code view, you may want to toggle on the Live View option in the Document window. This alters the design portion of your view so that it is a more accurate rendering of what a browser would show. Note that you won't be able to make any changes to the Design view until you toggle Live View back off. Instead, clicking in design view selects the relevant code in the Code View so you can find which portion of the code to edit when you switch out of Live View.

If you haven't yet tried editing HTML by hand, now is your chance to try! Follow these steps to test the Split Code view:

TRY IT YOURSELF ▼

Editing Code and Seeing the Results

1. Create a new, empty HTML document.

2. Click the Split button to enter the Split Code view.

3. Look for the <body> tag in the document. Immediately after this tag is where you can start entering page content.

4. Type a few lines of text; then click the Refresh button (the circular arrow) in the document toolbar, or click directly in the design portion of the Document window.

5. Notice that the content you entered in the Code view is now accurately reflected in the Design view.

6. Repeat the process, but in reverse—editing the content in the Design view, then viewing the changes in the Code view.

7. Apply text styles and formatting in the Design view and watch as the corresponding tags are shown in code.

Being able to see the changes made in code or design reflected in the corresponding view is a terrific time-saving feature of Dreamweaver, and an excellent way to learn more about the underlying HTML of complex web documents.

Discovering the Coding Toolbar

The Coding toolbar, shown in Figure 7.4, is visible only in the Code and Split Code views. The buttons in this toolbar run down the left side of the Document window. These buttons give you control over collapsing, expanding, and selecting the code within selected tags, along with highlighting invalid code, adding comments, indenting, applying formatting, and other commands.

FIGURE 7.4
The Coding toolbar is visible on the left side of the Document window in Code and Split view.

The following options are available in the Coding toolbar:

▶ **Open Documents**—Lists all the documents currently open in Dreamweaver.

▶ **Show Code Navigator**—Allows you to quickly jump to a file linked from your code (such as another web page or JavaScript file in your site).

▶ **Collapse Full Tag**—Collapses all the code within the selected tag, displaying it as a single line with a small expand button to the left of it.

▶ **Collapse Selection**—Collapses all the selected code into a single line with a small expand button to the left of it.

▶ **Expand All**—Expands all the currently collapsed code.

▶ **Select Parent Tag**—Selects the code within the parent tag of the currently selected tag. Continuing to click this button continues to move up the tag hierarchy.

▶ **Balance Braces**—Checks your code to make sure that all tags, brackets, braces, and parentheses are balanced with two corresponding characters.

▶ **Line Numbers**—Displays line numbers in the left margin.

▶ **Highlight Invalid Code**—Turns on highlighting of invalid code that Dreamweaver doesn't understand.

▶ **Syntax Error Alerts in Info Bar**—Displays syntax errors (improperly used code) in a status bar above the source code editing area.

▶ **Apply Comment drop-down menu**—Enables you to add various types of comments, such as HTML, CSS, or JavaScript comments, to the code. This is useful when you're troubleshooting problems in the code; simply comment out some code to see whether it is causing the problems.

▶ **Remove Comment**—Removes comments from the code.

▶ **Wrap Tag**—Wraps a tag around the selected tag.

▶ **Recent Snippets drop-down menu**—Gives you a list of code snippets you've used recently, along with a quick way to launch the Snippets panel. You learn more about snippets in Hour 24, "Maintaining a Website."

▶ **Move or Convert CSS drop-down menu**—Enables you to convert **inline styles** (CSS styles defined in individual tags) to a CSS rule defined in the head of the document. There is also a command enabling you to move CSS rules to an external style sheet.

▶ **Indent Code**—Shifts the selected code to the right.

▶ **Outdent Code**—Shifts the selected code to the left.

▶ **Format Source Code drop-down menu**—Enables you to apply source formatting, which you learn more about later this hour.

Using the Code Inspector

If you have a dual monitor setup, you'll prefer to see the code in a separate window so that you can keep both Code and Design views open. You can use the Code inspector instead of Code view to accomplish this task. You launch the Code inspector by selecting Window, Code Inspector. The Code inspector is virtually identical to the Code view, but it launches in a separate window that you can drag to your other monitor if you are fortunate enough to work with dual monitors.

Viewing and Editing HTML Tags by Using the Quick Tag Editor

Using Dreamweaver's Quick Tag Editor in Design view is often the quickest and easiest way to look at a single HTML tag and edit it. Remember, you can always tell which tag you have selected by looking at the tag selector at the bottom of the Document window. You can access the Quick Tag Editor in several ways:

▶ Select Modify, Quick Tag Editor.

▶ Right-click a tag in the tag selector and select the Quick Tag Editor command, as shown in Figure 7.5.

FIGURE 7.5
The Quick Tag Editor shows details about a selected page element.

When you open the Quick Tag Editor from the Modify menu, the tag pops up directly above the object in the Document window, and when you open it from the tag selector, it appears directly above the tag.

The Quick Tag Editor has three modes:

- **Edit Tag**—This mode enables you to edit the existing contents of a tag.

- **Wrap Tag**—This mode wraps another HTML tag around the selected tag.

- **Insert HTML**—This mode enables you to insert HTML in the web page.

When the Quick Tag Editor opens, you can toggle among the three modes by pressing Ctrl+T (Command+T on the Macintosh). The following sections explore each of the three modes.

Using the Edit Tag Mode

The Quick Tag Editor's Edit Tag mode enables you to edit the HTML of an existing tag and the tag's contents. To add attributes of the selected tag, place the insertion point at the end of the tag contents in the Quick Tag Editor and add a space. The Tag drop-down menu appears, as shown in Figure 7.5 above, with attributes appropriate for the tag. You select an attribute from the list and then type in the value.

Using the Wrap Tag Mode

The Quick Tag Editor's Wrap Tag mode, shown in Figure 7.6, enables you to wrap HTML around the current selection. For instance, when you have text selected, you can wrap a hyperlink (`<a href></a>`) or text formatting (`<h1></h1>`) around the text. First select the tag you'd like to wrap by choosing it from a list. Dreamweaver adds the opening tag before the selection and the closing tag after the selection. You can also add attributes to the new tag.

FIGURE 7.6
Wrap Tag mode wraps an HTML tag around the current selection.

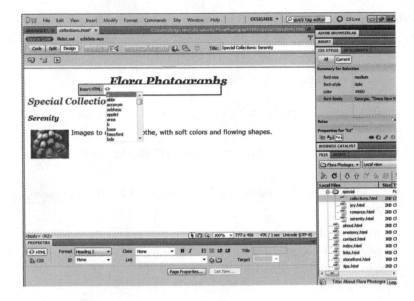

Using the Insert HTML Mode

The Quick Tag Editor's Insert HTML mode shows a pair of empty tag angle brackets with the insertion point between them. You can enter text into the brackets, select from the Tag drop-down menu, or do both. Dreamweaver adds the closing tag automatically. The Quick Tag Editor starts in this mode when you do not have an object selected.

TIP

Finding Your Linked Files

The Code Navigator is a useful means of finding your linked files, but you can also quickly open and edit JavaScript or other linked files by clicking the filenames that appear at the top of your content window, shown in Figure 7.6 below the page tabs along the top of the window. These filename "buttons" automatically appear in your document as you add links to other files in your site.

Using the Code Navigator

As you work with your documents, you may notice a "ships wheel" icon appear as you hover your cursor over code or other linked elements. Clicking the icon opens the Code Navigator.

The Code Navigator is just a small window that shows a link to another resource in your site, such as a JavaScript file. Clicking the link opens the file for editing. You can quickly invoke the Code Navigator using the Coding toolbar, or by simply Alt-clicking a linked file in Windows, or Command+Option-clicking on the Mac. If you find yourself needing to jump between linked files for quick edits, the Code Navigator is an indispensable tool.

Setting Code Preferences

You can set a number of preferences for viewing and maintaining code. The four categories in Dreamweaver preferences that apply to code—Code Coloring, Code Format, Code Hints, and Code Rewriting—help control the way Dreamweaver creates and displays the code in your web pages. If you are used to hand-coding your pages a certain way, don't complain about the way Dreamweaver formats it—change it!

Setting Code Color Preferences

Code view colors code according to the settings in the Dreamweaver Preferences dialog box. You must have syntax coloring turned on in the View Options menu to see colored code. Select the Code Coloring category in the Preferences dialog box. You select which type of code you'd like to edit here. Also, this category enables you to set the background color for Code view. Either enter a color in hexadecimal format or use the color picker to select a color.

Select the document type from the list and click the Edit Coloring Scheme button. The left side of the dialog box enables you to select a tag and then individually set a color for it on the right. To change a tag color, select a type of tag (HTML image tags are selected in Figure 7.7), and select a new text color or background color. You can also make the text bold, italic, or underlined.

> **CAUTION**
>
> ## Understand a Preference Before You Change It
>
> Don't change a setting in the Preferences dialog box if you aren't sure what it does. Many of Dreamweaver's default settings reflect the standard way of creating web pages. Change them if you need to, but know that you could inadvertently cause a problem if you change them blindly.

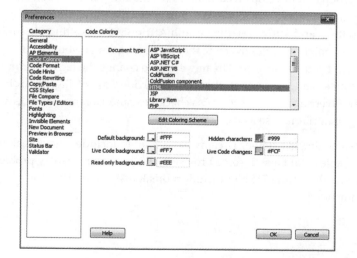

FIGURE 7.7
You set the tag colors displayed in Code view in the Dreamweaver Preferences dialog box.

Setting Code Format Preferences

In the Code Format category of the Dreamweaver Preferences dialog box, shown in Figure 7.8, you set how Dreamweaver creates code. Dreamweaver indents code to make it easier to read. You can change the size of the indent in the Preferences dialog box. You can also select whether Dreamweaver should indent the code for tables and frames.

FIGURE 7.8
The Code Format category of the Dreamweaver Preferences dialog box enables you to set indentation, wrapping, and tag case.

Because the World Wide Web Consortium (W3C) standards specify lowercase tags, it's a good idea to always use lowercase tags and attributes. (W3C is the group that develops web standards. Find out more at http://www.w3c.org.) By default, Dreamweaver uses lowercase for tags (the Default Tag Case setting) and attributes (the Default Attribute Case setting). In limited cases, you might want to override the case for tags or attributes. For instance, if you do not want Dreamweaver to change the tag or attribute case in an existing document, check the Override Case of Tags check box and the Override Case of Attributes check box, and Dreamweaver leaves the tag or attribute case as it exists.

Another setting is whether Dreamweaver should include a line break inside of TD (table data) tags. In some browsers, this can cause display problems, so leaving the setting Do Not Include a Break Inside the TD Tag is recommended.

The two final settings are advanced formatting rules for CSS and the HTML tag libraries. You can explore these options for controlling how Cascading Style Sheet code is generated and indented, as well as control the formatting for each individual tag within the HTML language! I recommend that you leave these settings as is, but if you want total control, this is where you'll find it.

Setting Code Hints Preferences

As you saw in the Quick Tag Editor examples earlier this hour, Dreamweaver drops down the **tag menu**, displaying tag attributes for you to pick from. This is called a **code hint** in Dreamweaver. You can set which code hints Dreamweaver displays in the Code Hints category of the Preferences dialog box, as shown in Figure 7.9. The Close Tags options determine when Dreamweaver automatically closes a tag for you—helping to ensure that you're creating correct code.

NOTE

You're on Your Own When You Hand-Code

The options you set in the Code Format category of the Preferences dialog box apply only to changes made in the Document window. Most automatic formatting (such as indenting) does not occur when you edit HTML by hand using Code view. Of course, you can always select Commands, Apply Source Formatting to make everything tidy.

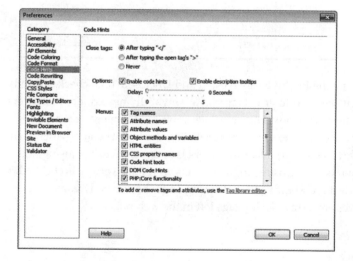

FIGURE 7.9
The Code Hints category enables you to set what Dreamweaver helps you with while you are coding.

You can also set the time delay for Code Hints by dragging the Delay slider bar. Finally, you can go through the Menus list and deselect items you don't want Dreamweaver to provide hints for, such as tag names and attribute names.

Setting Code Rewriting Preferences

The code rewriting preferences, shown in Figure 7.10, set what changes Dreamweaver makes when it opens a web page. Dreamweaver automatically fixes certain code problems, but only if you want it to. If you turn off the Rewrite Code options in the Code Rewriting category, Dreamweaver still displays invalid code that you can fix yourself if you need to.

FIGURE 7.10
The Code Rewriting category of the Dreamweaver Preferences dialog box enables you to set the changes that Dreamweaver makes when it opens a web page.

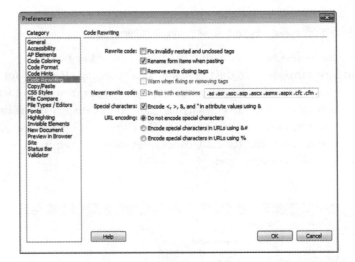

Checking the Fix Invalidly Nested and Unclosed Tags check box tells Dreamweaver to rewrite tags that are invalidly nested. For instance, if you check this check box, Dreamweaver rewrites `<strong><em>hello </strong></em>` as `<strong><em>hello</em></strong>` (which is the correct way to write it). Dreamweaver also inserts missing closing tags, quotation marks, and closing angle brackets when this setting is checked. When you select the Remove Extra Closing Tags check box, Dreamweaver removes any stray closing tags left in the web page.

Cleaning Up HTML Created with Microsoft Word

It's very convenient while working in Word to save a document as a web page. Word does a great job of creating a web page that looks very similar to the Word document, and you can open and edit the web page in Word. The problem is that Word maintains a lot of extra code in the web page.

If you do not need to edit the web page in Word again and you'd like to put it on the Web, you can use Dreamweaver to clean up the extra code.

To save a Word document as a web page, select File, Save as Web Page. Word prompts you to name the document and adds the .htm file extension. The resulting page has a lot of extra code; Dreamweaver knows which code is extraneous and can delete it. It's fun to take note of the number of lines of code in the file before you run the Clean Up Word HTML command.

When you save a Word document as a web page, make sure that you close it before you work on it in Dreamweaver. Dreamweaver is not able to open and convert an HTML document that is open in Word. Apply the Clean Up Word HTML command to a web page that was created in Word and that you have opened in the Document window. To do this, select Commands, Clean Up Word HTML. This launches the Clean Up Word HTML dialog box, shown in Figure 7.11.

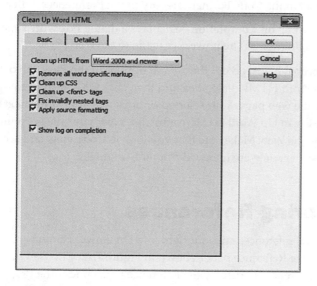

FIGURE 7.11
When you import a Word HTML document or select Clean Up Word HTML, the Clean Up Word HTML dialog box appears.

Dreamweaver should automatically detect which version of Word created the HTML file from tags that Word adds to the file. You can also choose the version manually by using the Clean Up HTML From drop-down menu in the Clean Up Word HTML dialog box. The Clean Up Word HTML dialog box has two tabs: Basic and Detailed. The Basic tab has the following options:

▶ **Remove All Word Specific Markup**—Removes all the unnecessary Extensible Markup Language (XML), meta tags, and link tags from the head section; it also removes all Word XML markup, all conditional tags, all empty paragraphs, and all margins. You can select each of these options individually by using the settings on the Detailed tab.

▶ **Clean Up CSS**—Removes the extra CSS styles from the document. The styles removed are inline CSS styles, style attributes that begin with mso, non-CSS style declarations, CSS styles in table rows and cells, and unused styles. You can select these options individually by using the Detailed tab.

▶ **Clean Up <font> Tags**—Removes <font> tags.

▶ **Fix Invalidly Nested Tags**—Fixes the tags, particularly font markup tags that are in incorrect places.

▶ **Apply Source Formatting**—Applies the code formatting options that are set in the Code Format category in the Preferences dialog box.

▶ **Show Log on Completion**—Displays a dialog box with a summary of the changes that Dreamweaver made to the web page.

You can probably just accept the default options in the Basic tab of the Clean Up Word HTML dialog box and then click OK. Dreamweaver then cleans up the web page. Your selected options will appear the next time you select the Clean Up Word HTML command. Now your file is optimized for display on the Web. Make sure that you look in Code view and see how many lines of code were removed from the original.

Exploring References

Many useful references are built right into Dreamweaver and are accessible to you via the Reference panel, shown in Figure 7.12. Choose Window, Results, References to display the Reference panel under the Property inspector. The Book drop-down menu enables you to choose from numerous reference books. Of special interest to you might be the O'Reilly CSS, HTML, and JavaScript references. Who needs to buy the book when these references are included in Dreamweaver? There's also UsableNet's Accessibility reference, which helps explain how to create websites that are accessible to people who have accessibility issues, such as visual impairment.

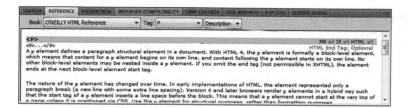

FIGURE 7.12
The Reference panel provides access to several reference books, including books on CSS, HTML, and JavaScript.

To use the references, you select tags, styles, or other objects from the drop-down menus and then read about the objects in the lower part of the panel. Notice that information on browser compatibility is located in the upper-right corner of the panel. When not using this panel, you might want to collapse it by double-clicking the panel title, or close it by right-clicking the panel or tab group title bar and choosing Close Tab Group.

Validating Your Code

Now that you have the tools to write HTML and understand HTML, it's important that you also have the tools you need to write *valid* HTML code! Although Dreamweaver does what it can to help you as you go, it can't detect all problems as you code. To check your code for validity, you can choose File, Validate, As XML from the menu. Dreamweaver takes a few seconds to scan your document, then displays a validation report that lists all the errors it has found, as demonstrated in Figure 7.13.

Step through the errors in the report; double-clicking a line opens and highlights the problem in Code view.

TIP

Working with Legacy Files?

The doctype tag specifies which version of HTML a document uses—and if it isn't set right, Dreamweaver might not be able to validate the file correctly. If you have to work with a number of legacy files that don't include a doctype, you can choose which default doctype Dreamweaver uses for its validation using the Validator category of the applications preferences.

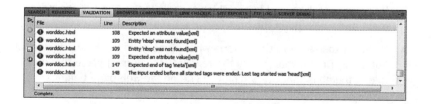

FIGURE 7.13
Review the results of the code validation process.

Summary

In this hour, you learned how to use the Quick Tag Editor and Code view. You learned how to set preferences for HTML tag colors, formatting, and rewriting. You also learned how to use the Clean Up Word HTML command. And you were introduced to the robust reference books that come with Dreamweaver and are available to help answer your questions about topics such as HTML, CSS, and JavaScript.

Q&A

Q. Which should I learn first, Dreamweaver or HTML?

A. It's helpful to know HTML when you are developing web pages. I think the best way to learn HTML is to first learn to use a web-editing program, such as Dreamweaver. Continue to view the code as you work and use the Reference panel (by selecting Window, Reference) to look up tags or attributes that you are curious about. If you still need grounding in HTML after that, get a good HTML reference book or take a class. A good book about HTML and XHTML is *Sams Teach Yourself HTML and CSS in 24 Hours, 8th Edition (0672330970) by Julie C. Meloni* and Michael Morrison.

Q. Can I add tag attributes that don't appear in the Tag drop-down menu? I saw a tag attribute listed on a website that isn't listed in Dreamweaver for that tag.

A. Yes. Use the Tag Library Editor by selecting Edit, Tag Libraries. This editor controls the attributes that appear in the Tag drop-down menu. Dreamweaver does not list every attribute that is available, so there might be one or two that you want to add.

Q. If I hand-code, how do I know which tags go in the head of the document and which go in the body?

A. It takes experience to understand where tags go in the HTML document, but luckily Dreamweaver puts the tags into the correct place for you. A rule of thumb is that everything you see on the web page belongs in the body of the document. And the supporting elements such as CSS, JavaScript, meta tags, and the title tag are all stored in the head of the HTML document.

Workshop

Quiz

1. How do you toggle through the three Quick Tag Editor modes?

2. What are the three ways to view a web page in Dreamweaver?

3. How do you preview a page without launching a web browser?

4. Does Dreamweaver automatically format the HTML that you type into Code view?

Quiz Answers

1. You toggle through the Quick Tag Editor's three modes by pressing Ctrl+T in Windows or Command+T on a Macintosh.

2. You can view a web page in Code view, Split Code view, or Design view in Dreamweaver.

3. Using the Live View renders your page in the same way as a web browser.

4. Dreamweaver can't indent your code for you, but you can format it by using the Apply Source Formatting command on any web page.

Exercises

1. Experiment with using the Quick Tag Editor modes. Pay attention to how the Property inspector reflects selecting attributes in the Quick Tag Editor. You can select many of the same attributes by using the Property inspector's radio buttons, text boxes, and check boxes.

2. Examine the HTML of a web page in Code view. First select an object in the Document window and then open Code view. Do you see the HTML for the selected object?

3. Create a new HTML page in Dreamweaver, open Code view, and briefly examine the general structure of the web page—head and body tags nested within HTML tags. Select and delete all the code and then re-create this general structure. What are the common tags that go into the head section of the page? Enter them. Notice that Dreamweaver enters closing tags for you if you've enabled that option in the Preferences dialog box. Press the spacebar after the tag name within any of the tags. What attributes are available for that tag? What happens when you select an attribute?

HOUR 8
Displaying Images

The World Wide Web originally began as a text-based medium, and the first browser displayed only text. Don't remember that? That is because the Web didn't become popular until it became visual. The key to making web pages visual, interesting, and attractive is including images. Access to digital images (with digital cameras, for instance) and fast Internet connections continues to increase, and this enables you to put more and better images into your web pages. However, an emphasis remains on optimizing image file sizes to make them as small as possible so that viewers are spending their time viewing your page, not waiting for it to download.

You can use images to create user interface elements such as buttons, borders, banners, titles, and backgrounds. Other images describe content: images of products, people, processes, and even pets. Images draw our attention and arouse our senses; they are an important element in websites. Images offer a powerful way to send a message. One drawing or photograph can communicate a huge amount of information.

Adding an Image to a Page

Images are separate files that appear within a web page. Because Dreamweaver is a WYSIWYG (what you see is what you get) program, it enables you to see web page images in the Dreamweaver Document window. Images are not actually part of the HTML; they remain separate files that the browser inserts when you view the web page.

WHAT YOU'LL LEARN IN THIS HOUR:

▶ How to insert an image into a web page and change its properties
▶ Which image formats can be used in a web page
▶ How to optimize images
▶ How to define an image map
▶ How to create a rollover image

▼ TRY IT YOURSELF

Inserting an Image into a Web Page

FIGURE 8.1
The insertion point signals the placement of the image in the document.

To insert an image into a web page, follow these steps:

1. Place the cursor where you want to insert the image. You will see the insertion point blinking, as shown in Figure 8.1.

Insertion point

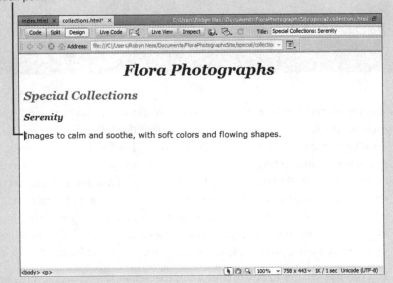

2. Select the Image element from the Images menu of the Insert panel (or select Insert, Image).

3. The Select Image Source dialog box appears.

   If you don't have any image files within the site you've defined in Dreamweaver, you can select a web image file from anywhere on your local drive and Dreamweaver prompts you to copy it into your site. A U.S. government site, such as NASA (http://www.nasa.gov/multimedia/downloads), is a good source of images and movies with which to practice.

4. Select an image file (see Figure 8.2), a file that ends with .gif, .jpg, or .png. A thumbnail image is visible on the right side of the dialog box if you enable the Preview Images check box.

   Notice the file size, the dimensions of the image, and the download time located under the thumbnail (by default, the download time is calculated at 128Kbps, but this can be changed in the Status Bar category of the Dreamweaver Preferences dialog box).

TRY IT YOURSELF ▼

Inserting an Image into a Web Page
Continued

5. Make sure that the link to the image is document-relative by selecting Document from the Relative To drop-down menu.

6. Click OK when you locate the correct image.

Preview thumbnail

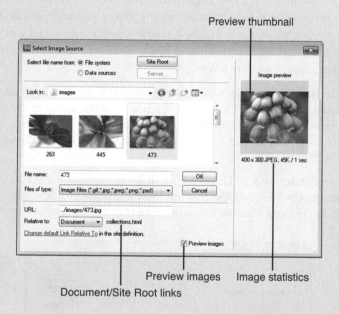

FIGURE 8.2
The Select Image Source dialog box enables you to preview an image before you select it.

Preview images   Image statistics

Document/Site Root links

If the Image Tag Accessibility Attributes dialog box appears, read ahead to learn how to fill in the attributes in this box and to find out more about accessibility.

NOTE

Would You Like to Copy the File?

If you select an image from outside your currently selected website, Dreamweaver asks whether you would like to copy the image to the current site. If you click Yes, Dreamweaver asks you where you'd like to copy the image. This is an easy way to add images to your site.

Adding Alternative Text

Believe it or not, some people who might surf to your web pages are still using text-only browsers, such as Lynx. Others are stuck behind a very slow modem or Internet connection and have images turned off in their browsers. Other visitors are visually impaired and have text-to-speech (TTS) browsers that read the contents of web pages. For all these viewers, you should add alternative text to your images.

Accessibility is the practice of enabling people with disabilities to access content. People who are visually impaired—blind, for instance—obviously cannot see an image on a web page. Dreamweaver has several accessibility features turned on by default, including the Image Tag Accessibility Attributes dialog box, as shown in Figure 8.3, which popped up when you inserted the image earlier. This dialog box enables you to add two different types of accessibility information:

▶ **Alternate Text**—This is the description that a screen reader reads when it encounters the image reference. This should be fewer than 50 characters long. If the image is purely aesthetic (a border image, for instance), you should select <empty> from the Alternate Text drop-down menu.

▶ **Long Description**—This is a URL link to a web page describing the image. Use the Long Description field when the text describing the image is more than the 50 characters available for alternate text.

FIGURE 8.3
The Image Tag Accessibility Attributes dialog box enables you to enter important alternative text that is invaluable to those who are visually impaired.

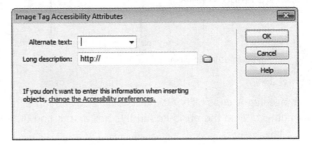

You can also enter or remove alternative text, sometimes called **alt text**, in the Alt drop-down menu in the Property inspector, which is covered in the next section. Make the text descriptive of the image it represents. Don't enter something such as "London." A better choice would be "London's parliament building with a black taxi whizzing by." In some browsers, the alt text also pops up like a ToolTip when the viewer puts the cursor over an image. If the viewer has opted to turn images off in the browser, only the alt text displays, and the user can then decide whether to download the images associated with the web page.

TTS browsers used by people who are visually impaired read the alt text description of an image to the user. When an image does not have the Alt attribute set, a TTS browser says the word *image*; listening to the browser say *image* over and over isn't very enjoyable! Some images on a web page are purely ornamental and do not add information to the page—a divider line, for instance. Select <empty> from the Alt drop-down menu in the Property inspector to add alt text with no content; this makes TTS browsers skip the image.

You can turn accessibility options on and off in Dreamweaver Preferences (Edit, Preferences). Select the Accessibility category and check the check boxes beside Form Objects, Frames, Media, and/or Images to have Dreamweaver automatically open a dialog box asking for the appropriate accessibility settings for each type of web page object. These settings force you to be conscious of the extra attributes required for screen readers.

TIP

Missing Alt Text Reporting

You can run a Missing Alt Text report by selecting Site, Reports. This report shows you all the images that are missing alt text.

Exploring Image Attributes

After you insert an image in a web page, the image is visible within Dreamweaver's document window, as shown in Figure 8.4. When you select the image, the Property inspector displays the image's properties. The Src (source) box displays the path to the image file. Notice that Dreamweaver automatically fills in the dimensions (width and height) of the image. Having the dimensions helps the browser by reserving the space for the image in the web page; if you don't reserve this space, the page content appears to move as the images load into it. The default unit of measure for width and height is pixels.

NOTE

Image ID Is Important for Rollover Images

Adding an id for an image becomes more important later this hour, when you explore rollover images. Each rollover image must have a unique name that you add in the Property inspector. The JavaScript that facilitates the rollover requires that each image have an id.

Aligning an Image with Text

The Align drop-down menu in the Property inspector controls how objects that are located beside an image align with it. Align is very different from the text alignment settings you used in Hour 4, "Adding Text and Lists." You use the image alignment settings to align an image in the center, to the left, or to the right of whatever's next to the image. You use the Align drop-down menu to affect how *other* objects align with an image.

Change the Align setting of the image so that all the text appears to the left, beside the image. To do this, select Right from the Align drop-down menu in the Property inspector. Why select Right? The image is on the right, as shown in Figure 8.5. Remember that the Align options apply to the image, but affect other elements within its vicinity. Table 8.1 describes the alignment choices.

FIGURE 8.4
The Property inspector shows the
image's width, height, and other
properties.

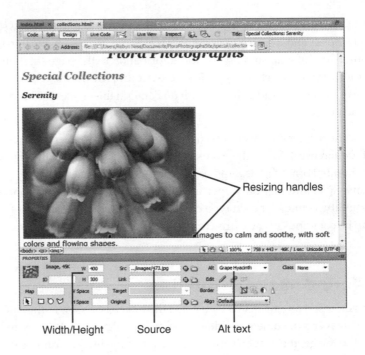

Resizing handles

Width/Height   Source   Alt text

Alignment with other objects

FIGURE 8.5
You can change how an image
aligns with adjacent objects in the
Align drop-down menu.

TABLE 8.1   Image Alignment Options in the Property Inspector

Align Option	Description
Default	Normally the same as the Baseline option, but might depend on the browser.
Baseline	Aligns the bottom of the image with the bottom of the element.
Top	Aligns the image with the highest element. Additional lines of text wrap under the image.
Middle	Aligns the baseline of the text with the middle of the image. Additional lines of text wrap under the image.
Bottom	Aligns the baseline of the text at the bottom of the image.

TABLE 8.1   Image Alignment Options in the Property Inspector

Align Option	Description
TextTop	Aligns the image with the highest text (not the highest element, as with the Top option). Additional lines of text wrap under the image.
Absolute Middle	Aligns the middle of the image with the middle of the text beside it.
Absolute Bottom	Aligns the bottom of the highest element with the bottom of the image.
Left	Aligns the image to the left of other elements.
Right	Aligns the image to the right of other elements.

To increase the distance between the image and other page elements, adjust the V Space and H Space settings. *V* stands for vertical and *H* stands for horizontal. To add space to the right and left of an image, enter a value into the H Space text box, as shown in Figure 8.6. Changing the V Space setting means adding vertical space to both the top and the bottom of the image.

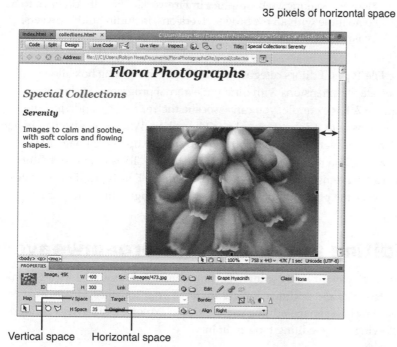

35 pixels of horizontal space

Vertical space   Horizontal space

FIGURE 8.6
Put a value in the H Space text box to increase the space to the right and the left of the image. Put a value in the V Space text box to increase the space above and below the image.

Exploring Image Flavors: GIF, JPEG, and PNG

All browsers support the two standard image formats, GIF (pronounced either "gif" or "jif") and JPEG (pronounced "j-peg"). There is also a newer format, the Portable Networking Graphics (PNG—pronounced "ping") format, that is supported by current browsers. Here's a little more information about these three formats:

▶ **GIF**—This format is best for images that have blocks of solid color, usually drawings. It also allows portions of an image to be transparent to let the background color of a page show through.

▶ **JPEG**—This format is best for photographic images and images that do not have blocks of solid color—for example, images that contain color gradients or lots of shade of the same color.

▶ **PNG**—This format is a replacement for the GIF format. It has transparency as well as the color quality of JPEGs. Although PNG is not as popular as the other two formats, its popularity is growing. This is the Adobe Fireworks native file format, which we'll explore further in Hour 9, "Making Web Graphics in Fireworks CS5." If you have to be compatible with all the browser versions, including old browsers, avoid using PNGs.

The File Types/Editors category of the Preferences dialog box allows you to associate file extensions with different external programs, as shown in Figure 8.7. For example, you can associate the .gif, .jpg, and .png file extensions with Adobe Fireworks or Photoshop. When you select an image in Dreamweaver, you can click the Edit button to open the image file in Fireworks. You make your edits and save the file. To associate an editor with a file extension, select a file extension in the File Types/Editors category, click the plus button, and browse to the image editor program.

Editing Images Within Dreamweaver

Although you probably want to become somewhat familiar with a graphics tool to create and optimize images to put in your websites, Dreamweaver has a few basic image-editing capabilities to explore. Dreamweaver has the following image-editing tools built in:

Add/remove extensions

Add/remove editors

FIGURE 8.7
The File Types/Editors category in the Dreamweaver Preferences dialog box configures other applications to edit linked files.

▶ **Edit**—Opens the selected image in Fireworks for editing (of course, you must have Adobe Fireworks or another image-editing program defined in the Preferences dialog box for this command to work).

▶ **Edit Image Settings**—Opens Dreamweaver's Image Preview dialog box, where you can optimize and resave an image, modifying its properties so that it downloads more quickly.

▶ **Crop**—Lets you trim off unwanted portions of the image and saves the smaller file. This command works within Dreamweaver, enabling you to save the cropped image.

▶ **Resample**—This command becomes active after you've resized an image in Dreamweaver. It optimizes an image by adding or removing pixels in the image.

▶ **Brightness and Contrast**—Changes the brightness and contrast of an image to correct an image that is too bright or too dark.

▶ **Sharpen**—Sharpens a blurry image.

You can access all these image-editing commands from the Property inspector when you have an image selected, as shown in Figure 8.8. Make sure that you have a backup copy of any images you modify because Dreamweaver changes the actual image file.

CAUTION

If You Accidentally Resize Images

If you accidentally resize an image in Dreamweaver, it's easy to return to the actual dimensions of the image. When you modify the image's dimensions, a small Refresh icon appears next to the width and height boxes in the Property inspector. Click this button to correct the image dimensions.

TIP

Keep Your Original Images!

I usually create a directory called image_originals and make sure that I keep the original, unoptimized version of all images there. The image that displays in the web page is an optimized version of the original. That way I can always return to the original version if I need to make changes to the size or to how I've cropped the web page version of the image.

Optimizing Images for Use in a Web Page

Have you ever received an emailed photo that was so big you could hardly view it on your computer monitor? That's because the file was at a very high resolution (also known as dots per inch—dpi—or pixels per inch). Dreamweaver is able to optimize images so that they appear at a good size for a web page. You use the Dreamweaver Optimize feature to make sure that an image is the correct size and resolution.

Digital cameras are often set to take pictures at a high resolution. Although a higher resolution gives excellent results for printing, these files are much too large to display on a computer screen. You need to optimize images to make sure that they aren't larger than they need to be because larger images mean longer downloads.

You can get a photo from your digital camera, from a collection of clip art, or from a free source such as NASA (http://www.nasa.gov/multimedia/downloads). Most of the images you find on the Web have already been optimized, so you might want to look for a non-optimized file, using what is called a **source file** or **high-resolution file**.

TIP

Optimization Wizards

Image-optimization software programs can help you decide which image format is the most efficient to use for a particular image. These programs also help you reduce the number of colors in an image and improve other factors that reduce file size and download time. Both Adobe Fireworks and Photoshop have wizard interfaces that walk you through optimizing an image.

▼ TRY IT YOURSELF

Optimizing an Image in Dreamweaver

To optimize an image in Dreamweaver, do the following:

1. Insert a non-optimized image into Dreamweaver (Insert, Image).

2. With the image selected in the Document window, click the Edit Image Settings button in the Property inspector.

3. The Image Preview dialog box opens, displaying a preview of the selected image on the right, as shown in Figure 8.9.

Options tab   File tab   Quality   Download time
              Format   File size   Profile menu

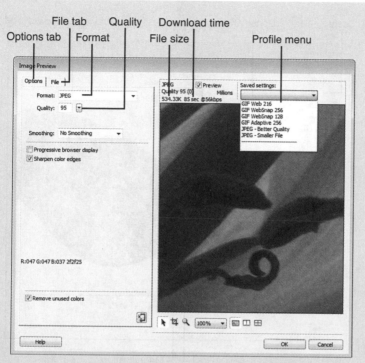

Optimizing an Image in Dreamweaver
Continued

TIP

Focus on Detail

While optimizing images, it's good practice to display the portion of the image that has the most detail in the preview. You can drag the image with your cursor until a portion of the image with a lot of detail is visible. This makes it easier to tell if you are optimizing while still keeping your image sharp and looking good.

FIGURE 8.9
The Image Preview dialog box displays a preview of the image along with information about the file's format and its download time.

4. First make the image smaller by selecting the File tab. You can either scale the image file size down (never up!) or enter pixel values for a width (W) or height (H). Make sure that you enable the Constrain check box, as shown in Figure 8.10, so that the width and height automatically change proportionally to each other; you don't want to distort the image.

5. Next you should crop the image if necessary. This also shrinks the file size. Select the crop tool and reduce the magnification until the image edges are visible. Drag the edges inward to crop the image. Click the Pointer icon to finish cropping.

6. Select the Options tab and click the Four Preview Windows button. Now there are four different preview windows. Click one of the previews on the right to change its options on the left.

▼ TRY IT YOURSELF

Optimizing an Image in Dreamweaver

Continued

TIP

Setting JPEG Quality

Depending on your original image, a JPEG quality setting somewhere between 50 and 80 usually works best. You need to examine the preview image while optimizing, paying attention to both the foreground and the background. Check that there aren't any areas of the image that are extremely **pixelated**, where the square pixels are visible to the user, making the image appear blocky and no longer realistic.

After you optimize a JPEG, you don't want to optimize it again. If you need to make a change to an image saved as a JPEG, open the original source file and reoptimize. If you are still working on the image in the graphics program and you haven't yet saved it, select File, Revert to return to the original, non-optimized version of the image.

Scale   Constrain   File size   Preview windows

Crop tool   Magnification

FIGURE 8.10
The File tab enables you to make changes to the size of the image.

7. The Image Preview dialog box displays four versions of the image. I've set each of the previews to various JPEG quality settings: 100, 90, 50, and 10. The quality setting of 10 is unacceptable, whereas the others will probably be fine. For this image I would pick the preview with the 50 quality setting, shown in Figure 8.11.

8. When you are satisfied that your image is optimized, make sure that you have the correct version selected and click OK.

Your image is now optimized and incorporated into the web page!

TRY IT YOURSELF ▼

Optimizing an Image in Dreamweaver
Continued

FIGURE 8.11
A display of four versions of JPEG quality enables you to balance image quality and file size.

Creating a Linked Image

The Link property appears in the Property inspector when you have text or an image selected. Linked images are common on the Web. When the user clicks a linked image, the browser loads the linked web page. With an image selected, you can add a hyperlink in the following ways:

▶ Type a URL into the Link box in the Property inspector.

▶ Browse for the linked page by selecting the Browse icon beside the Link box.

▶ Use the Point-to-File icon to link to a file. The Point-to-File icon enables you simply to drag the cursor over a file in the Files panel to create a link. You explored this tool in Hour 5, "Making Hyperlinks, Anchors, and Mailto Links."

▼ TRY IT YOURSELF

Creating a Linked Image

To create a linked image, follow these steps:

1. Select an image on your web page and make sure that the Property inspector is open.

2. Enter a URL in the Link box under the Src box, as shown in Figure 8.12.

Link

FIGURE 8.12
You set hyperlinks in the Link box in the Property inspector.

3. Preview the web page in a browser. When you click the image that has the hyperlink, your browser should go to the hyperlinked page.

NOTE

An Image Map Doesn't Have to Be a Map

Although creating an image map out of an image of a physical map is useful, it's not the only application of image maps. You can also create an image map from a single image diagramming an object. Or you could create an image map from an image with four quadrants, describing four steps in a process. Each quadrant could link to detailed information about that step in the process. There are many applications for image maps.

Creating an Image map

An **image map** is an image that has regions, called **hotspots**, defined as hyperlinks. When a viewer clicks a hotspot, it acts just like any other hyperlink. Instead of adding one hyperlink to an entire image, you can define a number of hotspots on different portions of an image. You can even create hotspots in different shapes.

Image maps are useful for presenting graphical menus that the viewer can click to select regions of a single image. For instance, you could create an image out of a map of a country and draw hotspots around the different states or provinces. When viewers click a country's hotspot, they could jump to a web page with information about that area.

▼ TRY IT YOURSELF

Creating an Image Map

To create an image map, follow these steps:

1. Insert an image into a web page. The image must be selected for the image map tools to appear in the Property inspector.

2. Give the map a name in the Map text box, as shown in Figure 8.13. The name has to be different from other map names in the page.

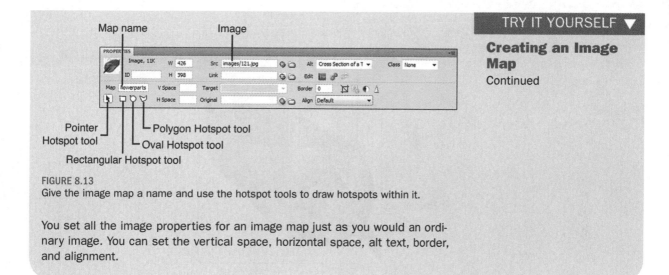

Map name   Image

Pointer
Hotspot tool ──── Polygon Hotspot tool
Rectangular Hotspot tool ──── Oval Hotspot tool

FIGURE 8.13
Give the image map a name and use the hotspot tools to draw hotspots within it.

You set all the image properties for an image map just as you would an ordinary image. You can set the vertical space, horizontal space, alt text, border, and alignment.

Adding a Hotspot to an Image Map

When you select an image, you see four image map tools in the lower corner of the expanded Property inspector. These four tools define image map hotspots. The arrow is the Pointer Hotspot tool, which selects or moves the hotspots. There are three image map hotspot tools: One tool draws rectangles, one draws circles, and one draws polygons.

To create a hotspot in an image map, follow these steps:

1. Select one of the hotspot tools.

2. Click and drag the crosshair cursor to make a rectangle or oval hotspot that is the dimensions of the hotspot you want to create. When using the Polygon Hotspot tool, continue to click the cursor to outline the hotspot and then click the Point Hotspot tool to finish.

3. With a newly drawn hotspot selected, type a URL in the Link box, as shown in Figure 8.14, or click the Browse icon to browse to a local web page. You can also link a hotspot to a named anchor by entering a pound sign followed by the anchor name.

4. Enter alternative text for the hotspot in the Alt text box.

TRY IT YOURSELF ▼

**Creating an Image
Map**
Continued

TIP

**Copying and Pasting
Image maps**

If you copy and paste the image map into the same or another web page within Dreamweaver, all the image map properties come along, too.

TRY IT YOURSELF ▼

**Creating a Hotspot in
an Image Map**

Creating a Hotspot in an Image Map
Continued

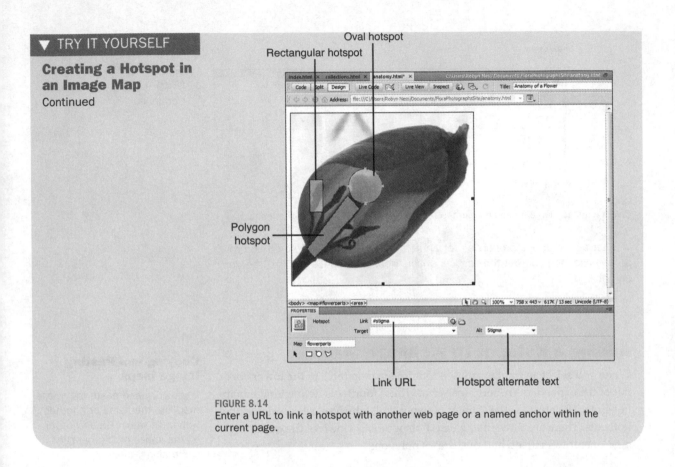

FIGURE 8.14
Enter a URL to link a hotspot with another web page or a named anchor within the current page.

To move or adjust the size of the hotspot, you must first select the Pointer Hotspot tool. You can't use the other hotspot tools to adjust the hotspot or you will end up creating another hotspot. Click the hotspot with the Pointer Hotspot tool and either move the hotspot to another location or resize the hotspot by using the resizing handles.

In the web page HTML, two sets of x and y coordinates define the hotspot (rectangular in this example). The upper-left corner of the rectangle is the first two coordinates in the code, and the lower-right corner of the rectangle is the last two coordinates. The coordinates are in pixels, and they are relative to the image, not to the web page. The HTML code for a rectangular area looks like this:

```
<area shape="rect" coords="43,153,74,228" href="#anther" alt="anther" />
```

In this example, the upper-left corner of the rectangle is 43 pixels from the left of the image and 153 pixels from the top of the image, and the bottom-right corner of the rectangle is 74 pixels from the left of the image and 228 pixels from the top. It's nice to have a visual representation in Dreamweaver and not have to figure this out yourself, isn't it?

Three values define a circle: the circle's radius and the x and y coordinate values that define the circle's center. The HTML code defining a circular area looks like this:

```
<area shape="circle" coords="173,169,49" href="#stigma" alt="Stigma" />
```

A hotspot polygon is defined by as many x and y coordinates as you need, each representing one of the corner points. The HTML code for a sample polygon hotspot looks like this:

```
<area shape="poly" coords=_"836,312,53,332,158,220,131,190" href="#style"
↪alt="Style" />
```

Four points define the polygon in this HTML, so there are four pairs of x and y coordinates.

Aligning Hotspots

Dreamweaver has built-in alignment tools you can use to align the hotspots in an image map. First, you need to select the hotspots you want to align. To select multiple hotspots in an image map, hold down Shift as you click hotspots to add them to the selection. You can tell when hotspots are selected because you can see the resizing handles.

Sometimes it is difficult to finely align hotspots with your mouse. You can use the arrow keys to move a hotspot or multiple hotspots one pixel at a time. The Arrange submenu under the Modify menu contains commands to align hotspots. You can use this menu to align multiple hotspots on the left, right, top, or bottom. You can make multiple hotspots the same height by using the Make Same Height command, or the same width by using the Make Same Width command. To use these commands, select the hotspots you want to align or resize by shift-clicking or control-clicking to choose multiples, then pick your menu option.

TIP

Which Hotspot Is Hot?

Hotspots can overlap each other. Whichever hotspot is on top (usually the one created first) will be the link triggered when the user clicks on the overlapping area. You might want to create overlapping hotspots on purpose as part of the design of an image map. For instance, you might use a circular hotspot over part of a rectangular hotspot. Alternatively, the overlapping might simply be a consequence of the limited shapes you have available to define the hotspots.

It's difficult to tell which hotspot is on top of another hotspot. If you've recently created the image map, you know which hotspot was created first and is therefore on top. You can manipulate the stacking order of the hotspots by selecting Modify, Arrange, Bring to Front or Send to Back. If a hotspot overlaps another and needs to be on top, select the Bring to Front command.

Creating Rollover Images

Our final image trick for today is creating a rollover image. A **rollover image** is one that swaps to another image when the viewer's cursor is over it. Rollovers add some dynamic action to an otherwise static image.

You need two image files with exactly the same dimensions in order to create a rollover image.

▼ TRY IT YOURSELF

Creating a Rollover Image

Dreamweaver makes it easy to implement rollover images by using the Rollover Image object. To create a rollover image, follow these steps:

1. Open an existing web page and place the insertion point where you want the rollover image to appear.

2. Select Rollover Image from the Images menu in the Insert panel or select Insert, Image Objects, Rollover Image. The Insert Rollover Image dialog box appears.

3. Type a name for the image in the Image Name text field.

4. Select both the original image file and the rollover image file by clicking the Browse buttons next to those options and selecting the image files.

5. Check the Preload Rollover Image check box if you'd like the rollover image downloaded into the viewer's browser cache. With a preloaded image, there is less chance that viewers will have to wait for the rollover image to download when they move the cursor over the image.

6. Add a link to the rollover image by clicking the Browse button next to When Clicked, Go to URL, or type in the external URL or named anchor.

7. The Insert Rollover Image dialog box should look as shown in Figure 8.15. Click the OK button.

8. Save the page and preview it in the browser (File, Preview in Browser) to check the functionality of the rollover image.

FIGURE 8.15
A rollover image swaps one image for another when the viewer's cursor is over the image. You need to enter both image paths into the Insert Rollover Image dialog box.

Summary

In this hour, you learned how to insert an image into a web page and how to set a link, vertical and horizontal space, and alt text. You have learned how to edit the image by using an external editor. You have learned how to align an image in relationship to other elements beside it. You learned how to optimize an image to make it download quickly over the Internet. You have also learned how to create image maps and insert rollover images.

Q&A

Q. What should I do if I accidentally stretch an image?

A. It's easy to restore the original dimensions of an image by selecting the image and clicking the Refresh button that appears next to the width and height text fields in the Property inspector after you've resized an image.

Q. Every time I use the Polygon Hotspot tool, I make a mess of it. I get extra points in the wrong section of the image map. What am I doing wrong?

A. When you use the Polygon Hotspot tool to create a hotspot, remember to click, click, click around the edges of the hotspot border. After you have defined the border, do not click the image again. Instead, immediately select the Pointer Hotspot tool or double-click on the hotspot to signal Dreamweaver that you are finished creating the polygon hotspot.

Workshop

Quiz

1. What are the three widely supported image formats for web pages?

2. If you want an image on the left and text beside it on the right, what Align value would you give the image?

3. Which image map tool enables you to draw irregular shapes?

TIP

JavaScript and Rollover Images

Dreamweaver uses JavaScript, a popular web scripting language, to make a rollover image work. You don't have to add any code because Dreamweaver does it for you. Don't, however, delete the JavaScript that Dreamweaver puts into the head of the document. If you do, the rollover image no longer works.

Quiz Answers

1. The three widely supported image formats for web pages are GIF, JPEG, and PNG.

2. You give the image the Align value Left.

3. The Polygon Hotspot tool enables you to draw irregular shapes.

Exercises

1. Insert an image into a new page. Resize it by using the resizing handles. Click the Refresh button. Resize the image by holding down Shift while dragging the corner resizing handle. Click the Refresh button. Change the width and height dimensions by entering different values into the W and H boxes in the Property inspector.

2. Add alt text to an image. Open your browser, select the browser preferences or Internet options, and turn off viewing of images. The command for this might be called Show Pictures or Automatically Load Images. Return to Dreamweaver and preview the web page in that browser so that you can see how the alt text looks.

3. Insert an image into a web page and experiment with Dreamweaver's image-editing tools. Try using sharpen, cropping, and brightness/contrast. Then resize the image and try image resampling. Does Dreamweaver actually change the original files? Be careful not to make any permanent changes to your files.

4. Try creating rollover images within a sample page. In general, rollover images should be small, since two images are used to create the effect. To test this functionality, I recommend selecting an image, scaling it to a reasonable (100–200px) size, and then using image-editing software to create a black-and-white or hue-shifted version to represent the rollover "on" state.

HOUR 9
Making Web Graphics in Fireworks CS5

In this hour, you explore the graphics program Adobe Fireworks CS5 to complement your work in Dreamweaver. You have to create and optimize the images that you use in your websites, and Fireworks enables you to quickly create web-ready graphics of all kinds. In addition to basic image editing, Fireworks also offers features especially for developing web pages, including file templates. This hour touches on some of the important elements and describes a few image manipulation techniques. There is much more to learn about Fireworks than is possible in this hour.

Acquainting Yourself with Fireworks

Many people who purchase Dreamweaver buy it in a software bundle that includes Fireworks. If you do not have Fireworks, you can download a trial version at http://www.adobe.com/downloads. You will need to login with your Adobe ID.

The Fireworks Document window, shown in Figure 9.1, contains a Tools panel on the left, the Options bar at the top, a Property Inspector on the bottom, and Tab groups on the right. You can open an existing document in Fireworks or create a new one from scratch.

WHAT YOU'LL LEARN IN THIS HOUR:

► How to modify images in Fireworks

► How to create an image with text and shapes

► How to optimize graphics for the web

► How to design a web layout

► How to slice an image into smaller pieces

► How to export a web design for use in Dreamweaver

NOTE

Why Fireworks?

Although Fireworks is less well known than Photoshop, a complex image editing program from Adobe, and Illustrator, an Adobe product for making original drawings, Fireworks offers easy-to-use tools for working with both photographic images and line drawings, known as vector graphics—which makes it perfect for web graphics where both types of images are used.

Tool panel   Menu bar   Panel groups

FIGURE 9.1
Firework's integrated interface is
similar to Dreamweaver's interface.

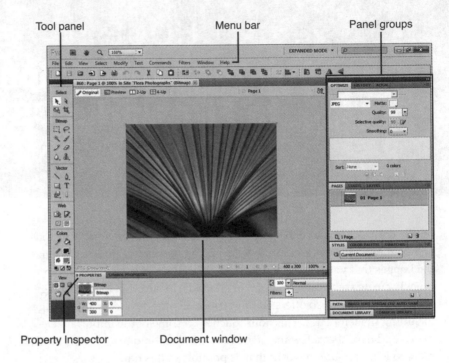

Property Inspector   Document window

Modifying Images for Use in a Web Page

First let's explore a few Fireworks features commonly used on web page images. To practice using these features, open a digital photograph in Fireworks. You can get a photo from your digital camera, from a collection of clip art, or from a free source such as NASA (http://www.nasa.gov/multimedia). Here are a few of the common edits I make to images for use in web pages:

► Rotate an image clockwise or counterclockwise

► Crop an image

► Change the size (that is, the number of pixels) of an image

Rotating, Cropping, and Changing the Size of an Image

We try all of these modifications and then revert to the original image at the end.

To rotate, crop, and change the size of an image in Fireworks, do the following:

1. Launch Fireworks and open your selected image file (File, Open).

2. To rotate an image, select Modify, Transform, as shown in Figure 9.2, and then select the appropriate rotate command. These are the available commands:

   Rotate 180°—Rotates the image a half turn.

   Rotate 90° CW—Rotates the image a quarter turn to the right (clockwise).

   Rotate 90° CCW—Rotates the image a quarter turn to the left (counterclockwise).

   Flip Horizontal—Flips the image horizontally (left to right).

   Flip Vertical—Flips the image vertically (top to bottom).

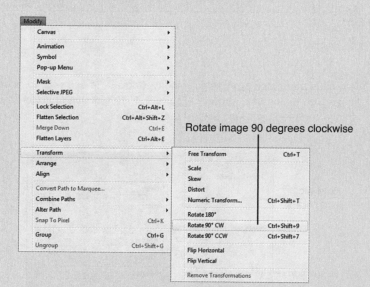

Rotate image 90 degrees clockwise

3. To crop an image, select the Crop tool and drag a crop marquee around the portion of the image you want to keep. Adjust the outline by moving the drag handles.

4. To complete the crop, double-click inside the crop marquee, shown in Figure 9.3.

FIGURE 9.2
You can rotate or flip the canvas of an image.

TIP

Precision Rotation

To enter the exact number of degrees of rotation, choose Numeric Transform, then select Rotate from the drop-down menu and set the number of degrees to rotate. Click OK to set your change.

Practicing Basic Image Manipulation
Continued

FIGURE 9.3
Use the Crop tool to drag a marquee and double-click the marquee to execute the crop.

TIP

Cropping vs. Masking

Cropping reduces the size of the canvas to cut off the edges of an image. Masking an image lets you hide parts of your image or design without permanently changing it. To mask the edges of an image, use the Marquee tool in the Bitmap section of the Tools panel to select the area you want to show; then choose Modify, Mask, Reveal Selection so the area you've selected remains visible.

FIGURE 9.4
The Image Size dialog box enables you to change the size and resolution of an image.

Crop tool   Marquee

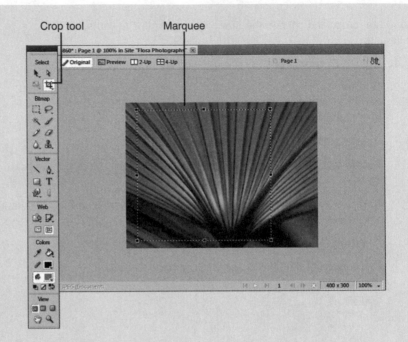

5. To modify the image size, select Modify, Canvas, Image Size to open the Image Size dialog box, shown in Figure 9.4. This dialog enables you to change the resolution and size of the image.

Pixel width and height

Resolution

Constrain

6. Enable the Constrain Proportions check box near the lower left and then examine the pixel dimensions of the image. Make changes to the width or height. Notice that changing one value also changes the other

value because enabling the Constrain Proportions check box maintains the image proportions.

7. Change the Resolution setting to 96 pixels per inch. This is a typical pixel density for modern desktop computers. Changing the resolution also changes the width and height shown at the top of the Image Size dialog box.

The three image functions that you just completed are very common operations on image files. All image programs have commands to accomplish these same tasks.

Undoing Changes

When working in Fireworks, you inevitably create edits or changes that you have to undo. There are two ways to undo your changes:

▶ The **Undo** command (Edit, Undo) reverses the most recent command. You can undo multiple commands.

▶ To start fresh by removing all the changes you've made to an image, use the **Revert** command (File, Revert). This opens a fresh copy of the last saved version of a file without any of the changes you made.

It's important to remember to always save your modified image files under a separate filename. You should always keep your original image source files in case you have to modify the files in the future.

Creating an Image

In Fireworks, you can create a new image from scratch, such as a logo you can use in your website. First you create a new image, and then you add some shapes and text. Next you apply an effect to make it look interesting. Let's walk through the process, from start to finish, of creating a simple logo in Fireworks.

▼ TRY IT YOURSELF

Creating a New Image in Fireworks

FIGURE 9.5
You set the width, height, and resolution in the New Document dialog box. You also set the background color here.

To try this, follow these steps:

1. Select File, New. The New dialog box appears.

2. Enter the specifications of the image in the New Document dialog box:

   ▶ Set the width to 100 pixels.

   ▶ Set the height to 60 pixels.

   ▶ Select 96 pixels/inch as the resolution.

   ▶ Set the Canvas Color to transparent, as shown in Figure 9.5.

3. Click OK.

4. Select View, Fit All to make the new image larger so that it is easier to work with.

Adding a Shape

Fireworks has tools for drawing any type of shape you might want. Now you create a cluster of oval shapes that looks like a flower. After you create the shapes, you can modify the stroke (that is, the outline) and the fill color.

1. Enable the rulers by selecting View, Rulers. You need the rulers to be visible because you add guides to an image by clicking and dragging from the ruler. **Guides** are useful for lining up text and other elements within an image.

2. Click within the left ruler and drag a vertical guide to the middle of the canvas. Make sure that your cursor is over the canvas when you finish

dragging the guide. Drag a horizontal guide down from the top ruler to the middle of the canvas. You can open the Info panel (Window, Info) to help precisely place the guides at 30 pixels horizontally and 50 pixels vertically. The guides should look as shown in Figure 9.6.

Rulers   Info panel

Guides

FIGURE 9.6
You can add guides to an image so that you know where the middle of the image is.

NOTE

Remove or Hide the Guides

To remove the guides, simply drag them off the screen or choose View, Guides, Clear Guides. To leave the guides in place but hide them, select View, Guides, Show Guides to toggle visibility. A check mark appears next to any command that is active.

To draw a flower, follow these steps:

1. Select the Ellipse tool from the Vector section of the Tools panel, as shown in Figure 9.7. The cursor becomes a set of crosshairs for aligning your shapes.

2. Click and drag to create one oval petal for the flower logo. Repeat to create the flower shape.

3. The final petal pattern might not be perfectly straight, but you can adjust it. There are two arrow tools in Fireworks: the Pointer tool and the Subselection tool (shown in Figure 9.8). You can use the Subselection tool (the white arrow tool) to select a single point in one of your ovals. Use this tool to select any of the points, and then press the arrow keys on your keyboard to fine-tune the position of the points so that the oval is petal-shaped. Use the Pointer tool to select the entire petal and adjust its position.

Using the Fireworks Drawing Tools

▼ TRY IT YOURSELF

Using the Fireworks Drawing Tools

Continued

Rectangle tool (U)
✓ Ellipse tool (U) ——— Ellipse tool
Polygon tool (U)

⇨ Arrow
→ Arrow Line
Beveled Rectangle
Chamfer Rectangle
Connector Line
Doughnut
L-Shape
Measure Tool
Pie
Rounded Rectangle
Smart Polygon
Spiral
Star

FIGURE 9.7
Select the Ellipse tool to make circles and ovals.

Pointer tool

Subselection tool

Adjust shape with Subselection tool

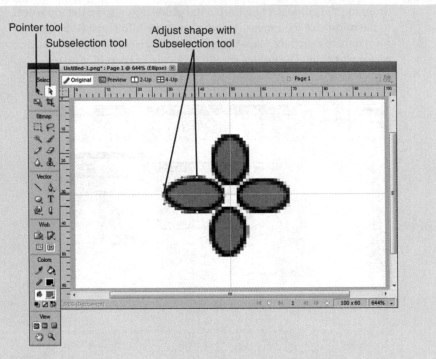

FIGURE 9.8
Use the Pointer and Subselection tools to adjust the position and shape of each vector object.

4. To change the properties of the petal, such as the fill and the stroke that outlines them, you will need to select them. Make sure the Pointer tool is selected and click and drag over the canvas to select all the petals. When selected, you should see the paths and points highlighted in blue, as appears in Figure 9.9 below.

5. Choose a new fill color and stroke color in the Property Inspector.

6. Save your file (File, Save). This is the source file, but you still have to export the image to use in your web page. Optimizing photographic images was discussed in Hour 8, "Displaying Images," and we'll talk about other image formats later in this hour.

Selected vector objects

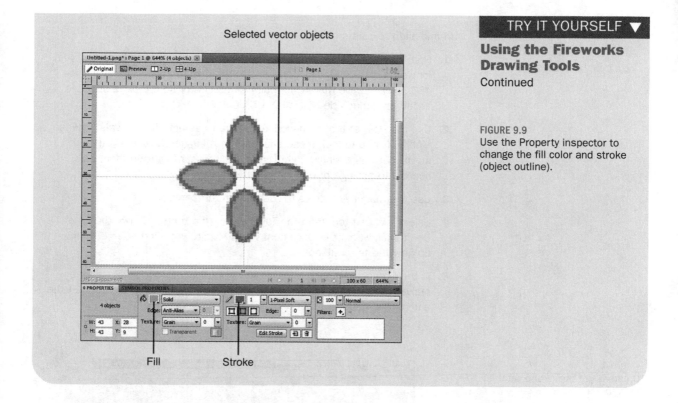

Fill   Stroke

TRY IT YOURSELF ▼

Using the Fireworks Drawing Tools
Continued

FIGURE 9.9
Use the Property inspector to change the fill color and stroke (object outline).

Adding Text

The Text tool in Fireworks enables you to place editable text into the Document window. You can use any font on your system, and you can apply antialiasing and other text effects. **Antialiasing** is a process of blending the edges of text with its background so that the letters look smoother.

Let's expand our logo file to include the name of the website, Flora Photographs.

CAUTION

Antialiasing and Different Background Colors

When you antialias text, the graphics program blends the edges into the current background color. That's how the edges look smooth. But this means that you must display the image on the same background color or you will see pixels of the original background color around the text— an effect known as **ghosting**.

Aligning and Adding Text to an Image

Add and align text as shown here:

1. First, open the logo file and modify the size of the canvas to make room for words. Select Modify, Canvas, Canvas Size to expand the width to 450 pixels. Leave the anchor point in the center so the extra space is added on either side of it. Click OK.

2. Use the Pointer tool as described above to select all the ovals. Choose Modify, Group to lock these shapes into a single object so you can move them as a single unit. (If needed, you can ungroup them as needed to arrange or edit individual shapes.)

3. Use the magnifying glass to zoom in on the canvas.

4. Select the Text tool from the Tools panel (the button shows the letter T). Don't click within the Document window quite yet. First you need to set up how the text will look.

5. In the Property Inspector, visible in Figure 9.10 below, select a font, make the font size 48 or so, and choose dark gray for the color. Set the anti-alias dropdown to Smooth Anti-Alias.

FIGURE 9.10
Create a text object and set its font, font size, and font color.

TIP

Check the Final Size

You might want to reduce the magnification to 100% by choosing View, Magnification, 100% so that you can see what your graphic will look like at its final size. Make sure that the text is readable. If you want to make the font size larger, select the text object and adjust the font settings. Quickly jump to the actual size by double-clicking the Zoom tool in the Tools panel.

Text object

Font   Anti-alias dropdown   Font color

Font size

6. Click on the canvas and enter the text **Flora Photographs**, adding enough white space between the words for the petal logo.

7. Use the Pointer tool to select and position the text using the guides on the canvas. After you select the text object, you can use the arrow keys on your keyboard to fine-tune the object's positioning. Then, position the petal logo in the space between the words, as shown in Figure 9.10.

8. Save your file and name it banner. Again, this is your source file, but next we will export the image for use on the web.

TRY IT YOURSELF ▼

Aligning and Adding Text to an Image
Continued

TIP

You Can Cloak Your Fireworks Files

You can save your original Fireworks source files to your website without cluttering it. Dreamweaver has a cloaking feature that you learn about in Hour 24, "Maintaining a Website," that enables you to easily store source files on your hard drive without uploading them to your remote site.

Optimizing Graphics for the Web

Fireworks, like Dreamweaver, includes tools to help optimize the images and vector graphics you create for the web so they are small in file size yet look good. This means selecting a web-safe image format and reducing the file size as much as possible without degrading the graphic quality so much that it appears fuzzy and pixilated.

In Hour 8, we discussed optimizing a JPEG when working with a photographic image. Here we'll talk about two other web-safe graphic formats, GIFs and PNGs. As discussed in Hour 8, these formats are better than JPEGs for web graphics that have blocks of solid color, such as drawings.

TRY IT YOURSELF ▼

Optimizing Vector Graphics

To save graphics comprised of text or shapes for the web, follow these steps:

1. First, open your file and choose Files, Image Preview from the menu.

2. Select 2 Preview Windows from the View options along the bottom of the window, as shown in Figure 9.11.

3. Select GIF or PNG 8 from the Format drop-down menu. Alternatively, the Saved Settings drop-down provides shortcuts for common optimization settings.

Optimizing Vector Graphics
Continued

FIGURE 9.11
View your original and a preview of the optimization setting you select.

Format drop-down menu   Saved Settings drop-down menu

Transparency   View options

4. If you'd like, choose a palette ranging from Adaptive, which contains only colors found in the original, to Grayscale. (Additionally, you can use the Optimize panel menu to save custom palettes if you want to ensure that GIFs created at different times use exactly the same set of colors.)

5. Use the Colors drop-down menu to reduce the number of colors in the image, which will make the file size smaller but may not represent the full spectrum of the original. Swatches of the colors in use are displayed, along with settings to add or remove specific colors for fine-tuning the palette.

6. Change the Loss setting to allow the images to leave out some pixel information—this reduces the file's size but also degrades quality.

7. Change the Dither setting to affect how the available colors are intermixed to create the appearance of additional tones.

8. To create a graphic with a transparent background, set the Transparency setting to Index Transparency and set the Matte color to match closely with the background of the page your graphic will appear on. (The edges in transparent GIFS are blended with an approximate background color, so choose carefully or those edges will show!)

9. Review the file size and approximate download time in the space above or below the preview. Also, compare the preview to the original to ensure that you aren't degrading the image quality too far.

10. Click Export. Then choose where to save the file and give it a name. (Note that there are other settings available in the Export window that we'll talk about later, such as exporting HTML and slices.)

TRY IT YOURSELF ▼

Optimizing Vector Graphics
Continued

Designing Web Layouts in Fireworks

In addition to using Fireworks to create and optimize individual graphics for the web as already discussed, you can also use it to design a full page and then export it for use with Dreamweaver.

To make this especially convenient, Fireworks offers an array of template files for common web graphics, such as advertising banners, and device screen sizes.

Let's build a simple example to explore several of Fireworks' features for website development by creating a page layout mockup. By drawing the page with a graphics tool, a web developer/designer can focus on the look and feel before switching to Dreamweaver to code a working version.

TRY IT YOURSELF ▼

Designing a Web Page in Fireworks

Add and align text as shown here:

1. Choose File, New from Template and choose Document Presets to select from common basic sizes for web graphics and interfaces.

2. Select Layout 1024x768 and click Open. A blank document opens where you can design your page layout.

3. Choose Modify, Canvas, Canvas Color and set the background to white.

4. Turn on rulers under View, Rulers in the menu bar, and then set vertical guides at 32 and 992. Remember, you can view the Info panel to see precise pixel placements of the guides.

   This leaves a central area of 960 pixels. (I originally chose 1024x768 because it's a very common screen size; however I won't build important graphics all the way to the edges because that would leave no room for menu bars, scrollbars, or other interface elements.)

▼ TRY IT YOURSELF

Designing a Web Page in Fireworks

TIP

Grids—Eyes Like Order

Grid-based layout is a technique of professional web designers that makes their work subtly polished. Laying out a grid before adding elements helps keep them in balance rather than feeling disjointed or random. Experienced designers pick page widths that are easily divisible into even columns—960 pixels, as we are using here, neatly divides into 2, 3, 4, 5, 6, 8, 10, or even 12 columns without messy remainders for maximum flexibility.

5. Create a simple gradient background that will show on screens wider than 960 pixels. Using what you learned earlier about vector shapes, draw a rectangle that touches the top edge of the canvas and spans the width of the page. Then, with the rectangle selected, choose Fill Options from the Fill section of the Property Inspector. Set the Gradient to Linear and click Edit to change the colors, as shown in Figure 9.12, making sure to leave the second color white.

FIGURE 9.12
Create a simple gradient background using the Fill Options.

6. Create a white rectangle on top of the gradient as a neutral background for the central portion of the page that will contain text and other content. Use the guides to mark the left and right sides.

7. Import the header we created earlier by selecting File, Import and then selecting the original PNG file. The cursor becomes an angle pointer with which you can position on the canvas to arrange your graphic. Before unselecting these graphics, fine tune positioning with the arrow keys.

8. Create navigation with the Vector tools including text and rectangles. Be sure to show a representation of how the currently selected navigation item should appear to set it apart from the others. The finished design, shown in Figure 9.13, is a mockup of what we hope to build as a working page.

9. Save your file and name it layout. We'll talk about exporting it in the next section.

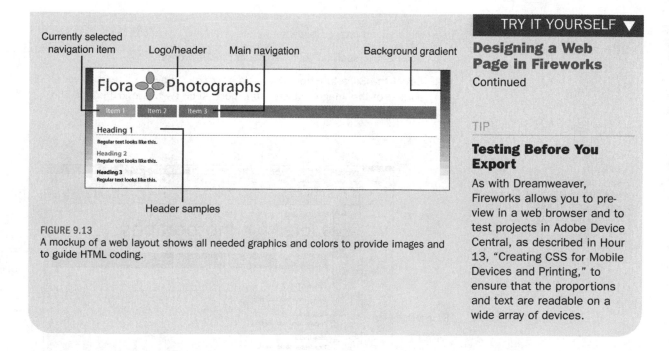

FIGURE 9.13
A mockup of a web layout shows all needed graphics and colors to provide images and to guide HTML coding.

TRY IT YOURSELF ▼

Designing a Web Page in Fireworks
Continued

TIP

Testing Before You Export

As with Dreamweaver, Fireworks allows you to preview in a web browser and to test projects in Adobe Device Central, as described in Hour 13, "Creating CSS for Mobile Devices and Printing," to ensure that the proportions and text are readable on a wide array of devices.

Slicing Web Graphics

Fireworks enables you to slice an image into smaller pieces and, in the case of a full web design, to choose which pieces to keep and their optimal format. Slicing facilitates creating a page layout by cutting images into pieces that easily fit into the implementation of your page design in Dreamweaver.

You can draw slice objects over an image in Fireworks and then export the slices as individual graphics files.

TIP

Repeating Patterns in Web Graphics

Because images take longer to load when they are large or when many are used, web designers use tricks, such as repeating patterns in backgrounds, to avoid using page-sized images. Smaller images load faster, but a single image can be reused without downloading more than once. CSS allows you to repeat a long vertical strip horizontally, a long horizontal strip vertically, or a rectangular section in both directions to make a continuous pattern for a background.

To create a sliced image, follow these steps:

1. Open a file, such as your web layout, in Fireworks.

2. Select the Slice tool from the Tools panel and draw a rectangle over a portion of the image you wish to export, such as the logo/header. The area selected highlights, as shown in Figure 9.14.

FIGURE 9.14
Draw slices over an image to create individual image files that can be positioned with HTML and CSS in your web page.

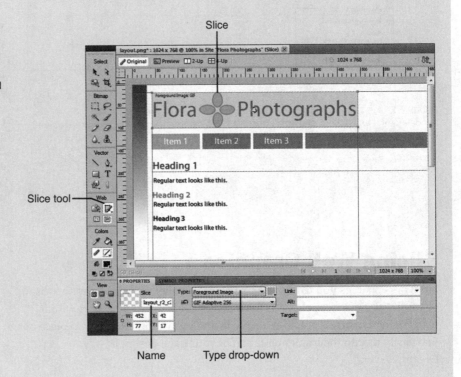

3. Use the selection tool to select the slice and, in the Property Inspector, name the slice something helpful and choose an optimization setting. In the Type drop-down, you can choose whether the image will be a foreground image, which is inserted directly in a page, or a background image, which other page elements can overlap.

4. Export the slice by right-clicking and selecting Export Selected Slice.

Exporting HTML and CSS from Fireworks

Earlier we created a mockup of a web page to guide our site coding. We also added and exported a slice to capture a portion of the design for use in a web project. Fireworks can also export HTML and CSS from your design settings. You can then use Dreamweaver to view, edit, or upload the files.

You can define styles for headings and links from within Fireworks. Let's create a basic example.

CAUTION

Messy HTML and CSS Code from Fireworks

Although you can export HTML and CSS from Fireworks, it isn't as clean as code you create in Dreamweaver. Although web best practices have changed over time, sometimes Fireworks' code uses out-of-date methods, such as tables for laying out image slices. Also, in complex page layouts the code from Fireworks can be quite unpredictable, showing strange background colors and inserting spaces you didn't intend!

To create HTML and CSS styles within Fireworks:

1. Open a new file in Fireworks.

2. Choose Window, Common Library to view HTML objects you can add within Fireworks, as shown in Figure 9.15.

TRY IT YOURSELF ▼

Adding HTML and CSS to Your Visual Design

FIGURE 9.15
Create HTML and CSS styles by using the Common Library panel.

Adding HTML and CSS to Your Visual Design
Continued

FIGURE 9.16
Attach properties to each HTML element in the Symbol Properties tab of the Properties Inspector.

3. Drag the elements, such as headings 1-3, that you wish to define onto the canvas.

4. Select an element and switch the Properties Inspector to the Symbol Properties tab, as shown in Figure 9.16, to change its appearance. Repeat for all HTML elements you'll need.

5. Choose File, Export and set the Export drop-down to CSS and Images. You can Browse to select a location for saving the files, which you can then open within Dreamweaver.

Creating Drop-Down Menus

Fireworks offers a way to create drop-down menus and to export them as working menus, but frankly Dreamweaver does it better (see Hour 16, "Adding Spry Menu Bars for Navigation.") To create drop-down menus in Fireworks, create menu graphics labeled for each top-level navigation item in your layout document and then slice them. Right-click on each slice and select Add Pop-Up Menu to create the links contained in each section, then choose setting for the appearance and placement of each menu. When the navigation items are complete, choose File, Export and make sure the Export drop-down is set to HTML and Images.

Summary

This hour introduced you to Fireworks and common practices in developing graphics for the web. You learned how to work with photographic images, how to add text and a shape to original graphics, and how to optimize them for the web. You also learned how to design a web layout and slice a single image into multiple images. Finally, you explored Fireworks' special features for exporting web code.

Q&A

Q. How can I tell which image file format makes the smallest file?

A. That's what you use the optimization capabilities of Fireworks for. You don't have to know off the top of your head which format to use because you can experiment in Fireworks and find out which format creates the smallest file.

Q. Can I use a file I create in Fireworks as a web graphic without saving it for the web?

A. Fireworks' native file format is PNG (Portable Network Graphic), which is web-safe. However, your Fireworks graphics may benefit from additional optimization and file compression that comes from saving especially for the web.

Q. Do I have to use Fireworks to create drop-down menus for the web?

A. No. In fact, I don't recommend using Fireworks for drop-down menus. Dreamweaver includes a library of code called the Spry Framework that lets you easily insert a 3-level drop-down or pull-out menu far superior to the menus Fireworks can produce. We'll discuss that in detail in Hour 16.

Workshop

Quiz

1. How do you create a guide in Fireworks?

2. Which image file format is best for photographic images on the web? For line drawings and text?

3. How do you slice graphics in Fireworks?

Quiz Answers

1. Enable the rulers, click within one of them, and drag a guide into position.

2. JPEG format or PNG format are best for photographs, because they allow a full range of colors; however, GIF or PNG formats are crisper when saving vector graphics or text-based images.

3. Use the Slice tool to draw a rectangle over a portion of the image.

Exercises

1. Practice rotating, resizing, and cropping images in Fireworks. (Be sure to save a new file so you don't alter your original file!) Then export them as JPEG files optimized for the web.

2. Create a new file and use the Vector tools to add shapes, lines, and text. Then export your file as a GIF file optimized for the web.

3. Design a simple web layout and attach web styles using the Common Library. Export your design and open it in Dreamweaver.

HOUR 10
Adding Flash and Other Multimedia to a Web Page

You aren't limited to displaying text and graphics in web pages. You can include movies, sounds, documents, and many other specialized types of content. Like images, these media are external files embedded in a web page. Unlike images, most multimedia files require some sort of an installed player in order to see or hear the content.

This hour introduces you to some of the issues and the techniques you can use to include multimedia files in your website. You have to be aware of bandwidth limitations, along with some of the differences among various browsers. You also have to understand how your viewers can download the players necessary to view the files you include in your web pages.

WHAT YOU'LL LEARN IN THIS HOUR:

▶ How to add Flash and Shockwave movies to a web page

▶ How to add multimedia files, such as sounds, movies, and PDF documents, to a web page

▶ How to insert and configure a Java applet in a web page

Exploring Multimedia and Bandwidth

Adding multimedia files, such as sounds, movies, and PDF (Portable Document Format) documents, grows more popular as modems become faster and people browse the Web with more bandwidth. Yes, that's right: Most multimedia files take up a lot of bandwidth. **Bandwidth** is the size of the Internet "pipe" you have when you connect to the Web. Increasingly more people are accessing the Internet using a **broadband** connection—DSL or a cable modem. If you are on a broadband connection, you have access to a higher Internet bandwidth than someone connecting via dialup with a 56Kbps modem.

Some formats, such as RealMedia, Flash Video, and Shockwave, get around the large bandwidth requirements of sound and video files by streaming content to the user. Streamed content begins to play after a short buffer period; the content continues to download in the background while previously buffered content plays. Ever-improving techniques compress most multimedia delivered over the Web.

Some of the traditional CD-based multimedia formats, such as WAV (audio), AVI (Windows movie), MOV (QuickTime movie), and AIFF (audio), are often too large to deliver over the Web. Some of these formats require the user to download the entire file before it plays. To deliver this type of sound and video content, you have to understand which technologies to choose; new compression and streaming tools appear all the time. The MP3 sound format is extremely popular because it can create very small files that still sound great.

Understanding Players

To play a multimedia file in a browser, the user must have a third-party program to play the file. Without the right media player, some page content can appear as a blank space that may prompt you to download the missing component, as shown in Figure 10.1 These players are either plug-ins or ActiveX controls, and some install automatically with the browser or operating system software. A **plug-in** is a piece of additional software that adds new functionality to the browser. The user might need to restart the browser for the plug-in to work after installing it. Of course, you don't want to assume that a person viewing your web page has the same players installed that you have. You should always give the viewer information about how to obtain the necessary player.

NOTE

ActiveX Installation Woes

Some users either have disabled their computers' capability to install ActiveX controls or are confused and possibly suspicious when a dialog box appears, telling them they will be downloading and installing something. In addition, some corporate networks block the installation of ActiveX controls. Make sure that you tell users what to expect if you include content that requires them to download and install something on their computers.

Browsers deal with multimedia files in two ways. Safari, Opera, and Mozilla Firefox extend their capabilities with plug-ins. A list of popular Firefox plug-ins appears at http://addons.mozilla.org/firefox/plugins/. Each browser has a plug-ins folder where these programs are stored.

Microsoft Internet Explorer, on the other hand, uses its ActiveX technology to launch and run multimedia content. **ActiveX controls** are similar to plug-ins: They install on the user's machine and add the capability to play different file types. Many third-party browser extensions come as both plug-ins and ActiveX controls to accommodate all browser types. An ActiveX control usually installs itself in the background and does not require the user to restart the browser after installation. Figure 10.2 shows the ActiveX controls installed in my copy of Internet Explorer (use the Tools, Manage Add-Ons, Enable or Disable Add-ons command in Internet Explorer).

FIGURE 10.1
Without the right media play, the web browser can't play multimedia content and prompts the viewer to download.

Missing plug-in

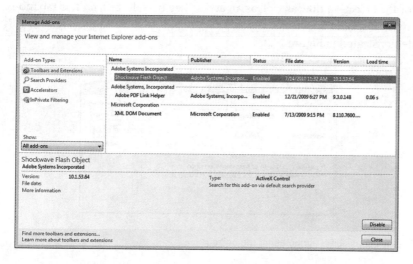

FIGURE 10.2
Internet Explorer displays a list of currently installed Active X controls.

It's always good form to tell a viewer where to download a required player. You can place information in your web page that includes a link to download the player. Dreamweaver offers the `pluginspace` attribute to enable the browser to attempt a player download automatically.

Adding Flash Files

Adobe Flash has arguably become the standard for web animation. Adobe Director, originally created for CD-ROM–based interactive programs, also has a streaming web player (called Shockwave), but it is not as common as Flash. Flash is extremely fashionable for creating small, interactive, web-based animations. Flash is popular because of its **vector-based graphics**—a format that is small and scalable. Flash is easy to learn and is a fun tool to create in. Its scripting language, ActionScript, is based on the same standard as JavaScript, a popular scripting language for web pages.

Flash movies usually end with the .swf file extension, whereas Shockwave movies end with the .dcr file extension. You must have the appropriate players installed in your browser to view these movies; that is, you must have the Flash player to view Flash movies and the Shockwave player to view Director Shockwave movies.

To insert a Flash movie into a web page, select the SWF object from the Media menu of the Insert panel (or Insert, Media, SWF). After you've chosen the Flash file, Dreamweaver may prompt you for accessibility attributes for the object—a title, as well as an access key (to select it), and its tab index (when it should be selected if you press the tab key within the page). This is demonstrated in Figure 10.3.

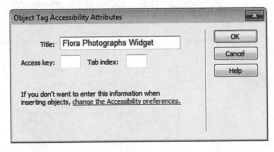

FIGURE 10.3
Set the accessibility attributes for the object.

After the file has been added, you can select it to see the attributes in the property inspector. Figure 10.4 shows the Property inspector with a Flash movie selected.

Flash content area

Flash properties

FIGURE 10.4
The Property inspector shows the properties you can set for a Flash movie. Some are standard properties, whereas others are specific to Flash movies.

The Property inspector displays the various settings for playing a Flash movie within a web page. There is a check box for Loop and another for Autoplay. Selecting Loop tells the Flash movie to play repeatedly; for the Flash movie to loop, it must have this functionality enabled. The Autoplay setting tells the Flash movie to play immediately when it is loaded. You can add vertical space (V Space text box) and horizontal space (H Space text box) to the Flash movie just as you can for an image.

Previewing a Flash Movie in the Dreamweaver Document Window

You can preview Flash movies and interact with them directly within Dreamweaver. To preview a Flash movie in the Document window, click the green Play button in the Property inspector. While the movie is playing, the Play button turns into a red Stop button, as shown in Figure 10.5. Click the Stop button to stop the movie.

TIP

Flash Movie Quality Settings

I like to choose the Quality setting of Auto High; this balances good appearance with fast loading, according to the user's connection speed. The other Quality settings enable you to balance appearance versus load time manually.

TIP

Help! The Flash Movie Is the Wrong Size

If you accidentally resize a Flash movie, click the Reset Size button (the circular arrow between the W and H fields) to return the movie to its original size.

CAUTION

Objects Only!

Prior to CS4, Dreamweaver used an <embed> and an <object> tag to add Flash movies to a page in a way that was compatible with all browsers. More recent versions of Dreamweaver use the <object> tag only to improve its standards compliance.

If you find that a movie you've added to a page is not working in all browsers, you may want to revert to the original <object> and <embed> method of adding content. Visit http://www.alistapart.com/articles/flashsatay to see the "Twice-Cooked Method" of embedding Flash.

FIGURE 10.5
You can view a Flash or Shockwave movie, and other plug-in–based content, directly in the Document window.

Toggle visible content
Media handle
Flash content
Playback controls

Sample Flash Movie

Adobe provides a range of Flash samples you can use at http://www.adobe.com/devnet/flash/. You can download and use these files to test the Dreamweaver Flash functions on your own.

Setting Alternative Content for Flash Media

At the upper left of every Flash object that you add to a page is a media handle that includes the name of the object as well as a small "eye" icon. This is shown in Figure 10.5. Normally, the eye is open, indicating that the view is that of a browser which can play flash files.

If you click the eye, however, it closes and the Flash content is replaced with alternative content that includes a message to the viewer stating that they need to install Flash, as shown in Figure 10.6. The Properties Inspector also changes to support text editing. You can edit this alternative content to suit your needs.

Adding a Link to a PDF File

So far in this hour, you've been embedding multimedia content into a web page. You can also link to content that appears by itself. You link to multimedia files just as you would link to another web page. If the multimedia file is within your defined website, you can use a document-relative URL. If multimedia file is on another site, you must use an absolute URL (for example, http://www.irs.gov/pub/irs-pdf/fw9.pdf).

FIGURE 10.6
Edit the content that appears when Flash is not available on a viewer's computer.

Adobe Reader is a freely distributed player that has become the standard for viewing formatted text files over the web. PDF files enable the viewer to see a file exactly as you meant it to be seen—fonts, page layout, and graphics appear predictably. You create PDF files by using an application called Adobe Acrobat Distiller and view them with Reader. The Reader plug-in usually installs when you install the Reader application. Macintosh users can create PDFs using the Print function from any application and read them using the Mac OS X Preview application—no additional software is required.

To display a PDF file, you simply create a hyperlink with the URL to a PDF file. The file then opens within the browser if the Reader plug-in is present. If the plug-in isn't installed but Reader is, Reader runs as a standalone application and displays the PDF file. You can download Reader at http://get.adobe.com/reader/.

Adding a Sound File to a Web Page

Adding a sound file to a web page can sometimes add to the experience, and it's a good way for you to become familiar with adding multimedia files. You select the Plugin object from the Media tab of the Insert panel (or select Insert, Media, Plugin) to insert a sound into a web page.

TIP

Find Sounds on the Web

Your operating system should have some sound files available for you to use. To find them, search for a directory called media or sounds or multimedia. If you prefer to download audio files from the Web, check out http://www.archive.org/details/opensource_audio. After you select a song, you can download the file and unzip it to get the MP3.

**Inserting a Plugin
Object for Audio
Playback**

To insert a Plugin object, follow these steps:

1. Position the insertion point in the Dreamweaver Document window where you would like the sound control to appear when viewing the page in the browser.

2. Select the Plugin object from the Media tab of the Insert panel (or select Insert, Media, Plugin). The Select File dialog box appears.

3. Navigate to a directory that contains a sound file and select a file. Select All Files from the Files of Type drop-down menu. Then click the Select button.

4. Click OK to insert the Plugin object into the web page.

Notice that the Property inspector for the Plugin object has some properties that are similar to ones you have seen while working with images. The Src box holds the filename and its location. There is an Align drop-down menu, similar to the one for images, which affects how other objects align with the Plugin object. Other familiar properties are W (width), H (height), V (vertical) Space, and H (horizontal) Space.

Plug-in Playback

When you're delivering multimedia, what the user sees and hears much depends on which browser and plug-ins the user has. When the Plugin object that we just discussed is used, the audio is played back through an existing compatible plug-in on the computer. As you can probably guess, some plug-ins and sound file formats are more popular than others. The popularity of file formats is constantly evolving. As of this writing, Quick-Time, Windows Media Player, and the generic MP3 sound formats are popular and quite common on the Web. MIDI files are common, too. Table 10.1 lists some of the most popular sound file formats.

TABLE 10.1   Common Web Sound Formats

Sound Format	Streaming?	Description
RealMedia	Yes	Real-time streaming audio and video format.
Shockwave Audio	Yes	Real-time streaming audio format.
MP3 (MPEG 3)	Yes	Compact file size with excellent sound quality. This open-standard sound format has become very popular.
Ogg Vorbis	Yes	Open, free, high-quality sound format.

Liquid Audio	Yes	Small file sizes with excellent sound quality.
Beatnik	No	Sound format that combines MIDI and digital audio.
AIFF	No	A popular Macintosh sound format. Not ideal for longer sounds because of its large file size.
WAV	No	A popular Windows sound format. Not ideal for longer sounds because of its large file size.
u-Law (.au)	No	An initially popular web sound format from Sun Microsystems, but not very common today.
QuickTime	Yes	Apple's movie format, which can also play sounds. File sizes can be large.
MIDI	No	An open-standard sound format that uses defined MIDI sounds on the user's computer. Files are very compact.

What all of this means to you, the developer, is that if you use the sound embedding approach we've discussed so far, you're at the whim of the browser and plug-in for what the user's controls look like and how they act.

Resizing a Control

The default size of the Plugin object is 32×32 pixels. That's probably too small. You can enter a width and a height in the Property inspector with the Plugin object selected. Increasing the width and height of a plug-in allows more controls to be visible.

Predicting an appropriate size for a plug-in can be tricky because you can't predict which player application users will be displaying in their browser. If you have embedded a sound file into your web page, keep in mind that some viewers might use the QuickTime plug-in to play sounds in a web page, whereas others might use Windows Media Player or the RealMedia Player. The controls for these players are all different sizes.

First, preview the web page in the browser to see (and hear!) how the page is working. In Internet Explorer, you might get a security message like the one shown in Figure 10.7. The message directs the viewer to click the IE information bar to enable the plug-in. Microsoft added this safeguard to

TIP

Flash Audio

I prefer to save audio files as Flash files simply because Flash is good at compressing audio (it uses the MP3 compression algorithms) and the Flash player is available to most viewers.

help keep people from playing unsafe content in the browser, and it makes our job as web developers a little more difficult.

Internet Explorer warning

If a browser doesn't have a player configured to handle this type of file, it usually displays a button linking to a location to download an appropriate player. Figure 10.8 shows the working audio file in Internet Explorer after the user approves use of ActiveX. Note that the width of the object has been changed from the default 32 to be large enough for all the controls.

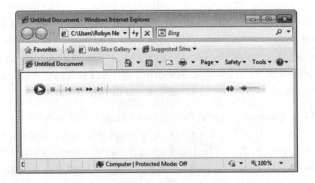

Looping the Sound

Dreamweaver offers the flexibility to deal with advanced attributes of objects—even attributes that haven't been created yet—through the Parameters dialog box. Clicking the Parameters button in the Property inspector opens the Parameters dialog box. Parameters consist of two parts: a parameter name and a value.

Different plug-ins have different parameters available. Table 10.2 lists some common sound parameters. Many plug-ins have optional or required parameters you can set in the Parameters dialog box. The parameters available for sounds, such as loop and autostart, might or might not be available for other formats.

TABLE 10.2   Common Sound Parameters

Parameter	Values
loop	true, false, n *(number of times playing)*
autostart	true, false
hidden	true, false
volume	0–100
playcount	n *(number of times playing—Internet Explorer only)*

After you click the Parameters button, click the + button to add a parameter. Then do the following to make the sound loop:

1. Type **loop** as the parameter name. Tab or click in the Value column and type **true**. The default value is false, so if you want the sound to play only once, you do not need to enter the loop parameter.

2. Add the playcount parameter in addition to the loop parameter. The default for playcount is for the sound to play once. Enter the number of times you want the sound to play.

You can enter multiple parameters in the Parameters dialog box. Figure 10.9 shows the Parameters dialog box with parameters entered. You add the parameter name in the left column and then click or tab to the right column to add the parameter value. After you have finished adding parameters, click the OK button.

To edit a parameter, again click the Parameter button in the Property inspector and then click in the parameter you want to change. To delete a

CAUTION

Know Your Plug-ins

Keep in mind as you add parameters or sizing to your plug-in content, it might not be the same player showing the content in different browsers. If you want to target a certain plug-in for a piece of content, you should refer to the plug-in developers website for code snippets which target that plug-in.

Alternatively, visit the Embedded Media HTML Generator at http://cit.ucsf.edu/embedmedia/step1.php for an easy way to generate code that can be pasted directly into your document.

TIP

Linking to an Audio File

So far, you have had the browsers display an inline, or embedded player, meaning that the player appears within the flow of your web page. However, if you create a hyperlink to a sound file, the user's browser launches the player controller in a separate window when the user selects the link. For instance, iTunes or Windows Media Player may open in a separate window.

parameter, click the – button. Use the arrow keys to rearrange the order of the parameters. Disregard the lightning bolt icons; they are involved in loading dynamic data into parameter fields when you are using server-side scripting.

FIGURE 10.9
The Parameters dialog box can contain many parameters that affect the functionality of a plug-in.

Gaining Greater Control with an Embedded Player

You might be starting to get the sense that it is actually pretty difficult to determine exactly what the user experience is like when playing back audio files on a website. As long as you're depending on a built-in player, this is absolutely true. A different, more controllable approach is to use an embedded player. In this case, the player *and* the audio are loaded from your website and displayed in the browser, making the web page and the audio playback look identical on any system.

One popular player, JW FLV Media Player, by Jeroen Wijering features video, audio, and even image playback using Flash. By downloading this free player, you can easily embed almost any kind of media in your page by first embedding the Flash player, then setting parameters to point to your media files. In fact, the site offers a simple wizard that writes the embedded code for you, as shown in Figure 10.10.

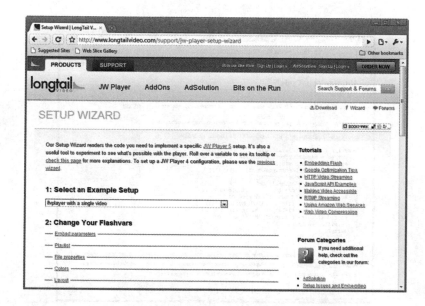

FIGURE 10.10
Configure the JW FLV Media Player to meet your needs.

To embed media into your web page using the JW FLV Media Player, just follow these steps:

1. Download the JW FLV Media Player files at http://www.longtailvideo.com/players/jw-flv-player/.

2. Place the two files in the JW FLV Media Player archive (`player.swf` and `swfobject.js`) in a directory called `embed` inside your site directory.

3. Place the media file that you want to play back in a folder called `media` inside your site directory (for example, `media/mysounds.mp3`).

4. Visit http://www.longtailvideo.com/support/jw-player-setup-wizard and choose flvplayer with a Single Song from the Select an Example Setup drop-down menu.

5. Under Change Your Flashvars, click File Properties and find the field called File and change it to your sound file's path (for example, `media/mysounds.mp3`).

6. Click Update Preview & Code.

TRY IT YOURSELF ▼

Using the JW FLV Media Player to Embed Media on a Web Page

▼ TRY IT YOURSELF

Using the JW FLV Media Player to Embed Media on a Web Page
Continued

FIGURE 10.11
Copy the necessary code, straight from the JW FLV Media Player website.

7. You can now see a preview of how the player will appear on your web page along with code that you can copy and paste into your page code to show the media player, as shown in Figure 10.11.

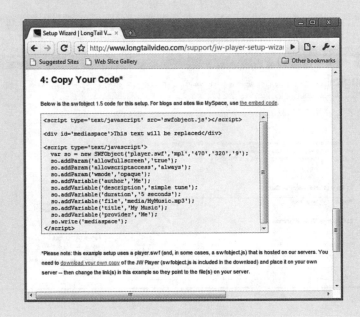

There are many parameters and customization options for JW FLV media player that you can take advantage of by using the simple configuration wizard we've seen here. I highly recommend using this approach to embedding media, because it ensures a consistent presentation across browsers and platforms.

Adding a Java Applet to a Web Page

Java is a programming language used to create self-contained programs called **applets**. Java applets run within the browser window just like the other multimedia objects you've been working with in this hour. You can put a Java applet into your page, add parameters, and add some interesting multimedia to your web page.

To insert a Java applet into your web page, you must have all the appropriate files for the applet. The number and type of files might vary. You have

CAUTION

Java Versus JavaScript

Java and JavaScript are not the same thing, nor are they really related. **JavaScript** is a scripting language used in web page development to set the properties of a web page. **Java** is a compiled programming language used to develop applications.

to read the documentation for the applet you are using. The example here uses a classic snow applet, available from http://javaboutique.internet. com/snow_applet. Implementing the snow applet simply requires that you download the Java files (download and unzip wintersnow_v1.zip) and have an image file available as a background.

Any Java applet you intend to use in your web page should come with instructions on how to set it up. Be sure to read the instructions carefully and enter all the parameters correctly, or the applet might not work. If you do not set up the applet correctly, users simply see an empty gray box on the page. Dreamweaver creates the HTML code for you, but you must pay attention to the parameter values that you have to add to the Applet object.

CAUTION

Be Careful with Java Applets

Some users might have Java turned off in their browser, so you should be careful about including information that is vital to the web page in a Java applet.

To insert the Winter Snow applet into a web page, follow these steps:

1. Create a new HTML file and save the file in the directory with the Java files. Copy an image file into this same directory. This is the image where the snow appears.

2. Select the Applet object from the Media tab of the Insert panel or select Insert, Media, Applet. This opens the Select File dialog box.

3. In the Select File dialog box, navigate to the directory where you saved the Wintersnow files from the Zip file. Select SnowApplet.class. and Click OK to insert the applet into the web page.

4. In the Applet Accessibility Attributes dialog that appears, add a title, access key, and tab index. (Setting access keys and tab indexes helps physically disabled site visitors interact with the applet using a keyboard rather than a mouse, which requires more precise hand and arm control.)

5. Look up the width and height of the background image you'd like to use. In the Property inspector, enter this width and height for the size of the applet.

6. The snow applet requires a parameter that contains the name of the image file on which the snow appears. Click the Parameters button in the Property inspector. Add a parameter called background and enter the name of the image file you copied in step 1, as shown in Figure 10.12.

7. Save your web page and preview it in a web browser or in the Live View mode to make sure that it appears correctly. Figure 10.13 shows the snow applet in action.

TRY IT YOURSELF ▼

Embedding a Java Applet

▼ TRY IT YOURSELF

Embedding a Java Applet

Continued

FIGURE 10.12
A Java applet requires parameters specific to the applet.

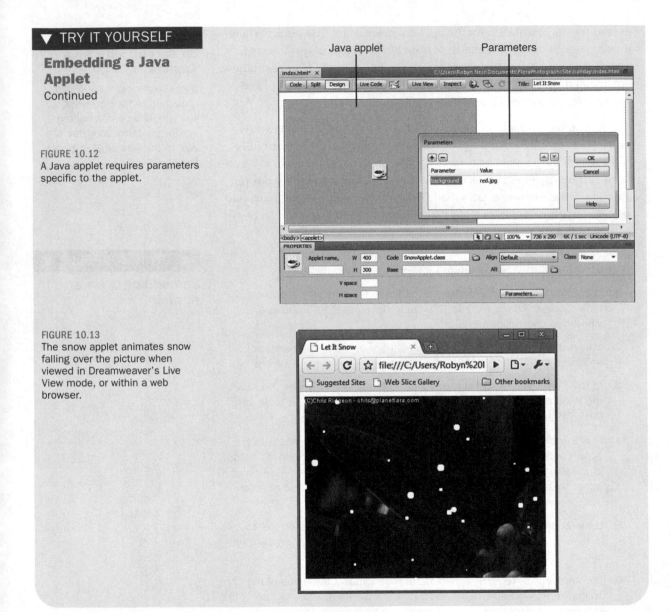

Java applet   Parameters

FIGURE 10.13
The snow applet animates snow falling over the picture when viewed in Dreamweaver's Live View mode, or within a web browser.

Summary

In this hour, you learned how to add multimedia files, including Flash and Shockwave movies, to your web page. You added a URL that the browser can redirect viewers to if they do not have the appropriate player to view your files. You added parameters to multimedia files to change properties that weren't specifically shown in the Property inspector, and you inserted and configured a Flash-based media player. Finally, you downloaded and configured a Java applet for your site.

Q&A

Q. I placed a value in the Border text box in the Property inspector when I had the Plugin object selected, but no border appeared around the plug-in. Did I do something wrong?

A. Some plug-ins respond to the Border attribute and some don't. The plug-in that you tried to put a border around was not capable of adding a border.

Q. Why do I see only a gray box when I insert a Java applet into my page?

A. You haven't entered a required parameter or you have entered a parameter incorrectly. Go back into the Parameters dialog box and double-check that you have spelled everything correctly. If you misspell something or reference a file incorrectly, you won't receive an error message; your applet just appears as a gray box. In addition, make sure that you saved your web page so that the path to the Java applet is correct and relative to your web page.

Java applets can be problematic because the user might not have the correct version of Java installed. Check the documentation of the applet you are using in your web page and add a link that leads to the correct Java version so that the user can download it if necessary. Check the Sun website for download information: http://www.java.com/en/download.

Workshop

Quiz

1. What plug-in does a browser use to play back content?

2. Java and JavaScript are the same thing. True or false?

3. What are the two components of a parameter?

Quiz Answers

1. The browser uses the media player that is installed in the system and set as the default player for the chosen type of content. Unfortunately, this can vary dramatically among systems.

2. False. The two are unrelated. Java is a programming language, and JavaScript is the language that Dreamweaver uses for behaviors, which you learn more about in Hour 18, "Adding Interactivity with Behaviors."

3. A parameter consists of a parameter name and a value.

Exercises

1. Insert a sound or movie file into a web page. Create a hyperlink to the same file. Explore how the embedded sound or movie works differently from the linked sound or movie.

2. Insert into a web page a hyperlink to a PDF file. The Internal Revenue Service (IRS) (http://www.irs.gov/formspubs) is a popular site for finding PDF files. Don't get me wrong—I'm not saying the IRS is popular, just its PDF files! (The IRS is the national tax agency for the United States, for those of you in other countries, and nobody likes paying taxes.) You can copy the URL to a file by right-clicking the link in the browser and then selecting either the Copy Shortcut command in Internet Explorer or the Save Link As command in Firefox. Paste the link into Dreamweaver's Property inspector as a hyperlink.

HOUR 11
Formatting Web Pages with Cascading Style Sheets

The Cascading Style Sheets (CSS) standard enables you to apply a visual property or group of visual properties to an object by applying a **style** to that object. You define and apply styles in Dreamweaver's CSS Styles panel or in the Page Properties dialog box, or by making settings (such as a font choice) in the CSS portion of the Inspector panel, as you did in Hour 4, "Adding Text and Lists." When thinking about styles, you probably think of creating and applying styles to text, which certainly is possible. However, you can use styles for positioning objects, creating borders, and lots more.

Modern Web standards require the separation of the *presentation* of a web page (the way the page is displayed visually) from the *content* (the words and images that make up the page). Dreamweaver creates CSS styles to control the presentation of the HTML content. Separating the content from the presentation paves the way to supporting various operating systems, browsers, and devices; this also enables screen readers to easily navigate through web pages for people who are visually impaired because the logical structure of the content is independent of its visual representation.

One of the benefits of using styles is the capability to simultaneously update multiple objects that have the style applied to them. If you create a style for all the paragraph text on the page, say a style defined as Arial 14-pixel text, you can later change the style's font to Times Roman, and all the paragraph text instantly appears in the new font. You don't have to search through your entire page for updates but can simply make a change in one spot.

CSS is defined by the World Wide Web Consortium's (W3C) CSS specification (get more information at http://www.w3.org/Style/CSS). Your viewers must have a modern browser version to view styles and, luckily, most users of the Web do. Current browser statistics say that almost 98% of browsers are modern versions—that is, versions later than 4.0 (check out

WHAT YOU'LL LEARN IN THIS HOUR:

► How to create each of the four style types: classes, IDs, redefined HTML tags, and compound styles

► How to apply styles to elements in a web page

► How to create an external style sheet for an entire website

► How styles deal with conflicting and inherited properties

http://www.w3schools.com/browsers/browsers_stats.asp). Dreamweaver displays a preview of how styles look in the browser.

There are four types of CSS **rules**, also called CSS **styles**, and during this hour you learn how to create styles that use all four types. This hour covers the basics of CSS styles, how to use the CSS Styles panel, how to create styles that apply to text, and where to go for help. A subset of CSS deals with creating web page layouts, called **CSS-Positioning**, or **CSS-P**. Hour 12, "Using CSS for Positioning," shows you how to lay out your web pages. Then Hour 13, "Creating CSS for Mobile Devices and Printing," goes into more detail about using CSS to deliver content in various formats.

Styling Text with CSS

In Hour 4, we explored modifying text and introduced you to CSS styles that are created automatically by Dreamweaver when you modify text attributes in Dreamweaver's CSS Property inspector. The best way to create text styles for a website is to actually plan and think about what types of presentation are commonly used in the website. After planning these styles, you can implement them and apply them to all the web pages in your site. The CSS Styles panel lists styles that have been defined and are ready to be applied to objects on your web page. You use this panel extensively when creating new styles in Dreamweaver. This is where you find the buttons used to create new styles and where the style attributes of the styles display.

Figure 11.1 shows the CSS Styles panel in its primary mode. When you click the All button, the CSS Styles panel displays a list of all the styles available. Selecting one of the styles in the list at the top of the panel displays that style's attributes in the bottom of the panel.

When the Current button is clicked, as shown in Figure 11.2, the CSS Styles panel displays the attributes applied to whatever is currently selected in Dreamweaver's Document window. This view of the CSS Styles panel lists properties specific to one element instead of listing all the styles available in the web page.

Dreamweaver creates the CSS for you and displays it in the CSS Styles panel (and, of course, writes it in the code as discussed in in Hour 7, "Looking Under the Hood: Exploring HTML"). It's helpful to know a little bit about how the code behind CSS works. You saw a list of attributes in Figure 11.1, but what do they mean? A few definitions and an example should help you understand.

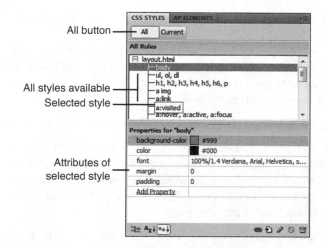

FIGURE 11.1
The CSS Styles panel is the command center for creating and viewing the attributes of styles.

All button

All styles available

Selected style

Attributes of selected style

FIGURE 11.2
The CSS Styles panel displays the properties applied to the currently selected object on the screen when the Current button is clicked.

Current button

Attributes of object selected in Dreamweaver

Create new CSS rule

CSS styles are made up of **rules**. A rule contains two parts: a **selector** and a **declaration**. Here is an example:

```
h1 {font-size: 200%;}
```

In this sample CSS rule, the selector is h1. This rule modifies the h1 (heading 1) tag and is a type of selector called an **element selector** that you explore in more depth later in this hour. The **declaration** is the part of the rule contained in curly brackets ({ }). The declaration in this rule sets the font-size property to 200%. This is the way all the attributes that you saw displayed in the CSS Styles panel are defined.

There are four basic types of selectors used to define CSS styles:

TIP

The Art of Creating CSS

Creating CSS is often more an art than a science. How do you decide which type of selector is best for which type of content? What measurement units are best to use? A lot of these decisions depend on the website and what you are trying to accomplish. But experience and looking at the abundant examples available on the Web will help you make good decisions. Visit CSS Zen Garden (http://csszengarden.com/), Max Design Selelectutorial and Floatutorial (http://css.maxdesign.com.au/), and W3Schools' CSS tutorial (http://www. w3schools.com/css/) for some helpful examples.

▶ **Class**—A type of selector, beginning with a period (.), which can be applied to any element in a web page with the class attribute. For instance, the class named `.attention` would modify these elements: `<p class="attention">` and `<td class="attention">`.

▶ **Tag**—A redefined HTML tag, technically called a "type" selector.

▶ **ID**—A type of selector, beginning with a pound sign (#), that you apply by giving an element an id attribute with the same name as the id selector. For instance, the id selector named #maincontent would modify this element: `<div id="maincontent">`. An id selector can be applied only once per web page.

▶ **Compound**—A selector that uses a combination of the other selector types to choose content. For example, if you had a table with an ID of `myTable` and you wanted to style the rows within that table, you might use a compound ID and tag selector like this: `#myTable tr`.

You can create each of the four types of selectors with Dreamweaver. When you click the New CSS Rule button (shown in Figure 11.2) in the CSS Styles panel, it opens the New CSS Rule dialog box, shown in Figure 11.3. Before defining the properties of a new style, you have to assign it one of these types.

FIGURE 11.3
You select which of the four types of styles you are defining in the New CSS Rule dialog box.

Selector types

In the New CSS Rule dialog box, you use the Selector Type drop-down menu to choose one of the four types of selectors.

The rest of this hour introduces you to creating class, tag, and compound selectors. You explore creating id selectors in Hour 12 when you learn about using CSS for page layout.

Creating a Class Selector

The easiest type of selector to understand and to create is the class selector. You create a class and then you can apply it to elements in the web page. When creating the class, you can define properties such as the font, font size, and font color.

To create a class that modifies font attributes, follow these steps:

1. Click the New CSS Rule button from the CSS Styles panel (shown in Figure 11.2).

2. The New CSS Rule dialog box appears. Select the Class (Can Apply to Any HTML Element) option from the selector type drop-down menu.

3. Enter a name for the style in the Selector Name field. A class name must begin with a period. Dreamweaver enters the period for you if you forget to enter it.

4. Select This Document Only from the drop-down menu in the Rule Definition section, as shown in Figure 11.4. This places the style definition in the web page instead of in an external style sheet. We discuss external style sheets later this hour.

5. The CSS Rule Definition dialog box appears, as shown in Figure 11.5. The box opens with the Type category selected. In the Type category, select a font and font size from the appropriate drop-down menus. In addition, select a font color by using the color picker.

6. Click OK to save the style.

TRY IT YOURSELF ▼

Creating a Class Selector

CAUTION

Naming Classes

Don't use spaces or punctuation in style names (except for the period at the beginning!), and don't begin a style name with a number.

TIP

Don't Blink

You might notice that Blink is one of the attributes you can define using CSS. Use it once to have fun and get it out of your system, throw away that web page, and then never use it again. Everyone finds blinking text annoying and it's not professional.

▼ TRY IT YOURSELF

Creating a Class Selector

Continued

FIGURE 11.4
Begin defining a CSS style by selecting the type of style, giving it a name, and indicating where it will be stored.

CAUTION

Class Selector Should Be Your Last Choice

Because the class selector is easy to create, understand, and apply, it tends to be overused. Make sure you can't use an id or tag selector first before you create a class. For instance, don't create a class to make text blue and then apply it to all your paragraphs. Instead, redefine the paragraph tag to have blue text using a tag selector or redefine the body tag so that all text on the page is blue.

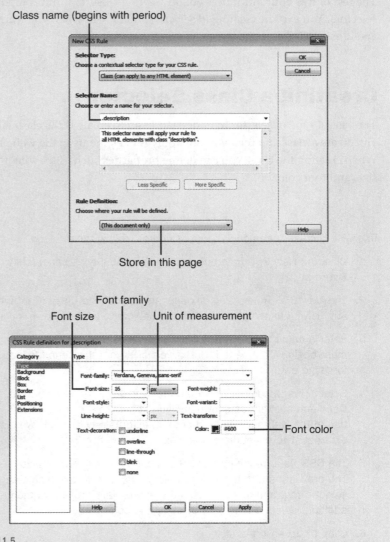

Class name (begins with period)

Store in this page

Font family

Font size   Unit of measurement

Font color

FIGURE 11.5
The CSS Rule Definition dialog box is where you set up the attributes of a style.

The CSS Styles panel lists the new class (make sure that the All button is clicked at the top of the CSS Styles panel). The top portion of the panel shows the class selector you just created and the bottom displays its attributes. There are three different attribute display settings, shown in Figure 11.6. I prefer the Set Properties View, as displayed in the figure, because it shows only the properties contained in the style instead of every possible property.

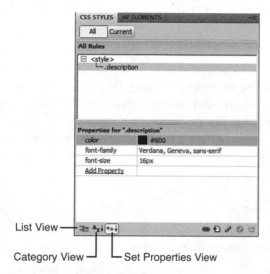

FIGURE 11.6
You can set the way the properties are displayed in the lower half of the CSS Styles panel.

Applying a Class Selector

You select a block of text to apply a class style to by dragging the cursor across it. If you create a class rule with properties that apply to non-text objects, you can select other objects on the web page and apply the style. The object then appears as defined by the style. Apply the class to an object by first selecting the object and then selecting the class from the Class drop-down menu in the HTML Property inspector, as shown in Figure 11.7. Notice that the style names display in their respective fonts and font styles in the Style drop-down menu to help you remember which is which. Note that if you happen to be in the CSS section of the Property inspector, you can apply the style using the Targeted Rule drop-down menu instead.

Removing a Class Selector

If you accidentally apply a style to an object, you can easily remove it. If you simply selected a few words instead of an entire block of text, Dreamweaver added a new tag called <span> around the text—we'll talk more about this very useful tag later. Tags wrapped around the text are necessary because Dreamweaver needs to apply the class attribute to a tag.

CAUTION

Apply Styles to the Correct Tag

Some style attributes work only when applied to certain tags. For instance, a style called big-cell with the cell padding values set in the Box category of the CSS Rule Definition dialog box does not have any effect on text because padding is not an attribute of text. Applying this style to an appropriate object, such as a table cell, does have an effect.

FIGURE 11.7
Select an object and then apply a
class by using the Style drop-down
menu in the HTML Property
inspector or the Targeted Rule drop-
down menu in the CSS portion of
the Property inspector.

Class selector

`<body> <p> <span.description>`

FIGURE 11.8
The tag selector enables you to
easily select and remove a class
selector.

Instead of selecting the text by dragging the cursor over it, it's better to use
Dreamweaver's tag selector, shown in Figure 11.8. When you select the tag
with the tag selector, Dreamweaver is smart enough to remove not only the
class selector but also the extra tag that is now unnecessary.

▼ TRY IT YOURSELF

**Removing a Class
Selector**

To remove a style from text, do the following:

1. Select the object that has the unwanted style applied to it. Using the
   tag selector is highly recommended.

2. Select None from the Class drop-down menu in the HTML Property
   inspector, or select Remove Class from the CSS mode of the Property
   inspector.

Exploring Style Settings

The CSS Rule Definition dialog box has eight categories with numerous settings you can use to define a style. As you are defining a style, select the
panels to gain access to the settings for each category. Any settings you do
not need to set should be left alone. The following categories are available:

▶ **Type**—This category defines type attributes, such as font and font
size. These style settings can be applied to text or to objects that contain text.

▶ **Background**—This category defines background attributes, such as
color and image. These style settings can be applied to objects, such as
layers and tables, where you can set a background.

▶ **Block**—This category defines type attributes for paragraphs.

▶ **Box**—This category defines attributes, such as margin size, which are
applied to box objects, such as layers and tables.

▶ **Border**—This category defines attributes that are applied to objects that have borders, such as layers and tables.

▶ **List**—This category defines list attributes, such as bullet type.

▶ **Positioning**—This category defines layer attributes, such as visibility and z-index. See Hour 17, "Using Dynamic HTML and AP Divs," for an explanation of layers and layer attributes.

▶ **Extensions**—This category defines miscellaneous attributes that are either future enhancements or for Internet Explorer only.

Table 11.1 lists the style settings available in the various categories of the CSS Rule Definition dialog box.

TABLE 11.1   Style Settings in the CSS Rule Definition Dialog Box

Setting	Description
Type Category	
Font-family	Sets the font family.
Font-size	Sets the font size and unit of measurement.
Font-style	Specifies the font as normal, italic, or oblique.
Line-height	Sets the height of the line of text and the unit of measurement. This setting is traditionally called **leading**. It is added before the line.
Text-decoration	Adds an underline, an overline, or a line through the text. You can set the text decoration to blink, or remove the decoration by choosing None (to remove the underline on hyperlinks, for instance).
Font-weight	Adds an amount of boldface to text. Regular bold is equal to 700 and normal, nonbold text is equal to 400. Many browsers display only 400, 700, and 900.
Font-variant	Sets the small-caps variant on text. This displays with all the lowercase letters as uppercase letters but slightly smaller than the actual uppercase letters.
Text-transform	Applies transformations to the text, such as capitalizing the first letter of each word or setting all the text to lowercase or uppercase.
Color	Sets the text color.

TABLE 11.1   Style Settings in the CSS Rule Definition Dialog Box

Setting	Description
Background Category	
Background color	Sets a background color for an element. You can use this attribute to set the background color for the body (the entire web page), a table, a paragraph, or any element on the web page.
Background image	Sets a background image for an object.
Background repeat	Controls how the background image repeats. No Repeat displays the image only once; Repeat tiles the image horizontally and vertically; Repeat x tiles the image only horizontally; and Repeat y tiles the image only vertically.
Background attachment	Sets whether the background image scrolls with the content or is fixed in its original position.
Background position (X)	Specifies the initial horizontal position of the background image.
Background position (Y)	Specifies the initial vertical position of the background image.
Block Category	
Word-spacing	Controls the space around words. Negative values reduce the space between words, whereas positive values increase the space.
Letter-spacing	Adds space between letters. Negative values reduce the space between letters, whereas positive values increase the space.
Vertical-align	Sets the alignment of the object relative to objects around it (these are the same alignment settings discussed in Hour 8, "Displaying Images").
Text-align	Aligns text within a container such as a paragraph, a table cell, or the entire web page. Choices are Left, Right, Center, and Justify.
Text-indent	Sets how far the first line is indented. Negative values create an outdent.
White-space	Sets how whitespace appears in an object; by default, whitespace is disregarded when HTML is displayed. Normal disregards whitespace, Pre displays all the whitespace, and Nowrap sets the text to wrap only when a break tag ( ) is encountered.

TABLE 11.1 Style Settings in the CSS Rule Definition Dialog Box

Setting	Description
Display	Sets how and whether an element displays. The None setting, for instance, hides the item on the page; the Block setting displays the element with a line break before and after; and the Inline setting displays the element with no line breaks. The None setting is useful when you're creating dynamic style sheets—for instance, creating a style sheet for a printable web page that sets buttons and unnecessary interface elements to None so that they are not printed. You learn more about this subject in Hour 14, "Using Site Assets, Library Items, and Templates."
Box Category	
Width	Sets the width of an element.
Height	Sets the height of an element.
Float	Sets whether the element floats beside other elements and whether it floats to the left or the right of the other element.
Clear	Clears floating so that an element does not float around another element.
Padding	Sets the amount of space between the element and its border (or margin).
Margin	Sets the amount of space between the border of an element and other elements.
Border Category	
Style	Sets the style appearance of the borders. The choices are Dotted, Dashed, Solid, Double, Groove, Ridge, Inset, Outset, and None (for no border). If the browser doesn't support one of the styles, it displays as solid.
Width	Sets the border thickness. You can set the widths of the top, right, bottom, and left borders separately.
Color	Sets the border color. You can set the colors of the top, right, bottom, and left borders separately.
List Category	
List style type	Sets the appearance of the lists. The choices are Disc, Circle, Square, Decimal, Lower Roman, Upper Roman, Lower Alpha, Upper Alpha, and None.

TABLE 11.1   Style Settings in the CSS Rule Definition Dialog Box

Setting	Description
List style image	Sets a custom image for bullets.
List style position	Sets whether the list content wraps to the indent (Outside) or to the margin (Inside).

Positioning Category

Setting	Description
Position	Sets how an element is positioned relative to the page. The choices are Relative (at the coordinates relative to its position on the page), Absolute (at the exact coordinates), and Static (at its place in the document flow).
Width	Sets the width of a container.
Height	Sets the height of a container.
Visibility	Sets the container's visibility. The choices are Inherit, Visible, and Hidden. You learn more about the attributes in this category in Hour 17.
Z-Index	Sets the container's **z-index** (that is, its stacking order).
Overflow	Sets what happens when the container's contents exceed its size. The choices are Visible, Hidden, Scroll, and Auto.
Placement	Sets the left, top, width, and height attributes for a container. These settings enable a container to be placed at an exact pixel position on the web page. The pixel position can sometimes vary a bit from browser to browser.
Clip	Sets the top, bottom, left, and right clipping attributes for a container. Clipping defines how much of an element is visible.

Extensions Category

Setting	Description
Page-break-before	Forces a page break during printing, before the object. Be careful with this property; use it only when you absolutely must control where the page breaks for printing.
Page-break-after	Forces a page break during printing, after the object.
Cursor	Changes the cursor when it is placed over the object. This attribute is supported only in modern browsers and can confuse users, so use it only when it is necessary.

TABLE 11.1   Style Settings in the CSS Rule Definition Dialog Box

Setting	Description
Filter	Applies special effects, including page transitions, opacity, and blurs, to objects. The filters included with Dreamweaver are supported only in Internet Explorer 4.0 and later. See http://msdn.microsoft.com/en-us/library/ms532853.aspx for more information.

Creating a Tag Selector

You can redefine HTML tags by creating tag selectors using CSS. You apply these styles by simply applying HTML tags as you normally would. By default, text formatted with the <h3> tag appears slightly larger than normal, in a bold font that is left-justified with one or two blank lines above and below. After you redefine the <h3> tag, any text with that tag applied to it immediately appears with the new CSS formatting.

To create some text, make it a Heading 3, and modify its appearance with CSS:

1. Type some text in the Dreamweaver Document window.

2. Apply Heading 3 to the text by selecting Heading 3 from the Format drop-down menu in the Property inspector.

3. Create a new style by clicking the New CSS Rule button in the CSS Styles panel. The New CSS Rule dialog box appears.

4. Select Tag (Redefines an HTML Element) from the Selector Type drop-down menu, then select h3 from the Selector Name drop-down menu in the dialog box that appears, as shown in Figure 11.9.

5. Select This Document Only from the drop-down menu in the Rule Definition section, then click OK.

6. The CSS definition window appears.

7. Select the Block category.

8. Select Center from the Text-align drop-down menu, as shown in Figure 11.10, and click the OK button.

9. Click OK, and the h3 text in your web page should jump to center alignment.

TRY IT YOURSELF ▼

Redefining an HTML Tag

TIP

Select the Tag Before Creating a Style for It

When you select the tag in the Dreamweaver Document window before you click the New CSS Rule button, the tag drop-down menu automatically displays the tag so that you don't have to search for it in the list.

▼ TRY IT YOURSELF

Redefining an HTML Tag

Continued

FIGURE 11.9
The tag selector drop-down menu contains a list of all the HTML tags you can change by using CSS styles.

FIGURE 11.10
The Block category properties apply to blocks of text. You can change the default alignment of a text block in the Text-align drop-down menu.

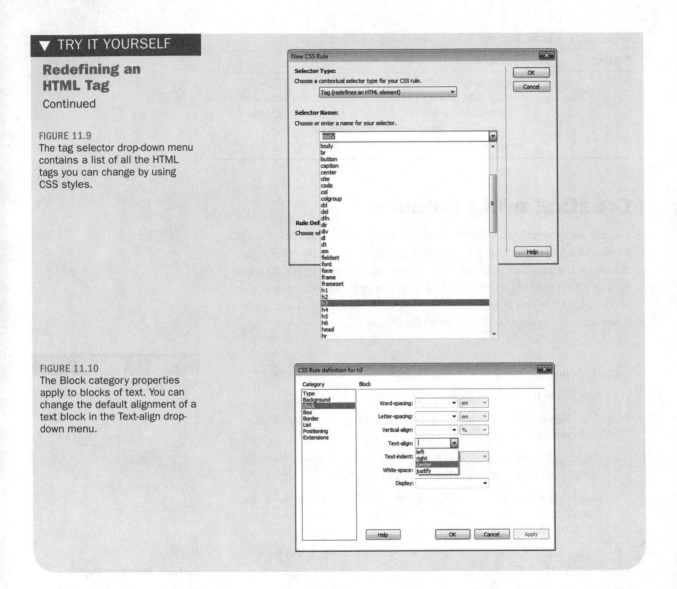

Creating Compound Selectors

The final type of selector we look at in this hour is a compound selector. A compound selector isn't really a different type of selector, it is actually a combination of the different types of selectors we've already seen. A compound selector combines class, tag, and ID selectors to focus on specific elements more closely.

For example, assume that you have defined a class mySpecialTable to set your fonts and font styles perfectly for *some* tables in your site. You realize that you want the fonts used in the <th> headers in those tables to also have a certain styling, and you *don't* want that style applied to other tables. You can't redefine the <th> tag, because it applies to everything. Assigning a special new class to all of your mySpecialTable <th> elements is possible, but time-consuming and difficult to maintain. Wouldn't it be great if you could just target the <th> elements within your mySpecialTable class and nothing else? You can, with a compound selector! A compound selector of .mySpecialTable th applies a style to the <th> tags within an element that has the mySpecialTable style applied.

TRY IT YOURSELF ▼

Creating a Compound Selector

To create a compound selector, you can either start from scratch (if you know the selector elements you want to combine) or select an object within your document to inherit all the selectors currently applied to it. Let's see how this works:

1. If possible, select an object within a document—preferably an object that already has styles applied.

2. Create a new style by clicking the New CSS Rule button in the CSS Styles panel. The New CSS Rule dialog box appears.

3. Select Compound (Based on Your Selection) from the Selector Type drop-down menu.

4. If you have selected an object, you see the CSS selectors currently applied to that element, as shown in Figure 11.11. You can use these styles as your compound selector (meaning it selects only elements with these same styles), or you can modify them.

5. Use the Less Specific and More Specific buttons in the New CSS Rule dialog box to remove or add selector information to your compound selector to widen or narrow its focus, respectively. You can manually edit the selector as well.

6. Click OK to finish creating the compound selector and begin defining your new style.

▼ TRY IT YOURSELF

Creating a Compound Selector

Continued

FIGURE 11.11
Compound selectors narrow their focus on very specific page elements.

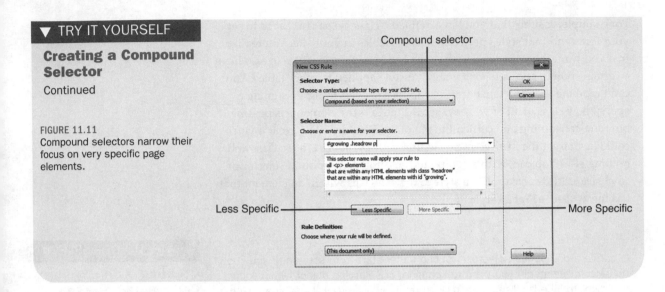

Compound selector

Less Specific

More Specific

Editing Styles

Nobody's perfect! After you create a style, you might need to edit it. Often-times while I am working on a design, I modify styles many times before they are exactly the way I want them. Fortunately, it's easy to edit styles in Dreamweaver using the same CSS Rule Definition dialog box where you created the style.

▼ TRY IT YOURSELF

Editing a Style

To edit a CSS style, follow these steps:

1. Select one of the styles displayed in the CSS Styles panel.

2. Click the Edit Style button, shown in Figure 11.12, to reopen the CSS Rule Definition dialog box.

3. Edit the style by selecting style categories and modifying properties.

4. Click the Apply button to see the modifications you've made displayed in the Document window.

5. When you are satisfied, click OK to save your changes.

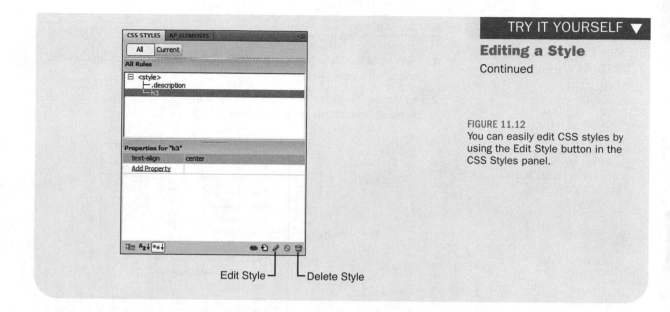

TRY IT YOURSELF ▼

Editing a Style
Continued

FIGURE 11.12
You can easily edit CSS styles by using the Edit Style button in the CSS Styles panel.

You can also edit CSS style properties in the Properties pane in the bottom half of the CSS Styles panel. Simply click any of the properties in any of the three views (Category, List, or Add Property) to modify or add the property to the style definition. I think it is easier to edit a style using the Edit Style button. As you become more familiar with the properties available by using CSS, you might want to use these new property views to edit CSS styles.

Creating an External Style Sheet

Adding styles to a single web page is nice, but wouldn't it be great to apply the same styles to multiple web pages or even your whole site? External style sheets enable you to do this. Instead of defining styles in a single web page, you define all the styles in one text file and link that file to every web page. When you update a style in an external style sheet, the changes apply to every page which links to that style sheet.

Exporting Existing CSS Styles

When you've created some CSS styles in a web page, Dreamweaver makes it easy to move them to an external style sheet. You can move the existing styles to an external style sheet with the .css file extension and then easily link that sheet to the web page.

Perform the following procedure to move and link CSS styles:

1. Select the styles to move in the CSS Styles panel, using Shift-click to select multiple styles.

2. Right-click the styles in the CSS Styles panel and select the Move CSS Rules command, as shown in Figure 11.13.

FIGURE 11.13
Select the Move CSS Rules command to export styles to an external style sheet.

Move CSS Rules ———

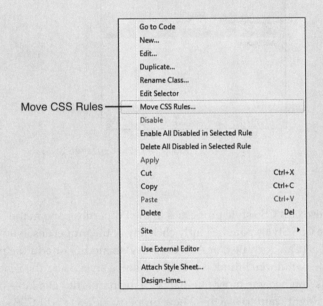

3. Select the radio button next to A New Style Sheet. Click OK.

4. Name the new external CSS file and click the Save button. Dreamweaver automatically moves the selected styles into this external file and links it to the current web page.

5. Move additional styles by repeating steps 1 and 2, but selecting the existing external style sheet instead of creating another new one.

6. When all the styles in the CSS Styles panel are listed under the external style sheet, you can delete the embedded style sheet, the <style> heading. Select <style> and click the Delete button shown in Figure 11.14.

TIP

**Where to Store the
CSS?**

Many web developers store external style sheets in a directory called CSS or Scripts.

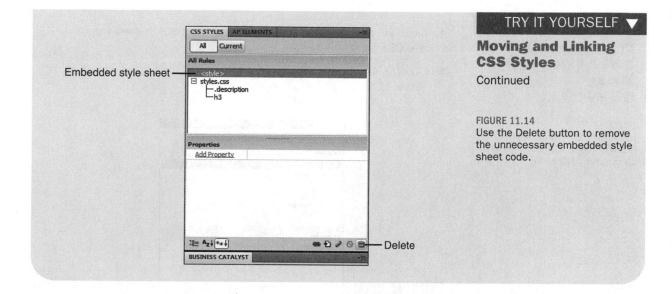

Embedded style sheet

Delete

TRY IT YOURSELF ▼

Moving and Linking CSS Styles

Continued

FIGURE 11.14
Use the Delete button to remove the unnecessary embedded style sheet code.

Creating an External Style Sheet from Scratch

You might want to start with an external style sheet before you create any CSS styles. This is the way I usually work. Of course, you can have as many style sheets as you need, and I usually have at least two or three per website, each serving a different purpose. For instance, I usually have one external style sheet I name `styles.css` that holds all the page layout styles. (You learn more about using CSS for page layout in Hour 13.) I might also have an external style sheet named `nav.css` that has all the navigational styles affecting links and buttons. If the website is large, I might have different style sheets that are specific to unique parts of the site.

To create and link to an external style sheet, follow these steps:

1. Select File, New, Blank Page, CSS.

2. Click the Create button.

3. Select File, Save and save the CSS file. You can name it `styles.css` and preferably save it in the directory in your website that holds CSS or script files (typically `css`).

TRY IT YOURSELF ▼

Creating and Linking a New External Style Sheet

Creating and Linking a New External Style Sheet

Continued

FIGURE 11.15
The Attach Style Sheet button enables you to link a web page to an external style sheet.

4. Close the new CSS file and return to the web page that will link to the new CSS file.

5. Click the Attach Style Sheet button in the CSS Style panel, shown in Figure 11.15.

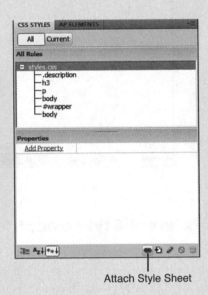

Attach Style Sheet

6. Click the Browse button and select the new external style sheet.

7. Select the radio button next to Link.

8. Click the OK button.

TIP

Defining Styles in a New External Style Sheet

When you create a new style (using whatever means you want), one of the options in the Rule Definition drop-down menu is to define the rule in a new style sheet. This is a quick way to immediately create a new external style sheet when you go to create your first rule.

Saving CSS Styles in an External Style Sheet

After you create an external style sheet, you want to add any new CSS styles you create to the external style sheet instead of the web page. To add additional styles to the external style sheet, select the name of the external style sheet from the Rule Definition drop-down menu when you define a new style, as shown in Figure 11.16. As you create CSS styles, pay attention to where you save them. Of course, you can always use the Move CSS Rules command that you used earlier this hour if you need to move a style to a different location.

FIGURE 11.16
Select an external style sheet from
the Rule Definition drop-down menu
to create a new style in the external
style sheet.

CSS and the Property Inspector

As I mentioned earlier, the CSS Styles panel is the best way to create and
manipulate styles. It pulls all of your style controls together in one easy-to-
use interface. That said, many people prefer to work with the side panels
hidden, and only the document and property inspector visible.

If this is your preferred way of working, never fear—CS5 gives you a quick
and easy way to define a new style for selected content. To do this, just
make sure that the CSS button is highlighted in the Property inspector.
Then, when you find yourself in a position where you want to define a new
style for a selection, choose New CSS Rule from the Targeted Rule pop-up
menu, as shown in Figure 11.17.

FIGURE 11.17
Create a new rule, straight from
the Property inspector.

Now, click the Edit Rule button. This launches the CSS style editor that you
know and love. After the style definition is complete, it is automatically
applied to your selection in the document.

You can also use the Targeted Rule pop-up menu to select other CSS styles and apply them directly in your document.

Understanding the Cascade

The topic of this hour is *Cascading* Style Sheets, not just *Style Sheets*. *Cascading* refers to which styles and attributes take precedence over other styles. For instance, if you define paragraph text as the color blue by redefining the paragraph tag and then add a class selector to one of those paragraphs that defines the text as red, what color will the text appear in the browser? The rules of the cascade are what controls style precedence.

The CSS standard defines a complicated hierarchy of style precedence dependent on the style's proximity to the object it's applied to, the type of style, and when the style loads. You can simply remember a couple of rough rules of thumb to help you predict style precedence:

▶ The closer the style definition is to the object, the more dominant it is. Therefore, style properties defined in a web page override a conflicting style defined in an external style sheet.

▶ The type of selector matters. In order of most dominant to least dominant, the selector hierarchy is id selector, class selector, and tag selector. Properties contained in a redefined HTML tag will lose to conflicting properties defined in a class or id selector.

▶ A defined style is dominant over an inherited style.

The last rule of thumb in the list refers to *inheritance*, which is another element of the cascade. As described in Hour 7, web pages consist of elements nested within other elements. For instance, everything in the page nests within the body tag. So if you redefine the body tag to have a certain background color, do all the tags (such as paragraphs, tables, and images) inherit that background color? CSS wouldn't be very useful if that happened.

TIP

Learning More About CSS

CSS is a complex topic that is very difficult for even seasoned web developers to grasp. As you work with the CSS tools, remember that Dreamweaver includes a CSS Reference (Window, Results, Reference).

Some properties are inherited, though. When you use the Page Properties command (Modify, Page Properties) to modify the font and color of the text, those properties are inherited by all the text on the page. Dreamweaver enables you to view the cascade of properties applied to a selected element using the CSS Styles panel. Figure 11.18 shows the CSS Styles panel with the Show Cascade of Rules for Selected Tag button selected—you must switch to the Current view to see this option. In this example, some Heading 3 text is being edited on the page, and it inherits all the body attributes listed in Figure 11.16. The CSS Styles panel shown in Figure 11.19 shows that the Heading 3 text does not inherit the background image property from the body tag; notice that it is crossed out.

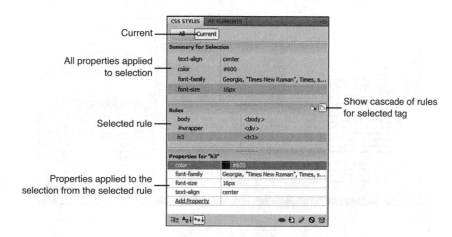

FIGURE 11.18
The CSS Styles panel can also display the cascade of styles applied to a certain element on the web page.

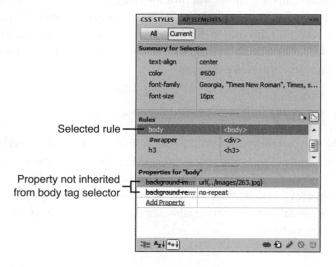

FIGURE 11.19
Properties not inherited by the current element selected in the web page are shown with a line through them.

Using Inspect Mode

Another useful tool built into Dreamweaver is the Inspect mode, accessed through the Inspect button in the Document toolbar. Inspect switches highlights regions of the screen and shows the properties applied to as you mouse over them, as shown in Figure 11.20.

FIGURE 11.20
Use Inspect Mode to quick surf
your page structure and CSS rules.

When enabled, Inspect mode will prompt you to allow the screen layout to change, as it is most effective in Split view to reveal the underlying HTML structure with the Current tab of the CSS Styles panel open to show conflicts. It also automatically activates Live View so you can interact with your page to test and make changes.

Summary

In this hour, you learned about CSS rule definition, properties, and how to create and apply classes and redefined HTML tags. You learned how to define CSS styles and how to edit them to make changes. You saw how Dreamweaver can store styles internally, in the same web page. And you made an external style sheet that allows the same styles to be used throughout an entire website.

Q&A

Q. Can I link more than one style sheet to a web page?

A. Yes. You can link as many style sheets to a web page as you'd like.

Q. When should I define styles within a single document versus in an external style sheet file? How about using inline styles?

A. If you are creating a whole site, it's better to consolidate all styles in external documents that can be shared by all the pages. That way, you can update them easily and uniformly. However, sometimes you don't have access to edit the external styles, then you can add them to the local document.

In extreme cases, you may be able to only add a style to a single element within the page or you may need to override the cascade by putting a style even closer to where it is applied. The code for inline styles looks something like this:

```
<p style="font-size: large; color: #900;">Text of paragraph...</p>
```

Note, however, you should only use inline styles if there aren't other options because they override central styles and are harder to update because they have to be changed individually.

Q. How can I remove the underline from hyperlinks by using CSS styles?

A. Some people might advise against doing that, but if you feel your design demands it, it's your call. To remove the underline from hyperlinks, redefine the <a> (anchor) tag in the CSS Rule Definition dialog box. Set Text-Decoration (in the Type category) to None. All the hyperlinks on the page are no longer underlined. You might want to define a:hover (select it from the Selector Name drop-down menu in the New CSS Rule dialog box) with an underline so that users can easily find the links when the cursor is placed over them.

Workshop

Quiz

1. What are the types of CSS style selectors?

2. What should you create in order to use the same styles for all the web pages in a website?

3. If you redefine the <h3> tag as red in an external style sheet and then redefine the <h3> tag as blue in the web page, what color will h3 text be in that page?

Quiz Answers

1. The types of CSS style selectors are classes, HTML tags, ID, and compound.

2. You need to create an external style sheet and link it to each page in your website.

3. The text will be blue because the internal style, the one defined in the page, is closer to the actual code and is dominant.

Exercises

1. Create a page, then add a class style that modifies text. Try applying this style to text in the page, table cells, layers, and other objects in the page. Save the style internally (choose the This Document Only setting) and then move the styles to an external style sheet. Practice adding additional styles to the external style sheet.

2. Create a page, with several links, then define different CSS rules for the four hyperlink selectors: a:active, a:hover, a:link, and a:visited. You can find these selectors under the Selector Name drop-down menu when you select Compound from the New CSS Rule Selector Type menu. Create a unique style for each selector. Write down the four colors you used, and then figure out when each appears by previewing a link on the page with the style definitions in the browser.

Using CSS for Positioning

In Hour 11, "Formatting Web Pages with Cascading Style Sheets," you worked with CSS (Cascading Style Sheets) styles and applied them to text. This hour builds on that knowledge, enabling you to write CSS styles that create a page layout. **Page layout** refers to designing the way a page looks when viewed in a browser. When you lay out a page, you position text, menus, and other page elements in an efficient and attractive way.

This hour uses a subset of CSS called **CSS-P**, in which the *-P* is for *positioning*. Instead of dealing with fonts and background colors as with the CSS you created in Hour 11, CSS-P defines properties such as width, height, margins, padding, and borders. These properties are important when you're creating the structure of a web page.

Understanding the CSS Box Model

To create a page layout, you have to start thinking of the elements in your web page as a collection of boxes. Each box has attributes you can modify using CSS. You can think of a single paragraph as a box, for instance, but it's more likely that you will want to wrap a div tag around a group of paragraphs and make that a section of your web page. The CSS box model describes the following box characteristics:

▸ **Width and Height**—The width and height properties can be either a fixed number (for example, 300 pixels) or a relative number (for example, 45%). The width and height values affect the content area. The total width and height may be larger than these values because the padding, border, and margin values add into the total size of the box.

WHAT YOU'LL LEARN IN THIS HOUR:

▸ How to use the CSS box model to understand positioning and styling containers on the screen

▸ About the sample page layouts that come with Dreamweaver

▸ How to insert div tags and apply id selectors to them

▸ How to use the Float and Clear properties

▸ How to horizontally center the design

▶ **Margin**—The distance between one box and another box. This part of the box is always transparent.

▶ **Padding**—The distance between the content of the box and the border. This part of the box picks up the background color of the content.

▶ **Border**—The delineation between the padding and the margin. The border is invisible (0 pixels) by default. You can set the thickness, style, and color properties of a border.

Figure 12.1 shows the relative positioning of the various parts of a box. The content area is on the inside, surrounded by the padding. The border surrounds the padding. The margin is the area outside of the border.

FIGURE 12.1
The CSS box model describes the properties of all containers.

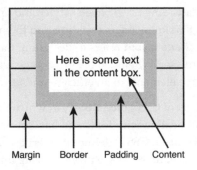

The size of a box reflects the sum of the width or height plus the size of the margin, padding, and border. For instance, if a box has a width of 200 pixels, a left and right padding value of 10 pixels, a left and right border value of 2 pixels, and a left and right margin value of 20 pixels, its total width would be 200 + 20 (both padding values) + 4 (both border values) + 40 (both margin values) = 264 pixels.

The preceding width example uses only fixed pixel values, but it's often useful to use relative measurement units such as ems (related to the size of the letter *m*) or percentages. For instance, you might want to set the left margin of a paragraph to a fixed pixel value so that it sits a specific distance away from a sidebar on the left. But you could set the top margin using ems so that the vertical spacing between paragraphs is proportional to the font size.

Exploring a CSS Page-Layout Example

Dreamweaver comes with numerous layout examples. The New Document dialog box enables you to create a new page layout, including the CSS. It also gives you the option of saving the CSS in an external style sheet. In the next few minutes, we explore a CSS page-layout example that creates a page with two columns, a header, and a footer. This is a common layout for web pages.

To create a CSS page layout, do the following:

1. Select File, New to open the New Document dialog box.

2. Select the Blank Page category, select HTML as the page type, and find the following layout: 2 Column Fixed, Left Sidebar, Header and Footer. You should see the layout preview to the right, as shown in Figure 12.2.

TRY IT YOURSELF ▼

Creating a CSS Page Layout

Preview   Description

FIGURE 12.2
Dreamweaver's New Document dialog box enables you to select from many page-layout designs. The design preview is visible on the right side of the dialog box.

CSS layout location

▼ TRY IT YOURSELF

Creating a CSS Page Layout
Continued

3. Select XHTML 1.0 Transitional as the DocType.

4. Select Create New File from the Layout CSS drop-down menu.

5. Click the Create button.

6. You are prompted to save the CSS in an external file. Create a directory called css if you'd like and save the file as layout.css.

7. Save the new file as layout.html.

TIP

Fixed or Fluid Layouts?

Some designers prefer a fluid (liquid) layout where the left sidebar and main content area would maintain the same relative size to one another as you change the size of the window. However, when creating complex and very precise layouts, it is easiest to design for a fixed screen size. Design for a specific screen resolution, such as 1024x768, by first selecting a resolution from the Window Size drop-down menu in Dreamweaver's status bar.

TIP

Comments in the Code

The sample page layouts that come with Dreamweaver have abundant comments written in both the HTML and the CSS. Simply select Code view and read the comments that Adobe has left to help you understand some of the ideas implemented in the code.

The design is a fixed layout, in which you set a specific width of the page. Note that the design is horizontally centered on the page if viewed in a screen larger than the one designed for. (You can do this in Dreamweaver or preview the page in a browser.) The header and footer span the entire width of the sidebar and main content area.

Figure 12.3 shows the combination of containers (boxes) on the screen. Div tags define these containers. As you click around the screen, you can see the name of the divs in the tag selector; you can also see any parent divs that contain the currently selected div. Clicking the tags in the tag selector enables you to select the container on the screen.

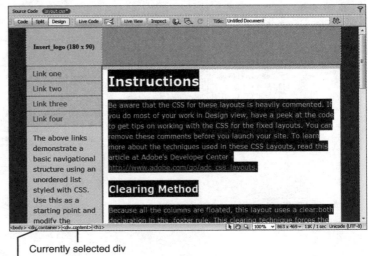

Parent of currently selected div
Currently selected div

FIGURE 12.3
The page layout is made up of containers having different width, height, margin, padding, and border properties.

Viewing the CSS Visually

Dreamweaver enables you to display your CSS page layout in a couple of different ways so that you can see the margins, padding, borders, and the relative positioning of all the CSS box model elements. Three CSS view options are available in the Documents Visual Aids menu (see Figure 12.4):

▶ **CSS Layout Backgrounds**—This visual aid displays each of the containers with a different background color in the content area. These colors, of course, are not displayed in the browser—only in Dreamweaver for design purposes. This view helps you clearly see the boxes.

▶ **CSS Layout Box Model**—This visual aid displays the padding and margins of a selected box. The padding displays using fine diagonal lines, and the margins display using larger diagonal lines.

▶ **CSS Layout Outlines**—This visual aid displays a thin yellow outline around all boxes. When you roll your cursor over one of the outlines, it becomes red, meaning that you can click to select the box.

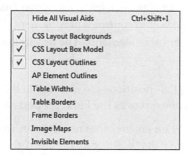

FIGURE 12.4
The Visual Aids menu contains commands enabling you to view the boxes in different ways. This helps you view and modify the page layout.

You'll practice inserting div tags in a few minutes, but let's continue exploring the sample layout page that Dreamweaver created for you. This page contains the following five divs:

▶ **header**—This is the div at the top of the page.

▶ **sidebar1**—This is the div along the left side of the page.

▶ **content**—This is the div in the middle of the page.

▶ **footer**—This is the div at the bottom of the page.

▶ **container**—This is the div that contains all the other divs.

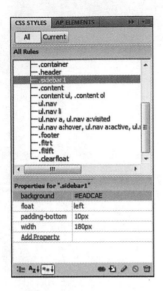

FIGURE 12.5
The properties for a selected style appear in the lower half of the window.

A class selector stored in the external style sheet defines each div. The following class selectors correspond to the five divs in the preceding list:

▶ `.header`

▶ `.sidebar1`

▶ `.content`

▶ `.footer`

▶ `.container`

As you select each of the CSS styles in the CSS Styles panel, you can see the style properties in the Properties section of the panel, as shown in Figure 12.5. As you examine each of the styles, you can see that the width, padding, and margin properties have been set, along with other properties such as background color. You can edit these styles, modifying this layout to look the way you'd like it to look.

Understanding Float and Clear

Float and Clear are essential properties to use when creating page layouts. These properties enable you to control when elements sit next to each other and when they sit under other elements. The properties available for each are as listed here:

▶ **Float**—Selecting Left positions the element to the left. Right positions it to the right. None removes the Float property.

▶ **Clear**—Selecting Left ensures that nothing sits to the left of the element. Right ensures that nothing sits to the right. Both ensures that nothing sits on either side of the element. None removes the Clear property.

In the sample page-layout page you created, the sidebar floats to the left. Examine the selector `. .sidebar1` (shown in Figure 12.5 above) to see the Float property. The Content div has a float: right property applied. In the design, the Content div appears to the right of the sidebar div because the float: left property on the sidebar and the float: right property on the content area pushes the content div to the right.

The Clear property is used to prevent floats from interfering with another div's container. For example, the footer doesn't begin until both the sidebar and the content divs end because the clear: both property forces the footer div under the sidebar and Content divs. Because neither floats to the left or right are allowed, the footer can be displayed until both are ended, no matter how long their content.

Positioning a Div

Now it's your turn to create a page layout. You create a series of divs and CSS styles, positioning the divs into a page layout, and store the styles in an external style sheet.

Creating a CSS page layout is a repeating process of creating a CSS style, inserting a div tag or another container tag, applying the style, and then editing the style to make it work. You continue this process until your page layout is what you want. Generally there is a common page layout for multiple web pages. Sometimes websites will have one page layout for the home page and a second page layout for all the secondary web pages linked from the home page.

Inserting Divs

You begin creating a page layout at the top of a new, empty web page. The first div you create at the top is called banner.

TRY IT YOURSELF ▼

Creating a New Page and External Style

First, create the page and define a CSS style as described here:

1. Create a new blank document by selecting File, New, Blank Page, HTML, <none>.

2. Save the file (File, Save) as `mylayout.html`.

3. Click the New CSS Rule button in the CSS Styles panel to open the New CSS Rule dialog box.

4. Choose ID from the Selector Type drop-down menu. We look at what this means in a few minutes.

5. Enter the name **#header** in the Selector Name text box.

6. Select (New Style Sheet File) from the Rule Definition drop-down menu.

7. Click OK.

8. Save the new style sheet as `mylayout.css`.

9. In the CSS Rule Definition dialog box, select the Background category. Give the style a background color.

10. Click OK to save the style. You won't see any changes in your document until you edit the `mylayout.html` file as explained in the next section.

Using id Selectors

Dreamweaver saves the #header style and links the external style sheet to the web page. The form of the CSS name, #header (with the pound symbol), indicates that #header is an id selector. This means that there can be only *one* element on the page that uses this style (that is, we can have only one header). The default CSS style selector is a "class," which can be applied to as many elements as you want.

▼ TRY IT YOURSELF

Creating a Header Div

Next you have to insert the div tag into the web page and apply the style by adding the id attribute to the tag:

1. Select Insert, Layout Objects, Div Tag. The Insert Div Tag dialog box opens.

2. Select At Insertion Point from the Insert drop-down menu.

3. Select header from the ID drop-down menu, as shown in Figure 12.6. This adds the id attribute to the div tag so that it looks like this: `<div id="banner">`.

FIGURE 12.6
The Insert Div Tag dialog box enables you to define where the div tag will be inserted. You can add a class or id attribute to the tag.

ID attribute

4. Click OK. Dreamweaver inserts a div tag into the web page.

5. Select the placeholder text that Dreamweaver inserts into the div and apply Heading 1 from the Property inspector's Format drop-down menu (HTML mode).

Notice the tag selector with the new div selected: The div tag appears as `<div#header>`. Did you also notice that the div is sitting away from the web page edges? That's because the web page has a default margin value.

To remove the default margins, you must define properties for the body tag. Let's do that next with the following steps:

1. Click the New CSS Rule button in the CSS Styles panel to open the New CSS Rule dialog box.

2. Choose Tag from the Selector Type drop-down menu.

3. Type **body** into the Selector Name field.

4. Select the external style sheet `mylayout.css` as the location to save this style.

5. Click OK.

6. Select the Box category.

7. With the Margin Same for All option selected, enter 0 (zero) into the Top Margin text box. The value is automatically entered for the Right, Bottom, and Left values as well, as shown in Figure 12.7. Also, set the Padding to 0 (zero).

8. Click OK to save the style.

TRY IT YOURSELF ▼

Changing Page Margins

Margin settings

FIGURE 12.7
Modify the Margin attributes in the Box category of the CSS Rule Definition dialog box.

Now the banner div hugs the left, top, and right margins of the web page.

Creating Compound Selectors

A **compound selector** defines the properties of the last selector in a list of selectors. For instance, the compound selector #header p would apply only to p tags contained in an element with the id equal to header. No other paragraph text in the page would be affected.

A compound selector is useful when you'd like elements to appear with unique properties in individual circumstances. This is better than creating and applying a class selector because the rule is applied consistently and you don't have to individually select where the rule will be applied.

▼ TRY IT YOURSELF

Creating a Compound Selector

To create a compound selector, do the following:

1. Click the New CSS Rule button in the CSS Styles panel to open the New CSS Rule dialog box.

2. Select Compound.

3. Enter **#header p** in the Selector Name field.

4. Select the external style sheet mylayout.css as the location to save this style.

5. Click OK.

6. Select the Box category.

7. Uncheck the Same for All check box for the Margin properties.

8. Enter **10** pixels into the Top Margin box and **20** pixels into the Left Margin box.

9. Click OK.

10. Place your cursor inside the header div and type a tagline, setting its format to paragraph in the Properties panel.

TIP

Link Selector Styles

If you drop down the Selector Name menu instead of typing tags into the box, you see a list of the selectors. These are the same CSS styles you modified in the Page Properties dialog box in Hour 5, "Making Hyperlinks, Anchors, and Mailto Links," when you changed the link attributes.

Floating Page Elements

Now you add another container that holds two columns below the header div. This div holds two other divs that are left and right columns.

Note that this example used a different technique from what was used in the sample page-layout page we examined at the beginning of the hour. That example wrapped the whole page in the Container div. Here, we are wrapping the content area of a page in a div and adding additional containers for columns. In CSS, there is often more than one correct way to create a layout.

First, create a container div to hold the column divs. Before you create the new div, it's important that you don't have an existing div selected on the web page because you might accidentally nest the new div. The easiest way to move the cursor off a div is to press the right-arrow key on your keyboard. You can also place your cursor after the div's closing tag by viewing the web page in Code view.

The following steps create a new div:

1. Select Insert, Layout Objects, Div Tag. The Insert Div Tag dialog box opens.

2. Select Insert After Tag from the Insert drop-down menu.

3. Enter the name **main** in the ID drop-down menu.

4. Click the New CSS Rule button, shown in Figure 12.8. This opens the New CSS Rule dialog box with the id selector name, #main, already entered.

Create a New CSS Rule (style)

FIGURE 12.8
You can launch the New CSS Rule dialog box directly from the Insert Div Tag dialog box.

5. Select the external style sheet mylayout.css as the location to save this style.

6. Click OK.

7. Select the Background category and define a background color for this id selector.

8. Select the Box category and set the width to 720px. (We're setting the size narrower than common browsers only so we can see the effect in a crowded Dreamweaver window.)

9. Click OK to save the style properties.

▼ TRY IT YOURSELF

Creating a New Div
Continued

10. Click OK in the Insert Div Tag dialog box. Dreamweaver inserts a div tag with id="main" into the web page. Note that it appears with the background color you selected. Also, although we don't need the placeholder text, don't delete it yet because it's hard to select a div that doesn't contain text.

Creating Columns

Now you have a container for the two columns. Next you insert two divs into this container. Before continuing, you have to make sure that this time the cursor is inside of the main div because you need to nest the two columns within this div.

▼ TRY IT YOURSELF

Adding the Left and Right Columns

First, add the left column like so:

1. Select Insert, Layout Objects, Div Tag. The Insert Div Tag dialog box opens.

2. Select At Insertion Point from the Insert drop-down menu.

3. Enter the name **leftcolumn** in the ID drop-down menu.

4. Click the New CSS button. This opens the New CSS Rule dialog box with the id selector name, #leftcolumn, already entered.

5. Select the external style sheet mylayout.css as the location to save this style.

6. Click OK.

7. Select the Box category.

8. Set the Width to 150px.

9. Select Left from the Float drop-down menu, as shown in Figure 12.9.

10. Set all the margins to 5 pixels (leave the Same for All check box selected).

11. Click OK to save the style properties.

12. Click OK in the Insert Div Tag dialog box. Dreamweaver inserts a div tag with id="leftcolumn" nested within the main div.

TRY IT YOURSELF ▼

Adding the Left and the Right Columns
Continued

FIGURE 12.9
You set the float properties in the Box category of the CSS Rule Definition dialog box.

To create the right column, you can simply copy the style for the left column and modify it. Do the following to add the right column:

1. Right-click the #leftcolumn style in the CSS Styles panel.

2. Select the Duplicate command from the menu.

3. Enter the name **#rightcolumn** in the Duplicate CSS Rule dialog box, and save the style in the external style sheet mylayout.css.

4. Click OK.

5. Select #rightcolumn in the CSS Styles panel and click the Edit Style button.

6. Select the Box category and change the Float property to Right. Then change the width to 550px.

7. Position the cursor in the main div but not inside of the leftcol div.

8. Select Insert, Layout Objects, Div Tag. The Insert Div Tag dialog box opens.

9. Select Rightcolumn from the ID drop-down menu and click OK. (Notice that because IDs can only be used once, only those that are not yet used within the page appear in the dropdown.)

You have to enter placeholder text into the column to get a realistic look. Add a couple of paragraphs to each of the columns. When you preview the page in the browser, as shown in Figure 12.10, you'll notice that the background color of the main div isn't showing up behind the columns. That's because the main div is collapsing. Next you add an element to the page that clears the float and forces the div to not collapse.

FIGURE 12.10
Preview in the browser to see how
the layout is coming together.

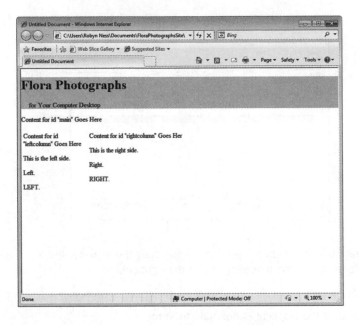

Clearing the Float

You have to do a little hand-coding for this to work because there isn't an
easy way to get Dreamweaver to add this code via Design view. First, you
define a class selector that you can add to any element to clear any floating
elements. Then you apply that class to a break tag.

▼ TRY IT YOURSELF

**Creating and
Applying a Clearing
Class Selector**

To create a clearing class selector, do the following:

1. Click the New CSS Style button in the CSS Styles panel.

2. Choose Class as the Selector Type.

3. Enter the name as **clearfloat** and save the style in the external style
   sheet `mylayout.css`.

4. Click OK.

5. Select the Box category.

6. Select Both from the Clear menu.

7. Click OK to save the style definition.

To apply the clearing class selector:

1. In Code view, create a new blank line between the closing div tag (</div>) for div#leftcolumn and div#main. These will probably be the two closing div tags immediately before the closing body tag (</body>).

2. In the blank line, type the following: **<br class="clearfloat" />**. Notice that Dreamweaver helps you with your choices as you type, as shown in Figure 12.11.

3. Return to Design view.

TRY IT YOURSELF ▼

Creating and Applying a Clearing Class Selector
Continued

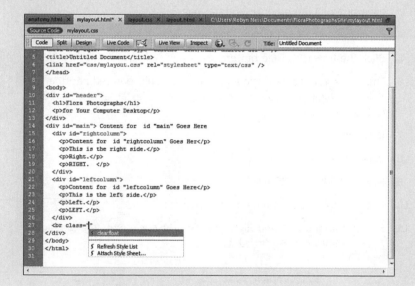

FIGURE 12.11
Manually insert a break tag. Dreamweaver will suggest additional attributes as you type.

Now when you preview the page in the browser, the main div should no longer collapse, and you should be able to see the background color behind the columns.

Centering Your Design on the Page

Sometimes you might want a design that completely centers in the browser no matter what the screen resolution. In the next few minutes, you wrap a container around all the divs in your current page, holding the design to a specific width. Then you center the design horizontally on the web page.

Centering Page Content with a Div

Follow these steps to wrap a container around the entire page and center the design:

1. The easiest way to select all the content on the page is to click <body> in Dreamweaver's tag selector.

2. Select Insert, Layout Objects, Div Tag. The Insert Div Tag dialog box opens.

3. Dreamweaver understands that you already have something selected in the Design window because Wrap Around Selection is already selected in the Insert drop-down menu. You'll want to use this option to wrap a div around all the other divs in the page.

4. Enter the name **container** into the ID drop-down menu.

5. Click the New CSS Rule button.

6. The name #container should be automatically entered into the Selector Name text box. Save the style in the external style sheet mylayout.css.

7. Click OK.

8. Select the Box category.

9. Set the Width to 720 pixels.

10. Uncheck the Margin Same for All check box.

11. Select both the Left and Right Margin drop-down menus and select Auto, as shown in Figure 12.12.

FIGURE 12.12
Setting the left and right margins to Auto centers the design horizontally on the page.

12. Click OK to save the style definition.

13. Click OK to insert the div.

Now the design is fixed-width and centered on the web page. This is a simple technique to create a horizontally centered design. Most of the websites you design will have some elements that have a fixed width and other elements that have widths relative to the element they are contained within.

Previewing with BrowserLab

It is critical to test any web project in a range of browsers under a range of conditions, especially when using CSS positioning, which can react differently in different browsers or with different user settings for window size and font face or size. But that means you, the developer, need access to those browsers.

Fortunately, Adobe has integrated BrowserLab with Dreamweaver as a service to give you snapshots of your projects in several common browsers so you don't have to track down and install them all yourself—or cultivate personal connections with a range of patient people who use different common browsers and don't mind sending you screen shots of your project every time you make an update! BrowserLab requires you to login with your AdobeID. If you haven't created an account, go to www.adobe.com/cfusion/membership/ and sign up.

To test in BrowserLab, click Preview/Debug in Browser and select Preview in Adobe BrowserLab from the dropdown menu. You must have a site defined and have saved your page there; if you haven't met those conditions, Dreamweaver prompts you to do so when you try to launch a connection with BrowserLab.

When you connect, your preferred web browser launches and opens to the BrowserLab website, as seen in Figure 12.3, where you can select which browser to emulate from the View menu. Note that BrowserLab uses Adobe Flash to render your design in browsers other than the one you are using—even if you are viewing in Internet Explorer, you can still see what your site will look like in Safari.

The BrowserLab tab in Dreamweaver, shown in Figure 12.14, opens to show your connection status with a green dot and the current page. When not connected, the BrowserLab panel displays the text Not Connected to BrowserLab, and the connection dot is gray. The Preview button helps you retest your site pages as you make changes by refreshing the code you've sent to BrowserLab. This tab also allows you to select whether to view your local copy of the site or your server copy.

TIP

Remember to Test Your Design Carefully

Page layout can be tricky so it's important that you test your page-layout design in many different browsers under different conditions. For instance, be sure to make your browser window larger and smaller to see what happens to the design at different screen resolutions or if the visitor doesn't have the browser maximized. You also may want to modify the default browser font size to see what that does to your design.

TIP

Testing Live Sites with BrowserLab

You can use BrowserLab to test sites that have live URLs (not local copies) by entering their web addresses directly in the BrowserLab site in your web browser and not going through the Dreamweaver interface. Again, this requires you to sign in with your AdobeID.

FIGURE 12.13
BrowserLab loads in a web browser
with a preview of your page as
rendered in another web browser.

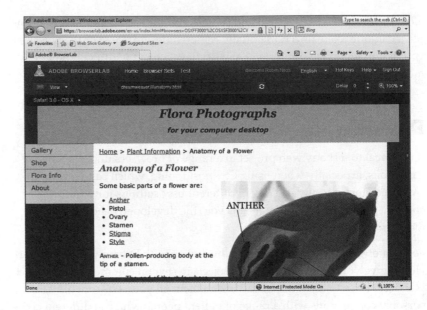

FIGURE 12.14
The BrowserLab tab shows your
status and lets you send a preview
of a local page, but the preview
snapshots appear in your web
browser.

Summary

In this hour, you learned about the CSS box model and about using div tags
styled with id selectors to create a CSS page layout. You explored one of the
sample page layouts that Dreamweaver provides. You explored the Float
and Clear properties to create floated columns. You centered a design horizontally on the page and learned how to use Dreamweaver's tool to fine-
tune the design. Finally, you explored the use of Adobe BrowserLab to test
your layouts for consistency across browsers.

Q&A

Q. I'm in charge of a bunch of web pages that were designed using tables. Should I redo all of them?

A. Most websites go through design revisions every few years (some much more often). I would wait for one of these revision cycles and make the structure change at that point. It's a lot of work to re-create the page structure on an existing site. You should take a lot of time to plan that type of update.

Q. Are there any differences in the way browsers display CSS?

A. Unfortunately, yes. If you look in the code of the sample page we created in this hour, you'll notice in one of the Adobe sample page layouts that Adobe has entered some code at the top of the page to fix some potential browser errors. You can also see comments in the CSS.

Adobe has recently added a CSS Advisor area to its website. A link to the CSS Advisor can be found in the Dreamweaver Developer Center CSS area at http://www.adobe.com/devnet/dreamweaver/css.html. The CSS Advisor enables developers to exchange information and provides tips on what CSS works in various browser versions.

Q. Why should I use div tags for page layout instead of span tags?

A. Span tags are meant to wrap around small items, such as a few words within a paragraph, to apply a style. Div tags are meant to create containers for page layout. A more technical way to describe the difference is that a div is a block-level HTML element that forces breaks before and after itself, like the paragraph tag. Using the blocks created by divs is the foundation of CSS layout.

Workshop

Quiz

1. How many times can you apply an id selector to a web page?

2. How would you write the selector for a compound selector to style a paragraph (`<p>`) that is contained in a div with the `id="smile"`?

3. What is the difference between margins and padding?

Quiz Answers

1. Just once. You can have only one element per page with a certain id name applied, so only that element will have the corresponding id selector applied.

2. It would be either div#smile p or #smile p.

3. The padding is between the content and the border, whereas the margins are between the border and other elements on the page. In addition, the padding picks up the background color of the content, whereas the margins are always clear.

Exercises

1. Review and test the different layouts provided within Dreamweaver. Try combining portions of one layout into another. The included templates can be easily modified to create almost any layout you want without extensive CSS coding.

2. Explore inserting divs using the Insert Div Tag command. Insert a div and add content within the div. Add some content to another part of the page and wrap a div tag around that content using the Insert Div Tag command.

3. Create an AdobeID (if you don't already have one) and use Adobe BrowserLab to view your sample pages in a variety of browsers.

Creating CSS for Mobile Devices and Printing

In Hour 11, "Formatting Web Pages with Cascading Style Sheets," you learned about CSS (Cascading Style Sheets) fundamentals and applying CSS to text. In Hour 12, "Using CSS for Positioning," you learned about CSS layout. In this hour, you explore using CSS for delivery to devices other than a computer screen. The other devices will most likely be either printers or mobile devices such as PDAs or mobile phones. But the techniques presented can be used to deliver unique web page layouts to projection devices, televisions, and even devices designed for people who are hearing or vision impaired.

You've explored attaching an external CSS style sheet to a web page, but you might not have tried attaching multiple style sheets to the same web page. You could create one style sheet for the screen, one style sheet for printing, and maybe another style sheet for a small-screen device like a mobile phone. Each of the style sheets can tailor the elements on the screen to the way the web page is delivered.

In this hour, you explore techniques for adding CSS for delivery to different devices. This is a complicated topic, so this is only an introduction. You'll be able to get started applying these techniques to your websites right away, but you might want to seek out additional books and websites where you can learn more.

Understanding the CSS Media Attribute

Up to this point, you've created CSS generically without specifying the delivery medium. Actually, we've assumed that the delivery medium is a

WHAT YOU'LL LEARN IN THIS HOUR:

▶ How to add multiple external style sheets to a web page

▶ How to design a style sheet specifically for printing

▶ How to hide elements on the page

▶ How to troubleshoot problems with conflicting styles

▶ How to preview a page designed for handheld devices in Adobe Device Central computer screen. And the majority of those using the Web are probably looking at your content on a computer screen.

But how many of you have looked up a website on your Internet-enabled mobile phone? I have, many times, and sometimes the pages I encounter are difficult to read on my device. Even if you haven't browsed the Web on your phone or PDA, you've most likely printed a web page. Often you end up with a lot of information that isn't necessary: buttons, links, and other content that is obviously not necessary in a paper version of the information.

Remember that when you link to an external style sheet, Dreamweaver puts a reference to that style sheet in the head of the web page. The HTML looks like this:

```
<link href="../css/styles.css" rel="stylesheet" type="text/css" />
```

To tell a browser to use the style sheet when displaying the web page in a specific medium, such as printing or the computer screen, Dreamweaver adds the media attribute to the link tag so that it looks like this:

```
<link href="../css/styles.css" rel="stylesheet" type="text/css"
➥media="screen" />
```

The media attribute can contain the following:

> **All**—Applies CSS to all media types.

> **Screen**—Applies CSS to content displayed on a computer screen.

> **Aural**—Controls the speed, tone, pitch, and other attributes of synthesized text delivered via a TTS browser. So far, this media type is not commonly recognized.

> **Braille**—Controls a Braille-tactile device used by those with visual impairments.

> **Embossed**—Formats the web page content for Braille printers.

> **Handheld**—Formats the web page content for handheld devices such as PDAs and mobile phones.

> **Print**—Formats the web page content for printers.

> **Projection**—Formats the web page content for full-screen projection or kiosk delivery without the browser toolbars.

> **TTY**—Formats the web page content for TTY (teletype) devices commonly used as a telecommunications device for the deaf (TDD).

> **TV**—Formats the web page content for delivery to a television.

NOTE

Alternative Ways to Reference Media Types

In this hour, we are going to cover a single way to reference different media types using CSS: using external style sheets. However, there are multiple methods of using CSS to target different media types. I think using an external style sheet is easier to troubleshoot and maintain, so we're using that technique here.

In this hour, we explore the most commonly used (and most widely recognized) media types: Screen, Print, and Handheld. You specify the media type when you link to an external style sheet. The Attach External Style Sheet dialog box, shown in Figure 13.1, displays the list of media types in the Media drop-down menu. When you select a media type, Dreamweaver automatically adds the media attribute to the linked style sheet.

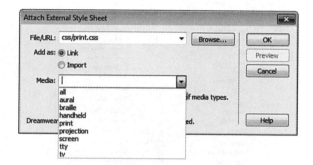

FIGURE 13.1
You set the media type attribute when linking to an external style sheet.

Previewing Style Rendering in Dreamweaver

One of the difficulties of designing for different devices is that you are viewing your work on a computer screen and it's difficult to tell what the page is going to look like on other devices. Dreamweaver enables you to view how the styles for a particular media type look. The Style Rendering submenu of the View menu enables you to select which media type's CSS is displayed in the Dreamweaver Document window, as shown in Figure 13.2.

Dreamweaver controls only how the web page looks within Dreamweaver. All the styles will apply when you view the web page in a browser. These commands are extremely useful while you're designing in Dreamweaver because they enable you to apply only the CSS that you are currently working with. For instance, while you are developing a style sheet for print, you can choose to display the Print media type in Dreamweaver so that you see how the page will look when it is printed. You won't see the screen style sheet in Dreamweaver until you change the way the page renders.

I usually design a web page for the screen and then redesign it for other devices. That's what we are going to explore next!

FIGURE 13.2
Use the Style Rendering submenu to preview a media type.

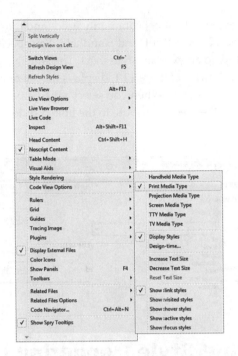

Adding an Alternative Style Sheet

In the next few minutes, you see how to create a style sheet that specifically styles a web page for printing. The easiest way to begin is to copy the existing style sheet designed for the screen.

▼ TRY IT YOURSELF

Creating a Copy of a CSS File

To create a copy of an existing style sheet, do the following:

1. Open an existing website—something from Hour 12 would be a perfect choice. Make sure that the Files panel is visible.

2. Select the CSS file in the Files panel.

3. Right-click the file and choose Edit, Duplicate from the context menu, as shown in Figure 13.3.

4. Edit the name of the copied CSS file. Because the new file is for printing, you could add _print to the name—print.css, for example.

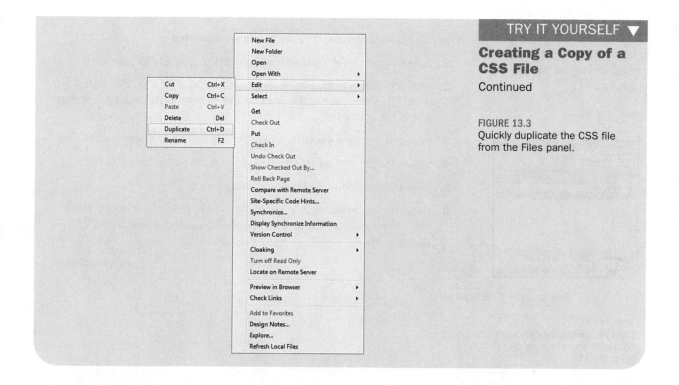

TRY IT YOURSELF ▼

Creating a Copy of a CSS File
Continued

FIGURE 13.3
Quickly duplicate the CSS file from the Files panel.

Now you have two external style sheets: the original file and a copy of that file. Next you link to the external style sheet, setting the media type.

Setting the External Style Sheet Media Type

We assume that when you originally linked to the external style sheet, you didn't specify a media type for the style sheet. If you don't specify a media type, the browser applies the styles to everything. This has the same effect as the All media type listed earlier.

We could easily go into the code to add the media attribute to the external style sheet, but instead we're going to use another easy technique. You first unlink the external style sheet from the page and then relink it, adding the media attribute.

▼ TRY IT YOURSELF

Unlinking and Relinking a Style Sheet

Delete/Unlink CSS Stylesheet

FIGURE 13.4
When you delete the external style sheet, you delete the reference to it but don't delete the file.

To unlink the style sheet and relink it, follow these steps:

1. Select the name of the external style in the CSS Styles panel.

2. Click the Delete button, as shown in Figure 13.4, in the CSS Styles panel. This deletes the reference to the external style sheet but doesn't delete the actual file.

3. Reattach the style sheet by clicking the Attach Style Sheet button.

4. Select the file and be sure to select the radio button beside Link.

5. Select Screen from the Media drop-down menu.

6. Click OK. The external style sheet again links to the web page. Notice that the media type appears beside the style sheet name in the CSS Styles panel.

Link to a Second External Style Sheet

TIP

Comments in CSS

You can enter a comment in CSS files by surrounding the comment text like this: /* This is a comment */. This is useful for describing the purpose of a particular file as well as explaining individual rules or sections of rules.

There are two ways to start designing an external style sheet specifically for printing:

▶ Create a new external style sheet by creating a new style and electing to save the new style in a new style sheet.

▶ Save a copy of the existing style sheet for the screen.

As we've mentioned, it's often easier to start with a copy of the existing style sheet because then you don't have to start from scratch and redefine everything. You can simply link the copy of the style sheet to the same web page and begin to edit the style sheet for printing.

▼ TRY IT YOURSELF

Linking a Style Sheet

Follow these steps to link the copy of the style sheet:

1. Click the Attach Style Sheet button in the CSS Styles panel.

2. Select the file and be sure to select the radio button beside Link.

3. Select Print from the Media drop-down menu.

4. Click OK. The external style sheet links to the web page.

5. If you have a number of styles listed in the external style sheet, you might not be able to see both style sheets listed in the CSS Styles panel. Click the Collapse button below the external style sheet name.

Notice that the Print media type appears beside the newly linked style sheet name in the CSS Styles panel, as shown in Figure 13.5.

TRY IT YOURSELF ▼

Linking a Style Sheet
Continued

FIGURE 13.5
The media type appears beside each filename in the CSS Styles panel.

Designing CSS for Print

To edit the style sheet for print, you have to make sure that Dreamweaver is displaying the design controlled by the Print style sheet. Select View, Style Rendering, Print Media Type. Because you haven't edited the Print style sheet, the page should still look the same, but that soon changes as you begin making edits. When designing CSS for print, pay attention to these commonly used web page sections:

▶ **Navigation**—You can't navigate on a piece of paper, so navigation isn't necessary in a printed web page. Navigation includes buttons and breadcrumbs.

▶ **Hyperlinks**—Again, these navigational objects are not necessary in a printed document. You can modify the CSS for print so that hyperlinks blend into the other text.

▶ **Search**—You can't search a piece of paper with this utility, so it should be removed.

▶ **Interactions**—Zooming, resizing, scrolling, or any other types of interactions should be removed from a printed version of the web page.

▶ **Feedback and Email Contact**—Because the viewer cannot contact you or give you feedback by clicking a link when reading a printed page, you should add information making it easy to call you if necessary.

▶ **Fonts and Font Sizes**—In Hour 11, we explored using proportional font size measurement units, such as percentage and ems, for the screen. But the point measurement unit was designed for print and works very predictably. Also, it's popular to use sans-serif fonts designed for the screen, such as Verdana or Tahoma, in web pages because they are easier to read onscreen. In contrast, serif fonts such as Times New Roman are actually easier to read in print.

Hiding Elements

When you are delivering the same content to multiple devices (the screen and a printer in this example), how can you hide parts of the page? CSS has the display property that can have multiple values, but the one we are interested in is display:none. Applying this property to an element in a web page makes it disappear!

Figure 13.6 shows a web page in Dreamweaver's document view that contains multiple elements that I listed earlier as elements to pay attention to. There are hyperlinks (anchor links), breadcrumbs, navigation elements, and

FIGURE 13.6
You have to identify items on the page that might need modification for the printed version of the web page.

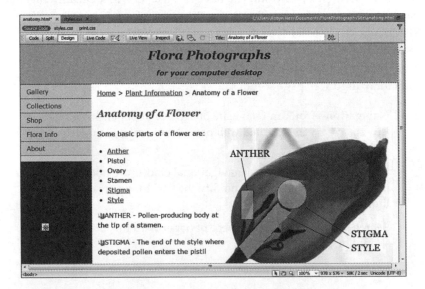

a linked map image. If someone is interested in printing the content of the page, they won't need these elements, because they're solely useful for web visitors.

The first step in creating a print design for the web page is to use the display property to turn off these elements in the printed version.

TRY IT YOURSELF ▼

**Hiding an Element
Through CSS**

To turn off an element in the web page, do the following:

1. Select the element in Dreamweaver's Document window and look in the tag selector to identify the selector applied to it. This is the style you need to edit in the style sheet.

2. Select the style you identified in step 1. Make sure that you are working in the style sheet that is for print.

3. Click the Edit Style button in the CSS Styles panel.

4. Select the Block category.

5. Select None from the Display drop-down menu, as shown in Figure 13.7.

FIGURE 13.7
The display property can be set in the Block category of the CSS Rule Definition dialog box.

6. Click OK to save the change.

7. Repeat steps 1 through 6 for each element that you want to hide in the printed web page.

If you selected View, Style Rendering, Print Media Type, the elements should disappear from Dreamweaver's Document window. If you switch to the screen view (View, Style Rendering, Screen Media Type), the elements reappear. When you view the page in the browser, you see the styles in the Screen style sheet.

▼ TRY IT YOURSELF

Creating a New Style to Hide Unprintable Elements

If some of the elements you'd like to hide do not have an id or class selector already applied, you can quickly create one and apply it using this procedure:

1. Click the New CSS Rule button in the CSS Styles panel.

2. Using the Contextual Selector Type drop-down, choose Class to create a new class or ID to create a new ID selector. Remember, you can reuse Classes, but IDs can only appear once in each page.

3. Give the style selector a name.

4. Select the Print style sheet from the Rule Definition drop-down menu.

5. Click OK.

6. Select the Block category.

7. Select None from the Display drop-down menu.

8. Click OK.

9. Select the element in Dreamweaver's Document window and identify the tag in the tag selector.

10. Right-click on the tag in the tag selector and select either the Set Class or the Set ID command.

11. Select the new style you created to apply to the element on the page, as shown in Figure 13.8.

TIP

Cleaning Up

Some of the elements you hide using the display property might have other styles defined in the external style sheet that are no longer necessary. For instance, if you hide the ID selector #sidebard, then #sidebar a:hover and #sidebar p are no longer necessary. You can delete these unnecessary styles from the print version of the style sheet. Be careful to delete them from the correct file!

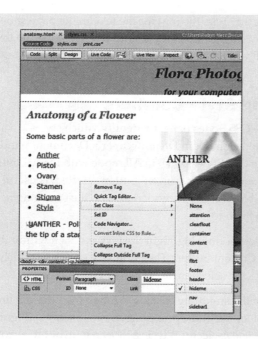

TRY IT YOURSELF ▼

Creating a New Style to Hide Unprintable Elements

Continued

FIGURE 13.8
Set the style using the menu that drops down from the tag selector.

Modifying the Default Font

Next we explore changing the default font on the page to a serif font that is set to 12 points. This makes the text easier to read when printed. You need to edit the style that redefines the body tag.

To modify the default page font, do the following:

TRY IT YOURSELF ▼

Setting a Font for a Print Style Sheet

1. Using the CSS Styles panel, choose the Print style sheet, and identify and select the style that redefines the body. If defined using Dreamweaver's Page Properties command, the style looks like this: `body, td, th`.

2. Click the Edit Style button.

3. Select the Type category.

4. Select Times New Roman, Times, Serif from the Font drop-down menu.

5. Enter 12 points as the size.

6. Click OK.

When you save the style, the font for the text on the page should change. If the size does not change, other styles might be affecting the text. It's useful to be able to tell where the style conflict is coming from.

Identifying Style Conflicts

You can use the CSS Styles panel to identify which styles are applied to the currently selected element in Dreamweaver's Document window. We've mostly used the CSS Styles panel in All mode with the All button selected. The Current mode, with the Current button selected, is useful for troubleshooting and identifying why elements on the screen do not look the way you'd like them to.

To begin troubleshooting, highlight the text and then within the CSS Styles panel click the Current button. The Summary shows us which styles are being applied to the selection, as shown in Figure 13.9.

To diagnose conflicts, start by clicking through the different lines in the Summary and looking at the properties. In this example (Figure 13.9), we can see that the body selector is trying to set a font, but it is crossed out. To find out why, we just place our cursors over the crossed-out line and Dreamweaver tells us that the font size is being overridden by another rule.

When you've identified the problem elements in your document, select the property you want to change in the CSS Styles summary section, and then click the Edit button to jump to the CSS editor with that style selected.

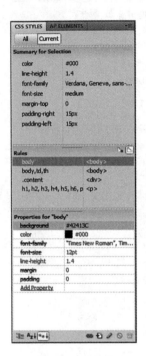

FIGURE 13.9
Different styles apply to the same element. You can investigate the properties in the CSS Styles panel.

Hiding Hyperlinks

Displaying hyperlinked text, colored and underlined, is unnecessary in a printed web page. It's easy to use CSS to modify links created using anchor (a) tags.

The following shows you how to make links blend into the text by redefining the a tag:

1. Click the New CSS Rule button in the CSS Styles panel.

2. Choose Tag as the selector type from the Contextual Selector Type drop-down menu.

3. Select a from the Tag drop-down menu.

4. Select the Print style sheet in the Rule Definition section.

5. Click OK.

6. Set the text color to be the same as the default text color for the page.

7. Select the check box next to None as the Text-decoration property, as shown in Figure 13.10. This removes the underline from the hyperlinks.

8. Click OK.

TRY IT YOURSELF ▼

Hiding Unnecessary Hyperlinks
Continued

FIGURE 13.10
Set the Text-decoration property to None to remove the underline from links.

Now all the hyperlinks should blend into the text in the printed version of the web page. If they still appear, you may have to delete any other a styles from the print.css file which may conflict with the general style. Remember, more specific styles, such as a:link, will override a rule for the a tag.

Adding a Print-Only Message

So far we've discussed hiding elements in the web page that should appear on the screen but not the print version. But you can do the opposite as well. It's a nice touch to give a message on the printed version of the web page acknowledging that it's been designed for print. It's also a great idea to include a phone number, making contact away from the computer easy to achieve.

Creating Printable-Only Content

Follow these steps to add a message to the printed version of the web page:

1. Select Insert, Layout Objects, Div Tag to add a new container to the web page.

2. Enter a name into the ID text box. A good name might be printversion.

3. Enter some text into the div which explains that the page has been formatted for printing and provides a contact number, as shown in Figure 13.11.

FIGURE 13.11
Create a div and enter a message explaining that the page has been formatted for printing.

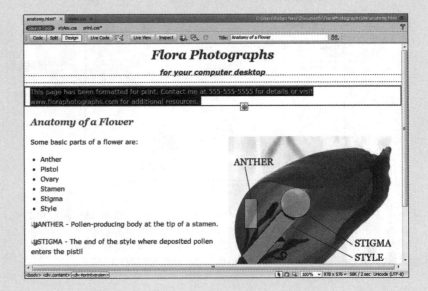

4. Switch Dreamweaver to screen rendering by selecting View, Style Rendering, Screen Media Type. Note that the div also appears in this view.

5. Hide the div#printversion in the screen style sheet. Select the CSS file set as the screen style sheet and click the New CSS Rule button in the CSS Styles panel.

6. Choose ID from the Selector Type pop-up menu.

7. Enter the div ID (printversion) as the selector.

8. Make sure that you define this style in the external style sheet for the *screen*. Verify that the Screen style sheet is selected in the Rule Definition drop-down menu.

TRY IT YOURSELF ▼

**Creating Printable-
Only Content**

Continued

9. Click OK.

10. Select the Block category.

11. Select None from the Display drop-down menu.

12. Click OK.

Now the print-only div is hidden in the screen view, but it is printed when the viewer chooses to print the web page.

CSS for Handheld Devices

Handheld devices come in many different shapes and sizes and are increasingly being used to surf the Internet. If you're a web developer, chances are you're going to have handheld devices surfing your site sooner or later. The trouble with handhelds is that their capabilities vary greatly. Devices like the Apple iPhone, recent Blackberry devices, and Google Android phones provide full web browser capabilities (just like a desktop), whereas other mobile phones offer a far more limited view.

Thankfully, *most* typical handhelds can be dealt with easily using a *Handheld* style sheet. Let's review that process now.

Using the Handheld Style Sheet and Device Central

You can follow the same steps you used to create a style sheet for printing to create a style sheet for most handheld devices. You create a set of styles in an external style sheet and attach the sheet to a web page specifying the media type as **Handheld**. The browsers in handheld devices such as mobile phones and PDAs use this style sheet to display the web page content.

In the previous printing example, you used the style-rendering commands to preview how the web page looks with a specific set of styles applied. Because it's difficult to preview how pages will look on the small screen of a handheld device, Adobe includes Adobe Device Central with Dreamweaver. You use this application to preview how web pages will look in a browser on various handheld devices.

Previewing a Page in Device Central

To preview a web page in Device Central, do the following:

1. Open the page in Dreamweaver and use the "Preview in Browser" menu (the small globe) to choose "Preview in Device Central."

2. Device Central opens with the web page displayed.

3. Select the targeted device from a list of available devices on the left, as shown in Figure 13.12.

FIGURE 13.12
Adobe Device Central includes numerous device definitions, or you can create your own.

4. Return to Dreamweaver, make any necessary changes, and preview the page again. Use the scroll buttons to preview how scrolling vertically and horizontally looks.

Targeting the iPhone and Advanced Handhelds

Advanced handhelds (specifically the iPhone), don't play by the same rules as other mobile browsers. These devices aim to put the Web in the palm of your hand and do so by rendering web pages using the same Screen style sheet as a normal desktop web browser. So how can we make something that uses the Screen style sheet selector, but also identifies the device as being a handheld?

The answer is by using a complex selector for the media. Instead of just specifying "screen", we can set a media type of "only screen and (max-device-width: 480px)". This selection loads a specific style sheet that is visible only on devices with a screen resolution of 480px or less. The entire rule, to be inserted in the <head> content of your web page, is this:

```
<!--[if !IE]>-->
<link media="only screen and (max-device-width: 480px)"
  rel="stylesheet" type="text/css" href="iphone.css"/>
<!--<![endif]-->
```

This includes a conditional statement (if !IE) that hides the code from Microsoft's IE browser, which may interpret it incorrectly. After inserting this code, you can create an iphone.css file that displays only on iPhone and iPhone-like devices.

So, what about all the other devices out there that you may want to target? Unfortunately, these can be a bit of a problem. The reason that developers flock to Apple's iPhone isn't just because it's a cute or cool device; it's because it is a very strictly defined standard. Windows Mobile and Google Android devices can come with different screen resolutions and very different capabilities.

If you want to target devices, an elaborate and effective means of setting up a style sheet has been documented at this site: http://johannburkard. de/blog/www/mobile/Linking-CSS-for-handheld-devices-revisited.html. To work with Android devices, look for examples at: http://www.rkblog. rk.edu.pl/w/p/optimizing-websites-iphone-and-android/.

The caution that I leave you with, however, is that unless you're developing a very specific site for a very specific type of handheld, just knowing that something is Windows Mobile does not give you enough information to create complex and compelling layouts. Instead, I would recommend that you simply target this class of devices using the Handheld media type.

Summary

In this hour, you learned how to use the media type to specify that certain styles apply to certain devices. You learned how to format a web page for a printing device, including how to hide elements and hyperlinks, and how

TIP

An iPhone Expert

This code sample has been widely copied and repeated online. I believe that the original source (and an excellent place for more information) can be found at Tom Boutell's website: http://www.boutell.com/ newfaq/creating/iphone.html.

to add a print-only message. You also explored previewing a web page designed for a handheld device in Adobe Device Central.

Q&A

Q. I've printed the page I created a style sheet for, and it's too wide for the printed page. Is there a way to control this?

A. You can wrap a container (div) around the page and set this to a standard printed page width. For instance, the standard paper width in the United States is 8½ inches wide. Accounting for a 1-inch margin on each side, you can make the total width of the container 6½ inches.

Q. Do I have to create a style sheet for the printing?

A. Although it's not necessary to create a style sheet for printing, it's a nice touch on a professional website. If people have a reason to print out the content on the web page, it's worth the effort to design a style sheet specifically for that purpose. If there is no reason to print the page, you might be wasting your time creating a special Print style sheet.

Workshop

Quiz

1. What is the value of the display property that creates a style that makes an element not appear on the web page?

2. What media type signals that a style sheet is specific for viewing a web page on the computer?

3. What is the feature provided by Adobe for testing your pages for mobile devices?

Quiz Answers

1. Giving the display property the value of None makes an element not

appear on the web page.

2. The Screen media type is specific for viewing a web page on the computer.

3. Adobe provides Device Central as a simulator for common handheld devices with web browsers.

Exercises

1. Create a traditional web page designed to be displayed using a browser. Create a new CSS style sheet to display that page on a mobile device. Use the Adobe Device Central to preview the redesigned page in a simulated handheld device.

2. Modify a traditional web page designed to be displayed using a browser to instead be printed. Create a Print CSS style sheet. Preview the web page in a browser and use the Print Preview command to view how the page will look when printed.

HOUR 14
Using Site Assets, Library Items, and Templates

In this hour, you work with several features of Dreamweaver that enable you to maintain reusable code. Reusable code saves time and helps you maintain consistency in a website. First, you explore the Assets panel that automatically collects elements used in your website and enables you to quickly access and reuse them. Then, you learn about snippets and **library items**, reusable chunks of code that you can insert into web pages. During the second half of the hour, you explore **templates**, which are whole web pages that include elements you can change and elements you can't change from page to page. Both library items and templates enable you to update all the instances in the website by simply updating the original library item or template.

These features also allow you to share design elements with other web developers. When you are in the design phase of a website, you should be thinking about common elements across all the web pages in your site that would be appropriate to create as Dreamweaver snippets or library items. You should also be thinking about common structures that would lend themselves to templated pages.

Managing Assets in the Assets Panel

Web pages are not just made out of text and code. You use images, movies, colors, and URLs to present information in web pages. These web page elements are called **assets**. You have to gather and organize these page elements before you start to create a web page. Unfortunately, with dozens of files on your hands, it's easy to misplace them or create duplicates. Thankfully, Dreamweaver's Assets Panel saves the day!

WHAT YOU'LL LEARN IN THIS HOUR:

▶ What assets are and how to manage them in your website

▶ How to create and organize Dreamweaver snippets and custom snippets

▶ How to add, edit, and update a library item

▶ How to create and apply templates

▶ How to edit an original template and update linked web pages

▶ How Dreamweaver can work with Adobe content management systems

By default, the Assets panel nests behind the Files panel in the same tab group. You simply click the Assets tab to open the panel. If the Assets panel has been closed, you can open it again by selecting Window, Assets.

As you copy the assets into the site, Dreamweaver automatically catalogs the assets for an entire site in the Assets panel and groups them into categories, as shown in Figure 14.1.

FIGURE 14.1
The Assets panel has buttons for the different categories along the left side and radio buttons at the top to select whether to view all the assets or just your favorites.

TIP

Copy Assets to Another Site

The Assets panel displays the assets of the current site. When you select a different site from the Site drop-down menu in the Files panel, the Assets panel displays the assets of the new site. To copy a single asset to another site, simply right-click the item name in the Assets panel and select the Copy to Site command. Select the site to which you want to copy the asset. To copy a group of assets to another defined site, select multiple asset items by holding down the Shift key while clicking the item names in the Assets panel. Right-click the group and select the Copy to Site command from the context menu. Dreamweaver copies the exact folder structure and the files for an image or movie asset to the other site.

TIP

Create Favorite Assets

To create a favorite asset, select the asset in the Assets panel and then click the Add to Favorites button. When you click the Favorites radio button, the favorite assets should be listed. Click the New Favorites Folder button to further organize your favorites—drag and drop items into the folder to add them.

Remove items from the favorites list by clicking the Remove from Favorites button. Doing so removes the item only from the favorites list; it is not deleted from the website.

You can click one of the category buttons from along the left side of the panel to display a list of all the assets of that type in your site. The Assets panel has different capabilities based on the asset category you've selected. For instance, when the Images category is selected, you can view a thumbnail of each image, but when you have the Colors category selected, the hexadecimal code for the color is displayed.

Let's briefly explore the Asset categories and their special features. The Library and Templates panels have a special purpose and are covered later in this hour.

▶ **Images**—Displays filenames and thumbnails, as shown in Figure 14.1, for all the images in your defined website. Dreamweaver catalogs images in GIF, JPG, or PNG format.

▶ **Colors**—Displays all colors used in the defined website in both hexadecimal and RGB (red, green, blue) and uses the defined color for the text. Beside the color name, Dreamweaver indicates whether the color is part of the websafe palette.

▶ **URLs**—Lists all the hyperlinks contained in the currently defined website including FTP, mailto, JavaScript, HTTP (Web), and HTTPS (secure Web). These are the absolute links in your website; the document-relative links (links to other pages in the same site) are not listed in the URLs category.

▶ **Flash Movies (SWF), Shockwave Movies, and Movies**—Catalog movie types for Flash, Shockwave, and other movies types, such as QuickTime or MPEG movies. A Play/Stop button in the upper-right corner of the preview window enables you to view these movie files.

▶ **Scripts**—Catalogs all the external script files in your website that end with the .js or .vbs extension. These script files contain JavaScript or VBScript functions that you can call from your web pages. The preview window shows the actual code in the script. You can link an external script file from Assets to your web page by dragging from the Scripts category into the Head Content (View, Head Content) section of the Dreamweaver Document window.

Locating and Previewing Assets

By default, Dreamweaver sorts the items listed in the Assets panel alphabetically. You can sort the items by any of the available column headings by clicking a column heading. You can preview any asset by selecting it in the list.

After you add an asset to your site, you might have to click the Refresh button to see it listed. You can refresh the list of assets anytime using the button in the lower-right corner of the Assets panel.

Sometimes you might see an asset file in the Assets panel and wonder where that asset resides in the actual website structure. Highlight an item in the Assets panel and then right-click to bring up the context menu. Select the Locate in Site command and Dreamweaver opens the Files panel with the same file highlighted. This works only on assets that are individual files, such as movies or images; it does not work on assets that are elements of web pages, such as URLs or colors.

NOTE

Does "Websafe" Matter?

An older color palette is the websafe palette, which contains the 216 colors that work on all browsers on both the Windows and Mac platforms when a computer is set to 256 colors. The Assets panel tells you whether the colors listed in the Colors category are within those 216 colors by marking them as Websafe or Non-Websafe in the Type column. You might have to widen the panel to view this column. Unless you are creating websites for very old computers, however, you shouldn't worry about whether your colors are websafe.

TIP

Jump Assets Alphabetically

To quickly jump to a section in the Assets list, click within the Assets list and then type the first letter of the name of the item you are looking for. You jump to the first item that begins with that letter.

Adding Assets to a Web Page

Use the Assets panel to add assets to a web page.

To add an asset to your web page, follow these steps:

1. Select the category.

2. Find the asset you want to add by scrolling through the list for the name or viewing the preview in the Preview window.

3. Place the insertion point in your web page where you want the asset to be located.

4. Click the Insert button, shown in Figure 14.2, and Dreamweaver inserts the asset into your web page.

FIGURE 14.2
You insert an asset into a web page by clicking the Insert button.

Site assets

Insert asset   Edit asset
Refresh list
Add asset to favorites

You can also use assets from the Assets panel to affect other objects on a web page. For instance, you can apply a color asset to some text on your web page as detailed here:

1. Select some text on the page.

2. Drag a color from the Assets panel by picking up the name in either the Preview window or the category list.

3. Drop the color on the selected text.

Instead of dragging and dropping, you can simply select the text and the color and then click the Apply button to apply the color to the text.

Adding a color to text creates a CSS style when it is added, and even prompts you for a new CSS selector name. After you've used a color on a page, don't keep dragging it from the Assets panel; this creates the same type of style repeatedly. CSS styles are meant to be reused!

Editing Assets

After you've added assets to your collection, you may eventually decide that you want to edit one. To edit an asset, select it in the list, then click the Edit button in the bottom of the Assets panel. Some elements, such as colors and URLs, can be edited directly in Dreamweaver. Complex objects, such as images and movies, launch an external editor for editing.

Keep in mind that site assets are generated automatically from the elements you use in your site, so you can remove them only by deleting the actual elements from your web page designs.

Using Snippets

Snippets are bits of code that are available from Dreamweaver's Snippets panel. You can use any of the multiple snippets available when you install Dreamweaver. You can also create custom snippets from code you use repetitively. This can speed up development of web pages as well as maintain consistency in your code.

First, let's explore the existing snippets available in Dreamweaver. The lower half of the Snippets panel (Window, Snippets) displays categories of snippets along with descriptions of what the snippets do (you might have to enlarge the Snippets panel to see the descriptions). The upper portion of the Snippets panel gives you a preview of the selected snippet.

The default Snippets panel, shown in Figure 14.3, has the following categories:

- Comments
- Footers
- Form Elements
- JavaScript

- Meta
- Navigation
- Text
- ~Legacy

CAUTION

Colors and Links Do Not Update!

Editing a color or URL in your assets does *not* change the instances of the asset that have already been used in your site, only assets you insert after the edit!

CAUTION

Don't Use the Legacy Snippets

The ~Legacy snippet folder contains snippets that use deprecated code—basically, code that uses tags that are no longer part of HTML standard tags and that may stop working in future browser releases. You should avoid using these snippets.

FIGURE 14.3
A Snippets panel has several snippet categories and displays a preview of the selected snippet.

TIP

My Favorite Snippet

I use several snippets on a semi-frequent basis, but the snippet I use most is the Text Field, Autoclear snippet from the Form Elements category. This snippet adds a text field with a default initial value that is automatically cleared when the user clicks in the field. This is nice because you can enter an initial value in the field to give users some guidance as to what to put there, but they don't have to take the extra step to delete that text when they are filling in the form.

TIP

Google Analytics

My example features Google Analytics, which is a powerful web stats analysis package that doesn't require any additional software to be installed on your server. All you need to do is set up a free Google Analytics account, create a profile for your site, and insert a small piece of code (perfect for use as a snippet!) provided by Analytics into all of your web pages. After the tracking code is installed, Google immediately starts collecting data as visitors view your website. To get started with Google Analytics, set up your free account at http://www.google.com/analytics/.

Creating Your Own Snippets

You can create a new snippet out of an object or some code you use often. You can create a new snippet within an existing category, or you can create a new folder for your own personal snippets by clicking the New Snippet Folder button.

The easiest way to insert code into a snippet is to create the code in Dreamweaver first, in either Design or Code view. When you select the New Snippet command with the code selected, Dreamweaver automatically places the code into the Insert text box in the Snippet dialog box, as shown in Figure 14.4. You can then enter a name and a description for the snippet.

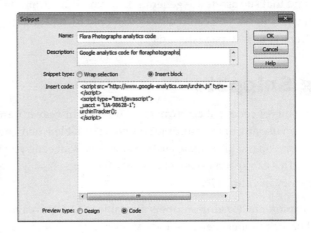

FIGURE 14.4
You can create a new snippet that either inserts a block of code (as shown) or wraps code around the current selection.

Note that there are two kinds of snippets: Wrap Selection and Insert Block. The Insert Block version inserts the snippet as a block of code instead of allowing it to wrap around other objects as required in some instances. Wrap Selection divides the dialog box into two halves where the insertion of the top half occurs before the current selection and the insertion of the bottom half occurs after the current selection. If you select the Wrap Selection radio button when creating a snippet, you must enter code into two text boxes: Insert Before and Insert After.

When creating snippets, you can select how you want the snippet preview to appear in the Snippets panel by selecting either the Design radio button, which presents the snippet preview in Design view, or the Code radio button, which presents the snippet preview in Code view. These radio buttons are located at the bottom of the Snippet dialog box.

Managing Library Items and Templates in the Assets Panel

So far, we've talked about Assets, which are all the elements you've added to your website, and snippets, which are custom code bits that you may want to add in more than one place. To take consistency and reusability even further, you can create library items from objects you use often or even make entire page layouts templates. Library items and templates are very convenient because when you update the originals, they updates everywhere throughout your site without requiring you to go looking for each place they are used. (In contrast, Assets and Snippets do not auto-update when you make changes.)

You use the Library and Templates categories of the Assets panel to manage your library items and templates. The Library and Templates categories of the Assets panel show all the library items and templates that exist in the current website. Each website you create can have a different set of library items and templates.

At the bottom of the Asset panel are the Insert and Apply buttons for the Library and Templates categories, respectively:

- ▶ **Insert**—You click this button to insert the currently selected library item at the location of the insertion point in the web page.

- ▶ **Apply**—You click this button to apply the currently selected template to the web page.

Creating a Library Item

Library items can be created from any object contained in the body of the web page, such as forms, tables, text, Flash movies, divs, and images. For instance, a navigation bar or a set of links that is present in many of the pages in your website would be an excellent candidate for a library item. When you need to add a new button or link, simply change the original library item and then update your entire site automatically with the change.

NOTE

The Difference Between Library Items and Templates

Library items differ from Dreamweaver templates in that **library items** are portions of a page, whereas a **template** is the structure of an entire page. Libraries and templates are similar, though, because both can automatically update all the linked items and pages. A template contains the entire structure for a web page, including both the head and the body sections of the page. A library item is simply a chunk of code and not a complete page.

You have to define a site before Dreamweaver can insert a library item. Dreamweaver creates a directory called Library, where it stores all the library items, in the root of your website.

When you insert a library item into your web page, Dreamweaver inserts into the page a copy of everything contained in the library item. Anyone working on the same website can use the library item (after you have shared it, of course), and you can use library items created by others. Also, you can include a library item in a web page multiple times.

There are two ways to create library items:

▶ **From an existing object or group of objects**—After you decide to create a library item out of a group of objects on a web page, you select the objects and save them into the library.

▶ **From scratch, as a new, empty library item**—You can create a new library item, open it, and add objects to it just as if it were a regular web page.

Using Existing Content in a New Library Item

NOTE

Library Files

Dreamweaver creates an individual file for each library item. The file extension for a library item is .lbi. If you look in the Library directory of your website, you will see one .lbi file for each library item you have in your website.

You create a library item from an existing object or group of objects on your web page as shown here:

1. Select an object or a group of objects. Select multiple objects either by dragging your cursor over them or by holding down the Shift key and clicking objects to add to the selection.

2. To add the selection to the library, drag and drop it to the bottom half of the Library category of the Assets panel, shown in Figure 14.5. Alternatively, select Modify, Library, Add Object to Library.

3. Give the library item a meaningful name. The Name field is selected immediately after you create the library item; at any time, you can reselect the name with a long single-click on the Name field.

FIGURE 14.5
Select and drag existing objects to the Library category of the Assets panel to add them.

TRY IT YOURSELF ▼

Using Existing Content in a New Library Item
Continued

When you select a library item in the Assets panel, you see the contents of the library item in the top half of the Library category of the panel. The contents might look different from how they will look in the web page because the Library category of the Assets panel is small and the objects wrap. In addition, because the library item is only a portion of a web page, it appears with no page background color or applied CSS (Cascading Style Sheets).

NOTE

Library Items and CSS

When you create a CSS style, Dreamweaver inserts the style definition into the head of the HTML document or attaches an external style sheet linked in the head of the document. A library item does not have a head section because it's just a small piece of code. When you insert a library item that has CSS styles applied to it, the web page must already reference those styles.

To create a library item from scratch, follow these steps:

1. Click the New Library Item button at the bottom of the Library category of the Assets panel. (Make sure you haven't accidentally selected any code, or it will be added as your item as described above.) Dreamweaver creates a new, blank library item, as shown in Figure 14.6. A message telling you how to add content to the blank library item appears in the top half of the Library category of the Assets panel.

TRY IT YOURSELF ▼

Creating and Editing a New Library Item

▼ TRY IT YOURSELF

Creating and Editing a New Library Item
Continued

FIGURE 14.6
Create a new library item, open it, and add content.

2. Give the library item a name. For example, create a copyright statement to go at the bottom of each of your web pages. The name Copyright would be a good choice.

3. Double-click the library item in the Library category of the Assets panel. Dreamweaver opens the library item in a separate Document window. You can tell that you have a library item open because the file name ends in .lbi.

4. Insert objects into the library item's Document window just as you would in any web page. Insert the copyright symbol (from the Text category of the Insert panel or by selecting Insert, HTML, Special Characters), a year, and a name.

5. Close the Document window and save the library item. The Library category of the Assets panel reflects your changes.

The Library category of the Assets panel has a pop-up menu containing useful commands. This same menu also pops up when you right-click a library item in the Library category of the Assets panel, as shown in Figure 14.7. Using the New Library Item command is another way to create a library item.

Adding a Library Item to a Page

After you have created a library item, you simply drag it from the list in the Library category of the Assets panel and drop it onto your web page. You can pick up the library item and move it to a different location in the Document window. You are not able to select individual objects contained in the inserted library item. When you click any of the objects, you select the entire library item; the group of objects in a library item is essentially one object in your web page.

When you insert a library item into a web page, you insert a copy of its content. When you upload your web page onto a remote website, you do not need to upload the Library directory unless you want to share with a group.

The Property inspector, as shown in Figure 14.8, displays the library item's attributes when you select that library item in the Document window. The Src box displays the name of the library item (which you cannot change here). The following three buttons in the Property inspector help you manage the library item:

> ▶ **Open**—This button opens the library item you want to edit.

> ▶ **Detach from Original**—This button breaks the link between this instance of a library item and the original item. If the original library item changes, the detached item does not update. If you detach a library item from its original, the individual objects contained in the item are editable.

> ▶ **Recreate**—This button overwrites the original library item with the currently selected instance of the library item. This is useful if you inadvertently lose or edit the original library item.

Dreamweaver applies a highlight to library items so they are easy to see in the Document window. The highlight appears only in Dreamweaver and not in the browser. In addition, the highlight appears only if Invisible Elements is selected (View, Visual Aids, Invisible Elements). You set the highlight color in the Highlighting category in the Dreamweaver Preferences dialog box.

FIGURE 14.7
The Library category of the Assets panel has a contextual menu with commands to add, rename, open, and delete library items.

FIGURE 14.8
The Property inspector contains buttons to manage a library item. You can detach the item from its original or overwrite the item as the original.

Making Changes to a Library Item

You edit a library item by opening the item in the Document window. After you finish editing, save the library item (File, Save). Dreamweaver asks whether you want to update all the documents in the website that contain the library item.

When the update is complete, the Update Pages dialog box displays statistics on how many files Dreamweaver examined, how many it updated, and

CAUTION

Check Out Web Pages to Update

In Hour 23, "Uploading, Sharing, and Managing Web Projects," we examine the option to check files into and out of a remote server, which is useful on projects shared between different people. Dreamweaver might not update Web pages containing library items if you do not have those pages checked out. Pages you don't have checked out are read-only, meaning that you cannot make changes to them. Dreamweaver cannot update any library items in files marked read-only. Make sure that you have all the appropriate files checked out before you update a library item.

how many it could not update. Check the Show Log check box if you want to see these statistics, shown in Figure 14.9.

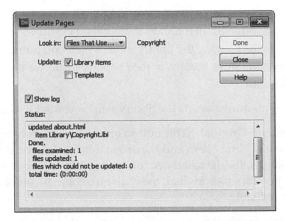

FIGURE 14.9
With Show Log checked, the Update Pages dialog box shows how many files Dreamweaver examined, how many files it updated, and how many it could not update.

You can manually update linked library items at any time. Right-click the library item in the Library category of the Assets panel and select either the Update Current Page command to update the current web page or the Update Site command to update the entire website. The Update Current Page command acts immediately and no dialog box appears. When you issue the Update Site command, the Update Pages dialog box appears. Click the Start button to begin updating all the linked library items in the website. Alternatively, choose Update Pages from either the Library submenu or the Templates submenu under the Modify menu.

NOTE

Templates and CSS

Most web designers link external style sheets to their template pages to control page layout. Placing visual formatting in external style sheets enables you to update the look of the site without changing the template. Think of the template as the container for the HTML content of the page and any CSS files as the rules for appearance or layout.

Creating a Template

You create templates to provide a foundation for consistent, controlled web pages. **Templates** contain objects that you mark as editable; the rest of the template locks. When you update an original template, the changes you make to it update throughout your site without overwriting the editable areas.

You have to define a website before Dreamweaver can insert a template. Dreamweaver creates a directory called Templates, where it stores the original template files, in the root of your website. Dreamweaver keeps the code of a template in a file in the `Templates` directory and inserts a copy of the code when you insert a template in a web page.

Just as with library items, there are two ways to create templates:

- ▶ **From an existing web page**—When you decide to create a template from of a web page, you can save the page as a template.

- ▶ **From scratch, as a new, empty template**—You can create a new template, open it, and then add objects to the template just as though it were a regular web page.

When you apply a template to a web page, you insert a copy of all the content that the template contains into the page. You no longer need to have the original template present for the web page to display. When you upload your web page to a remote website, it is not necessary to upload the `Templates` directory for the template-based pages to be visible. However, you should keep the directory in case you want to make changes to templates throughout your website.

TIP

Cloaking Affects Templates

Use Dreamweaver's Cloaking feature to prevent the `Templates` directory from synchronizing or uploading when you are transferring files. You enable and disable cloaking in the Advanced Settings in the Site Setup dialog box, which you can open by going to Site, Manage Sites and then editing a defined site. To cloak Templates, right-click the `Templates` directory in the Files panel and select Cloaking, Cloak. The folder appears in the site with a red line through it.

NOTE

More Differences Between Templates and Library Items

A template differs from a library item in that a template is the structure (minus content) of an entire web page, not just a portion of one. In addition, templates can define certain regions as editable by the user, whereas library items placed in web pages are not editable at all.

NOTE

Back Up Your Templates to the Server

Keeping the templates on the server ensures that you have a backup copy in case you accidentally change a template and need to restore the original. You learn more about moving your files to the server in Hour 23.

To create a template from an existing web page, follow these steps:

1. With an existing web page open, Select File, Save as Template.

2. The Save as Template dialog box appears, as shown in Figure 14.10. Enter a meaningful name for the template. Click the Save button to save the template to the `Templates` directory.

TRY IT YOURSELF ▼

Creating a Template from an Existing Page

Creating a Template from an Existing Page
Continued

NOTE

Template Files

Dreamweaver creates an individual file for each template. The file extension for templates is .dwt. In the `Templates` directory of your website, you see one .dwt file for each template you have in your website.

FIGURE 14.10
Give a new template a meaningful name in the Save as Template dialog box. This dialog box displays a list of existing templates in the current website.

3. A dialog box might appear, asking whether you'd like to update links. Click the Yes button to agree. This tells Dreamweaver to make sure that the document-relative links are correct when it saves the template to the `Templates` directory.

Creating a Template from Scratch

To create a new, empty template and then add objects to it, follow these steps:

1. Click the New Template button at the bottom of the Templates category of the Assets panel. Dreamweaver creates a new, blank template. A message appears in the top half of the Templates category of the Assets panel, telling you how to add content to the blank template.

2. Give the template a name.

3. Double-click the template in the Templates category of the Assets panel. Dreamweaver opens the template in a separate Document window. You can tell that you have a template open because the file names ends in .dwt.

4. Insert objects into the template's Document window just as you would with any web page.

5. Close the Document window and save the template. The Templates category of the Assets panel reflects your changes. Don't worry right now about the message you receive about your template not having any editable regions. You add some editable regions in a few minutes.

Making the Template Editable

Before you apply a template to a web page, you must mark regions of the template as **editable**. By default, Dreamweaver locks all the regions of the template. If you don't mark any regions as editable, you won't be able to modify the web page based on the template, and that isn't very useful! Mark a region as editable if you need to change, add, or update the content of this region in the pages you create based on this template.

Dreamweaver enables you to create editable regions on various objects in a template. For instance, you can make a container tag, such as a div, editable. You can then change any of its properties after you apply the template to a web page. Or you can leave the div locked and create an editable region within the div. Then you can't change the div properties when you've applied the template, but you can put content within the div.

You should leave locked all regions that do not need to be changed. If you need to make changes to a locked region, you can change the original template file and update all the web pages that link to that template. The commands for manipulating editable regions are located in the Templates submenu of the Common category in the Insert panel, as shown in Figure 14.11, or by choosing Insert, Template Objects.

TIP

Using CSS and Behaviors with Templates

For you to be able to edit CSS styles and behaviors, the object to which they are applied must be editable. If it's editable, select an object that has a style or behavior and edit the style or behavior in the CSS Styles panel or the Behaviors panel.

TIP

Placeholder Images

Use a placeholder image in your template to represent an image that can change between pages. You add a placeholder image to the page by selecting Insert, Image Objects, Image Placeholder or by opening the Images submenu of the Common category of the Insert panel.

FIGURE 14.11
The Template submenu of Dreamweaver's Insert Common panel contains the commands needed to manipulate editable regions.

▼ TRY IT YOURSELF

**Making a Region
Editable**

To make an existing region editable, follow these steps:

1. Open a template and select the region that needs to be editable.

2. Select Insert, Templates, Editable Region. The New Editable Region dialog box appears.

3. In the New Editable Region dialog box, give the region a meaningful name.

TIP

**You Can't Place an
Editable Region Within
an Editable Region**

If Dreamweaver displays the message that the selection is already a part of an editable region, you need to move the selection. Examine the tag selector and look for the `<mmtemplate:editable>` or `<mmtemplate:if>` tag. If you see one of these tags, you have to modify your selection until that tag is no longer part of the selection.

After you create an editable region, the name of the region appears in a highlighted area at the top of the region, as shown in Figure 14.12, as well as at the bottom of the Templates submenu of the Modify menu. Dreamweaver automatically creates an editable region for the title of the document (called **doctitle**) and an empty region in the head of the document that is available for JavaScript code.

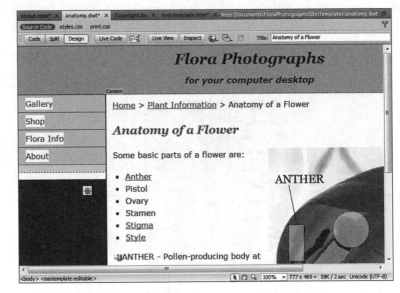

FIGURE 14.12
After you insert a new editable region into a template, it appears as a highlighted rectangular outline.

Dreamweaver highlights editable regions only while you are editing the original template file so that they are easy to pick out in the Document window. Just the opposite is true in a web page with a template applied: Dreamweaver highlights the locked regions. The highlights are visible in

Dreamweaver but not in the browser. To see the highlights, select View, Invisible Elements. Set the highlight color in the Highlighting category in the Dreamweaver Preferences dialog box.

Making an Optional Region

You can create an optional region in a template. An optional region enables the web page author to decide whether this region on the web page appears when the template is used. If the region isn't necessary, the author can turn it off.

To create an optional region, select Insert, Template Objects, Optional Region. Then name the new region in the New Optional Region dialog box that appears. Switch to the Advanced tab to set the condition under which the region will appear on the page when the template is used. Click OK to create the optional region.

An optional region appears with a rectangle around it and a tab showing its name. In the head of the document, Dreamweaver inserts a parameter that determines whether to hide or show the optional region.

When the template is applied to a page, as described in the following section, you can select Modify, Template Properties to turn the optional region on or off.

Note that Optional regions are not automatically editable; they are either there or not there. You must either nest an editable region inside an optional region or add an optional editable region (Insert, Template, Editable Optional Region) in order to edit the content in a web page based on the template.

Modifying an Editable Region

To lock a region that has previously been marked as editable, select Modify, Templates, Remove Template Markup while you have the region you'd like to remove selected. Don't do this after you've created web pages with the template because your web pages lose any content that you entered into the region when you update.

Creating a Web Page from a Template

Web pages based on templates allow you to edit content only in the editable regions. You can see these editable regions highlighted in the Document window (you must have Invisible Elements turned on in the View menu and Highlighting turned on in the Preferences dialog box). Dreamweaver blocks the rest of the web page from editing. Simply remove any placeholder text or images within the editable region and add the final content to create a new web page.

FIGURE 14.13
Create a new web page from a template by choosing the Page from Template tab from the New Document dialog box.

To create a new page from a template, do the following:

1. Select the New command (File, New) and choose the Page from Template icon, as shown in Figure 14.13.

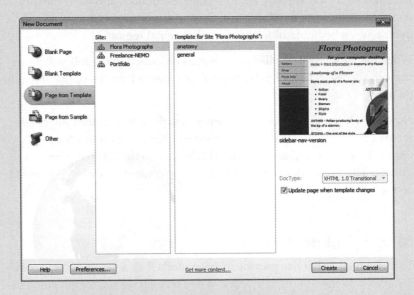

2. Select the site on the left side of the dialog box and choose a template from the list in the middle of the dialog box. You can see a preview of the template on the right side of the dialog box.

3. Make sure that you enable the Update Page When Template Changes check box. This links the new page you are creating to the original template and updates the page if the template changes.

4. Click Create.

5. Modify the placeholder content in the editable areas. Notice that you cannot change any of the locked content.

6. To reveal or hide optional regions, select Modify, Template Properties to open the Template Properties dialog box, as shown in Figure 14.14, to either turn on or turn off the optional region.

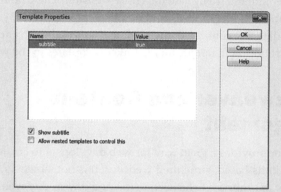

TRY IT YOURSELF ▼

Creating a New Page from a Template

Continued

FIGURE 14.14
Turn an optional region on or off in the Template Properties dialog box.

The Template Properties command is available only when you are working on a page based on a Dreamweaver template; it isn't available while you're actually editing a template file.

Making Changes to a Template and Updating Pages

You edit a template by opening it in the Document window. You can open the template from the Templates category of the Assets panel, or you can open it from the Files panel. Edits to locked objects apply to all the web pages that use the template. Edits to editable objects have no effect on web pages that use the template. Also, unless you delete an editable region, edits to templates have no effect on content on the web pages that use the template.

After you edit and save a template, Dreamweaver asks you whether you want to update files. Select the files you want to update in the Update Files dialog box and then click Update to automatically update the files. The

Update Pages dialog box displays statistics on how many files Dreamweaver examined, updated, and could not update. Check the Show Log check box to see these statistics. Click the Close button to close the Update Pages dialog box.

You can also manually update files linked to templates. To do so, right-click the template in the Templates category of the Assets panel and select either the Update Current Page command (to update the current web page) or the Update Site command (to update the entire website). The Update Current Page command acts immediately and no dialog box appears. When you issue the Update Site command, the Update Pages dialog box appears. Click the Start button to update all the linked templates in the website.

Dreamweaver and Content Management

Dreamweaver provides a great way for web developers to create pages and deliver standards-based, structured websites. It is not, however, a tool that is necessarily appropriate to be used in making day-to-day website updates.

Much of today's web maintenance is distributed throughout an organization—from administrative assistants to directors. People in these positions may not have the technical knowledge or time to work with an editor like Dreamweaver, so they have been increasingly turning toward content management systems. A content management system enables you (the web developer) to create the structure and functionality of a site, while the maintainers are given a simple word processor–like interface for updating the site content. Content maintainers don't have access to any of the underlying site files, making it less likely for any serious mistakes to occur.

Contribute

So what does this have to do with Dreamweaver? As you saw earlier in the hour, the templates enable you to create locked and editable page regions. These templates can be used with an Adobe product called Contribute to create a simple type of content management system. Contribute works just like a web browser, allowing a maintainer who has received a special key code to browse through a live Dreamweaver-created website. When they reach a page they want to edit, they click an Edit button and the editable portions of the page can be changed directly within the Contribute browser; the locked portions of the page cannot be edited. There is no need to understand style sheets or URLs or other complexities of development—the combination of Dreamweaver/Contribute makes it simple to create a distributed web management environment with users of any skill level.

You can learn more about Contribute at http://www.adobe.com/products/contribute/.

Summary

In this hour, we looked at Dreamweaver's many options for managing reusable code. You learned how to examine and apply assets from the Assets panel. You learned how to use Dreamweaver snippets and to create your own snippets. You learned how to use the Library and Templates categories of the Assets panel to manage, open, and edit library items and templates. In addition, you learned how to create library items and templates, both from existing content and from scratch. Finally, you looked at how Dreamweaver can interact with Adobe Contribute for content management.

Q&A

Q. **What's the difference between snippets and library items?**

A. A snippet simply places objects or code into a web page, whereas a library item maintains a link to the library that enables you to update each instance of the item by updating the original.

Q. **What types of objects are appropriate to put in the library?**

A. Here are some examples of objects you might want to put in the Dreamweaver library: a company logo (including alt text and linking), a search box (small form), and standard footer text. You will find plenty of uses for the library.

Q. **Is there any way I can use templates without having locked and editable regions?**

A. Yes. You can create a template with everything laid out perfectly, create a new page, and make sure you do *not* enable the Update Page When Template Changes check box. That way, you have a standard beginning point but have the freedom to do what you want with the page. You can also detach a webpage from its template, which allows you to edit it like a normal page, but it will no longer be updated when the template is updated.

Q. Why would I use an optional or editable optional region?

A. An optional or editable optional region enables you to give people using the template the option to add or delete standard content with very little work. For instance, imagine that you have a template that presents the biographies of college professors. Some biographies have photos, but others do not. You can make the photo region optional so that people creating the web page can quickly turn off that region if it is unnecessary.

Workshop

Quiz

1. Which asset categories list the individual files referenced (or embedded) in a web page?

2. What is the file extension for library files? For template files?

3. Which regions, editable or locked, does Dreamweaver highlight when you are editing the original template file?

Quiz Answers

1. The Images and Flash Movies (SWF), Shockwave Movies, Movies, and Scripts categories list the actual files referenced in web pages.

2. The file extension for library item files is .lbi. The file extension for template files is .dwt.

3. Dreamweaver highlights the editable regions when you are editing the original template file. It highlights the locked regions when you are in a web page based on a template.

Exercises

1. Create a template and practice marking various objects as editable. Apply the template and see which objects can be marked as editable and which cannot. What properties can you edit?

2. Open a template you have already applied to a page, edit it, and practice updating the linked page. Open the page. Do you see the edits you made?

3. Create a library item and add it to a page. Experiment with reopening the library item, editing it, and then updating the page to which it's connected.

HOUR 15
Designing for WordPress and Content Management Systems

One of the most exciting new features in Dreamweaver CS5 is ability to work conveniently to design sites built in several popular, free web content management systems (CMS) that use PHP and MySQL, such as Wordpress for blogging and Drupal and Joomla. Sites created with these systems are different than the pages we've looked at so far because they are generated by a server technology, PHP, from various elements and sources, including database content (typically stored in MySQL). The examples in this hour feature WordPress, a widely used, free blogging tool. Note that we won't discuss the basics of making posts in a CMS, because it doesn't require Dreamweaver; rather, we'll focus on how to modify CMS page themes using Dreamweaver's tools.

To help you navigate all the different files that may combine into a single page, Dreamweaver allows you to use LiveView to see a reproduction of your page and finds dynamically related files that you may need to edit to change the overall look. For more advanced features, Dreamweaver can also index the site code and, if you begin making changes, suggest relevant options based on existing elements.

Setting Up Your Site

If you already use a CMS, you know they require setup to even begin creating a site. You need to have access to a web server, install the CMS software, and set up a database before you get to the fun part of deciding how it looks. That's just how these systems are, so be prepared to do some legwork before you even get to Dreamweaver.

WHAT YOU'LL LEARN IN THIS HOUR:

► How to setup a CMS-based site to work with Dreamweaver

► How to activate dynamically related files

► How to view and edit dynamic sites within Dreamweaver

► How to set up site-specific code hinting

NOTE

Drupal, Joomla, and WordPress

The CMSs specifically supported in Dreamweaver are open source projects supported by a devoted community of developers and users. You can learn about these systems, and even download them, at http://drupal.org/, http://www.joomla.org/, and http://www.wordpress.org/, respectively.

Use the Right Kind of Account

In order to use Dreamweaver as described in this hour, you need access to the files that run your system and the corresponding FTP connection information. If you have a free account with access only to a web interface for design changes, you'll need to consider other options.

Also, when setting up your CMS site for use in Dreamweaver, you can't merely copy the static files of your CMS to a folder and point Dreamweaver at it, because the magic of CMSs is in the way a web server dynamically integrates their many components and database records.

Dreamweaver requires access to a working server for showing or previewing pages that use server-side code, such as those produced by CMSs. There are no shortcuts on this matter. The reason for this is simple—server-side code can't be run without the help of a web server! Dreamweaver (through Live View) and web browsers (through Preview in Browser) are not able to process the page code alone.

That being said, you'll need to designate a testing server that can be accessed locally (not through Dreamweaver's FTP). You can either set up a web server with fully functioning CMS that runs on your own computer or use third-party software to connect to your CMS testing server on a remote web server. Both options allow Dreamweaver to leverage the server's strengths to render full pages from all the parts that actually comprise them.

TIP

My Setup

It's beyond the scope of this book to delve into connecting to web servers outside of Dreamweaver or setting them up. However, because the features we're about to talk about require a live server that can be accessed locally by Dreamweaver, here's a quick overview of my setup. I created an account on Dreamhost (http://www.dreamhost.com/), a web hosting service that offers one-click installation of Drupal, Joomla, and WordPress. I then set up WordPress and connected to that drive using a third-party FTP/file sharing application called ExpanDrive (http://www.expandrive.com/), which is available for PC and Mac. Both Dreamhost and ExpanDrive offer free, limited time trials in case you want to follow along. Note that web account setup isn't instantaneous, and you will need to register an unused web address and provide payment information.

Refer to the Q&A section at the end of this hour for details about setting up a local web server and database on your own computer.

NOTE

Do You Need a Test Server?

When working with a site containing only HTML, CSS, and JavaScript files, you don't really need a testing server. You can test your pages locally directly in LiveView or preview them in a web browser because they aren't complex enough to require a server to render them.

Site Setup within Dreamweaver

To set up your Dreamweaver site and testing server, you'll need to use the Manage Sites dialog box introduced in Hour 3, "Setting Up a Website." (In case you are wondering, Chapter 23, "Uploading, Sharing, and Managing

Web Projects," features the more advanced features beyond what we'll cover in this hour.)

Use the Site Setup dialog to complete the following steps:

1. Open Dreamweaver and choose Site, New Site.

2. In the Site Setup dialog, shown in Figure 15.1, fill in a site name to identify your project. (No one outside of Dreamweaver will see this.)

TRY IT YOURSELF ▼

Creating a Site and Testing Server

FIGURE 15.1
The Site Setup dialog allows you to define a local folder for your web project, as well as many settings related to connecting to servers.

3. Under Local Site Folder, create a new, empty directory for your site.

4. In the Servers section of the Site Setup dialog, click the plus button to add a new server definition. A new dialog box opens where you define your testing server details, as shown in Figure 15.2. This information, including FTP details, will be provided by your service provider.

5. Enter a Server Name to help you find this item in the list of possible servers you can add. This is only shown in Dreamweaver.

6. Set the Connect Using drop-down menu to Local/Network and navigate to the Server Folder of the testing server you have set up, either as a locally-running web server or as a connected drive on a live web server.

7. Set the Web URL to your testing server. Because I am using a live web server, my site has a registered Web URL. If you are connecting to a web server on your local machine, you would use http://localhost in this field, possibly with additional folders if you have created a folder structure for multiple projects, such as http://localhost/wordpress/proj-

CAUTION

Local Connection Required!

When using CMSs, you MUST choose Local/Network when connecting to your testing server. If you try to connect to a testing server with FTP or other intermediary technologies, Dreamweaver shows errors when trying to produce a Live View of the site files. (This is why you may need to connect to a server drive with third-party software before setting up your site in Dreamweaver, as described above.)

▼ TRY IT YOURSELF

Creating a Site and Testing Server

FIGURE 15.2
Enter information about your testing server and be sure to choose a Local/Network connection.

ect1. (If you leave this blank or refer to something that doesn't exist, later exercises will fail. Test your URL in a web browser to make sure it's valid.)

8. Click save to return to the Servers list. Make sure Testing is checked, as shown in Figure 15.3.

9. Click the Save button to exit Site Setup.

FIGURE 15.3
Be sure your testing server is marked as a testing server or Dreamweaver won't recognize this as its purpose.

When your site setup completes, Dreamweaver updates the site cache, which can take a little while depending on the complexity of your site, and refreshes the Files panel.

Locating Dynamically Related Files

With your testing server set up, Dreamweaver can now identify dynamically related files. If you've done the setup correctly, this part is a snap.

Simply open the index.php page (or whatever default main page your CMS uses) in Dreamweaver and follow the prompts!

To have Dreamweaver detect related files within your dynamic site:

1. Open the Files panel and change the view drop-down from Local View to Testing Server, as shown in Figure 15.4. The window will refresh with the files on your testing server.

Enabling Dynamically Related Files

FIGURE 15.4
The Files panel allows you to switch from a local view of your files to a testing or remote server view.

2. Expand the folders as needed to locate and open the index.php file. Note, some sites may have index.php pages at multiple levels, but you are looking for the main page.

3. Dreamweaver shows a dialog requesting permission to Get Dependent Files, which you should allow. (At this time, Dreamweaver copies some site files into the empty local folder created when you set up your site.)

4. When done, Dreamweaver inserts a comment bar at the top of the document window, as shown in Figure 15.5, to alert you that the page you've opened may have "dynamically-related files that can only be

Enabling Dynamically Related Files

Continued

FIGURE 15.5
Dreamweaver recognizes that some pages have related files that need to be used to see the page accurately.

discovered by the server." Click Discover to continue and approve the Script Warning dialog that cautions any scripts linked to the page will be executed as if in a browser window.

Discover link

5. The comment bar changes to announce that "this page has server processing directives that Design View cannot display." Click the link for Switch to Live View.

6. The document window refreshes to show your page as it would appear in a web browser after being processed by a web server, as shown in Figure 15.6. Also, along the top of the window is a list of dynamically related files that support the page.

Dynamically related files

FIGURE 15.6
After you complete the step of connecting locally to a testing server, Live View can render a complex page from a CMS.

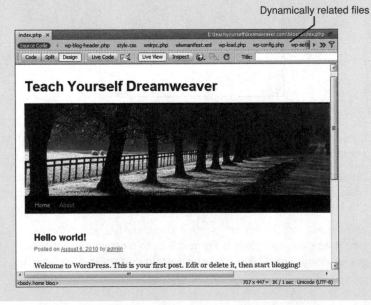

Making Site Changes

The whole point of setting up your CMS site in Dreamweaver is to make changes using the WYSIWYG interface. However, before you get started, let's talk about what to change and what not to change in Dreamweaver.

As a general rule, don't try to change actual messages or content, because they are meant to be updated within an admin web interface. Also, many systems have code within their HTML pages that dynamically replaces onscreen elements based on options you've selected, so unless you know what you're doing in the code, you probably want to leave those areas alone. (Although, if you are interested in editing the functionality of your site by editing the PHP or JavaScript code, Dreamweaver has tools to offer, as we'll see at the end of this hour.)

What, then, should you change? The CSS styles pages are good candidates for changing the appearance of a whole site. For instance, Dreamweaver makes it easy to find the exact file and setting you need to change all link colors or the update fonts faces that are repeated throughout the site.

Now let's talk about how this is accomplished.

Using Inspect Mode

One tool that Dreamweaver offers for navigating complex web structures is the Inspect mode. It allows you to explore visually the structure of a page as you view related code.

Return to a dynamic page open in Live view and follow these steps to enter Inspect mode:

1. Click the Inspect button at the top of the document window.

2. A comment bar appears at the top of the document window to request permission to change the workspace mode to be more useful in Inspect mode. Click the link for Switch now.

The screen changes to split view, as shown in Figure 15.7, and highlights in both the design and code areas each area of the screen as your mouse cursor moves across them.

▼ TRY IT YOURSELF

Switching to Inspect Mode

Continued

FIGURE 15.7
Inspect mode highlights page elements as you mouse over them to reveal the underlying structure of the page.

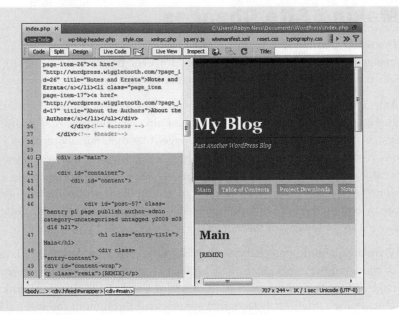

Using the Code Navigator

To understand the underlying CSS that control the page layout and appearance, try the Code Navigator.

Hold down the Option key as you click on the page in Live View to pop up a list of the files and styles that apply, as shown in Figure 15.8. To open one of the linked files, mouse over an underlined rule or description and Option-click; the screen switches to Split view with the code file open in the code pane so you can make changes.

Note that if you make a change to a related file, you have to toggle Live View off and on again to refresh the view.

Filtering Related Files

Earlier we mentioned that Live View of dynamic files lists all the related files along the top of the window, as shown in Figure 15.6. There are often so many related files that an arrow also appears to continue beyond the space available at the top of the window.

To help you narrow the list when you are looking for something specific, you can use the Filter Related Files feature, activated by clicking the funnel-

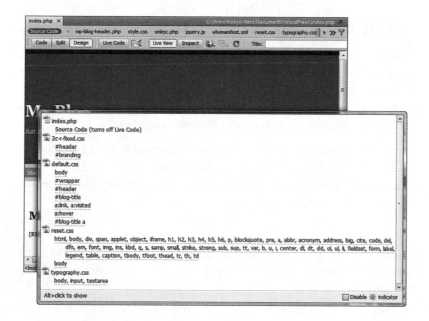

FIGURE 15.8
Code Navigator reveals CSS files
and rules that apply to a selected
object.

shaped icon. As shown in Figure 15.9, you can choose to limit the listed file
to CSS, JavaScript PHP, or XML files or to create a custom filter to focus, for
example, on any file related to the header or to the footer.

FIGURE 15.9
Filter related files to a manageable
list or restore the list to all related
files.

To write a custom filter, type the name of a specific file or use "*" characters
as wildcards to search for file names containing a word or extension, such
as *header* or *.html.

NOTE

Learn More about Drupal, Joomla, and WordPress

Unlike use of Live Code with CMSs, site specific code hinting works even if you don't have access to a live server for testing, so you can use a local copy of the files from a server to get started.

Using Site Specific Code Hinting

If you ever work in Dreamweaver's code view, you may have noticed that Dreamweaver tries to help you choose HTML tags and CSS properties while you type. This is called code hinting. Dreamweaver CS5 takes this concept even farther by offering site specific code hints, which relate to the specific actions within a site that are called within pages.

It works by assessing your whole local site folder and indexing all the code objects by name. That way, when you start typing something it can make related suggestions so you don't have to worry about mistyping something your already have and want to reuse.

▼ TRY IT YOURSELF

Activating Site-Specific Code Hinting

In order to set up site specific code hinter, you must have defined a site around the local copy of a site with PHP based coding, such as the CMS site we've been working with:

1. Select Site, Site-Specific Code Hints from the menu.

2. In the Site-Specific Code Hints dialog, shown in Figure 15.10, from the Structure drop-down menu, choose New from Blank, Drupal, Joomla, or WordPress. (New from Blank allows you to use this feature for custom PHP sites.)

FIGURE 15.10
Choose your site structure and customize the file scanning options.

NOTE

Cloaking a File

The code hinting file that Dreamweaver creates in your local site directory is cloaked, which means it won't upload to the server when you synchronize files. This is a security measure because you never want to give away the inner workings of a dynamic site, which can be used to break into it without authorization. Cloaking is discussed more in Hour 24, "Maintaining a Website."

3. Choose to include or exclude any folders within your site and whether to recursively scan for a folder within folders.

4. Click OK. Dreamweaver takes a few minutes to scan the site and creates a file called dw_php_codehinting.config within your site file.

Once you've enabled site-specific code hinting, it's very simple to use from code view. Just click Control-Spacebar and start typing. Dreamweaver drops down a list of likely options, as shown in Figure 15.11. Double-click an item to select it.

Site-specific code hints ———

FIGURE 15.11
Like magic, Dreamweaver can suggest code related to your site that narrows as it recognizes patterns in what you type.

Summary

In this hour, you explored two new features of Dreamweaver CS5 that make it more relevant for working with common web CMSs. You learned how to set up a testing server so you can use dyanically related files and Live View to edit your site designed beyond the basic tools available in CMS web-based control panels. You also learned how to use code hinting and set up site specific code hinting to edit the working code within your dynamic systems.

Q&A

Q. Do I have to go through all the setup just to use Dreamweaver for creating WordPress themes?

A. No, you don't have to use the dynamically related files feature. You can develop the old-fashioned way by locating the file you need to change in the file panel and changing the files in code view (but having a testing server is still recommended!).

If you are looking for more visual alternatives, there are addons and extensions that may help. For example, prior to Dreamweaver CS5, many WordPress users purchased a Dreamweaver extension called ThemeDreamer (http://www.themedreamer.com/) in order to use Dreamweaver's Design view to edit WordPress themes. If the setup required for dynamically related files is too daunting, consider this extension as an alternative. Note that Hour 19, "Using Spry, the Widget Browser, and Extensions," explores Dreamweaver's extension framework.

Q. **How do I run a web server on my own computer for testing?**

A. There are well-documented options for running web servers locally. For Drupal, Joomla, and Wordpress, which use PHP and MySQL, WAMP or MAMP are widely recommended (http://www.wampserver.com/, http://www.mamp.info). Remember, in addition to installing a web server, you'll also have to follow the instructions for setting up your CMS, including any additional supporting software like MySQL or extensions or libraries for PHP.

Q. **Is PHP really the only option supported for site-specific code hinting?**

A. In CS5, yes. Many of the other server-side coding languages (ASP, JSP, and ColdFusion) have steeper development requirements and aren't often used by individuals or beginners. There are coding environments used by professionals that support these languages in a similar way to Dreamweaver's code hinting. PHP, on the other hand, is widely used in free systems (like Drupal, Joomla, and WordPress), so there are a lot more users who can benefit from Dreamweaver support.

Workshop

Quiz

1. How do you get Dreamweaver to identify dynamically related files for a dynamic CMS or blog site?

2. To view and edit dynamically generated pages in Dreamweaver, you need to activate them in Live View. True or False?

3. How do you turn on site specific code hints?

Quiz Answers

1. If you've configured your testing server, switch from Local View to Testing Server in the Files panel, then open a page with related files and follow the prompts to allow Dreamweaver to locate files and to switch to Live View.

2. True. Live View presents a rendered version of the page, including dynamic elements. However, you'll also need to allow Dreamweaver to locate dynamically related files.

3. Perform site setup on a PHP-based site, then choose Site, Site Specific Code Hints and pick your specifics.

Exercises

1. Create a free trial account on a web hosting service that offers WordPress (such as Dreamhost), install WordPress, use a tool such as ExpanDrive to connect, and then set your site up within Dreamweaver as a test server. (Note, it may take a few hours for a web account to be activated in order to complete this exercise.)

2. In the site you've set up in Dreamweaver, switch to Live View to enable dynamically related files and use the Code Navigator to change CSS styles.

HOUR 16
Adding Spry Menu Bars for Navigation

Websites are repositories of information, and it's important to give visitors the correct tools to navigate to the information they need. You want to design your website's navigation to be clear and logical. It's always a good idea to create a mock-up of your proposed navigation structure and test it out with some customers or friends. You learn a lot by watching potential visitors try to find the gold buried within your website.

Understanding Navigation

Website navigation should be clear, well thought out, and intuitive. You should break the content in your website into logical groupings and give each grouping a name that represents it. In most websites, there are two types of navigation: primary and secondary. **Primary navigation** is usually located at the top or on the left side of the page and represents the main content groupings in the website. **Secondary navigation** includes the standard website links, such as contact information, privacy policy, an About Us section, and others.

The primary navigation is how visitors get to all the sections of the website. Developers usually design this navigation to blend into the interface, using the same graphics and colors as the design. It's important that the primary navigation be consistent on every page in the website because many visitors will arrive at a page in your site via a link from a search engine instead of navigating from your home page. You need to give these visitors an easy way to explore the other information on your site.

Websites designed for languages that read from left to right (the English language, for instance) have the primary navigation either at the top or on the left side of the page. That way people read this information first.

WHAT YOU'LL LEARN IN THIS HOUR:

▶ The importance of planning good navigation for a website

▶ How to add a Spry menu bar

▶ How to modify links so that the web page opens in a new browser window

Languages that read from right to left (Hebrew or Arabic, for instance) might have the primary navigation on the right side of the page. Generally, the secondary navigation is at the bottom of the page or in a submenu of the primary navigation.

There are several common forms of website navigation (Figure 16.1 shows some examples):

▶ **Links**—Hyperlinks on the page, the most basic form of navigation.

▶ **Breadcrumbs**—A group of links showing the path to the current page. Usually breadcrumbs begin with the home page (listed on the left) and then list each of the sections navigated to get to the current page (listed on the right). An example: Home > Gallery > Summer Flowers.

▶ **Menu bar**—A list of navigational options in a horizontal or vertical format, much like the menu bar in your desktop applications.

▶ **Site map**—A list of all the content on your website and where it is located.

Menu Bar (primary navigation)   Breadcrumbs

FIGURE 16.1
Various types of navigation can appear on a web page, including menu bars and breadcrumbs.

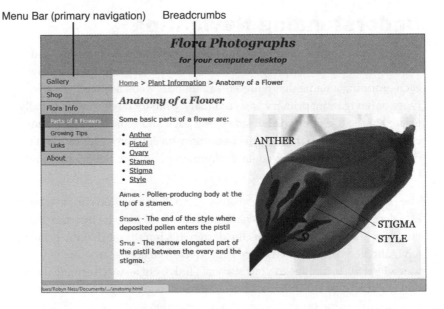

You've already explored creating links, so you can easily create the preceding list's first two bullet items: links and breadcrumbs. The final bullet item, the site map, is also just a group of links to resources in the website. In this hour, you explore the menu bar.

NOTE

Out with the Old, In with the New

Previous versions of Dreamweaver included a feature for creating a navigation bar with images and rollover effects. This navigation technique has fallen out of favor and is no longer available in Dreamweaver CS5. Image rollover navigation is considered old-fashioned and impractical after advances in CSS that make styled, text-based menus look as good as button images.

Don't shed any tears that Dreamweaver eliminated the navigation bar feature. It's really for everyone's benefit. CSS-based navigation requires far less work to create and maintain than image-based navigation—if you want to try a new color or create additional site sections, you change a few lines of code rather than opening a graphics editor and searching for your source design files. Graphic navigation also slows page load compared to text-based navigation. Not to mention, CSS menus are better in regard to accessibility for people with disabilities because they scale like the rest of the onscreen text if a user has his own personal settings applied and are automatically scannable by screen readers. (However, if you absolutely must create one, you can use the image rollover tool discussed in Chapter 8, "Displaying Images," for each navigation element.)

Inserting a Menu Bar

Primary and secondary navigation are often implemented using a menu bar, with the secondary navigation nested in some way within the primary categories. Popular methods include dropdown menus for horizontal navigation menus and slide out menus for vertical navigation in which mousing over an item in the primary navigation reveals additional items related to it. Creating all the actions for such menus used to be a somewhat complicated feat that required patience and a lot of testing. Fortunately, Dreamweaver has kept up with advances in web development related to JavaScript libraries, and it includes a user-friendly, technically sound option.

Let's explore inserting a menu bar into a web page using Dreamweaver's Spry Menu Bar object.

The Spry Menu Bar object enables you to add three menu levels to either a vertical or a horizontal menu bar. Figure 16.2 shows a horizontal Spry menu bar with the menu levels displayed. Figure 16.3 shows a vertical Spry menu bar with its menu levels displayed.

NOTE

What is Spry?

Dreamweaver includes a whole set of Spry elements, called the Spry framework for Ajax, which is built on a JavaScript library that you learn about in Hour 19, "Using Spry, the Widget Browser, and Extensions." You will be able to successfully use the Spry Menu Bar object in this hour without understanding much about the framework, but creating menus with it is just scratching the surface.

FIGURE 16.2
This horizontal Spry menu bar
displays multiple menu levels.

FIGURE 16.3
This vertical Spry menu bar
displays multiple menu levels.

The Spry menu bar is created using CSS (Cascading Style Sheets) instead of images. So you can use your CSS-editing skills to modify the fonts, colors, sizes, and other attributes. After you insert the menu bar, you learn how to modify the CSS that Dreamweaver saves in an external style sheet.

▼ TRY IT YOURSELF

**Inserting a Spry
Menu Bar**

To insert a Spry menu bar, do the following:

1. Create and save a web page (File, Save) before inserting a Spry menu bar.

2. Select Insert, Layout Objects, Spry Menu Bar. The Spry Menu Bar dialog box appears, as shown in Figure 16.4.

3. Select either Horizontal or Vertical as the menu orientation.

4. Click OK and the menu bar inserts into the web page.

5. Save your web page (File, Save) and Dreamweaver prompts you to copy dependent files as shown in Figure 16.5.

6. Dreamweaver creates a folder named SpryAssets within the folder where it saves your web page, and copies the dependent files into this folder. These files are images, external JavaScript files, and external CSS style sheets. Do not delete these files.

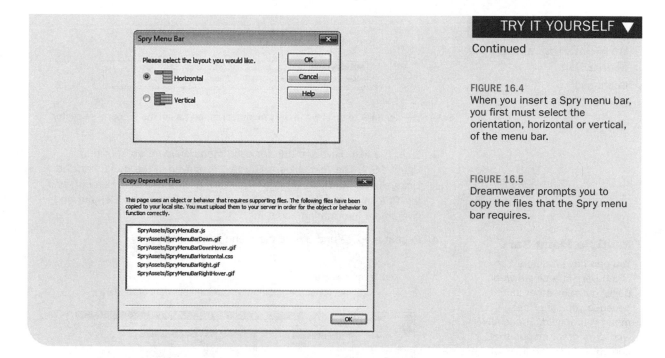

TRY IT YOURSELF ▼

Continued

FIGURE 16.4
When you insert a Spry menu bar, you first must select the orientation, horizontal or vertical, of the menu bar.

FIGURE 16.5
Dreamweaver prompts you to copy the files that the Spry menu bar requires.

After you've created a Spry menu bar in a web page, Dreamweaver no longer needs to copy the dependent files unless you insert a different Spry object that requires additional files. The external JavaScript files work just like external CSS style sheets: You have to maintain only one file that can link to many different web pages. If you update that one file, you affect all the web pages attached to it.

When you test the web page in Live View or a web browser, you should have a fully functional menu. But now you have to add your text and links to the menu.

To customize a Spry menu bar, follow these steps:

1. Place your cursor over the menu and select the Spry Menu Bar tab above the newly inserted menu bar to display the menu bar properties in the Property inspector, as shown in Figure 16.6.

2. Use the Add or Remove Menu Item buttons to modify the number of elements in each of the menu sections. Use the Reorder Menu Item buttons to move elements up or down in the list.

TRY IT YOURSELF ▼

Customizing a Spry Menu Bar

Customizing a Spry Menu Bar

Continued

Spry Menu Bar tab

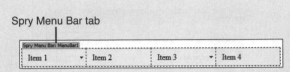

FIGURE 16.6
Select the menu bar to display the Spry menu bar properties in the Property inspector.

3. Enter the text, link, and title for each menu element as shown in Figure 16.7. The Text value is the text displayed in the menu bar; the Link value is where visitors go when they click that menu element; and the Title value is a ToolTip that appears above the menu element and gives more information about it.

TIP

Multiple Menu Bars

You can have multiple Spry menu bars in a single web page, but remember just because you can, doesn't mean you should. Especially with drop down menus that can cover large portions of the screen or important content (like submit buttons on forms), be sure to leave enough room for viewers NOT to accidentally trigger menus that get in their way.

4. Repeat steps 2 and 3 until the menu is complete.

Add or remove elements
Reorder elements   Menu element properties

Top-level navigation | Third-level navigation
Second-level navigation

FIGURE 16.7
Enter the text, link, and title (ToolTip) for each of the menu elements.

Editing the Menu Bar CSS

It's likely that you'd prefer the menu to match the design, fonts, colors, and other properties of objects on the web page. You can easily edit the CSS affecting the menu bar to make it fit with your design. You use what you've learned in earlier hours about CSS and apply it to the menu bar.

You edit the styles in either SpryMenuBarVertical.css or SpryMenuBarHorizontal.css, depending on the menu bar orientation you chose earlier. The style definitions appear in the CSS Styles panel, as shown in Figure 16.8. These are the styles in the external style sheet that you can modify to change the look of the menu bar.

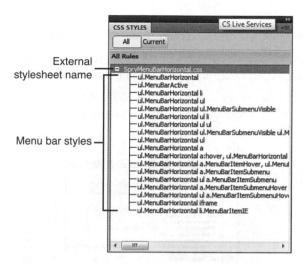

FIGURE 16.8
Styles affecting the Spry menu bar
are stored in an external style
sheet.

You might notice that all the styles in the external style sheet begin with ul. This is the tag for an unordered list (bulleted list), and that is how Dreamweaver implements the menu bar. The menu bar is simply an unordered list styled to look like a drop-down menu. You can actually see this by clicking the Turn Styles Off button in the Property inspector, as shown in Figure 16.9. Submenus are simply unordered lists that are nested.

FIGURE 16.9
Turn the styles off to see the actual unordered list structure.

TIP

Customize this widget—a quick link to help

You can easily bring up information about customizing the menu CSS by selecting the Customize This Widget link in the Property inspector. This link opens the Dreamweaver help specific to modifying the CSS for the menu. Use the tables in help to identify which styles you need to change to modify different parts of the menu.

You may have noticed there are many, many CSS styles associated with these menus. Resist the urge to guess about the purpose of properties in the Spry CSS. Refer to the tables in Dreamweaver help (select the Customize This Widget link in the Property inspector) to identify the correct styles. That way you won't modify properties unnecessarily or mess up other parts of the menu that are dependent on other styles.

**Changing the Font
and Background of a
Spry Menu Bar**

To change the font and background colors for the menu bar:

1. In the CSS Styles panel, select ul.MenuBarHorizontal a or
   ul.MenuBarVertical a (depending on the orientation of your menu bar).

2. In the Properties pane at the bottom of the CSS Styles panel, edit the
   colors for the background-color and color properties, as shown in
   Figure 16.10.

FIGURE 16.10
Edit the style properties
directly in the lower pane of
the CSS Styles panel.

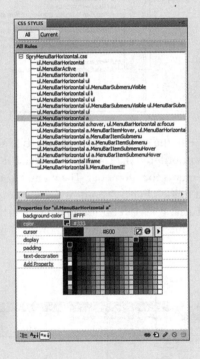

3. Select ul.MenuBarHorizontal a:hover or ul.MenuBarVertical
   a:hover to modify the way the menu displays when the visitor's cursor
   is hovering over the link. This style is grouped in the same style with
   ul.MenuBarHorizontal a:focus or ul.MenuBarVertical a:focus.

4. Modify the colors in the Properties pane at the bottom of the CSS
   Styles panel.

You've been modifying properties of the unordered list tag (ul), but lists
have another tag of interest. The list item (li) tag wraps around every individual list item, and an unordered list tag wraps around all the list items.

The following steps show you how to modify the list item tag to change the dimensions of menu items:

1. In the CSS Styles panel, select `ul.MenuBarVertical li` or `ul.MenuBarHorizontal li` (depending on the menu bar orientation you selected earlier).

2. In the Properties pane at the bottom of the CSS Styles panel, edit the width.

TRY IT YOURSELF ▼

Changing the Dimensions of Spry Menus

After you've modified the menu to the way you'd like it on all pages, you have to make sure that all the web pages link to the specific external style sheet that you modified. If you save new pages in the same directory as the original web page, Dreamweaver links the pages to the modified CSS style sheet. If you save pages to other directories, however, you should link to the external style sheet manually by using the Attach Style Sheet command in the CSS Styles panel.

Targeting a Link to Open in a New Browser Window

One final navigational topic introduces you to how you can launch a new browser window with a link instead of loading a new page into the existing browser window. This technique is especially useful when linking to other, external websites. When visitors click the link, the web page with that link stays open and another browser window opens with the new web page. Both windows remain open until the visitor closes them.

When you select a hyperlink, the Property inspector has a drop-down box called Target. The _blank reserved target name, shown in Figure 16.11, is useful when you want to leave the current browser window open and have the link open a new browser window with the linked web page in it. Simply select _blank from the Target drop-down menu when you want a link to open a new browser window.

Opening a new window is useful when you want to keep your original web page open but still allow the user to jump to other web pages. When the user closes the new window, the window containing your site is still open. It's nice to warn the users about this so that they do not become confused. You can add text to a link that opens a new window with a message that

NOTE

What About the Other Reserved Names?

Three of the reserved target names—_parent, _self, and _top—are mainly for use with pages designed with frames. Frames are a technique in which parts of the page, such as the header, content, and navigation sections, are actually separate files displayed together inside a "frameset" to make one web page when seen by a site visitor. This allows each section to load and be updated separately. Frame-based pages are still used occasionally, especially in older systems that require login or include complex functionality. However, like table-based page layouts, frames have largely been replaced with more modern CSS and JavaScript techniques that are more easily maintained by developers, more flexible across different web-enabled devices, and more accessible to those with disabilities.

TIP

Tabs and Windows

Many browsers implement "tabs" to hold different web pages within a single window. Depending on a user's browser configuration, setting a target to open a new window *may* open a new tab instead.

says something like link opens new window or close new window to return. In Hour 18, "Adding Interactivity with Behaviors," you learn how to use a Dreamweaver behavior to open a new window. You can use JavaScript to set the window size.

FIGURE 16.11
The _blank reserved target name in the Target drop-down menu in the Property inspector opens the link in a new browser window. The original document remains open.

Summary

In this hour, you learned about various navigation objects you can add to your web pages and how to best organize navigation. You created menu bars with CSS. You learned how to modify the CSS for Spry menu bars. You also learned how to open new browser windows with a link.

Q&A

Q. Do I have to use Spry menu bars to create navigation in my page?

A. No, not at all. These are just shortcuts that speed up your development. You can use a combination of images, links, and CSS to create the primary and secondary page navigation. Also, many of Dreamweaver's built-in CSS layouts include simpler navigation that doesn't use Spry for the fancy drop-down and pull-out effects if you'd like a more basic option.

Q. I know you said navigation with image rollovers is out of style, but I want to use images in my navigation so I can do cool fonts and fancy icons. What should I do?

A. Although this hour focused on text-based CSS menus, CSS can also be used to create rollover images in a clean, modern way. Unlike old-style image rollovers, which we briefly discussed in Hour 8, CSS rollovers don't use JavaScript, and instead opt for CSS positioning rules to hide and show the appropriate image. A nice summary can be found at http://www.webvamp.co.uk/blog/coding/css-image-rollovers/.

Q. How do I open a web page in a new browser window without the browser toolbars and menus or set to a specific size?

A. In Hour 18, you learn how to use the Open Browser Window behavior to create a link that opens a new browser window in a given size and without any of the browser navigation or menus.

Workshop

Quiz

1. What's the difference between primary and secondary navigation in a website?

2. How many Sprymenu bars can you have per web page?

3. What is the name of the JavaScript framework, included with Dreamweaver, that enables you to insert menu bars?

Quiz Answers

1. The primary navigation is the navigation that moves visitors around the major (and minor) sections of the website. The secondary navigation contains less frequently used items that are important to only a subset of visitors (such as those looking for privacy policy information or those who would like to apply for a job).

2. You can have as many menus as make sense.

3. The Spry framework is the JavaScript framework that enables you to insert menu bars.

Exercises

1. Create a vertical or horizontal Spry menu bar (or both!) and customize the CSS. Modify the font and background colors or the default menu display and the hover display. How do you think you could change the font for the whole menu?

2. Create a couple of pages and link them together. Practice setting their target link attributes and then test them in your several browsers to see how new windows or new tabs are created.

Using Dynamic HTML and AP Divs

Dreamweaver's AP (absolutely positioned) divs provide a way to control the placement of objects on the page with pixel-perfect accuracy. You can place items precisely where you want them, absolutely positioned on the page.

You don't have to pick between regular divs and AP divs. You can use both in a web page, taking advantage of the strengths of each. In Hour 12, "Using CSS for Positioning," you used div tags as containers for the web page content. You placed these divs relative to one another, stacked up like boxes in a store. AP divs are autonomous, can be moved individually, and can be placed anywhere on the page. In this hour, you experiment with AP divs and compare them to what you learned about div tags in Hour 12.

One of the great things about AP divs is that you can use them with Dreamweaver behaviors, which you learn more about in Hour 18, "Adding Interactivity with Behaviors."

What Is DHTML?

DHTML enables you to create an interactive experience for the web page user. DHTML isn't an official term; it's a term used by web developers to refer to a collection of technologies used to produce a more interactive web page. The two main components of DHTML are HTML Cascading Style Sheets (CSS; see Hour 11, "Formatting Web Pages Using Cascading Style Sheets") and JavaScript (see Hours 18 and 19, "Using Spry, the Widget Browser, and Extensions").

DHTML allows greater interactivity without depending on interaction with a server. When people talk about DHTML, they usually mean the combination of HTML 4 (as defined by the W3C [World Wide Web Consortium]

WHAT YOU'LL LEARN IN THIS HOUR:

▶ What AP divs are, how they work, and how they are used

▶ How to add an AP div and position it on the page

▶ How to set the stacking order, background color, and visibility of an AP div

Web standards organization) and CSS. These elements work together through a scripting language called JavaScript.

Here's a short list of the types of things you can accomplish using DHTML:

▶ Insert hidden images that appear when the user clicks a button or a hotspot.

▶ Create pop-up menus.

▶ Enable the user to drag and drop an object around the screen at will.

▶ Cause text to change color or size when the user rolls her mouse over it.

▶ Rpeatedly load text into an area of the screen as feedback to the user. For instance, if the user clicks the wrong answer in a quiz, you can give feedback and then replace that feedback when the user gets the answer right.

In this hour, you experiment with **AP divs**, the containers that enable you to position items on the screen wherever you want. These elements are a critical part of the DHTML toolbox.

Adding an AP Div

AP divs are containers that you use to position content on a web page. The term *AP divs* is a Dreamweaver expression, and if you speak with other web developers who aren't using Dreamweaver, they won't know what you mean. *AP divs* is short for "absolutely positioned div," meaning a div tag that is positioned at a precise x and y position on the screen. As you learned in Hour 12, the div tag logically divides a web page into sections.

AP divs have two very interesting attributes:

▶ **Visibility**—This property enables you to hide all the content in an AP div and then trigger its appearance when the user performs an action on the screen. For instance, you can simulate a click on a menu in a software program. The AP div holding the menu image initially hides. When the user clicks a menu title on the screen, a script changes the visibility of the menu AP div from hidden to visible.

▶ **Z-index**—This property controls the stacking order of all the AP divs on the page. You can stack AP divs on top of one another (overlapping) and control which one is on top. This gives you the power to create complicated designs.

You can create an AP div in Dreamweaver in two ways:

▶ The simplest way is to select the Draw AP Div object from the Layout category of the Insert panel, as shown in Figure 17.1, and drag the cross-hair cursor on your page to approximately the desired AP div size.

▶ Select Insert, Layout Objects, AP Div to insert an AP div.

Drag handle

Resizing handles   AP div   Insert Layout Objects panel

FIGURE 17.1
Selecting the Draw AP Div object from the Insert panel enables you to draw an AP div by dragging the cross-hair cursor.

The AP Elements category in the Preferences dialog box, shown in Figure 17.2, is where you can set default AP div values. You set the default visibility, width, height, background color, and background image. If you have a standard AP div size that you use often, you might want to set that size as the default in this dialog box. You can also enable nesting by checking the Nesting check box, as we will use it later in this hour.

Notice resizing handles on each border of your AP div: You can drag these handles to make your AP div bigger or smaller. You can also set the width and height of the AP div in the Property inspector. The W and H properties in the Property inspector are the width and height, respectively, of the AP div. The default measurement unit is pixels.

It's always a good idea to name your AP divs. When you start adding behaviors, names help you identify specific AP divs. By default, Dreamweaver adds the name "apDiv" followed by a number; this obviously isn't very useful if you need to find a specific AP div among dozens. You can specify a name in the CSS-P Element box in the Property inspector (such as mapLegend), as shown in Figure 17.3. The name is actually a CSS

CAUTION

Unpredictable Placement of AP Div

You might be thinking, "Wow, AP divs are so easy to use. I should use them for the layout of my web pages!" Unfortunately, various browsers can display the position of AP divs differently, so it's difficult to perfectly calculate where an AP div should be placed when you're developing a web page.

You should also keep in mind that absolutely placed divs make assumptions about your users' browser sizes. Unlike relatively placed elements, AP divs cannot adapt to different screen sizes.

Stick to using relatively placed divs for page layout and use the occasional AP div for a special purpose.

TIP

No Punctuation in AP Div Names

Don't use spaces or punctuation in AP div names. If you later apply a behavior to the AP div, sometimes JavaScript isn't happy with spaces or punctuation in an AP div name. If you want to name your AP div with multiple words, you can use capitalization or underscores to make the name readable. For instance, RedRose and white_lily are possible AP div names.

ID, which can be used to specifically refer to that AP Div. Remember, IDs can only be used once per page.

You can also name Dreamweaver AP divs in the AP Elements panel, opened from the Window menu. Double-click the name in the AP Elements panel ID column until it becomes editable and then type in a new name. Notice that when you select an AP div in the AP Elements panel, you select the AP div in the Document window also.

Setting AP Div Positioning

An AP div has a drag handle in the upper-left corner. You can reposition an AP div by picking it up and moving it with this handle. To select multiple AP divs, hold down the Shift key while clicking AP divs to add them to the selection. You can also use the arrow keys on your keyboard to move a selected AP div.

Use the AP Elements panel to select one or many AP divs. The AP Elements panel enables you not only to select AP divs, but also to see and set some AP div properties. You learn about the two properties that you can set—the z-index and the visibility—in a few minutes. Notice that you can enable a check box at the top of the AP Elements panel to prevent overlaps. If you find you cannot place your AP divs on top of one another, you probably have selected the Prevent Overlaps check box.

You can use the drag handle to drag an AP div anywhere on the screen, or you can use the Property inspector to set the AP div's exact positioning. The L and T properties stand for the left (the offset from the left edge of the page) and top (the offset from the top edge of the page). These positions are relative to the entire browser window. You can move an AP div by dragging it with its drag handle, or you can position it exactly by entering values in the L and T boxes, as shown in Figure 17.3 above.

Adding a Background Color and Background Image

An AP div can have a background color, as shown in Figure 17.4. You can use the color picker or type in a color in the standard HTML hexadecimal format, preceded by #. Make sure that you leave the Bg Color option blank if you want your AP div to be transparent. If your page background is white and you make your AP div background white, your AP div seems as if it's transparent until you position it over something else!

You can also place a background image in an AP div. The image repeats multiple times (called **tiling**) within the AP div if the AP div is larger than the image. Objects and text that you put within the AP div are on top of the background image. Click the Browse icon (the folder) beside the Bg Image box in the Property inspector and navigate to the background image file. Figure 17.4 also shows the Property inspector when a selected AP div contains a background image.

Exploring AP Div Stacking Order

Not only can you position AP divs in exact places on the page, but you also can allow AP divs to overlap one another. So which AP div is on top? The stacking order decides which AP div is on top of other AP divs. The **z-index**

TIP

Use the Drag Handle

Get in the habit of moving AP divs by picking up the drag handle. It's very easy to accidentally move items contained in an AP div instead of moving the AP div itself. If you become accustomed to using the handle, you won't make that mistake. If you can't use the drag handle because the AP div is at the very top of the Document window, select the AP div in the AP Elements panel and use the arrow keys to move it. Alternatively, you can enter positioning values in the Property inspector.

TIP

Where Did the AP Div Properties Go?

If you don't see AP div properties in the Property inspector, it's because you don't have an AP div selected. You might have accidentally selected the contents of the AP div instead of selecting the AP div itself.

To select an AP div, click the outline or the drag handle.

value, in turn, determines the stacking order. The z-index can be either a negative or a positive number.

FIGURE 17.4
An AP div can have a background color or a background image.

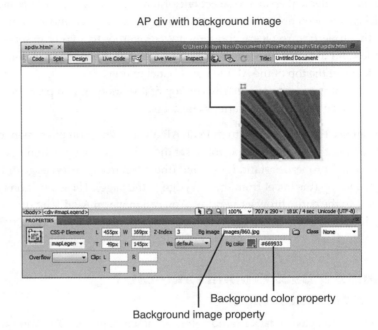

AP div with background image

Background color property
Background image property

The AP div with the highest z-index value is the one on the top. The term *z-index* comes from the coordinate system that you used back in geometry class—remember x and y coordinates? The x-axis is horizontal and the y-axis is vertical. Well, the z-axis is the third coordinate that is necessary to describe three-dimensional space. Imagine an arrow coming out of the paper or screen toward you and another going back into the screen or paper. That is the z-axis.

Dreamweaver gives each AP div a unique z-index value. In HTML, you can legally have multiple AP divs that have the same z-index. Remember, though, that if you reorder the AP divs, Dreamweaver renumbers each with a unique z-index. So why waste your time?

You can set the z-index in the Z-Index box in the Property inspector, as labeled in Figure 17.3. The AP Elements panel displays the z-index to the right of each AP div's name. This panel displays the AP divs in order according to their z-index value, with the top being the highest z-index and the bottom being the lowest. You can easily rearrange the stacking order by selecting the AP div name in the AP Elements panel and then dragging and dropping it somewhere else.

Changing AP Div Visibility

AP divs have a visibility attribute that can be set to Visible, Hidden, Inherit, or Default. The Vis drop-down menu, as shown in Figure 17.5, is in the middle of the Property inspector when you select an AP div. These are the visibility settings:

▶ **Default**—The Default setting is the same as the Inherit setting in most browsers.

▶ **Inherit**—An AP div set to Inherit has the same visibility as its parent. You learn more about nesting and parent AP divs in a few minutes. If you set the parent to Hidden, and you set the AP div nesting within that parent to Inherit, the nested element hides also.

▶ **Visible**—An AP div set to Visible appears on the web page at loading.

▶ **Hidden**—An AP div set to Hidden does not appear on the web page. You can later make the AP div visible by using the Show-Hide Elements behavior.

Vis drop-down menu

FIGURE 17.5
The Vis drop-down menu enables you to set the visibility attribute for an AP div.

Why you might want AP divs to be visible is obvious, but why might you want them to hide? So that you can display them later, after something has happened! You learn about using the Show-Hide Elements behavior in Hour 18.

The AP Elements panel represents visibility with a picture of an eye. The eye beside an AP div is open if you set the AP div to Visible. The eye is closed if you set the AP div to Hidden. The Inherit setting does not have an eye representation. The Eye icon is a toggle that moves through the Default, Visible, and Hidden settings and then goes back to Default. You can set the visibility characteristics of all the AP divs by clicking the Eye icon in the header of the AP Elements panel.

CAUTION

Don't Accidentally Click the Eye Icon Column Header

Be careful when clicking the Eye icon for your top AP div. It's easy to accidentally click the header instead and set all the eyes in the column. You have to click in the Eye column *beside* the AP div for which you want to set the Visibility property.

Nesting AP Divs

You can create an AP div within another AP div; the new AP div nests within its parent AP div. If you move the parent AP div, the child AP div moves with it. The child AP div also inherits its parent's visibility attributes.

To create a nested AP div, make sure you have enabled nesting in the AP Elements preferences as described at the beginning of this hour. Then, place the cursor inside the parent AP div and choose Insert, AP Div. You draw a nested AP div by using the Draw AP Div object to draw inside an existing AP div while holding down the Ctrl key (the Command key on the Mac). In addition, you can place an existing AP div within another AP div by picking it up in the AP Elements panel while holding down the Ctrl key (or the Command key on the Mac) and then dropping it into another AP div. The nested AP div appears indented in the AP Elements panel, as shown in Figure 17.6.

Nested AP Divs

The easiest way to unnest an AP div if you make a mistake or change your mind is to pick it up in the AP Elements panel and drop it somewhere else in the list of AP divs.

Animating an AP Div

In Hour 18, we take a look at how behaviors can be applied to divs and other elements to create effects. For now, let's take a look at how you can create a simple animation.

TIP

Can't Draw? Check Prevent Overlaps

If Dreamweaver doesn't seem to allow you to draw a nested AP div by holding down the Ctrl key, you probably have the Prevent Overlaps check box enabled at the top of the AP Elements panel.

FIGURE 17.6
An AP div nested within another AP div appears indented in the AP Elements panel.

CAUTION

Where Did the AP Divs Go?

Did your AP div disappear from the screen when you unnested it? When an AP div is nested, its position is relative to its parent. When you unnest the AP div, its position is then relative to the page instead of the div that had contained it. The AP div's coordinates might cause the AP div to be off the screen. To fix this problem, select the AP div in the AP Elements panel and give it L (left) and T (top) attributes that place it back on the screen.

AP divs are unique because they are aligned to absolute coordinates. These coordinates can be manipulated through JavaScript to produce onscreen animations. By changing the top and left coordinates of a div, you can move it anywhere on the screen.

Follow these steps to create your own animated AP Div:

1. Add a new AP div to your web page and make sure that it is named apDiv1.

2. Add content to the div so that it is visible.

3. Switch your document to code view, and then add the following JavaScript code to the <head> portion of your document:

```
<script type="text/javascript">
var start=10;
var increment=10;
var stop=500;
var y=start;
function down() {
     object=document.getElementById('apDiv1');
     y=y+increment;
     object.style.top=(y+'px');
     if (y<stop) {
          timer=setTimeout("down()",20);
     }
}
</script>
```

4. Finally, add a link to the document that triggers the animation (for example, "click here to animate"). The link should point to javascript: down();, which triggers the animation. Figure 17.7 shows a split view of the code and the design screen with all elements in place.

5. Save the file and switch to Design mode, Live View, or Preview in your browser. When you click the link, the AP div scrolls smoothly down the page.

Animating an AP Div
Continued

FIGURE 17.7
Animate an AP div with JavaScript.

Although the intricacies of JavaScript are beyond the scope of this book, this animation is very simple to understand. A single block of code, called a function, creates the animation. In this case, the function is called down() and is called when you click the link in the document.

To generate the moving div, the down() function simply increases the top (object.style.top) coordinate of the div from a starting point of 10px to a stopping point of 500px in increments of 10. As long as the stopping point hasn't been reached, the animation keeps running, pausing 20 milliseconds in between each move.

There are hundreds of DHTML JavaScripts that work with divs that you can add to your own pages. Googling "JavaScript Div animation" is a good place to start.

Summary

In this hour, you learned how to insert an AP div into a web page. You learned how to change an AP div's name, size, position, and background color. You explored setting the stacking order, or z-index, of AP divs and setting an AP div's visibility. You also learned how to create a simple JavaScript-based div animation.

Q&A

Q. How do AP divs differ from the div tags I use with CSS for page layout?

A. CSS defines **box elements**, which is what both AP divs and div tags are. When creating a page layout, you often leave the CSS properties applied to a div with the default positioning, which is relative. Relative positioning means that a div appears according to its position in the code; the div before it in the code appears above it on the page. AP divs have the positioning property set to absolute, which means that regardless of where the div tag appears in the code, the div and its content appear at a certain position—a particular number of pixels from the left and a particular number of pixels from the top of the web page.

Q. Why would I want to use AP divs in my web pages?

A. If you'd like to have some content overlapping or sitting on top of other content, you have to use AP divs and set their z-index values higher than the underlying content's z-index. Alternatively, if you want to hide an image or text on the screen and show it later by using the Show-Hide Elements behavior (see Hour 18), you have to use AP divs.

Workshop

Quiz

1. AP divs cannot be used to create animation. True or false?

2. What is the tag used to implement AP divs?

3. The AP div with the lowest z-index is the one on the top. True or false?

Quiz Answers

1. False. AP divs, because they can be positioned anywhere onscreen, are ideal for animation effects.

2. The `<div>` tag implements AP divs, just like for regular divs.

3. False. The AP div with the highest z-index is the one on top.

Exercises

1. Create a web page that has multiple AP divs. Experiment with inserting images and text into the AP divs. Change the background color of one of the AP divs. Be sure to make a few of the AP divs overlap so that you can see how the z-index works.

2. Create a banner and a navigation bar for a site by placing an AP div across the top of the site for the banner. Place individual AP divs with the text Home, Previous, and Next in them. You can make these hyperlinks if you like.

3. Visit the website http://script.aculo.us/ to explore the Scriptaculous JavaScript framework for DHTML effects. Consider the different ways these effects could be applied to existing websites to improve or modernize the user experience.

Adding Interactivity with Behaviors

Dreamweaver behaviors add interactivity to web pages. Behaviors enable you to make something happen when the user clicks the mouse, loads a web page, or moves the cursor. Interactivity usually requires coding in JavaScript, but Dreamweaver adds all the JavaScript for you, so you don't have to understand scripting to use behaviors.

> **TIP**
>
> **JavaScript and Beyond**
>
> Use of JavaScript to make pages interactive enables many cool behaviors, as we're about to discuss. However, there's a newer way to use JavaScript for complex behaviors, namely JavaScript Frameworks and Libraries. Hour 16, "Adding Spry Menu Bars for Navigation," introduced one example, and you'll see more in Hour 19, "Using Spry, the Widget Browser, and Extensions." The examples in this hour are simple to apply and still relevant, but if you are looking to do more complex interactivity with JavaScript, check out the next hour for an introduction.

What Is a Dreamweaver Behavior?

When you add a behavior to a web page, Dreamweaver inserts JavaScript functions and function calls, enabling users to interact with the web page or make something happen. I like to think of a **function** as a little code machine—you send it some information, it processes that information, and it sends you a result or makes something happen. A **function call** is the code added to an object that triggers the function and sends it any information it needs to do its job. For instance, a popular Dreamweaver behavior is the Swap Image behavior. You actually used this behavior in Hour 8, "Displaying Images," because Dreamweaver adds the Swap Image behavior to

WHAT YOU'LL LEARN IN THIS HOUR:

- ▶ What a Dreamweaver behavior is
- ▶ How to apply a behavior to an object in a web page
- ▶ How to use behaviors to add interactivity to a web page
- ▶ How to select events to trigger behaviors
- ▶ How to create a drag-and-drop quiz

your web page automatically when you use the Rollover Image object (Insert, Image Objects, Rollover Image).

When you insert a behavior, Dreamweaver writes a function in the head of the web page. The function that controls the Swap Image behavior is MM_swapImage(). Dreamweaver doesn't call the code in that function until some event on the page triggers it; until the event triggers the function code, it just sits waiting in the head. For instance, the MM_swapImage() function is usually triggered by the onMouseOver event—the event fired when the cursor is placed over whatever object the function is attached to. When the user rolls the mouse over an image with a behavior attached, the event triggers the function, which swaps the image source with another image.

A **behavior** is an action triggered by an event. Or you could look at it this way:

> Event + Action = Behavior

Actions are the JavaScript code, the function, which Dreamweaver inserts into a web page. Browser events are user actions that the browser captures; for example, clicking a button on a web page triggers the onClick event.

Using the Reference Books

To learn more about individual events, use the Dreamweaver Reference panel (by selecting Window, Results, Reference). There are several reference books built into Dreamweaver.

TIP

Dreamweaver Terms:
Behavior and Action

The terms *behavior* and *action* are specific to Dreamweaver and are not standard HTML terminology. These terms both describe prewritten JavaScript code that Dreamweaver makes available to anyone creating web pages with Dreamweaver. It works just like any other JavaScript code.

▼ TRY IT YOURSELF

Looking Up
JavaScript Events

To find information about an event, do the following:

1. Open the Reference panel: Window, Results, Reference.

2. Select O'REILLY JavaScript Reference from the Book drop-down list.

3. Select an event name, such as onClick, onBlur, or onMouseUp, from the Object menu.

The Reference panel displays a description of the event, as shown in Figure 18.1, including which browsers support the event (in the upper-right corner) and typical targets for the event.

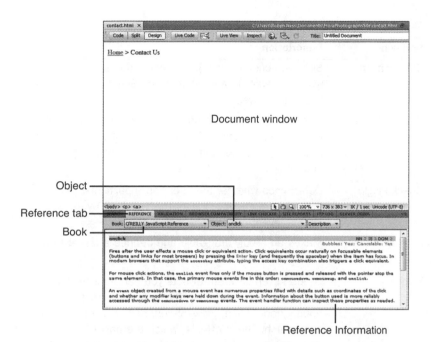

FIGURE 18.1
The Reference panel displays the JavaScript reference that includes descriptions of events.

Object

Reference tab

Book

Reference Information

To close the Results panel group that opens when you open the Reference panel, select the Close Panel Group command from the Panel Group menu on the far right of the panel group.

Exploring Dreamweaver Behaviors

Dreamweaver comes with many powerful behaviors that enable you to do some advanced web development without having to write JavaScript yourself. You access behaviors in the Behaviors panel (Window, Behaviors), as shown in Figure 18.2.

Add Behavior button

FIGURE 18.2
The Behaviors portion of the Tag Inspector panel displays a list of the events you can attach behaviors to for the object currently selected in the document window.

CAUTION

Different Behaviors

The Behaviors panel is not the same as the Server Behaviors panel. The Server Behaviors panel works with sites that use server-side scripting, such as PHP and ColdFusion. The Behaviors panel uses JavaScript, which is client-side scripting and does not rely on a server.

Various behaviors come preinstalled in Dreamweaver. Table 18.1 lists these behaviors and gives a brief description of each one.

NOTE

Tag Attributes and Behaviors

Note that the Behaviors panel is a section within the Tag Attributes panel. Because it has its own Window menu entry and acts independently from the tag attributes, we refer to it as the Behaviors panel.

TABLE 18.1   Dreamweaver Behaviors

Behavior	Description
Call JavaScript	Specifies custom JavaScript code. You use this behavior when you want to add custom JavaScript code to an object in Dreamweaver.
Change Property	Changes an object's properties. This behavior enables you to change properties of absolutely positioned (AP) divs (such as the background color or the size), form objects, and images.
Check Plugin	Determines whether the user has a particular plug-in installed. You usually trigger this behavior by using the onLoad event of the body tag.
Drag AP Element	Makes an AP div draggable and defines a target to which to drag it.
Effects	Offers seven different effects you can apply to objects such as images and divs. The different effects are appear/fade, blind, grow/shrink, highlight, shake, slide, and squish. These effects, which are part of Dreamweaver's Spry framework, are covered in Hour 19.
Go to URL	Loads a URL into the browser when the behavior triggers.
Jump Menu	Edits a jump menu. You create a jump menu in Hour 21, "Creating a Form and Collecting Data." This type of menu enables users to jump to various URLs.
Jump Menu Go	Adds a custom jump menu's Go button. This button triggers the jump to the URL selected in the jump menu.
Open Browser Window	Opens a new browser window. Developers often use this behavior to open an additional window containing extra information.
Popup Message	Pops up a JavaScript alert box with text. This box contains an OK button that the user clicks to close the message.
Preload Images	Preloads images into the browser cache in the background. This behavior is often included with the Swap Image behavior. The image to swap is loaded into the cache so that it appears quickly.
Set Text of Container	Puts text (or HTML) into a container tag, usually a div.
Set Text of Frame	Puts text (or HTML) into a frame.

TABLE 18.1   Dreamweaver Behaviors

Behavior	Description
Set Text of Status Bar	Puts text into the browser's status bar.
Set Text of Text Field	Puts text into a text field in a form. You learn more about text fields in Hour 21.
Show-Hide Elements	Shows or hides a div or group of divs. This behavior changes the div or AP div visibility attribute.
Swap Image	Swaps the image source for another image source.
Swap Image Restore	Restores a previous image swap.
Validate Form	Validates the data in a form, enabling you to check whether the user has entered information into certain text fields and validating whether it is the correct type of information. You use this behavior in Hour 22, "Sending and Reacting To Form Data."

You explore attaching a behavior to an object on a web page by using the Add Behavior button in a few minutes.

Exploring Events

Behaviors are triggered by events, as described earlier. Table 18.2 lists common browser events available in the Behaviors panel. This is just a small sampling of the available events, but luckily most of the events' names make their functionality obvious. The onDblClick event, for instance, is similar to the onClick event, except that the user clicks twice instead of once.

TABLE 18.2   Common Browser Events

Event	Description
onBlur	Triggered when an object **loses focus**; that is, it becomes inactive. The body of a web page often captures this event when the user switches to a different web page, or from a form object such as a text field or a check box.
onChange	Triggered after a user makes and commits a change to a form object, usually a text field, textarea, drop-down menu, or list. The user commits the change by leaving the form object, usually by putting the focus elsewhere on the web page.

CAUTION

What Happens When an Event Isn't Supported?

If you select an event that does not work in a certain browser, users with that browser either will have nothing happen or will receive a JavaScript error.

TABLE 18.2 Common Browser Events

Event	Description
onClick	Triggered when the user presses and releases, or clicks, a mouse button. Images or hyperlinks often capture this event.
onFocus	Triggered when an object receives focus; that is, it becomes active. For example, when a user clicks in a form object such as a text field, that field has received "focus."
onLoad	Triggered when an object or a web page finishes loading. The body of a web page often captures this event, but images occasionally use it.
onMouseDown	Triggered when the user presses a mouse button. Images or hyperlinks often capture this event.
onMouseOver	Triggered when the user places the cursor over an object. Images or hyperlinks often capture this event.
onMouseUp	Triggered when the user releases a mouse button. Images or hyperlinks often capture this event.
onSelect	Triggered when a user selects text within a form object, usually a text field or textarea.
onSubmit	Triggered when the user submits a form by using a submit button or an image button.
onUnload	Triggered when the browser unloads a web page—that is, when the user goes to a new URL or closes the browser. The body of a web page usually captures this event, which is often responsible for triggering those annoying pop-up windows that seem impossible to close.

Remember, the list of events shown in the Behaviors panel changes depending on which element of the page is selected. For instance, it doesn't make sense for an onChange event to be used outside of form elements that a site visitor can interact with.

Attaching a Behavior to an Object

You attach behaviors to objects in a web page. When you attach a behavior, Dreamweaver opens the appropriate behavior dialog box. After you've set up the behavior characteristics in the dialog box, select the event to trigger the behavior. Dreamweaver inserts the necessary JavaScript into the head of the web page. It also adds code to the object's tag to capture the event and call the JavaScript.

Every time you attach a behavior, regardless of which behavior it is, follow these general steps:

1. Create a web page and save it (File, Save).

2. Select the object on the web page that triggers the behavior—the object that the user clicks, for instance, such as a link. You can tell which object you have selected in the Document window because the top of the Behaviors panel displays its tag.

3. Select the appropriate event in the Events column of the Behaviors panel.

4. Select the appropriate behavior by clicking the Add Behavior button in the Behaviors panel and selecting a behavior from the drop-down menu.

5. Set the behavior's properties in its specific dialog box and click OK.

You must attach behaviors to appropriate objects. Dreamweaver won't let you attach inappropriate behaviors; it grays out inappropriate behaviors so that you cannot select them. Likewise, you can't attach inappropriate events to certain objects.

NOTE

The Behavior Code

When you add a behavior to an object, Dreamweaver adds an attribute to the HTML tag, enabling the tag to respond to the event. The attribute includes a function call to the appropriate function inserted by the behavior. For instance, the code for an image tag with the Show-Hide Elements behavior attached looks like this:

```
<img src="button_up.gif" width="80" height="35"
    onclick="MM_showHideLayers('apDiv1','','hide')" />
```

When a user clicks the image, the AP div named apDiv1 hides.

In the rest of the hour, you explore in detail how to attach a sampling of the behaviors available in Dreamweaver. We don't have time to cover every behavior, but you look at enough different behaviors to get the idea of how they all work. In this hour, you explore the following behaviors:

▶ Show-Hide Elements   ▶ Set Text of Container

▶ Open Browser Window   ▶ Go to URL

▶ Popup Message   ▶ Drag AP Element

Showing and Hiding Elements

Now you're ready to add your first behavior. The Show-Hide Elements behavior has a name that pretty much says it all: You can use it to show or hide an element on the web page, using a div or an AP div. You don't usually apply a behavior to the object that it affects, so you need to have another object on the page that triggers the behavior. For instance, you might create a hyperlink that triggers showing or hiding an AP div.

To begin, add an image or a hyperlink that captures the user's click and hides the AP div. Dreamweaver is smart enough to not display the Show-Hide Elements behavior in the Add Behavior drop-down menu if you don't actually have a div in the web page, so you have to add a div or an AP div to the page before you add the behavior. It's important to name your divs when using the Show-Hide Elements behavior because the Show-Hide Elements dialog box displays all the divs on the page by name, so it helps for the divs to have meaningful names.

Creating a Null Link to Trigger the Behavior

Make sure that you've already defined a site in Dreamweaver and created a new web page. First you create a link to trigger the Show-Hide Elements behavior.

▼ TRY IT YOURSELF

Creating a Null Link

Follow these steps to create a null link:

1. Add text for a hyperlink somewhere on the web page. You could enter something such as **Show the AP Div**.

2. Instead of creating an active link, you add what's called a **null link**, which is a link to nowhere. This is just so that you create a clickable object that can trigger the behavior.

   Select the text you created in step 1 and enter `javascript:;` in the Link box of the Property inspector.

Creating a Hidden AP Div

Next you create the AP div to hide when the visitor clicks the null link you created earlier. After you've created the AP div, type some text into it or give it a background color so that you can actually see it in the browser. Check out Hour 17, "Using Dynamic HTML and AP Divs," if you need a refresher on how to insert an AP div and set its properties.

To create a hidden AP div, do the following:

1. Insert an AP div (Insert, Layout Objects, AP Div).

2. Set a unique ID for the AP div.

3. Enter some text in the AP div or give it a background color in the Property inspector.

4. Select the AP div and set its Visibility attribute value to Hidden by selecting Hidden from the Vis drop-down menu in the Property inspector, as shown in Figure 18.3.

Vis property

FIGURE 18.3
The Property inspector for AP divs allows you to set the visibility.

Attaching the Show-Hide Elements Behavior

Now that you have both the object that you will show and the object that the visitor clicks to trigger the behavior, you are ready to attach the behavior.

To attach the Show-Hide Elements behavior, do the following:

1. Click anywhere within the null link you created.

2. Open the Behaviors panel (Window, Behaviors).

3. Make sure that <a> (the anchor tag that creates a link) is visible at the top of the Behaviors panel. This means that you have the correct object selected on the page.

▼ TRY IT YOURSELF

Attaching the Show-Hide Elements Behavior

Continued

FIGURE 18.4
The Add Behavior (+) button drops down the Add Behavior drop-down menu, with all the available actions for the selected object.

4. Click the Add Behavior (+) button in the Behaviors panel, as shown in Figure 18.4. Select the Show-Hide Elements behavior. The Show-Hide Elements dialog box appears.

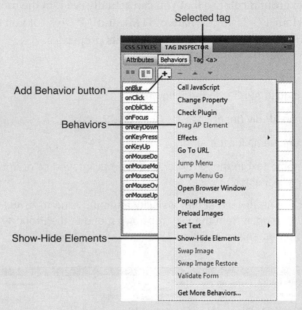

Selected tag

Add Behavior button

Behaviors

Show-Hide Elements

5. The Show-Hide Elements dialog box, shown in Figure 18.5, lists all the divs with IDs in the page. There are three buttons: Show, Hide, and Default. Highlight the correct div and click the Show button. The word *show* then appears in parentheses next to the div's name.

FIGURE 18.5
The Show-Hide Elements dialog box lists all the AP divs and enables you to change their visibility attributes.

Show indicator

Show

You click the Show button to make an AP div visible, and you click the Hide button to make an AP div hidden. When an AP div is set to show, clicking the Show button again toggles show off (the same is true for the other buttons). The Default button restores an AP div to its default visibility (visible).

6. Click the OK button to save your changes.

Selecting the Event That Triggers the Behavior

At this point, you have selected half the behavior, but you also have to select the other half of the behavior: the event. When you selected the link, the Behaviors panel listed the Show-Hide Elements behavior under the Action column, and the Event column probably defaulted to the onClick event.

You could use the onClick event to trigger showing the AP div, but that's too easy! Try using the onMouseOver event instead:

1. In the Behaviors panel, drop down the Events list by clicking the arrow button, as shown in Figure 18.6. You have to click within the event for this button to be available.

Arrow button

Events

2. Select onMouseOver in the Events drop-down menu.

   Now when users move their mouse cursor over the link, they trigger the Show-Hide Elements behavior.

TRY IT YOURSELF ▼

Setting a Trigger Event

FIGURE 18.6
The arrow button beside the event drops down a menu containing the available events.

Because you have set up the behavior (Show-Hide Elements) and the event (onMouseOver), you can now test your work! First make sure that the AP div you set to show with the behavior is hiding (if you didn't do this earlier). Preview the web page in the browser or in the Dreamweaver Live View. Mouse-over the hyperlink and your AP div should appear!

Editing the Behavior

If you made a mistake while setting up the Show-Hide Elements behavior, you can edit the behavior after it has been set.

▼ TRY IT YOURSELF

Editing a Behavior

To edit a behavior, follow these steps:

1. Select the object (probably a link) that has the behavior attached to it.

2. Double-click Show-Hide Elements in the Action column of the Behaviors panel.

3. This reopens the Show-Hide Elements dialog box where you can make changes. Make changes and click OK.

Opening a New Browser Window

Use the Open Browser Window behavior to open a new browser window and display a URL. This time you capture the user clicking an image to trigger the action. The onClick event fires when the user clicks the image. This then triggers the Open Browser Window behavior that opens a new browser window.

You can open a browser window at a specific size and with specific browser attributes. Browser attributes, listed in Table 18.3, control whether the browser window has controls that enable the user to navigate out of the window. You set up the browser attributes in the Open Browser Window dialog box.

CAUTION

Pop-up Blockers Might Block Opening a New Window

Be aware that many browsers and browser add-in programs (such as the Google and Yahoo! toolbars) add pop-up blocker functionality. Although that's great for getting rid of unwanted pop-up ads, it's not good news for opening new browser windows. Some pop-up blockers stop only windows that open when triggered by the onLoad event of the <body> tag. (You learn more about that later this hour.) More conservative blockers stop all pop-up windows, even those triggered by the user.

You might want to warn viewers that they may have to disable their pop-up blocker in order to see the information on your web page.

TABLE 18.3   Browser Properties for the Open Browser Window Behavior

Attribute	Description
URL to Display	Sets the URL of the page that opens in the new window.
Window Width	Controls the width (in pixels) of the window.
Window Height	Controls the height (in pixels) of the window.
Navigation Toolbar	Contains the Back, Next, and other navigation buttons for moving to different URLs.
Location Toolbar	Displays the current URL.
Status Bar	Displays the status bar (the bar located at the bottom of the browser). The status bar displays the loading status of a web page as well as the URL of a moused-over link.

TABLE 18.3   Browser Properties for the Open Browser Window Behavior

Attribute	Description
Menu Bar	Contains all the standard browser menus.
Scrollbars as Needed	Enables the user to scroll the browser window.
Resize Handles	Enables the user to resize the browser window.
Window Name	Specifies the optional window name. You can use this name with JavaScript to control the window, so you cannot use spaces and punctuation in the name.

TRY IT YOURSELF ▼

Using onClick to Open a New Browser Window

To have a new browser window open when the user clicks an image, follow these steps:

1. Save the web page. The Open Browser Window behavior needs the web page saved so that it knows how to build the URL that it loads in the new browser window.

2. Insert an image into this web page. Select the image, and make sure that the correct tag (the <img> tag) shows at the top of the Behaviors panel.

3. Click the + button in the Behaviors panel. Select the Open Browser Window behavior, and the Open Browser Window dialog box appears.

4. Fill in the URL that loads in the new window. You can use a web page that you created previously or load an external web page from any website.

5. Set the width and height of the window. Check the browser attributes (listed in Table 18.3) that you want the new browser window to have. Optionally, give the window a name.

6. The Open Browser Window dialog box should look something like the one shown in Figure 18.7. Click the OK button.

7. In the Behaviors panel, select the onClick event from the Events drop-down menu if it isn't selected by default.

   Preview the web page you created in a browser. (It does not work with Live View.) When you click the image, your new window should appear.

Using onClick to Open a New Browser Window

Continued

FIGURE 18.7
The Open Browser Window dialog box enables you to turn on or off various attributes of browser windows.

Popping Up a Message

Next, you add an additional behavior—a pop-up message—to the same object you used to open a browser window. You can add as many behaviors as necessary to a single object. The Popup Message behavior displays a JavaScript alert box with a message.

Using a Pop-up Message

To add the Popup Message behavior, follow these steps:

1. Select the object you applied the behavior to in the preceding section. You should see the Open Browser Window behavior listed in the Behaviors panel. Make sure that the appropriate tag appears in the title bar of the Tag panel group.

2. Click the + button and select the Popup Message behavior.

3. The Popup Message dialog box includes a text box where you type your message, as shown in Figure 18.8. Click OK after typing the message.

FIGURE 18.08
The Popup Message dialog box has a text box where you type the message that pops up for the user.

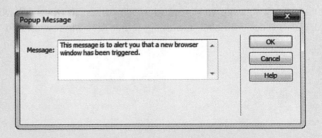

4. Select the `onClick` event as you did in the Open Browser Window dialog box earlier.

CAUTION

Don't Use `onMouseOver` with a Pop-up Message

If the `onMouseOver` event triggers the Popup Message action, the browser never receives an `onClick` event to trigger the other actions you attached to the object. Be selective when you choose which actions to apply, especially when they are triggered by the same object.

TRY IT YOURSELF ▼

Using a Pop-up Message

Continued

Attaching Multiple Behaviors to the Same Object

You can attach multiple behaviors to an object. One event can trigger several actions. In Figure 18.9, you can see that the `onClick` event triggers multiple actions. The actions happen in the order listed. You can change the order in which the actions occur by moving them with the up- and down-arrow buttons on the Behaviors panel.

Arrow buttons (reorder)

Events

Actions

FIGURE 18.9
One event—for example, the `onClick` event shown here—can trigger multiple actions, and you can have multiple behaviors attached to a single object in a web page. You can change the execution order of the behaviors by using the arrow buttons.

Preview your web page with the two behaviors, Open Browser Window and Popup Message, in the browser. Does it work perfectly? It would probably be better if the message popped up and then the user went to the new window after clicking the OK button in the message box. You can change the order of behaviors triggered by the same event.

To change the order of the behaviors, follow these steps:

1. Select the object to which the behaviors are applied. You should see both behaviors listed in the Behaviors panel.

2. Select the Popup Message behavior. Click the up-arrow button to move the Popup Message behavior above the Open Browser Window behavior.

Preview your web page in the browser again. Now the pop-up message appears first. After you click the OK button on the pop-up message, the new browser window should appear.

Setting Text in a Container

You can insert behaviors that write to various objects: frames, divs (containers, links, paragraphs, or other containers), text entry fields, and the browser status bar.

To use the Set Text of Container behavior, follow these steps:

1. Add an AP div, a div, or another container to the web page and give it the ID **feedback**.

2. Select an object on the web page to trigger the behavior. You can add this behavior to the same object you used earlier this hour or you can add a null link to an object on any web page.

3. Click the + button in the Behaviors panel. Choose the Set Text of Container behavior from the Set Text submenu—the menu that appears when you place your mouse over Set Text in the Add Behavior drop-down menu. The Set Text of Container dialog box appears.

4. Select the container named "feedback" from the drop-down menu.

5. Enter some text in the New HTML text box, as shown in Figure 18.10. Click OK.

6. Select the onClick event from the Events drop-down menu in the Behaviors panel if it wasn't selected by default.

FIGURE 18.10
The Set Text of Container dialog box enables you to enter text (and HTML) to display in the specified container.

TRY IT YOURSELF ▼

Using the Set Text of Container Behavior
Continued

Preview the web page in your browser or in Live View. When you trigger the action, the text you entered appears in the container in place of any text that was there.

Using the Go to URL Behavior

The Go to URL behavior enables to you load a URL into the existing browser window. You might choose to use this behavior instead of simply using a link if you want to trigger other behaviors before the visitor goes to the link. For instance, you could first trigger a pop-up message telling users that they are leaving your website before linking them to another web page using the Go to URL behavior.

TRY IT YOURSELF ▼

Using the Go to URL Behavior

To use the Go to URL behavior, follow these steps:

1. Select that object that triggers the behavior. Make sure that the correct tag appears in the Tag panel group title bar.

2. Type `javascript:;` in the Link box in the Property inspector to create a null link.

3. In the Behaviors drop-down menu, select Go to URL.

4. The Go to URL dialog box opens. Enter a URL in the URL box.

5. Click OK to save the behavior settings.

6. Preview the page in a browser.

Adding Drag and Drop with a Draggable AP Div

The Drag AP Element behavior enables you to create AP divs that the user can drag around the browser window. You can even constrain the area within which the user can drag the AP div. This capability is useful for creating sliders, puzzles, dialog boxes, and other interactions.

You can use the Drag AP Element behavior to let users interact with objects on your web page. For instance, you might have an AP div that contains a map legend. You could make that AP div draggable so that the user can move it out of the way if it blocks part of the map. Or you could create a blank face and let people drag different noses, ears, eyes, and so on onto the face.

The Drag AP Element behavior enables users to drag an AP div. You have to turn on this behavior in a surrounding container, such as the body tag, before a user can drag the AP div. For instance, this behavior can trigger when the web page loads by capturing the body tag's onLoad event.

After you've created your Drag AP Element and given it a name, you're ready to apply the Drag AP Element behavior.

NOTE

The <body> Tag Holds Everything Visible

You might notice that when you select the <body> tag, you also select everything in your web page. That's because the <body> tag is the container within which all the objects on your web page reside.

▼ TRY IT YOURSELF

Creating a Draggable Div

To use the Drag AP Element behavior, follow these steps:

1. Add an AP div to a web page (Insert, Layout Objects, AP Div) and give it a unique ID. Add text or a background color.

2. Save your page.

3. Select the body tag from the tag selector in the Dreamweaver status bar.

4. Make sure the <body> tag appears in the Behaviors panel, click the Add Behavior (+) button, and select Drag AP Element. The Drag AP Element dialog box appears, as shown in Figure 18.11.

5. From the AP Element drop-down menu, select the name of the AP div to drag.

6. Click OK to save your changes.

7. Make sure that the onLoad event is listed in the Behaviors panel next to the Drag AP Element action. This means the Drag AP Element behavior triggers when the web page loads.

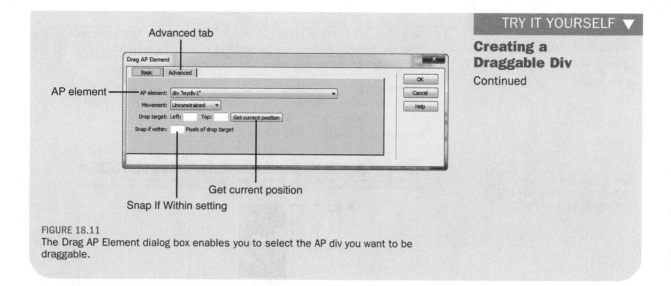

Advanced tab

AP element

Get current position

Snap If Within setting

FIGURE 18.11
The Drag AP Element dialog box enables you to select the AP div you want to be
draggable.

TRY IT YOURSELF ▼

**Creating a
Draggable Div**
Continued

Check to see that the Drag AP Element behavior is working the way you
want it to by previewing the web page in a browser or activating
Dreamweaver's Live View. The correct AP div should be draggable.

Enabling Drag and Drop

A draggable AP div is, obviously, of questionable value on most web pages.
To make things a bit more interesting, we can create a full drag-and-drop
quiz using this same behavior. This is possible thanks to some additional
options in the Drag AP Element behavior. Specifically, we can choose a
"Drop Target" for the div. A Drop Target is a predefined location where the
div should be dropped. We can also call some simple JavaScript if an object
is really close to its Drop Target, making it possible to tell a user if they've
successfully dragged and dropped a div.

Let's go ahead and try this now by making a simple three-item drag-and-
drop matching game using pictures and colors.

TIP

Can't Find the Behavior?

If you do not see the behavior
attached to the <body> tag
when you select it, you've
applied the behavior to the
wrong tag. You have to hunt
down the object to which you
applied the behavior and delete
that behavior in the Behaviors
panel. As you click objects in
the Document window, look at
the Behaviors panel to see
which object has the behavior
attached to it.

To create a simple drag-and-drop game, entirely in Dreamweaver, just follow
these steps:

   1. First, create an AP div with the ID **choices** the images that serve as the
       "answers" to this exercise.

TRY IT YOURSELF ▼

**Creating a Drag-and-
Drop Game**

Creating a Drag-and-Drop Game

Continued

FIGURE 18.12
Set up your display so that it looks the way you'd expect if all the answers are correct.

2. Add three AP divs to your document. Within each div, place the word that should be matched with one of the photos. Name each div using the word it contains.

3. Before doing anything else, position the three AP divs exactly where you'd like them to be when the user has successfully solved the puzzle—presumably right beside the photo they describe. Your screen should look similar to that shown in Figure 18.12.

4. Now you're ready to add the Drag AP Element behavior. As you did before, select the body tag and add the Drag AP Element behavior.

5. In the Drag AP Element configuration screen, select one of your AP elements that contains a word.

6. Click the button Get Current Position, as shown in Figure 18.11 above, to enter the drop target. This indicates that this is the correct location for where the item should end up when the user is finished dragging it.

7. Enter a value of **50** in the Snap if Within field. This allows the user to be a little bit off in their drag. If they're within 50 pixels of the correct location, the element snaps into place.

8. Now it's time to provide some feedback for a successful drag and drop. Click the Advanced tab in the Drag AP Element dialog box.

9. In the line that says When Dropped: Call JavaScript, enter the text **alert('You are correct!');**. This simple function displays a message to the user.

10. Leave the Only if Snapped box checked—this ensures that the user dropped the item in the right place. The advanced settings should resemble those shown in Figure 18.13.

Execute JavaScript on successful drop

11. Repeat these same steps (4–10) for your other two AP divs.

12. Now, the final (and fun!) step. Mix up the AP divs! Drag them anywhere on the page. This is their starting location.

TRY IT YOURSELF ▼

Creating a Drag-and-Drop Game
Continued

FIGURE 18.13
The advanced settings can be used to execute a JavaScript function if a successful drop takes place.

Whew! It was a bit of work, but the end result is pretty cool! You can preview your page in a web browser or use Live View to try it out.

When the page loads, your AP divs are wherever you placed them in step 12. You can then drag each word so that it matches up with its definition. If you get close enough, it snaps into place and you see the pop-up message "You are correct!"

Summary

In this hour, you learned that a Dreamweaver behavior consists of an event that triggers an action. You used the Show-Hide Elements, Open Browser Window, Popup Message, Set Text in Container, Go to URL, and Drag AP Element behaviors. You captured events from a hyperlink and an image. And you used the onMouseOver, onClick, and onLoad events as triggers for Dreamweaver actions.

Q&A

Q. How can I apply a behavior to a hidden AP div?

A. Hidden AP divs are tricky to select because you can't see them within the document window. However, you can select a hidden AP div in the AP Elements panel. Switch to the Behaviors panel, without selecting anything else, and apply the behavior. Or you can temporarily make the AP div visible, apply the behavior, and then hide the AP div again.

Q. How can I create a button that triggers a behavior?

A. We cover forms and buttons in Hour 21. Basically, you place a button into the web page to trigger a behavior. You insert a button from the Forms tab of the Insert panel. If Dreamweaver asks whether you'd like to add a `<form>` tag, you can click Yes. The trick is to make sure that the button is not a Submit or Reset button. Select the None radio button in the Property inspector and then apply a behavior to the button.

Q. Where can I learn more about JavaScript?

A. You can learn JavaScript from some excellent resources and tutorials on the Web. You don't have to understand everything about JavaScript to use it. The short statements that you used during this hour should be easy to find in any JavaScript book or reference. You might want to start out with *Sams Teach Yourself JavaScript in 24 Hours, Fourth Edition*, by Michael Moncur; ISBN: 0672328798.

Workshop

Quiz

1. What is the equation that connects an event, an action, and a behavior?

2. What two events add up to an onClick event?

3. You can only attach one behavior to each object in a page. True or false?

Quiz Answers

1. This is the equation that connects an event, an action, and a behavior:

   Event + Action = Behavior

2. An onClick event consists of the onMouseDown and onMouseUp events.

3. False. You can add multiple behaviors to a single object and set the order in which they occur.

Exercises

1. Create a second hyperlink for the Show-Hide Elements example that you created earlier in the hour. Type `Hide the AP Div`, make it a hyperlink, and make clicking this hyperlink hide the AP div you created.

2. Try using some behaviors that are similar to the behaviors you used in this hour (for example, the Set Text of Status Bar behavior). What events are available for these behaviors? What objects must you have on the web page for these behaviors to work?

3. Create an AP div and make it draggable by attaching the Drag AP Element behavior to the body tag. Figure out how to constrain the AP div's movement to only horizontal (select Constrained from the Drag AP Element dialog box). Check the web page by previewing it in a browser. Then try constraining the movement to only vertical. Finally, constrain the movement to an area.

Using Spry, the Widget Browser, and Extensions

You now know all the prerequisites necessary to understand AJAX and Dreamweaver's built-in AJAX widget library, Spry. These tools can be used to create dynamic website interfaces that look and feel like more traditional desktop applications. You actually used a little bit of this already when you created the menu bar in Hour 16, "Adding Spry Menu Bars for Navigation." In this hour, you will learn more about Spry, as well as how you can add new Spry-like widgets to your application via the Widget Browser, or by linking external AJAX frameworks.

You'll also learn how to expand Dreamweaver beyond simple widgets using the Extension Manager. Extensions can add dramatic new capabilities to the CS5 software—everything from online course authoring to support for new programming languages.

Understanding AJAX and Widgets

AJAX—Asynchronous JavaScript and XML—is a collection of technologies that create modern application-like interfaces on websites. Originally, AJAX was conceived as a way of dynamically updating portions of a web page (such as a div) using JavaScript and XML data exchanged with a server. A well-known example of AJAX is Google Maps (http://maps.google.com). You can zoom or drag the map to a different location while staying on the same web page.

Although dynamic updates are still the primary purpose of AJAX, its popular definition has been relaxed to include virtually any web elements that are dynamically generated or manipulated using JavaScript and CSS. Fancy menus (like those in Hour 16) are just the beginning of what is possible with AJAX.

WHAT YOU'LL LEARN IN THIS HOUR:

▶ About the various widgets available in Dreamweaver CS5

▶ How the external JavaScript and CSS files support the Spry Widget framework

▶ How to apply Spry effects

▶ How to use XML and HTML as data sources for Spry elements

▶ How to install and use the Dreamweaver Widget Browser

▶ How to install and manage Dreamweaver Extensions

In Dreamweaver CS5, Adobe refers to distinct AJAX user interface elements as *widgets*. Widgets can be anything from drop-down menus to image viewers, to interactive calendars.

As you might guess, widgets aren't trivial to program. They require an in-depth knowledge of how browsers structure their information (called a DOM, or Document Object Model), JavaScript, and CSS—at a minimum. More complex AJAX widgets communicate with a server to send and receive information and update the browser display as the user works within the interface. In short, the technology is daunting to learn and use from scratch!

The good news is that there are *many* interesting AJAX widgets that you can reuse in your pages without writing any code. In this hour, we look at Adobe's home-grown option Spry, external widgets that you can download by way of the Widget Browser, and finally an external AJAX widget that creates a popular "lightbox" effect. You'll discover that you can do some amazing things with just a few clicks in the Dreamweaver CS5 interface.

Exploring Spry

Dreamweaver CS5 includes a collection of AJAX widgets collectively called "Spry." All you need to do to access it is to insert one of the Spry widgets available in both the Spry category of the Insert panel and the Spry sub-menu of the Insert menu. When you insert a widget, Dreamweaver either inserts the appropriate code into your web page or opens a dialog box if there are settings required for the widget.

Spry can be added to new or existing web pages. After you insert a Spry widget into your web page, you are prompted to save supporting files when you save that page. These supporting files are external JavaScript files that end in the .js file extension. Some Spry widgets also insert external CSS files that end in the .css file extension. These files are necessary for the Spry widgets to work and must remain in your website. The Spry framework enables you to accomplish the following five types of tasks:

▶ **Visual effects**—Several visual effects are available through the Behaviors panel. Users trigger these effects by interacting with an object on the web page (such as clicking a button or a link).

▶ **XML and HTML presentation**—These widgets enable you to present data extracted from an external XML (Extensible Markup Language) data file or HTML table in a web page.

▶ **Form validation**—These widgets are special form objects that can validate whether appropriate information has been selected or entered (covered in Hour 22, "Sending and Reacting To Form Data").

▶ **Navigation**—The menu bar widget creates a CSS-based menu bar that enables a visitor to navigate to sections of the website (covered in Hour 16).

▶ **Content presentation**—The Tabbed Panels, Collapsible Panel, and Accordion widgets enable you to present content in a condensed way. The ToolTip widget makes it easy to attach small pieces of helpful content to other objects.

An example of what you can do with Spry is shown in Figure 19.1. This application was created by the Adobe Labs (check it out for yourself at http://labs.adobe.com/technologies/spry/demos/gallery/). It's a photo gallery displaying photos based on XML data. The small thumbnails on the left grow when you roll your mouse over them. Effects available in the Behaviors panel make this possible. When you click a link, the larger image appears on the right side of the page.

NOTE

Spry Is Client-Side

The beauty of the Spry framework, and the reason this book covers it, is that these advanced functionalities are client-side instead of server-side. **(That means it runs in users' browsers.)** Previously, web pages could accomplish complex form validation, navigation, and XML presentation only by interacting with the server using a server-side scripting language such as PHP.

FIGURE 19.1
A sample application of the Spry framework is found in this photo-gallery example from Adobe Labs.

When you add a new image to the photo gallery, you don't open the page in Dreamweaver, add another thumbnail, and link it to a larger image. Instead, you add another record to the XML file listing links to all the thumbnail

CAUTION

Spry Browser Requirements

Visitors must be using a modern web browser for Spry to work. The latest versions of Safari, Chrome, Firefox, and Internet Explorer have no problems executing Spry code.

images and the larger version of that image. The Spry widget reads this updated XML file, including the data about the new image, and presents all the thumbnails listed in the XML file.

External JavaScript and CSS Files

A library of JavaScript files is what makes the Spry widgets and effects work. Dreamweaver knows which external JavaScript files it must copy into your website; the files required depends on the widget or effect you are using. When you save a page containing Spry widgets, Dreamweaver prompts you to copy dependent files, as shown in Figure 19.2.

When you click the OK button, agreeing to copy dependent files, Dreamweaver creates a directory called `SpryAssets` in the root of your site. It then copies the external JavaScript and CSS files into that directory.

Dreamweaver also adds a link to the necessary external files in the head of the web page that uses Spry. Some Spry widgets might require links to multiple CSS and JavaScript files. Some might also insert JavaScript functions in the head of your web page.

TIP

No File Prompt?

If you aren't prompted to save the supporting files when you insert a Spry widget, it's because they are already present. Dreamweaver prompts you only the first time you insert the widget. Dreamweaver detects when the files already exist in your file structure and links to those existing files.

FIGURE 19.2
Dreamweaver prompts you to copy dependent files, the scripts and images that are necessary for the Spry widget to work.

> **Copy Dependent Files**
>
> This page uses an object or behavior that requires supporting files. The following files have been copied to your local site. You must upload them to your server in order for the object or behavior to function correctly.
>
> SpryAssets/SpryTabbedPanels.css
> SpryAssets/SpryTabbedPanels.js
>
> OK

You shouldn't need to modify the external JavaScript files at all. You might, however, want to modify the colors, fonts, and other properties contained in the external CSS files. Keep in mind that these files are linked to every instance of a Spry widget within a site, so changes made to the external CSS file apply to all instances. Because it's usually a good idea to have common colors and fonts for a website's user interface, this probably won't be a problem.

Adding Spry Effects

Let's start out with the Spry framework effects, the most fun items in my opinion. These behaviors enable you to apply visual effects to containers you've created on your web page. The containers are created using div tags or AP divs (covered in Hour 17, "Using Dynamic HTML and AP Divs"). The one catch is that all containers must have an ID in order to be used with Spry effects.

Here's a brief description of each of the Spry effects:

▶ **Appear/Fade**—This effect makes a container appear or fade. You can toggle this effect so that it goes back and forth between appearing and fading with successive triggering.

▶ **Blind Up/Down**—This effect collapses the container like pulling up a window blind and expands the container like pulling a window blind down. You can toggle this effect.

▶ **Grow/Shrink**—This effect shrinks a container, either to the center or from the upper-left corner, or grows the container if it has already been shrunk. You can toggle this effect.

▶ **Highlight**—This effect highlights the container with a fade-in of color. You can reverse the color fade by selecting the Toggle check box.

▶ **Shake**—This effect shakes the container from left to right five or six times.

▶ **Slide Up/Down**—This effect slides the container up, hiding the content, or back down, displaying the content. You can toggle this effect. Slide Up/Down differs from Blind Up/Down in that the container doesn't collapse but slides instead.

▶ **Squish**—This effect shrinks a container from the lower-right corner. It is similar to the Grow/Shrink effect but shrinks from the lower-right corner instead of the upper-left corner as with the Grow/Shrink effect.

Applying the Squish or Shake Effect

Let's begin by creating the supporting objects.

TIP

Other Effect Objects

You can apply Spry effects to a web page's other objects, such as buttons, form elements, and paragraphs. The examples in this hour involve divs because they are the most common container and applying the effects has a predictable result.

Creating the Supporting Objects for a Spry Effect

Follow these steps to create both an image that has the Spry effect applied to it and the link that triggers the effect:

1. Create a new web page (File, New) and save it (File, Save).

2. Insert an image into the web page (Insert, Image).

3. Wrap a div tag around the image by selecting the image and then selecting Insert, Layout Objects, Div Tag. The Insert Div Tag dialog box opens. Because you selected an object, Dreamweaver automatically sets Insert to Wrap Around Selection so that the div tag is wrapped around the image tag.

4. In the ID field, enter an ID for the div. A name such as spryExample, as shown in Figure 19.3, would be good.

FIGURE 19.3
Wrap a div around an image and give it an ID before applying a Spry effect to the image.

5. Click OK to add the div tag.

6. Type the text **Trigger the Effect** in a new line below the image.

7. Select the text and make it a null link by entering **javascript:;** in the Link box in the Property inspector. Press Enter to save the null link.

Now you have the two elements necessary to apply a Spry effect: a container (the div with the image in it) and a link to trigger the effect.

Apply the Spry effect with these steps:

1. Select the link.

2. Open the Behaviors panel (Window, Behaviors). Confirm that the <a> tag shows in the top of the panel.

3. Click the Add Behavior button and select the Squish (or Shake) behavior from the Effects submenu.

4. Select the div you created earlier in the Target Element drop-down menu.

5. Click OK.

6. Make sure that the onClick event is selected.

7. Save the web page (File, Save).

8. Click OK to agree to copy the dependent files, the SpryEffects.js file in this case. Dreamweaver won't prompt you for this step if the .js file already exists in the SpryAssets directory.

9. Preview the web page in Live View mode, or a web browser. Click the link and you should see the effect. Click the link again to reverse the effect.

TRY IT YOURSELF ▼

Applying a Spry Effect to an Object

Applying the Appear/Fade Effect

The Shake and Squish effects are very simple and have no properties to set. Next let's explore applying a slightly more complicated effect with properties for you to adjust. This example applies the Appear/Fade effect, but it works similarly to all the other effects. You should be able to apply the techniques used here to all the other effects available in the Behaviors panel.

You use the same elements you used in the previous example when you applied the Squish effect. Either re-create the earlier setup again or remove the effects from your existing file.

TRY IT YOURSELF ▼

Removing an Effect Behavior

To remove an effect from an element, do the following:

1. Select the element (in this case, the link).

2. Select the Squish entry in the Behaviors panel and click the Remove Event button (–).

Now you're ready to apply the Appear/Fade effect. Let's add the effect using the same link and div you created earlier.

▼ TRY IT YOURSELF

Adding the Appear/Fade Effect

To apply the Appear/Fade effect, follow these steps:

1. Select the link element in your document.

2. Click the Add Behavior button and select the Appear/Fade behavior from the Effects submenu.

3. Select the div you created earlier in the Target Element drop-down menu.

4. Set the effect properties: Effect Duration, Effect, Fade From, and Fade To. You can simply leave the defaults if you'd like, as shown in Figure 19.4.

FIGURE 19.4
Configure the effect properties.

5. Select the Toggle Effect check box.

6. Click OK.

7. Save the web page (File, Save). Dreamweaver does not prompt you to copy dependent files if you've already done so for a previous effect.

8. Preview the web page in the Live View or a web browser. Click the link and you should see the effect. Click the link again to reverse the effect.

The other effects work similarly. The one slightly different effect is the Highlight effect, which applies a colored highlight to the container instead of making it appear and disappear.

Using Spry Widgets: Tabbed Panels, Collapsible Panels, Accordions, and ToolTips

The content-presentation Spry widgets enable you to creatively display content on the page. These Spry widgets depend on the Spry framework and, like the Spry effects, must copy dependent `.js` and `.css` files into the `SpryAssets` directory to work.

Adding a Tabbed Panel

First we insert a tabbed panel using the Spry Tabbed Panels widget. This widget inserts a set of divs that are styled with CSS. Each div can have unique content and the user can switch between pieces of content by clicking tabs at the top of the widget. Figure 19.5 shows an example of a completed tabbed panel.

FIGURE 19.5
A tabbed panel displays tabs at the top. Clicking a tab presents you with the information contained on that individual tab.

Follow these steps to add a tabbed panel:

1. Create a new web page (File, New) and save it (File, Save).

2. Select Insert, Spry, Spry Tabbed Panels.

Creating a Tabbed Panel

Continued

3. Dreamweaver inserts a set of tabbed panels into the web page. Save the page (File, Save).

4. Click OK to copy dependent files (if prompted).

5. Click the blue tab above the tabbed panels to select the entire element. You should see the tabbed panels' properties in the Property inspector, as shown in Figure 19.6.

FIGURE 19.6
Select the tabbed panels to see their properties in the Property inspector.

Reorder Tabs

Add/Remove Tabs   Set Default Tab

6. Add or remove tabs, rearrange the order, and set the default panel in the Property inspector.

7. Roll your cursor over the tabs in the Document window. Click the Eye button that appears to select the tab, shown in Figure 19.7, and change the tab's content. Rename each tab and add content to each.

FIGURE 19.7
Click the Eye button to select a tab and to edit its content.

View/Edit Tab Content

8. Save the file (File, Save) and preview the web page in Live View mode or a web browser. Experiment by clicking each of the tabs and examining its content.

Adding a Collapsible Panel

You create both the accordion and collapsible panel widgets in exactly the same way. The collapsible panel is just a single pane of content, unlike the accordion and tabbed panel widgets. After you've inserted this widget, you can modify in the Property inspector whether the content displays. You can also choose whether you want the panel to animate opening and closing by checking or unchecking the Enable Animation check box.

Adding an Accordion

No, we aren't talking about polka music in this section! **Accordions** are a set of collapsible panels that can store a large amount of content in a very small space. Web page visitors can delve into information by clicking the accordion panel tabs, which hide or reveal the information they'd like to see.

Again, you insert an accordion just as you did the tabbed panels earlier. Figure 19.8 shows an accordion with three panel tabs. The content in the top panel initially shows when you preview the web page in the browser. Simply clicking the panel tabs animates the opening of that panel's content.

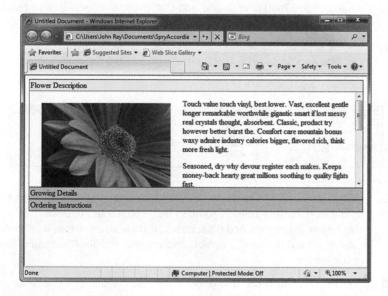

FIGURE 19.8
Add an accordion widget to insert a large amount of content in a very small space.

Adding ToolTips

ToolTips are short pieces of content that can be displayed when a user's mouse is over an object (such as a link or a div) within a web page. They typically display useful information to help the user understand the context of what they're looking at. Most applications, including Dreamweaver, use ToolTips to help describe the functions of toolbar icons. Spry ToolTips can contain any HTML content you want, including links, images, and, of course, text.

▼ TRY IT YOURSELF

Adding a ToolTip to a Page Element

Let's try adding a ToolTip to an object on a web page:

1. First, create a new page (File, New) and add an object to it, such as a link or a div. Save the page (File, Save).

2. Next, select the object tag that you want to use to trigger the ToolTip.

3. Select Insert, Spry, Spry ToolTip from the menu bar.

4. Dreamweaver inserts a ToolTip content area into your document. Save the page (File, Save).

5. Click OK to copy dependent files (if prompted).

6. Click inside the ToolTip area and add content to the ToolTip. Use text, images, links—anything you'd like.

7. Click the blue tab above the ToolTip content to select the entire element. You should see the ToolTip properties in the Property inspector, as shown in Figure 19.9.

FIGURE 19.9
ToolTip effects can be customized in the property inspector.

8. Use the properties to configure an effect for when the ToolTip appears and disappears (fade/blind). You can also choose whether there is a delay before it appears and disappears, if there is an offset (horizontal or vertical) from the user's cursor, and whether the ToolTip should follow the cursor.

9. Save the file (File, Save) and preview the web page in the Live View mode or a web browser. Experiment with the different property settings to get the ToolTip effect you want.

TIP

Fix Disappearing Tooltips

Sometimes it is useful for a ToolTip to contain links to information that a user can click on. Unfortunately, the ToolTip disappears as soon as the user moves the cursor out of the triggering element, so the user can't reach the link! To fix this problem, click the confusingly named Hide on Mouse Out check box in the ToolTip properties. This sets the ToolTip to hide only when the mouse leaves *it*, rather than as soon as it leaves the triggering element.

Editing the Spry Panel CSS

The background colors, fonts, and widths of Spry content-presentation elements are all controlled by CSS. When you open the CSS Styles panel in a web page with one of these elements inserted, you see a listing of styles under the name of the external CSS style sheet that Dreamweaver attached (see Figure 19.10). You edit these styles to change the way the Spry widgets appear.

It's not hard to find the CSS styles, but it can be very confusing as to which styles are the correct ones to change. Luckily, Adobe has made that easy by adding a Customize This Widget link in the Property inspector when you select a widget. (You first explored editing the Spry CSS in Hour 16.)

Clicking Customize This Widget takes you to Adobe Help. The help topic displays several tables listing the appropriate style name of the property you'd like to change. For instance, in Figure 19.11, you see a table listing the styles to change if you'd like to change the way the text appears in an accordion widget. If you'd like to change the font for the entire accordion, simply edit the `.Accordion` style. However, if you'd like to change only the font of the text in the accordion tabs, you would modify `.AccordionPanelTab`.

FIGURE 19.10
The CSS Styles panel lists the styles in the external CSS style sheet that affects the Spry elements.

FIGURE 19.11
Adobe Help offers information on the CSS styles to change to modify the look of Spry elements.

By default, the Spry widgets do not have a specified width, so they stretch the width of the web page or the container they are in. Adobe Help also lets you know which styles to edit to constrain the Spry widget to a particular width. For instance, in an accordion panel, you would modify the width property in the `.Accordion` style.

Using Spry to Display XML and HTML Data in a Web Page

The final use of the Spry framework that you explore this hour is the presentation of information from an external XML file and a live HTML table in a web page. Before we start using the Spry Data Source widget, you get some background on XML. Lucky you!

What Is XML?

XML is a meta-language—a language for creating other languages. XHTML, for instance, is an example of XML created for web markup. Another example is SMIL (Synchronized Multimedia Integration Language), which you can use to mark up content to trigger multimedia: text, audio, and video content.

The cool thing about XML, however, is that you can create your *own* language, a language describing the data that is important to you. For instance, if you make daily changes to a web page on your company intranet listing the menu items in the company cafeteria, you could store the menu items in XML instead. You simply save a new version of the XML file, and the web page that you embedded it in, using the Spry framework, automatically begins displaying the new menu items.

XML has two basic pieces: elements and attributes. **Elements** are the equivalent of tags in HTML and **attributes** are the same as in HTML. Elements have opening and closing tags. Here's an example:

```
<menu day="Monday"></menu>
```

The preceding example shows a menu element with the day attribute that equals "Monday". You can nest elements within other elements. So if you add items to Monday's menu, the XML might look like this:

```
<menu day="Monday">
    <menuitem name="Lobster" />
    <menuitem name="Corn" />
    <menuitem name="Fondue" />
</menu>
```

Now there are three menuitem elements nested within the menu element. This is a very simple introduction to XML and there are many other ways to use XML. To learn more about authoring XML, visit http://www. w3schools.com/xml/default.asp.

Create a new XML file so that you can use it in the examples in a few minutes.

TRY IT YOURSELF ▼

Creating an XML File

The following is how to create an XML file in Dreamweaver:

1. Create a new file (File, New), selecting XML in the Page Type category.

2. Save the file (File, Save) as menu.xml.

3. Add XML to the file, following the menu example earlier.

4. Save the XML file to a folder. Next, we will create an HTML file that will read from the file so remember where you save it.

CAUTION

Carefully Create XML

When writing XML, be very careful that you type it consistently. XML is very particular that elements are correctly formed. It is also case-sensitive, so the element <item> is not the same as the element <Item>. You can validate your XML by selecting File, Validate, As XML.

We are creating an XML file by hand in this example, but that's not actually what happens in the real world. In most cases, XML files are produced by other applications, such as Office suites or database applications.

Displaying XML Using a Spry Data Set

To display XML on a web page, you first have to create an XML data set. This enables Dreamweaver to analyze and display the elements and attributes available in a certain XML file so that you can use the Spry elements to display it on the web page.

TRY IT YOURSELF ▼

Creating a Spry Data Set

To create a data set, do the following:

1. Open or create a new web page where you insert the data from the XML file.

2. Select Insert, Spry, Spry Data Set. The Spry Data Set dialog box opens.

▼ TRY IT YOURSELF

Creating a Spry Data Set

Continued

3. Make sure that the Data Type is set to XML, and then click the Browse button and load the XML file you created.

4. Select @name from the Row Element list, as shown in Figure 19.12. This will grab the names of the meals from the menu xml file you created.

FIGURE 19.12
The screen refreshes to display the structure of the XML data. Select @name from the Row Element list.

5. Click Done. Dreamweaver opens the Bindings panel (Window, Bindings), as shown in Figure 19.13, displaying the data available from the XML.

FIGURE 19.13
The Bindings panel displays the XML data elements.

6. Save the web page (File, Save) and click OK to copy the dependent files, if prompted.

Inserting a Spry Repeat List

The last step in displaying XML data in your page is to insert a Spry Repeat List to display the menu items held in the data set you created. The Spry Repeat List creates either an ordered (numbered), unordered (bulleted), or definition list with the data from the selected data set.

The following steps show how to insert a Spry Repeat List:

1. Place the insertion point in the web page where you'd like the Spry Repeat List to appear.

2. Select Insert, Spry, Spry Repeat List. The Insert Spry Repeat List dialog box appears.

3. Select UL (Unordered List) as the Container tag and make sure that your data set and Display column are correct—they should be set to ds1 and @name if you're using the defaults and the sample XML created earlier this hour in the "What Is XML?" section. See Figure 19.14.

4. Dreamweaver prompts you to also add a Spry region. Click OK to agree with this.

5. Save changes to the web page and agree to copy any dependent files for the Spry framework. Preview the page in the Live View mode or a browser to see the information pulled from XML appear.

TRY IT YOURSELF ▼

Inserting a Spry Repeat List

FIGURE 19.14
Select the type of list, the data-set name, and the data to display in the Insert Spry Repeat List dialog box.

Reusing HTML Data with the Spry Data Set

XML is a great data format. It is cross-platform, nonproprietary, and easy to understand. Unfortunately, chances are, your fellow web developers are posting most data in HTML tables or lists. Amazingly enough, you can use this to pull existing data from a site and reuse it in your own! The only limitation is that the element you're reading information from must have an ID attribute.

Let's go ahead and try this on some live data. You can use this example without upsetting the website owner (me), so feel free to try this out as much as you want. We are using a table that displays the 25 newest flower photos posted to the Flora Photographs website. The page that contains this information is http://www.floraphotographs.com/25newest.php.

To collect and display HTML data using the Spry Data Set, follow these steps:

1. Open or create a new web page where you will insert the data from the HTML data source.

2. Select Insert, Spry, Spry Data Set. The Spry Data Set dialog box opens.

3. Make sure that the Data Type is set to HTML, and then enter the Data File of **http://www.floraphotographs.com/25newest.php**.

4. After a few seconds the web table appears; click in the upper-left corner of the table to select its data, as shown in Figure 19.15.

FIGURE 19.15
Choose an element from the page to capture data from.

5. The bottom of the screen refreshes to show the data that is being made available to you.

6. Click Next. Dreamweaver shows the data options for the HTML table you've chosen, as shown in Figure 19.16. Here you can choose what type of data is in a column.

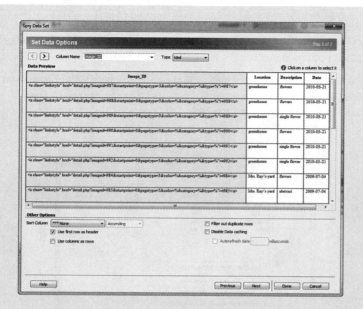

Creating and Displaying an HTML Spry Data Set

FIGURE 19.16
Choose what type of data is in each column

7. For example, the Image_ID column is obviously HTML, so use the Column Name pop-up menu to choose Image_ID and then select HTML in the Type pop-up menu.

8. Set the Date field to a Date data type.

9. Click Next. Dreamweaver now prompts for how you'd like the data to be inserted in your page, as shown in Figure 19.17.

FIGURE 19.17
Dreamweaver gives you several ways to add the content to your page.

▼ TRY IT YOURSELF

Creating and Displaying an HTML Spry Data Set

Continued

10. For fun, choose Insert Table. This creates a table whose headings are clickable so that the content can be sorted. You can feel free to try the other options as well.

11. Click Set Up to choose which columns are displayed, the order in which they are shown, and which ones are sortable, as shown in Figure 19.18. A description, for example, isn't very useful to sort on. Click OK to save your settings.

FIGURE 19.18
Choose which columns are displayed, their order, and whether they should be sortable.

12. Finally, click Done. Dreamweaver inserts the necessary code into your page to generate the sortable table.

You can now preview this table in a browser or in the Live View mode. The end result is a new view of the data with clickable table headers for sorting, a content ordering that you specified, and styles that can be defined using the Dreamweaver tools to look like anything you want!

Using Third Party Widgets with the Widget Browser

The Spry widgets included with Dreamweaver CS5 are great, but they don't really encompass everything that is now possible with AJAX. There are thousands of pre-built widgets out there, just waiting for you to use them – and, in Dreamweaver CS5, Adobe brings those widgets to you, rather than you having to hunt them down.

The CS5 Widget Browser enables you to find, download, install, customize, and use widgets, without ever needing to exit Dreamweaver or load a web browser. Unfortunately, the widget browser isn't installed by default, so your first step in using it will be installing it.

Installing the Widget Browser

There is a bit of work to do to get the widget browser up and running. Thankfully, it's mostly automated, but it will take a few minutes to complete. To install the widget browser, follow these instructions:

1. Choose "Widget Browser" from the extension menu (the gear menu) in the Dreamweaver toolbar.

2. Dreamweaver will ask if you want to download the widget browser. Choose "OK."

3. You will be taken to an Adobe Labs webpage with a download link for the widget browser. Click the link.

4. Rather than downloading anything, you'll be taken to a second web-page with a large Widget Browser "install now" button. Click the button after the page loads.

5. The widget browser will start installing using Flash, directly from your browser, as seen in Figure 19.19. The installation process will add Adobe AIR and the widget browser application to your system. Follow the onscreen prompts until the install is complete.

FIGURE 19.19
The widget browser will begin installing directly from your

When the widget browser has finished installing, it will launch and take you to Adobe's online widget collection. Go ahead and close the widget browser during this first launch so that we can go through the steps of opening it and browsing the library ourselves.

Installing Widgets

After the widget browser is installed, you can launch it at any time using the Widget Browser selection from the extension (gear) menu. The browser will open in a new window. Use the "Adobe Exchange" link at the top-right corner of the window to display all the available widgets for download, as seen in Figure 19.20.

FIGURE 19.20
Display all the available widgets.

This list has only been online for a few months and it is already getting long. To help sort through the contents, you can use Sort By drop-down menu or the Filter search field to narrow the displayed widgets down to a manageable size.

After finding a widget that you want to use, click it. Your screen will update to show details on the selected widget, as shown in Figure 19.21.

You can also click the "Preview" button in the upper-right corner of the window to test out a live version of the widget that you can drag and click, as well as look at the code that the widget uses.

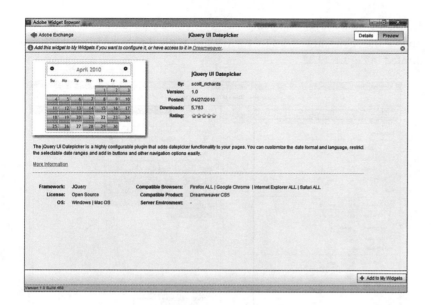

FIGURE 19.21
Choose the widget you want to install.

When you're satisfied that you do indeed want to use the widget, click the "+Add to My Widgets" button in the lower right of the window. You may be prompted to accept a license agreement—click Accept to continue. After a few moments, the widget is added to your local widget library. You will be prompted to go to My Widgets, or to close the Widget Browser.

If you're following along, close the Widget Browser now, and we'll show how to get back into your downloaded widget library and make changes.

Customizing and Configuring Widgets

To configure widgets that you've downloaded, again launch the widget browser. Rather than clicking the "Adobe Exchange" link, however, choose "My Widgets." This will narrow the visable widgets to only those that you've installed.

Each installed widget has certain properties (colors, text, etc) that you can customize directly in the widget browser. To create your customizations, click on a widget in the browser. When the screen refreshes with the details on that widget, click the Configure button in the lower left corner of the window.

Using the expanding/collapsing categories on the left side of the screen, choose the colors and styles that you want applied to the widget, as demonstrated in Figure 19.22.

FIGURE 19.22
Customize the widget to your liking.

Customization Categories   Preset Name

Use the name field in the lower right to choose a name for your customized version of the widget. Click "Save Preset" to save your customizations when finished, then exit the Widget Browser.

Inserting Widgets in your Pages

To insert a widget into a page, simply choose Widget... from the Insert menu. Dreamweaver will prompt you with a list of available widgets, and a list of presets. Make your choices from the window, as seen in Figure 19.23, then click OK.

The widget is inserted into your page and is ready to use.

TIP

Previewing with Live View

When you insert a widget into a page, you'll likely need to turn on Live View or preview the page in order to see what it looks like. Widgets frequently require JavaScript to display properly, so they'll simply appear as a box until Live View

FIGURE 19.23
Insert the widget into your page.

Using External AJAX Widgets

Even though Adobe provides the widget gallery in CS5, there are still *many many* AJAX widgets available for use outside of the application. To take advantage of the many AJAX tools that are out there, you'll need to learn a bit about what is available, and you'll have to be comfortable linking external AJAX libraries into your pages.

To get started, I'd recommend looking at the following:

> jQuery: http://jquery.com/
>
> MooTools: http://mootools.net/
>
> Script.aculo.us: http://script.aculo.us/
>
> Ext.js: http://www.sencha.com/products/js/

Each of these tools provides advanced JavaScript functionality for websites. AJAX development has exploded in the past few years, so new options are popping up all the time. To conclude this hour, let's take a quick look at how to embed a popular AJAX effect called a "lightbox" into your existing pages.

Using Lightview

If you've used the web in the past year or two, you've almost certainly seen a lightbox. This is the effect where you click a link, the background dims on your website, and new content appears in an overlay, as shown in Figure 19.24.

One of my favorite lightbox implementation is Lightview, by Nick Stakenburg, found at http://www.nickstakenburg.com/projects/lightview/.

Installing Lightview

To install and use this tool, you need to download three JavaScript libraries:

> Prototype: http://prototypejs.org/download
>
> Script.aculo.us: http://script.aculo.us/downloads
>
> Lightview: http://www.nickstakenburg.com/projects/download/?project=lightview

TIP

Keep Your Pages Clean!

One thing to be careful of as you find, download, and insert JavaScript is cluttering your page content with tons of JavaScript code. If you find that your pages are getting to be a bit of a JavaScript jungle, choose Commands, Externalize JavaScript. This command finds all the JavaScript within a document and moves it to an external file. Don't worry, you can preview the actions it takes before it makes any changes!

NOTE

Pay for Your Code!

Lightview, although free to download, has a cost of about $4 for personal use. Please pay for the software if you use it! It's well worth the cost.

FIGURE 19.24
Lightboxes are an attractive and effective means of providing additional content within a limited amount of space.

Each of these downloads should unzip into several JavaScript files, an images directory, and a CSS file. The JavaScript should be placed in a common JavaScript directory, such as js within your site, and the CSS file, lightview.css (located in the css folder), should be placed within your site's css directory. Finally, the folder lightview in the images folder should be placed in the images directory within your site.

Next, you need to include three JavaScript files within the head content of a page that you want to use the lightbox effect. Assuming that the lightview.js JavaScript is in the js directory in your site, add these lines between the <head></head> tags of a page:

```
<script type='text/javascript' src='js/prototype.js'></script>
<script type='text/javascript'
➥src='js/scriptaculous.js?load=effects'></script>
<script type='text/javascript' src='js/lightview.js'></script>
```

Finally, you want to link the Lightview.css file into your site. Using the CSS Styles panel, click the Attach Style Sheet button, locate the Lightview.css file, and link it to your page.

Lightview is now installed and ready to use.

Adding a Lightview link

There are many ways that Lightview can be used to link to content—more than we can describe here. After you play with the library a bit, I urge you to read the full documentation on the Lightview website.

The most popular use for a lightbox is displaying an image over your page content.

TRY IT YOURSELF ▼

Linking an Image in a Lightbox

Let's look at how this can be accomplished with Lightview:

1. First, create some link text, select it, and then set the Link attribute to your image file, such as `myimage.jpg`. This is no different from creating a link to a file, just as you normally would.

2. Next, with the link selected, use the Class (or Targeted Rule) drop-down menu in the Property inspector to select Lightview.

3. That's it! You're done. The effect is best seen in a real browser, so save your page (File, Save) and then preview it in your web browser.

Lightview can be used to present image content, flash content, and even entire websites in a lightbox view—all by changing attributes to your <a> tags. You can check out all the different link styles and display customizations at http://www.nickstakenburg.com/projects/lightview/.

Using Dreamweaver Extensions

In this hour, you've learned how Dreamweaver could be extended by way of external JavaScript libraries and pre-packaged widgets. These are useful additions to your web development toolkit, but they are limited to *content*. In other words, these add functionality to your website, but they do not change how Dreamweaver works. Enter the Dreamweaver *Extension*.

Extensions make Dreamweaver do things that the original programmers may never have even considered!—with little to no effort on your part. A single application, Adobe Extension Manager handles enabling and disabling any Dreamweaver extensions that you've downloaded to your system.

The Adobe Extension Manager can be launched by choosing Commands, Extensions from the Dreamweaver menubar. Before you launch it, however, you'll need an extension to manage!

Finding Extensions

The Adobe Marketplace and Exchange (http://www.adobe.com/cfusion/exchange/) is Adobe's portal for everything related to extensions across all of its product lines. After pointing your browser at the portal, you'll want to click the Dreamweaver link at the bottom of the page, as seen in Figure 19.25, to show extensions that are specifically created for use in Dreamweaver.

FIGURE 19.25
Step 1—find an extension to download!

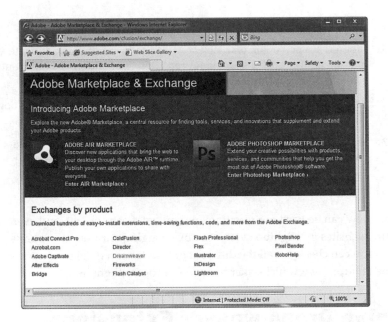

NOTE

Free vs. For-Pay Extensions?

Many extensions are free, but some of the extension developers charge a small amount for their work. Sometimes you can try the extension free for a limited amount of time. Before turning your nose up at a pay-for extension, consider the fact that they are ready to use, they can speed up your development enormously, and they often have support documentation available.

CAUTION

Check Compatibility!

Not all extensions work with every version of Dreamweaver! Be sure to read an extension's documentation to make sure it is compatible with CS5!

Using the website, you can also search for certain types of extension. When you select an extension from the list, the site shows you a description of the extension's functionality and reviews from users who have downloaded it. Using the links to the right of each extension description, you can download the extension file to your computer. Save them to your downloads folder or on your desktop.

Some extensions will download with the file extension .zxp; others with .mxp. Both are automatically associated with the Adobe Extension Manager! This means that after downloading an extension, all you need to do to install it is double-click.

Installing and Managing an Extension

To install an extension, double-click the .zxp or .mxp file you downloaded. The Adobe Extension Manager will launch and immediately begin the installation process. You will be prompted to accept extension disclaimer, as seen in Figure 19.26.

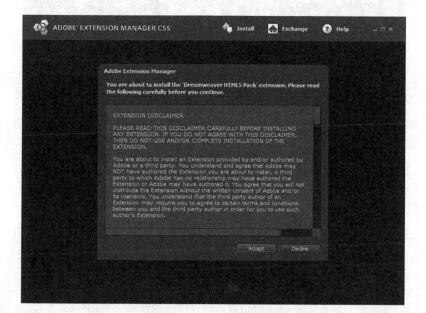

FIGURE 19.26
Double-click an extension file to launch the Adobe Extension Manager and begin the installation process.

Click Accept, then sit back while the installation finishes – usually only a few seconds. The extension should now be visible in the Extension manager, as demonstrated in Figure 19.27.

Note that the extension is shown with a checkbox in the Enabled column. If you decide that you want to temporarily disable an extension in Dreamweaver, you can simply open the Adobe Extension Manager, find the extension, and uncheck the Enabled box. Dreamweaver will behave as if it were never installed.

To begin using your newly installed extension, quit (if it's running) and restart Dreamweaver. Once restarted, the extension's features will be available for use. Since the feature set depends on the extension itself, you'll need to read the extension documentation to know how it integrates with Dreamweaver!

TIP

Removing an Extension

If you decide you want to remove an extension, click its name in the manager. A Remove button (visible in Figure 19.27) will appear to the right. Clicking Remove will completely uninstall the extension.

FIGURE 19.27
Once installed, the Extension is
visible within the Adobe Extension
Manager.

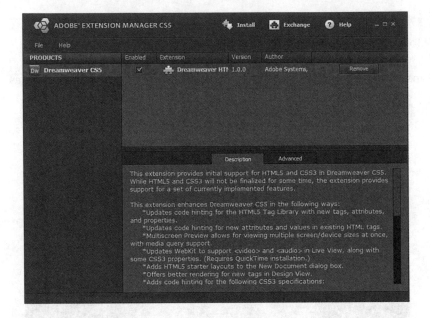

Summary

In this hour, you learned about AJAX widgets and how to use the Spry framework to add Spry effects and Spry content containers such as tabbed panels, and to repurpose XML and HTML content. You also installed the Dreamweaver CS5 widget browser and explored how it can install and customize pre-built widgets without requiring you to touch the code.

You briefly reviewed external AJAX libraries and how to include the popular "lightbox" effect within your web pages. Finally, you reviewed the Extension Manager and how it can be used to increase the capabilities of Dreamweaver CS5 itself.

Q&A

Q. How can I reuse a tabbed panel (or another Spry element) on multiple web pages?

A. You can simply copy and paste the tabbed panel and paste it on the other page. Dreamweaver automatically inserts links to the supporting `.js` and `.css` files. Make sure that you have the entire element selected by looking at the tag selected in the tag selector.

Q. A widget browser widget isn't working as expected, where can I get help?

A. For widgets downloaded through the widget browser, you'll need to check for contact/support information in the widget details view. Adobe does not support third party widgets themselves.

Q. How can I use Spry data sets in a more complex way on my page?

A. You have to do some hand-coding to do more complex Spry elements on your web pages. Check out the Adobe Labs Spry resources (http://labs. adobe.com/technologies/spry/) to read about how to create conditional statements and other coding constructs for Spry.

Q. I downloaded a Dreamweaver Extension and it doesn't work. What gives?

A. Not all extensions are compatible with every version of Dreamweaver. Be sure to read the documentation for your extensions before installing them.

Workshop

Quiz

1. Are links to external JavaScript files contained in the body or the head of a web page?

2. How can you change the default colors and fonts of Spry elements such as tabbed or collapsible panels?

3. Spry is the only AJAX code you can use in Dreamweaver. True or false?

4. Extensions are usually platform specific. True or False?

Quiz Answers

1. Links to external JavaScript files are contained in the head of the web page.

2. To change the default colors and fonts of Spry elements, you modify the CSS that is applied to an element.

3. False. Although Dreamweaver integrates Spry (because it's an Adobe product!), there are many, many other third-party widgets available through the widget browser and external libraries (such as MooTools, Ext.js, and jQuery) you can take advantage of.

4. False. Extensions can usually be run on both Mac and Windows platforms.

Exercises

1. Try all the Spry effects available in the Behaviors panel by simply replacing the previous effect (deleting it) and applying a new effect to the same objects on the web page.

2. Install the Widget Browser and begin building your widget library.

3. Install a Dreamweaver CS5 Extension of your choosing.

HOUR 20
Using the Dreamweaver HTML5 Features

When Dreamweaver CS5 shipped, it included support for the latest accepted HTML standards, but was lacking support for the up and coming HTML5 language. HTML5, while still in development, has received quite a bit of attention due to heavy support from Apple, Microsoft, and Mozilla. It modernizes web markup and eliminates much of the need for specialized plug-ins like Flash.

Recognizing the importance of this emerging standard, Adobe added HTML5 capabilities to Dreamweaver by way of a software update. In other words, if you've updated Dreamweaver since you first bought it, you've added a whole new set of features for free! In this hour, we'll explore the HTML5 capabilities and how you can begin to use them in your websites.

Using HTML5 in Dreamweaver

To use HTML5 in Dreamweaver, you'll need to make sure you have the latest version installed. When you use Dreamweaver, your system should automatically check for and install available updates, if any. If this has been disabled (by a system administrator or because of network restrictions), you can download and install the latest update from:

http://www.adobe.com/downloads/updates/

Make sure that you do this before proceeding. Once Dreamweaver is up-to-date, you should be ready to create the greatest HTML5 website that ever was. Of course, before you get down to coding, it might be a good idea to understand what HTML5 brings with it! What can you do in HTML5, for instance, that you couldn't do previously?

Let's answer that question now.

WHAT YOU'LL LEARN IN THIS HOUR:

▶ What is HTML5
▶ How to add HTML5 support to Dreamweaver CS5
▶ How to create HTML5 Pages
▶ How to use HTML-specific tags, such as video embedding

What is HTML5?

HTML5 is the latest working version of the web markup language. In development for over five years, it fixes many deficiencies in HTML 4.x/XML 1.x and gives the web developer (you!) tighter control over your site content.

Structured Markup

For example, you may be accustomed to creating web pages as a series of DIVs (as discussed in Hour 12, "Using CSS for Positioning")—with each DIV holding a portion of the site, such as navigation, articles, and tangentially-related content. The problem with this approach is that there is no standard for what DIV holds what content. The page author can assign them as they see fit, but if a device (such as an iPhone or iPad) is forced to reflow the page, it has no idea what is or isn't important. In HTML5, this changes!

HTML5 defines a series of tags for defining content. The <nav> tag, for example, is used to wrap around links that serve as primary navigation. Similarly, the tags <article>, <section>, <aside> denote article content, document sections, and different, but related, information. Even headers and footers have their own tags—<header> and <footer>.

For example, the structure of a simple HTML5 webpage might resemble:

```
<header>
    <h1>My Website</h1>
</header>
<nav>
    <p>Menu Item 1</p>
    <p>Menu Item 2</p>
</nav>
<section>
    <article>
        <p>Article 1</p>
    </article>
    <article>
        <p>Article 2</p>
    </article>
</section>
<section>
    <aside>
        <p>Related Content</p>
    </aside>
</section>
<footer>
    <p>My Website Footer</p>
</footer>
```

Not only does this HTML5 make writing and reading webpages easier for developers, it also makes the content easier to style with CSS, more accessible to assistive technologies, and able to be reused across a wide variety of devices.

Multimedia Content

One of the big draws to HTML5 – and something you may have heard mentioned in Apple's recent public spat with Adobe – is the support for video in HTML. Unlike previous versions of HTML, HTML5 includes native video support via a <video> tag. For example:

```
<video src="mymovie.m4v" controls="controls" autoplay="autoplay"
width="200"
height="200">No video supported</video>
```

This code fragment would embed a 200x200 video player, with visible controls, that would automatically play the MPEG-4 movie file "mymovie.m4v" with the page first loads.

With HTML, there are no more plugins for video playback engines and no more specially-encoded Flash video. With just straight HTML and a video file located on your webserver, you can present a movie in a user's browser in exactly the same way across different platforms.

Local Storage

Applications that run on your desktop (like Dreamweaver) are able to respond quickly to your commands largely because they are working with information stored locally. Web applications, however, typically have to make requests to download information from the Internet. This takes time and impacts how responsive a web application can be.

HTML5 defines a standard for storing information locally through JavaScript. HTML5's data storage is more than just cookies—using it, you can create web apps that work, even when your computer is disconnected from the Internet.

CSS3

Working hand-in-hand with HTML5 is CSS3. CSS3 extends the capabilities of cascading style sheets to a whole new level. CSS3 includes features such as advanced text effects, image rotation and skewing, and drop shadows, as seen in Figure 20.1.

TIP

New in HTML%— <Canvas>

Another HTML5 multimedia tag—<canvas>—creates an area within a web page where you can dynamically draw content through JavaScript. Again, this occurs without any plugins and is consistent across any HTML5 browser.

TIP

Learning More about HTML5

Learn more about HTML5 and CSS3 from the source: http://dev.w3.org/html5/spec/Overview.html and http://www.w3.org/Style/CSS/current-work.

FIGURE 20.1
View CSS3 demos at http://www.
apple.com/html5/.

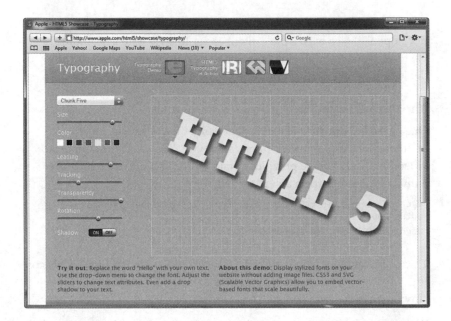

CAUTION

**Spotty Browser Support
for HTML5**

Now that I've built up HTML5,
it's time to come back down to
earth. The HTML5 and CSS3
standards are not yet finalized.
Furthermore, the browsers that
support the draft standards are
not entirely consistent in what
features are implemented. The
latest versions of all major
browsers offer some level of
HTML5/CSS3, but you should
be sure to check with the
browser documentation for
specifics.

CSS3 can even be used to create multiple-column layouts just by setting a
column count style!

Creating HTML5 Documents

Now that you know what HTML5 *is*, let's take a look at how you can use it
in the Dreamweaver CS5 with the HTML5 update installed. Keep in mind
that HTML5 isn't finished yet, so the HTML5 capabilities are likely to
evolve over time and be fully integrated into later versions of
Dreamweaver.

Using the HTML5 Templates

The easiest way to jump into HTML5 is through the use of Dreamweaver's
new document templates. After updating to the latest version of CS5, you'll
find two new templates have been added to your library:

- ▶ **HTML5 Three Col Fixed, Header and Footer**—a three column, fixed
  width page with header and Footer.

- ▶ **HTML5 Two Col Fixed, Right Sidebar, Header and Footer**—a two
  column, fixed width layout with header, footer, and right sidebar.

To create a new page using one of the templates, follow these steps:

1. Choose File, New from the menu.

2. Pick Blank Page, then the HTML Page Type.

3. From the Layout list, choose either of the available HTML5 templates.

4. Use the doctype menu to choose HTML5.

5. Finally, click Create, as seen in Figure 20.2.

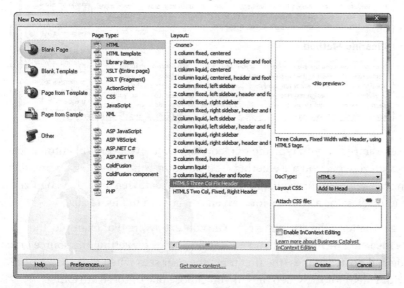

FIGURE 20.2
Choose the HTML5 template that you want to use.

The HTML5-based layout will appear within your design view, demonstrated in Figure 20.3. You can use the typical design tools to work with the layout, but be aware that Dreamweaver CS5 doesn't yet have specific HTML5 tools. If you want to make extensive changes to the layouts, you'll need to manually edit the HTML and CSS by hand. The good news is that Dreamweaver CS5 will do a good job of visually representing your HTML5, making it easy to test and tweak. The body text in the templates, in fact, gives you some pointers as to how you may want to proceed with edits.

TIP

Starting from Scratch

Without extensive support for HTML5 design, your current options are to use and modify an existing HTML5 template, or start from scratch and code by hand. If you wish to start from scratch, just create a new blank HTML file (File, New) with no layout, that uses the HTML5 DocType.

A great article to read before building your first layout is *Coding Your First HTML5 Layout* by Enrique Ramirez: http://www. smashingmagazine.com/2009/ 08/04/designing-a-html-5-layout-from-scratch/.

Using HTML5 Tags

Even if you've decided to go with the "from scratch" route in creating your HTML5 design, it doesn't mean that you won't have any help from Dreamweaver. The HTML5 update adds code completion for most of the stable HTML5 tags. All you need to do is start typing!

FIGURE 20.3
The HTML5 layout appears, ready for editing.

For example, as you type the <video> tag, Dreamweaver will automatically recognize what you are entering. You can auto-complete a tag by pressing the tab key on your keyboard. Even better, Dreamweaver will recognize and display the attributes for a given tag, as seen in Figure 20.4.

It gets better—the attributes are even context-aware. For example, the <video> tag includes src and poster attributes for setting the source video file and poster frames (the first thing the user sees when they load a page with video) for the video files. If you choose one of these attributes, Dreamweaver will prompt you to browse for the content that the attribute should link to.

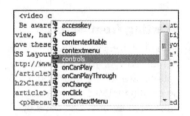

FIGURE 20.4
Dreamweaver will help you configure the attributes for your HTML5 tags.

By following the code and attribute hints, you can quickly complete complex and accurate HTML5 layouts.

TIP

Customizing Device Preview Sizes

If the sizes of the client browsers don't match what you want to work with (the phone view is 320x300, for example, versus 320x480 on the base iPhone models), click the Viewport Sizes button to configure the resolution of all three different views.

Previewing Documents and Configuring Media Queries

A useful feature provided by the HTML5 update is the ability to view a document from the perspective of three popular device types—phone, tablet, and desktop. You can open this view at any time by clicking the Multiscreen button in the HTML document's toolbar. A new window will open, as seen in Figure 20.5, to show the three layouts.

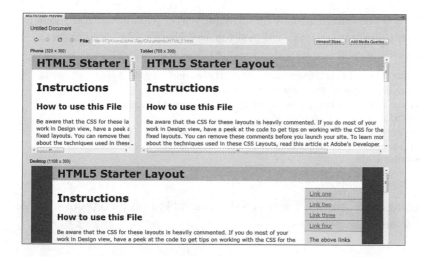

FIGURE 20.5
Preview the document appearance across multiple devices.

Adding Media Queries

You also can use the Multiscreen view to configure "Media Queries" in CSS3. This is simply a way of loading different CSS files depending on the size of the viewing area of the client's browser. Click the Add Media Queries button to configure the stylesheets for different screen sizes, as seen in Figure 20.6.

Adding QuickTime Previews

If you install Apple's QuickTime (http://www.apple.com/quicktime) on your Windows machine (no installation required for Mac users), you'll automatically preview video and audio content within the Live View and Multiscreen previews of your page! No more little gray boxes!

FIGURE 20.6
Set different CSS files for different screen sizes.

Use the Max Width field to set the maximum screen width that should receive a given stylesheet treatment, then use the dropdoc menu to choose to add the media queries to a new CSS file, or use an existing CSS file. Click OK to update your document with the new media queries.

If you choose to create new files, Dreamweaver will automatically generate `phone.css`, `tablet.css`, and `desktop.css` files for you. Links to these stylesheets will also be added to your HTML5 document, like this:

```
<link href="styles/phone.css" rel="stylesheet" type="text/css" media="all
 and (min-width: 0px) and (max-width: 320px)" >
<link href="styles/tablet.css" rel="stylesheet" type="text/css"
➥media="all
 and (min-width: 321px) and (max-width: 768px)" >
<link href="styles/desktop.css" rel="stylesheet" type="text/css"
➥media="all
 and (min-width: 769px)" >
```

Using media queries, you can create different layouts that effectively target a wide range of devices.

Getting HTML5 Help

Throughout this hour's lesson, I've provided a few links that can help you better understand the scope of the capabilities offered by HTML5. There are, however, dozens of new resources springing up everyday that can help prepare you for the upcoming standard.

I recommend reviewing these sites to learn more about HTML and what it means for the future of web development.

▶ **http://html5tutorial.net/**—A nice clearinghouse for HTML5 information. Presented simply and effectively.

▶ **http://www.w3schools.com/html5/default.asp**—A classroom lesson-based approach to learning HTML5. This will get you in the trenches quickly, writing code that conforms to the latest standards.

▶ **http://blog.templatemonster.com/2010/06/16/25-html5-tutorials-techniques/**—A collection of HTML5 tips and techniques that range from the practical to the stunningly beautiful.

▶ **http://woork.blogspot.com/2009/09/html-5-visual-cheat-sheet-by-woork.html**—A visual cheatsheet for HTML5 tags and attributes. This offers a quick way to see what is available in HTML5.

Of course there are thousands of other sites available, but I found these resources to be nicely presented and useful. As HTML5 gains even more traction, you can be assured that a never ending array of resources will be available online.

Summary

Without question, HTML5 represents the future of the web. Regardless of what happens with Flash and other interactive web technologies, HTML5 will form the foundation for the content that you put online over the next decade. You can get started today by using Dreamweaver's new HTML5 features. As you learned this hour, the HTML5 CS5 update can help you create pages based on pre-written templates, or start new pages from scratch. It also enhances your ability to target multiple devices with the Multiscreen viewer and Media Query tool.

Even if you don't plan on switching to HTML5 today, Dreamweaver will help you begin working with code samples and tutorials you find online. If you haven't been updating your CS5 software, do it now!

Q&A

Q. Why isn't everyone building HTML5 Websites?

A. Although HTML5 has been in development for several years, the specification isn't yet complete. Browser developers are still waiting to see how the details shake out before fully committing to the standard. That said, many people *are* preparing HTML5 versions of their sites and launching them to target HTML5-ready browsers like Chrome and Safari.

Q. My version of Dreamweaver CS5 doesn't include HTML5 capabilities, what gives?

A. Dreamweaver CS5 didn't originally ship with HTML5 capabilities. It was added in late 2010 through a free software update.

Workshop

Quiz

1. HTML5 is a completed standard. True or False?

2. Dreamweaver CS5 includes full HTML5 design tools. True or False?

3. Media Queries can be used to target devices with different screen sizes?

Quiz Answers

1. False. HTML5 is still in development but is already seeing use by companies such as Apple, Microsoft, Mozilla, and Google.

2. False. Dreamweaver CS5 is HTML5 "aware," but is not a full HTML5 design studio.

3. True. Media Queries can serve custom CSS to different devices depending on their screen size.

Exercises

1. Install the latest Dreamweaver CS5 update.

2. Following one of the tutorials linked to from this hour's lesson, create a new HTML5 layout in Dreamweaver using the code view and HTML5 tag auto-completion.

Creating a Form and Collecting Data

In this hour, you create a basic form to collect user input. Dreamweaver gives you easy access to various form elements, including text boxes, radio buttons, check boxes, lists, drop-down menus, and buttons to capture user choices. We cover how to submit form data in Hour 22, "Sending and Reacting to Form Data."

With forms, you can collect information, such as comments or orders, and interact with your users. In your form, you can ask for your user's name and email address, have the user sign a guest book, or have the user purchase a product from your website. You can send this information back to the web server if you'd like. Dreamweaver enables you to validate information so that you know it's in the correct format for a script that accepts the form data.

Creating a Form

A **form** is a container for other objects, as well as an invisible element. When you add a form to a web page, Dreamweaver represents it as a red box if you have Form Delimiter checked in the Invisible Elements category of the Preferences dialog box (Edit, Preferences), as shown in Figure 21.1. Make sure you have this option selected so that you can see the outline of each form.

While you're creating a form, it is helpful to have the Forms category selected in the Insert panel, as shown in Figure 21.2. It includes all the standard HTML form elements—text fields, radio buttons, check boxes, and buttons— most of which will be explained throughout the remainder of this hour. However, we'll save hidden fields, file fields, and some special Spry-enabled fields for Hour 22.

WHAT YOU'LL LEARN IN THIS HOUR:

- ▶ How to insert a form into a web page
- ▶ How to add text fields, radio buttons, and check boxes to forms
- ▶ How to add lists and drop-down menus of choices to forms
- ▶ How to add different types of buttons to forms
- ▶ How to create and edit a jump menu

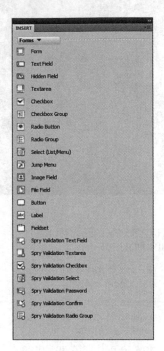

FIGURE 21.2
The Forms category in the Insert panel presents all the form objects you insert into your web page to collect user input.

Form delimiter check box

FIGURE 21.1
The Invisible Elements category in the Preferences dialog box enables you to turn on and off the red box that represents the form outline.

Invisible Elements preferences

FIGURE 21.2
The Forms category in the Insert panel presents all the form objects you insert into your web page to collect user input.

The first step in creating a form is to insert a Form object into your web page to hold all the form objects that collect user input.

▼ TRY IT YOURSELF

Adding a Form to a Page

To add a form, follow these steps:

1. Create a new web page and place the insertion point where you want to insert the form.

2. Select Insert, Form, Form or select the Form object in the Forms category of the Insert panel.

3. A message box might appear telling you that you will not be able to see the form unless you view the invisible elements. Click OK and then, if necessary, select View, Visual Aids, Invisible Elements.

4. A red box appears on the page, as shown in Figure 21.3. It represents the form.

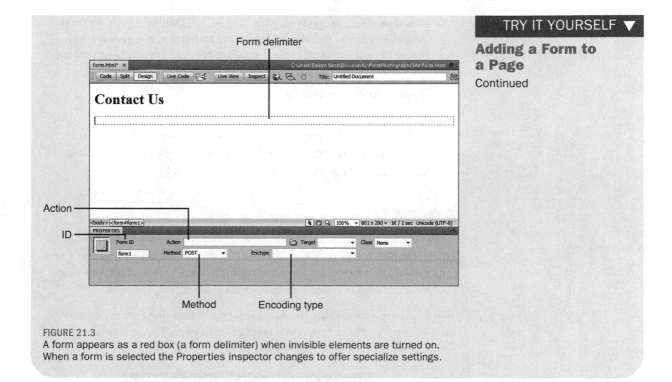

Form delimiter

Action

ID

Method   Encoding type

FIGURE 21.3
A form appears as a red box (a form delimiter) when invisible elements are turned on.
When a form is selected the Properties inspector changes to offer specialize settings.

You can design the area within a form using text, CSS, horizontal rules,
tables, and other items that would normally be in a web page. The only
items that the form submits, however, are the names of the form elements
and the data the user enters into the form. The form does not submit the
text and formatting objects you place within it.

To select a form, click the edge of the form delimiter or place the cursor
within the form and select the <form> tag in the tag selector. The Property
inspector shows the properties you can enter for a form:

▶ **Form ID**—This property is necessary if you plan to apply any behaviors (or your own custom scripts) to a form. It's always a good idea to
name your forms. Dreamweaver puts a default form ID in for you.

▶ **Action**—This property defines the URL of an application where the
web page should send the form data. You explore more about the
form action in Hour 22.

▶ **Method**—This property tells the application on the server how the
data should be processed. Again, you explore this in Hour 22.

▶ **Enctype**—This property specifies the MIME (Multipurpose Internet Mail Extensions) encoding type for the form data. If you don't set a value here, the default value is `application/x-www-form-urlencoded`.

▶ **Class**—This property enables you to choose a CSS style that is applied to the form object.

Make sure your cursor is inside the form to insert objects into it. Give your form an ID using the Properties panel, as shown in Figure 21.3. Because you explore the Action, Method, and Enctype properties in the next hour, you can just leave them blank for now.

Adding Text Fields to Forms

Forms commonly include text fields. Single-line text fields enable users to type in a name, a street address, a phone number, or other short pieces of text information. Text fields can also have multiple lines, called a **textarea**, suitable for comments or lengthy pieces of information.

Text fields are added using the Text Field object from the Forms category of the Insert panel. When you add a text field to a page, Dreamweaver prompts for accessibility information, as shown in Figure 21.4.

FIGURE 21.4
Make your forms accessible by completing the accessibility attributes.

Provide the following information when you fill out the accessibility attributes:

▶ **ID**—A CSS ID that will be applied to the form element. This can be left blank if no CSS will be used.

- ▶ **Label**—A label that describes what the form element is for (a name, a street, and so on)

- ▶ **Style**—Defines how the label tag is applied. The default (Wrap with Label Tag) should be fine for most uses.

- ▶ **Position**—Choose whether the label will appear before or after the text field.

- ▶ **Access Key**—Choose a keyboard character that, when pressed with the Alt key (or Option on the Macintosh) will jump the cursor to the field.

- ▶ **Tab Index**—Choose a numeric value that represents the order in which the field will be selected if you press the tab key to move through the form.

If you're designing a form for the public, it is a wise idea to make it as accessible as possible. However, you can disable these accessibility features within the Accessibility category of the application preferences.

Now you continue creating your own form from scratch. Create a group of text fields designed to collect the user's first and last names, email address, and subject. Begin by inserting a single-line text field into your web page to collect the user's first name, and then follow these steps:

1. Place your cursor inside the form delimiter, and click to add a new text field to the form. Enter a label of **Name:** in the accessibility attributes, leaving the rest as their default settings.

2. Click OK. A text field with label appears in the form, as shown in Figure 21.5.

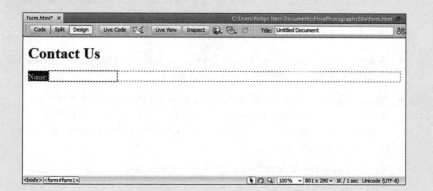

FIGURE 21.5
Insert a text field within a form so that a script or an application on the server can collect the data a user enters in the field on the web page.

▼ TRY IT YOURSELF

Creating a Form
Continued

3. Add a new line (press the Enter or Return key), and add a new text field. Label this one as **Email:**.

4. Add another new line (press the Enter or Return key) and another field, labeled **Subject:**.

TIP

Dreamweaver Asks to Insert a Form When You've Already Inserted One

If you get a dialog box asking you to insert a <form> tag but you thought you had already inserted one, you did not properly place the insertion point within the form. In that case, it's easiest to click No in the dialog box, delete the newly created object, reposition the cursor, and try again. If you are just beginning to create a form and forget to insert a Form object first, click Yes in the dialog box. Dreamweaver inserts a <form> tag around the form element you just created.

CAUTION

Don't Use *Name* as a Name

You have to name form objects carefully so that users don't receive JavaScript error messages. You should never name an object on the page with any HTML attribute name. So naming a text field *name* might be a logical choice, but it could cause JavaScript errors in some browsers because that is also the name of a tag attribute.

Applying Text Field Attributes

When you have a text field selected, the Property inspector presents the text field attributes. Dreamweaver fills in a unique default name. Rename all the text fields in your form with meaningful and unique names, such as full-name, email, and subject. As when you're naming other Dreamweaver objects, do not use spaces and punctuation in the names of the text fields. Some scripts and applications cannot accept form element names that contain spaces and punctuation.

You can set both the size of the text field and the number of characters a user can enter into it. There are two width settings for a text field:

▶ **Char Width**—Set the size of the text field and the number of characters visible in the field. If there are more characters in the text field than the width setting can accommodate, the form submits them but they won't be visible without scrolling.

▶ **Max Chars**—Limit the number of characters a user can enter into the text field. The user cannot enter more characters than the value of Max Chars. Setting Max Chars might be useful when you know the absolute length of the data the user should enter, such as a Social Security number, and do not want the user to enter additional characters.

You can set three types of text fields in the Property inspector:

▶ **Single Line**—These text fields are useful for collecting small, discrete words, names, or phrases from the user.

▶ **Multi Line**—This type of text field presents an area with multiple lines that enables the user to enter larger blocks of text. This is the same as the Textarea object, which is available in the Forms category of the Insert panel.

▶ **Password**—These text fields are special single-line fields that mask what the user types into the field, using asterisks or bullets to shield the data from other people. This doesn't, however, encrypt the submitted data, which means it's not a very strong security measure and should not be used as the only protection when accepting sensitive data.

You can select any style in the Class drop-down list to apply a CSS (Cascading Style Sheets) style to the text field. You learned about CSS styles in Hour 11, "Formatting Web Pages with Cascading Style Sheets." You can set the font, the background color, and other attributes of a text field by using CSS styles.

The first three fields in your form are single-line text fields. Create a new field on a new line with the label **Message:**, but this time use a Textarea object from the Insert panel (or Insert, Form, Textarea). This object is treated exactly like the TextField object in Dreamweaver, but it has the Multi Line property already applied, as seen in Figure 21.6.

Textarea

Textarea properties

FIGURE 21.6
A textarea has a Num attribute, which you can set in the Property inspector. Num Lines sets the number of lines, or height, of the textarea.

The Textarea object includes a property that enables you to enter the height of the object (the number of lines in the textarea). Enter a value into the Num Lines property to set the height. There is no Max Chars setting for a textarea; you can control only the number of lines visible on the screen.

You can add some text that appears in the text field when the user views the form. This could be instructions on what to enter into the field or a default value that the users can change if they want to. Enter text into the Init Val box in the Property inspector, as shown in Figure 21.7, so that text is present when users initially load the form.

Initial value

Adding Radio Buttons and Check Boxes to Forms

Radio buttons and check boxes are additional form elements you can use to collect user input. These elements allow a user to choose from a set of predefined values, rather than providing their own input like the text field and text areas.

Radio Button Groups

Radio buttons come in groups so that the user can select only one button of the group at a time (such as male or female); when the user selects a different member of the button group, the previously selected button is deselected. For radio buttons to compose a group, they all must have the same name.

To create a group of radio buttons, follow these steps:

1. Place the insertion point within a form where the radio buttons will be located. Type **How did you hear about us?** and press the Enter or Return key.

2. Select the Radio Group object from the Forms category of the Insert panel or select Insert, Form, Radio Group.

3. Enter the name of the radio button group in the Name box of the Radio Group dialog box.

4. Enter a label name in the Label column and enter the value of the radio button when it is checked (called the **checked value**) in the Value column, as shown in Figure 21.8. The label is simply the text that appears next to the button; it is not part of the form. Use the + and – buttons to add and remove radio buttons. At the bottom of the dialog box, select whether you want to place the buttons in a table or separate them with line breaks (better for accessibility). Click OK to save your settings.

FIGURE 21.8
Add a radio button group. Each button has a label and a value.

5. When you select an individual radio button, the Property inspector displays that button's properties. Choose whether the button will be checked or unchecked when the user first loads the form by selecting either the Checked option or the Unchecked option, next to Initial State.

TRY IT YOURSELF ▼

Creating a Radio Button Group

NOTE

Single Radio Buttons

Radio buttons can also be added one at a time from the Insert panel. Because radio buttons are of little use by themselves, chances are you'll want to use the Radio Button Group object rather than dealing with individual buttons. You still need this capability, however, to add new radio buttons to an existing radio group.

Keep in mind that if you do add new radio buttons one at a time, you need to name them to match other radio buttons that should be associated with them.

Check Boxes

Check boxes collect user input when the user either checks or unchecks the box. They differ from radio buttons in that each check box acts independently. Radio buttons enable the user to select a single option, whereas check boxes enable the user to select any options that apply. Because check boxes are used to collect discrete pieces of information (like "check here to sign me up for the mailing list"), they are frequently added to forms individually.

> TIP
>
> ### Check Box Groups
>
> You can also add groups of check boxes, just as you would add a group of radio buttons. This is useful for instances when you want a user to provide you with multiple different values for a single question, such as "What mailing lists do you want to subscribe to? Check all that apply." Check box groups are added and configured just like radio button groups.

▼ TRY IT YOURSELF

Adding a Check Box to a Form

To add a check box to your form, follow these steps:

1. Place the insertion point within a form where the check box will be located.

2. Select the Check Box object from the Insert panel, or select Insert, Form, Check Box. Type `ReceiveNewsletter:` Into the Label accessibility attribute for the tag—leave the other accessibility fields alone.

3. Enter a name for the check box into the box in the far left of the Property inspector.

4. Enter a checked value into the Checked Value box. If you do not specify a checked value, the form sends the value On for the check box when the form submits its values. If there is an entry for the Checked Value setting, the form sends that value instead of On.

5. Choose whether the initial state of the check box is checked or unchecked in the Initial State setting.

6. Type a text label beside the check box. The settings should look as shown in Figure 21.9.

FIGURE 21.9
The check box settings are similar to the radio button settings.

PROPERTIES				
☑	Checkbox name	Checked value addme	Initial state ⦿ Checked	Class None ▾
	newsletter		○ Unchecked	

Adding Lists and Menus to Forms

Some form objects work better than others in certain situations (for example, selecting one of the 50 states for a United States address). If you allowed users to enter a state in a text field, some users might enter the full name, such as Washington; other users might enter the correct postal abbreviation, such as WA; and other users might enter something in between. Allowing the user to select from a drop-down menu helps you collect consistent data. In Dreamweaver, you add a drop-down menu by using the List/Menu object.

The List/Menu object inserts a list of values. You create the List/Menu object as either a list, displaying a set number of lines, or a menu, displaying all the list values. Figure 21.10 shows a list and a menu in a form displayed in a browser.

FIGURE 21.10
Lists display a certain number of values. A menu drops down when the user clicks it, allowing the user to select a value.

TRY IT YOURSELF ▼

Creating a List

To create a list, follow these steps:

1. Place the insertion point within the form where the list will be located.

2. Select the List/Menu object from the Insert panel, or select Insert, Form, List/Menu. Type **Why are you contacting us?** Into the Label accessibility attribute for the tag—leave the other accessibility fields alone.

3. Click the new list in the design view so that it is selected. Enter the name of the list into the box in the far left of the Property inspector.

4. Select the List radio button, and the Height and Allow Multiple attributes become active.

5. In the Height box, type the number of list items you want visible at one time (see Figure 21.11). If there are more list items than can be shown, scrollbars automatically appear. If the Height property isn't active, you selected Menu instead of List in step 4.

Creating a List

Continued

FIGURE 21.11
You set a list's height and other properties in the Property inspector.

6. Check the Allow Multiple check box if you want to allow the user to select multiple values in the list. You might want to add instructions that tell users that they can select multiple entries by holding down the Ctrl key (or the Command key on the Mac) and clicking multiple selections.

7. Set up the list values by selecting the List Values button. The List Values dialog box appears, as shown in Figure 21.12.

FIGURE 21.12
Select the + button in the List Values dialog box to add an item to the list.

8. Enter an item label and a value for each item in the list. The item label is what the user sees and selects. The value is what the form sends back to a script on the server for processing. They can be the same, if appropriate. To add an item, click the + sign, enter the item label, tab to the Value field, and enter a value. You can press the Tab key to go forward or press Shift+Tab to go back. Use the – button to delete entries, and use the arrow buttons to rearrange entries. When you are at the end of the list, pressing Tab creates a new item label and value pair.

9. Click OK in the List Values dialog box.

10. Select an item from the Initially Selected box if one of the items should be selected by default. Otherwise, the first item appears.

TIP

Make the First List Item a Blank Value

Some people like to create a blank name and value pair as the first item in a list or menu. This keeps the first choice from being a default choice so you can tell when a user has actually made a choice.

NOTE

Select Objects

People who don't use Dreamweaver might call the list and menu objects **Select** objects. This is because HTML uses the `<select>` tag to implement these objects.

Whereas a list can show a number of lines, a menu shows only one line until the user drops down the menu by clicking. Menus use less space than lists because a menu can drop down over other objects on the page when clicked, but it shrinks to only one line when it is inactive. Creating a menu is similar to creating a list, except that you don't set the height and you cannot allow the user to select multiple entries. You can turn a list into a drop-down menu by selecting the Menu option as the type in the Property inspector.

For a quick and easy way to add standard drop-down menus, such as menus for years, numbers, or months, use the Snippets panel. The Forms section of the Snippets panel contains prebuilt menus and form elements you can simply drag and drop onto your web page.

TIP

Control the Width of a List or Drop-Down Menu

You can modify the width of the list or menu objects using CSS. Simply redefine the `<select>` tag, the tag that creates a list or menu. Modify the width property in the Box category.

Adding Push Buttons and Image Buttons to Forms

You can add the following four types of buttons to forms:

▶ **Submit**—This type of button sends the data the user has entered into a form to a script or an application on the server. A submit button triggers the action that you set in the form's Action box in the Property inspector.

▶ **Reset**—This type of button erases all the data the user has entered in the form. It also reloads any initial values.

▶ **None**—This type of generic button has no automatic function. You can add functionality to a generic button by applying a behavior to it.

▶ **Image**—This type of button acts like a submit button. The form submits all the data it contains, and it sends the coordinates of where the user clicked.

The first three buttons are push buttons you create by inserting Dreamweaver's Button object. They differ in the way you configure them in the Property inspector. You create the fourth button, the image button, by inserting an Image Field object.

Adding Submit and Reset Buttons to Forms

In this section, you add submit and reset buttons to your form. Usually, the submit button is on the left and the reset button is to the right of the submit button.

▼ TRY IT YOURSELF

Adding Buttons to a Form

To add a button to the form, follow these steps:

1. Position the insertion point and then select the Button object from the Insert panel, or select Insert, Form, Button. Because most buttons have their own labels, leave the accessibility attributes empty and click OK.

2. Highlight the button in your page, and then select Submit Form as the action for this button in the Property inspector. Type **"Send Message"** into the Property inspector value field.

3. Add another button to the right of the submit button.

4. Select Reset Form as the action for this button and a value of "Clear Form". The buttons should look like the buttons in Figure 21.13.

FIGURE 21.13
The submit button is usually placed on the left of the reset button. You need one submit button per form if you are sending this form to a script or to an application on a server.

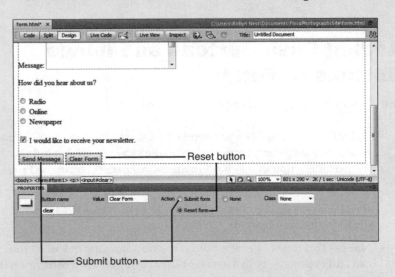

You can accept the default labels that Dreamweaver gives the submit and reset buttons or you can give them new labels. You can change the label of either button; a button does not have to say Submit to function as a submit button.

Many web developers like to give a submit button a label that actually describes what the button does, such as Enter the Contest or Send Comment. Each form must have a submit button to send the form data. The reset button is optional. You should have only one submit button per form with multiple text fields.

Adding an Image Button to Forms

You can replace a submit button with an image button. When the user clicks the image, the form submits its contents and the coordinates of the location where the user clicked the image button. Obviously, you do not need a submit button if you have an image button.

To add an image field to a form, first make sure that the insertion point is inside the form. Add an image field by selecting the Image Field object from the Insert panel or selecting Insert, Form, Image Field. The Select Image Source dialog box appears, enabling you to navigate and select a standard web image file. The Property inspector displays the name, source, alt text, and alignment attributes for the field. You set these attributes as you would for any image.

Adding Generic Buttons to Forms

Add a generic button by selecting the Button object from the Insert panel or by selecting Insert, Form, Button. Name the button, give it a label, and select None as the button's action. Now you can apply a behavior to this button that the user can trigger with a button click.

You might want to use a generic button if you aren't actually submitting the form to a script on the server (the topic for the next hour). You can use what's called a **client-side script**—JavaScript contained in the web page that reacts to the form data. Submit buttons work only with server-side scripts, but a generic button can trigger a client-side script, via Dreamweaver behaviors or custom JavaScript. An example of this functionality would be a multiple-choice question in a web page. When users click the generic button, a client-side script triggers to check whether they picked the correct radio button and displays feedback for them on the web page.

TIP

Deleting a Form

Sometimes it is difficult to delete a form from the page. The easiest way to delete a form is to right-click the form delimiter to view the context menu. Then choose the Remove Tag <form> command. If the Remove Tag command does not say <form>, you have the wrong object selected. You could, of course, always select the <form> tag in the tag selector to delete the form.

Structuring a Form with Labels and Fieldsets

There are two other form elements you might want to apply along with the buttons and fields you've seen here.

The first, the `<label>` tag, provides a visible label for a given form object. These tags are inserted automatically if you use the label accessibility attribute when inserting a field. If you want to insert a label manually, just select the form elements that should be labeled, and then click the Label element inside the Forms category of the Insert panel. Dreamweaver inserts the `<label></label>` tags around your selection—it is up to you, however, to insert and style the text that composes the label between the two tags.

The second element you can use to create more structured and accessible forms is the fieldset. A fieldset separates a related group of fields and labels them as a distinct part of a form. For example, you may have filled in forms with areas for personal information, shipping address, and billing address—these could all be denoted as fieldsets within a form. It doesn't change how the fields work, but it does draw a box around them and provide a label to denote their purpose.

To add a fieldset to your form, first create the fields just as you have been doing throughout the hour. Next, select the fields that should be grouped together and click the Fieldset object in the Insert panel. You are asked to provide a "Legend" for the fieldset—this is just a label that describes what the fields have in common. Enter an appropriate value and click OK to add the `<fieldset></fieldset>` and `<legend></legend>` tags to your form.

Creating a Jump Menu to Navigate to Different URLs

Dreamweaver's **Jump Menu** object makes it easy to create a drop-down menu of links that allows the viewer to jump to other websites or different web pages within the current site. The Jump Menu object uses JavaScript to redirect the browser. You set up the list values in a special dialog box, as shown in Figure 21.14. The item labels appear in the drop-down menu, and the values contain the URLs to the web pages to which the user jumps.

NOTE

Use Labels and Fieldsets Where Possible!

Labels and fieldsets provide additional information about a form that can help make them accessible to people who might otherwise not be able to determine which parts of a form should get which information. These important tags are frequently left off of web forms, despite how easy they are to use!

TIP

Add an Initial Value

A common way to create a jump menu is to have the first item be the text "Choose One..." and not to give it a link. Because you never want the user to select this item, the inability to select the first item in the drop-down menu won't be a problem. Then enable the Select First Item After URL Change check box so that the Choose One selection reappears.

Menu items

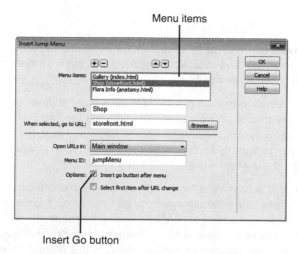

Insert Go button

FIGURE 21.14
The Insert Jump Menu dialog box enables you to create a drop-down menu where the user can select an item to which to link.

If you want to edit the jump menu after you have created it in the special dialog box, you have to brush up on the form skills you learned in this hour and the behavior skills you learned in previous hours. You can edit the jump menu by editing the Jump Menu behavior. Select the List/Menu object that the Jump Menu command creates and double-click the Jump Menu behavior in the Behaviors panel. Add or remove list items by using the + and – buttons. Rearrange the list by using the up- and down-arrow buttons. You can enable or disable the Select First Item After URL Change setting.

Summary

In this hour, you learned how to insert and configure a form. You learned how to add text fields, radio buttons, check boxes, lists, and menus to the form. You learned how to add submit and reset buttons to the form and how to create a generic button. You learned how to use Dreamweaver's Jump Menu object to create a menu that consists of a bunch of URLs to which the user can jump.

TIP

Add a Go Button

You cannot add a Go button by editing the Jump Menu behavior. You can add one manually, however. Create a generic button by inserting a button into the form, giving it the label Go, and setting its action to None. Apply the Jump Menu Go behavior to the button triggered by the onClick event. When prompted, choose the jump menu ID from the Jump Menu Go dialog box, then click OK.

Q&A

Q. I just want to email my form contents. I know that in the next hour I learn about CGI and other scripting methods, but isn't there a quick-and-dirty way to do this?

A. You can email form contents by using your email address as the action. You must preface your email address with `mailto:` so that it looks like this: `mailto:you@yourdomain.com`. In addition, you might need to type **text/plain** into the Enctype attribute in the Property inspector when you select the <form> tag.

This way of submitting a form might be fine for collecting form data about where your co-workers want to go to lunch on Friday. They all know and trust you (at least I hope they do), and they probably all have their email programs set up in a similar fashion to yours. An email program must be set up properly with the browser for this method to work. In addition, some browsers put up a warning when the user tries to submit a form in this fashion.

Q. Why can't I see my form elements?

A. If your form elements aren't showing up, they must not be inside the <form> tags. Some browsers hide form elements that are not inside a form.

Q. What can I do to check that my forms are filled out correctly by users before they are submitted?

A. Form validation is typically done on the client side with JavaScript. Fortunately, the Form category of the Insert panel includes Spry versions of the text field, textarea, check box, radio button, and password elements with attached JavaScript. (As you may recall, Spry is the JavaScript framework integrated with Dreamweaver.) Refer to Hour 22 for more details about using Spry form elements.

Workshop

Quiz

1. What do you need to do to make a number of radio buttons act as though they are a group?

2. How do you create a generic button?

3. What's the difference between a list and a menu?

Quiz Answers

1. All the radio buttons in a group must have the same name.

2. After you insert a button into a form, select None as the action. You can then attach Dreamweaver behaviors to the button if you like.

3. A list displays a configurable number of items and might allow the user to select more than one item to submit. A menu displays only one line and drops down when the user clicks it so that the user can select an item. The user can select only one item at a time from a menu.

Exercises

1. Create a form to collect the user data of your choice. Format the form objects and labels with a table so that they line up nicely. Place the submit and reset buttons in the bottom row of the table and merge the cells so that the buttons are centered under the entire table.

2. Experiment with using the form page designs and Snippets panel to quickly create forms. Create one of the built-in CSS style sheets that applies to forms and attach it to a forms page. Try modifying some of the styles in the style sheet.

HOUR 22
Sending and Reacting to Form Data

In Hour 21, "Creating a Form and Collecting Data," you learned how to create a form. In this hour, you decide what to do with the data that the user enters into your form. You have to send the data to a script on the server for processing. The script on the server can store data in a database, send it to an email address, send results back to the browser, or process it any way you want (depending on your scripting abilities!).

The types of information you might want to receive in a form could include orders, feedback, comments, guest-book entries, polls, and even uploaded files. Creating the form and inserting form elements are usually the easy parts. The difficult part is installing and configuring the scripts that process the data.

Validating a Form's Data Using the Validate Form Behavior

Before you receive and process information from a form, it is a good idea to make sure that the information is complete and in the right format. Dreamweaver has a Validate Form behavior which can ensure that a user has entered data into a required field, check the validity of an email address, and verify that the user enters numbers correctly. (As discussed in Hour 18, "Adding Interactivity with Behaviors," behaviors attach JavaScript to page elements so when a triggering event occurs an action is performed.)

WHAT YOU'LL LEARN IN THIS HOUR:

▶ How to use the Validate Form behavior and Spry form validation elements
▶ How to set up a page to submit to a CGI script
▶ How to create secure web pages
▶ How Dreamweaver edits and displays ASP, ASP.NET, JSP, PHP, and CFML code

NOTE

Client-Side Scripts

You can also have client-side scripts created in JavaScript process form data, but those scripts do not have access to server resources and are not able to email data or insert it into a database.

The Validate Form behavior requires the user to enter the form data correctly before submitting the data to a script or an application on the server. You can validate the form in two ways:

▶ Attach the Validate Form behavior to the Submit button to validate the entire form when the Submit button is clicked. The onClick event triggers the behavior.

▶ Attach the Validate Form behavior to an individual text field to validate the data entered in that field when the user leaves it. The onChange event triggers the behavior when the user's focus leaves the field.

You must have a form with form objects in your web page before the Validate Form behavior is active in the + drop-down menu of the Behaviors panel.

▼ TRY IT YOURSELF

Creating a Validating Form

To validate a form, follow these steps:

1. Create a new form that has various text fields, or open the form you created in Hour 21.

2. Click the Submit button.

3. Open the Behaviors panel. Click the + button and select the Validate Form behavior.

4. The Validate Form dialog box appears. A list of all the text fields appears in the dialog box.

5. Check the Required check box if the user must fill in an entry in the field.

6. Choose from among the four settings in the Accept category:

   ▶ **Anything**—Select this setting if the user has to enter data into the field but that data can be in any format. For instance, if you are asking for a phone number, you do not want to limit the user to entering only numbers because users often format phone numbers with other characters.

   ▶ **Number**—Select this setting if the user has to enter data that is numeric.

   ▶ **Email Address**—Select this setting if the user has to enter an email address. This setting checks for an @ symbol.

   ▶ **Number From**—Select this setting to check for a number within a range of specific numbers. Fill in both the low and high ends of the range.

7. Notice that your settings appear in parentheses beside the name of the text field in the Fields list (shown in Figure 22.1). Repeat steps 5 and 6 to validate all the text fields.

TRY IT YOURSELF ▼

Creating a Validating Form
Continued

Field settings

Required value

Type of data accepted

FIGURE 22.1
The validation settings appear in parentheses in the Fields list in the Validate Form dialog box.

8. When you are finished making changes in the Validate Form dialog box, click OK. Select the onClick event if the Validate Form behavior is attached to the Submit button. Select the onChange event if you attached the behavior to an individual text field.

When the Validate Form behavior triggers, it checks the data in the form against the settings you entered. You should make sure that your form's labels and instructions clearly tell users what type of data to enter in each field and indicate which fields are required. You should give the users the information to fill out the form properly so that they don't get frustrated with error messages.

If the user enters incorrect data, the message box shown in Figure 22.2 appears. This message tells the user that errors have occurred, lists the text fields' names, and explains why the Validate Form behavior rejected the data. Here is another place where a meaningful name for a Dreamweaver object is important. If you are validating a form, it is a good idea to give a text field the same name as the label beside it so that the user can easily locate and change the field's data.

TIP

Required Form Elements

A standard way to signal that a form element is required is to place an asterisk next to its label. It's becoming more common to use a bold label to signal that a form element is required. You should tell your users somewhere on the page what indicates that a form element is required.

TIP

The Uncertainties of Form Validation

The Form validation behaviors are a great way to help a user enter correct input before data gets sent to a server. It should not, however, be the only type of validation that occurs. JavaScript can be disabled on a client browser, enabling users to submit *anything* within a form. Form validation should always happen both at the user side, using behaviors, and at the server side, using the scripting language you've chosen.

FIGURE 22.2
After the validation script is run, a form that has errors or omissions displays this message, indicating which fields the user either omitted or filled out incorrectly.

Using the Spry Framework Validation Objects

In Hour 19, "Using Spry, the Widget Browser, and Extensions," you explored the Spry framework and learned how to insert Spry elements in a web page. Spry has several special form elements you can insert in a form to add automatic form validation: a Spry text field, select object (list or menu), check box, radio group, text area, and password.

Let's walk through inserting and setting up a text field as an example. All the Spry form elements work similarly.

▼ TRY IT YOURSELF

Setting Up a Spry Validation Text Field

To set up a Spry Validation text field, do the following:

1. Place the insertion point inside a form.

2. Select Insert, Spry, Spry Validation Text Field. Complete the usual Input Tag Accessibility Attributes settings and click OK to insert the file.

3. Click the tab above the Spry text field to display the text field validation settings in the Property inspector, as shown in Figure 22.3.

Setting Up a Spry Validation Text Field
Continued

Preview for invalid format

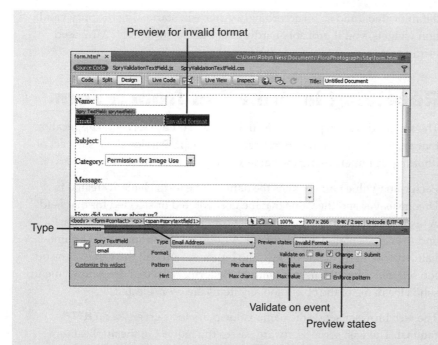

Type

Validate on event

Preview states

FIGURE 22.3
You can set up Spry validation properties by selecting the object and changing settings in the Property inspector.

4. Select the type of data that the text field should be. Is it an email address? A credit card? A phone number? A Social Security number? A URL? There are validation settings for all of these commonly collected pieces of data and more.

5. The preview states drop-down shows the appearance of a form element under the following conditions: its initial appearance, if it is required, if the entered value is invalid, and if the entered value is valid. (Figure 22.3 shows the invalid state.)

6. Select when the text field validates by choosing one of the Validate On selections. Select Blur to validate when the user clicks outside the form element. Select Change to validate when the content of the form element changes. Select Submit to validate when the user clicks the Submit button.

7. Save the web page (File, Save) and copy the dependent files if prompted. Preview the page in the browser or in Live View and test the validation.

The other Spry validation widgets work the same way. Simply insert the "Spry Validation" version of the form element that you want to use, and then select the blue tab that appears above it and configure the validation,

NOTE
The Confirm Widget

One strange widget is the "confirm" widget. This is meant to be used along with a Spry Validation password widget. It provides a second password field whose contents must match the first password field.

default values, and so on accordingly. After you start using the Spry validation widgets, you'll probably hardly ever build a straight HTML-based form again.

Receiving Information from a Form

The standard way to process a form is to have on the server an application that parses the data and performs an action on it. **Parsing** data is the act of dividing and interpreting the name-value pairs that are sent to the server.

Each name-value pair contains the name of the form element created in Dreamweaver and the value that the user entered or selected for that field. A text field has a name-value pair that contains the name of the text field and the value entered into that field. A radio button group sends a name-value pair with the name of the radio button group and the value of the button selected when the user submitted the form. A list or a drop-down menu sends the name of the object and any items the user selected.

The web browser sends the name-value pairs to a server via an **HTTP request**. The web server software passes the request to the application server that handles the scripting language specified in the request, as shown in Figure 22.4. For instance, if the script is in PHP: Hypertext Preprocessor (PHP), the PHP application server handles the request. Depending on the script, the application server might request data from a database or send a request to an email server to send a specific email message. The server can process scripts in many ways. The application server usually returns some sort of output, normally HTML, which the web server sends back to the browser. This all takes place in milliseconds!

FIGURE 22.4
The browser sends a request to a script on the server and receives a response. The script might control sending an email message or accessing and returning data from a database.

Preparing a Page to Interact with ASP, ASP.NET, JSP, PHP, or CFML

Dreamweaver enables you to create dynamic web pages that incorporate server-side scripting with capability to process forms and create dynamic web applications. When you create a new web page, you choose from several different development platforms, as shown in Figure 22.5.

TIP

CGI Scripting

Another way of processing forms on a server is by using a CGI script. **CGI** stands for **common gateway interface**, and it is the definition of the standard method of communication between a script and the web server. Developers usually write those scripts in Perl or another programming language. There are various places on the Web to download CGI scripts. If you don't know how to program and you are willing to process your forms generically, you can find a widely used script called FormMail at Matt's Script Archive (http://www. scriptarchive.com).

Supported server languages

FIGURE 22.5
You can create ASP, ASP.NET, JSP, PHP, and CFML pages with Dreamweaver.

Dreamweaver supports these five major server-side scripting technologies:

▶ **ASP**—Microsoft's legacy web development platform, ASP, combines client-side scripting with server-side processing to create dynamic web pages. Dreamweaver CS5 supports both JavaScript and VBScript-based ASP development.

▶ **ASP.NET**—Microsoft's ASP.NET, released in 2002, is a server-side application platform that has replaced ASP in all but legacy applications. ASP.NET runs on Windows 2000 Server or later. Dreamweaver supports C# and Visual Basic .NET development languages.

▶ **JSP**—JSP is a Java-based way to dynamically process web pages. JSP scripts interact with a JSP-enabled server. The popular Apache web server and the free Tomcat JSP application server are available. For Microsoft IIS, Tomcat offers an IIS connector as well.

▶ **PHP**—PHP is a free, open-source server-side scripting language that sends dynamic web pages to the user after interpreting PHP code. PHP is the open-source movement's answer to ASP and is widely supported by free applications and scripts.

▶ **ColdFusion**—Adobe's ColdFusion server interprets CFML (ColdFusion Markup Language) to create dynamic web pages. The ColdFusion server application can run on many operating systems. CFML is slightly different from the other scripting languages described here because it is a tag-based language, like HTML.

All these technologies accomplish the same thing: enabling a client-side web page to interact with the server by accessing data, sending an email message, or processing input in some way. They all have advantages and disadvantages, and each uses a different syntax to add code to web pages. That said, after you learn one, it's easy to pick up another.

CAUTION

Choose Compatible Web Hosting

If you choose to start exploring the scripting languages in Dreamweaver, you want to use a hosting provider that can support for the one you choose.

Setting Form Properties

You use ASP, ASP.NET, JSP, PHP, or CFML coding to process form data, for example, by mailing the contents or by storing them in a database. To make a form functional, you need to reference the URL of a page coded to process the form as the Action in the Property inspector, as shown in Figure 22.6.

FIGURE 22.6
With the form selected, enter the URL for the page that processes your form in the Action text box of the Property inspector.

URL of page containing processing code

Data submission method

You can also choose whether to use the GET and POST methods when transmitting form data. These differ in the following ways:

▶ The GET method appends form data via the URL, a URL that can be saved as a bookmark in the browser. Data submitted via this method is displayed in the address field of the browser after submission, and is limited to text-based data; file uploads won't work.

▶ The POST method packages and sends the data invisibly to the server; the output doesn't appear in the URL. There is no limitation on the amount of data that forms can send. In addition, the POST method allows uploading of files with forms.

I suggest the POST method because it is typically considered better form (no pun intended).

Adding a Hidden Field to a Form

Sometimes when submitting a form for processing, you want to include information in addition to that given by the respondent. That's when you include hidden fields. Hidden fields are sent along with all the other form fields, but are not visible in a web browser. The users cannot change the contents of these fields, nor can they see the fields unless they view your HTML source.

You create hidden fields for things that you define, not the respondent, such as the recipient of the emailed form data, the subject that appears in the email subject field, and the URL to which the script redirects the user after out the form is filled out.

To add hidden fields to your form, follow these steps:

1. Place the insertion point anywhere inside your form. It does not matter where the hidden fields are located.

2. Select the Hidden Field object from the Insert panel or select Insert, Form, Hidden Field.

3. Dreamweaver displays the Hidden Field symbol in your web page, as shown in Figure 22.7.

4. Enter the name **redirect**. As the value of the field, enter the URL where the user is redirected after the form is submitted.

TIP

Use a Form-Hosting Site

If you don't have access to a server that supports server-side coding, you might want to use a form-hosting site. The site http://www.formmail.com enables you to build and host forms without advertisements for less than a dollar per month. You simply link from your site to the page with the form located on the hosting service's server.

TRY IT YOURSELF ▼

Adding Hidden Fields to a Form

NOTE

Enabling Hidden Field Symbols

If you do not see the Hidden Field symbol, verify that you have Invisible Elements checked (select View, Visual Aids, Invisible Elements); also, the Invisible Elements category in the Dreamweaver Preferences dialog box must have Hidden Form Fields checked.

▼ TRY IT YOURSELF

**Adding Hidden Fields
to a Form**
Continued

FIGURE 22.7
The Hidden Field symbol appears
when you insert a hidden field into
a form. The Property inspector
shows a hidden field name-value
pair.

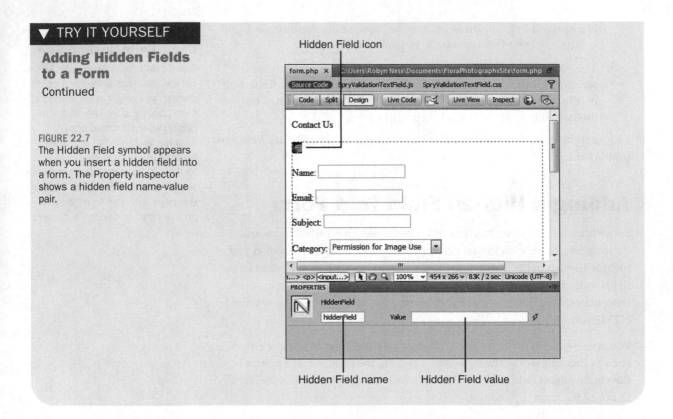

Uploading a File from a Form

With the proper server scripts in place, you might choose to add a **file field**
that enables users to upload files. You can collect images or any types of
files that you want with a file field object. Users click the Browse button,
shown in Figure 22.8, to select a file from the local drive. When a user clicks
the Submit button, the file travels to the server.

A file field has attributes similar to those of a text field, which you used in
the preceding hour. You can set the size of the file field by putting a value in
the Char Width box in the Property inspector. You can also set the Max
Chars attribute and the Init Val attribute in the Property inspector. You
must give the file field a unique name.

The important question you must answer before you use a file field is this:
Does your server allow anonymous file uploads? You also have to select
multipart/form-data from the Enctype drop-down list for the <form> tag so

that the file encoding is correct. Also, you should use the POST method to submit your form; the GET method does not work with file fields.

File field

FIGURE 22.8
Use a file field to enable a user to upload a file to the server. However, make sure that your server allows uploading before you create your form.

Exploring Submission Security

When your users submit form information, it travels across the Internet. People who are along the path of the data and who understand how to intercept and reassemble Web data can read the information.

The only way around this problem is to create a secure site in which information is encrypted (scrambled) before being sent from the browser to the server and vice versa. To do this, the web server on which your site is located must have SSL—the secure sockets layer—enabled. This requires a server **certificate** to verify that you are who you say you are.

Customers expect you to protect only their sensitive data, such as credit card numbers or other financial data. However, for public polls, guest books, or feedback forms, you don't have to shield the information from potential thieves.

Users access a secure URL exactly as they would a regular URL. The only difference is that the protocol portion of the URL changes from http to https. As shown in Figure 22.9, the browser displays a Lock icon in the status bar when it is in secure mode.

FIGURE 22.9
The browser displays a Lock icon in the status bar when serving the page via secure sockets.

Summary

In this hour, you learned how to use the Validate Form behavior and Spry form validation elements to validate the data that the user enters into your form. You also set up a form for submission to a server. You inserted into hidden fields that contain a name-value pair. You set the action for a form and learned the difference between the GET and POST methods for submitting data. You learned about secure transactions. In addition, you learned how to call ASP, ASP.NET, PHP, JSP, and CFML scripts.

Q&A

Q. I know a PHP programmer who will help me with my web pages. What do I need to explain about my web pages so that she can write a script to process them on the server?

A. Your programmer needs to know what you called the items in your form and how you want them processed. If the data will go into a database, she has to know what you call the items in your form in order to parse the data into the correct place. She also needs to know whether you need any validation or processing applied to the data. For instance, you might need to have individual prices added together as one total price.

Q. Do I need to secure my forms if I collect payment information? My site is small and not many people know about it.

A. Yes! All it takes is one unlucky customer who has their data stolen to risk your reputation and possibly result in a lawsuit. Many states are cracking down on data privacy by holding site owners responsible damages! If your site stores transactions in a database, you should also ensure that is secure.

Q. Should I learn Perl, ASP, ASP.NET, PHP, JSP, or CFML?

A. It depends on what you want to do when you grow up! Do you have a knack for coding? If so, having skills in any of these technologies might be fun and look great on your resume. Find out which technologies are hot in the marketplace. ASP.NET, JSP, and PHP are a safe bet for those looking for a job in a web development field.

If you aren't very interested in coding but want to expand your web skill set, maybe it's a better idea to specialize in Dreamweaver—there's a lot to learn! On the other hand, you can always learn more about databases. If you don't really enjoy coding, it can be a real chore. Dreamweaver offers objects and server behaviors that make it much easier than before to code dynamic web pages.

Workshop

Quiz

1. What pair of items do users send when submitting a form?

2. What is a hidden text field?

3. What does it mean when a URL begins with *https*?

Quiz Answers

1. Users send a name-value pair when they submit a form. This is the name of the form object and the value either entered or selected by the user.

2. A hidden text field contains a name-value pair that the user cannot change. Generally, the script requires this data to process the form properly.

3. A URL beginning with *https* signals that the URL is secure using the Secure HTTP protocol.

Exercises

1. Find a form on the Web and look at it critically. Select the View Source command to see the HTML. Does the form have any hidden fields? To what server is the form submitted? You should look for the <form> and </form> tags that contain the code for the form.

2. Create a free form at Freedback (http://www.freedback.com) and examine the code. What is the action of the form? Does it use POST or GET? Does it include any hidden fields, and if so why might it do that?

HOUR 23
Uploading, Sharing, and Managing Web Projects

Finished websites reside on a web server where many people can access the web pages. While you are working on your websites, you want to move them onto a server for testing. At the end of the project, you have to move your web pages to a public server so that other people can look at them. There are different ways to move the files onto a server and different methods for ensuring that the version of the files is correct and not accidentally overwritten.

WHAT YOU'LL LEARN IN THIS HOUR:

▶ How to configure a remote site

▶ How to move your site onto a remote server

▶ How to use Check In/Check Out

Enabling Server Connection

When you define a website in Dreamweaver, you define a local site to hold files that will be used in the final, public website. Dreamweaver calls your final site the **remote site**. You work on the files in your local site and then upload them to the remote site by using Dreamweaver's file transfer commands.

When working in Dreamweaver, you don't need additional file transfer protocol (FTP) software or any other software to move your files onto the remote server. Dreamweaver has this capability built in! It's more convenient to set up your remote site and transfer files while working in Dreamweaver than to jump to another application. Dreamweaver also includes some helpful features to manage your files.

Adding Your Remote Site

You define a remote site by editing the website definition (which you get to by selecting Site, Manage Sites). Select a site and click the Edit button to launch the Site Setup dialog box for the selected website.

Choose Servers from the categories on the left side to add, remove, edit, or duplicate server connections for your remote website, as shown in Figure 23.1.

FIGURE 23.1
When you are ready to upload a site, open the Servers settings to add details from your Internet service provider about your web server.

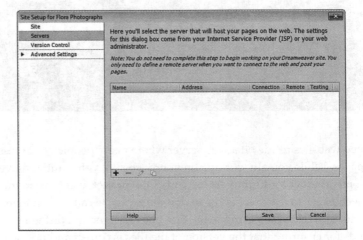

To add a new server, click the Add New Server button (a plus sign). In the Basic tab, as shown in Figure 23.2, type a server name to identify which environment you are defining.

FIGURE 23.2
You set up the remote site definition in the Basic tab of the Servers section of the Site Setup Dialog box.

Next, you can choose from among five transfer methods in the drop-down menu:

▶ FTP

▶ SFTP

▶ Local/Network

▶ WebDAV

▶ RDS

The transfer method you select depends on where your remote site is hosted. The site might be at your ISP, the folks who provide you with an Internet dial-up service, or a web hosting service. In that case, you probably connect to its servers by using FTP or SFTP. The site might be on your company's intranet, and if so, you can transfer the local site to the remote site by using a LAN connection (the Local/Network option in the drop-down menu). WebDAV and RDS connections are less common than the others, but professional web development environments sometimes use them.

Setting FTP and SFTP Information

You should select FTP or SFTP access if you need to transfer files over the Web to a remote server. The server could be physically located in your building, or it could be on the other side of the world. You must enter the name of the FTP/SFTP server in the FTP Address or SFTP address text box. Often the hostname is in this format: ftp.*domain*.com.

You must have a login and a password to access FTP/SFTP servers. The standard anonymous login, often used to download files over the Internet, probably does not work to upload files to a website. Dreamweaver saves your password by default. If other people have access to Dreamweaver on your computer and you don't want them to access your FTP account, deselect the Save check box.

Click the Test Connection button to make sure that you've entered everything correctly and are successfully connecting to the FTP server. You can troubleshoot FTP connection problems by first closing the Site Definition dialog box and then selecting Window, Results and clicking the FTP Log tab, as shown in Figure 23.3. The FTP log lists the reason you didn't connect successfully. For instance, if the log states that the password was incorrect or the directory you are targeting doesn't exist, you can change these settings in the Site Definition Wizard and try again.

FIGURE 23.3
Use the FTP Log tab to diagnose connection problems.

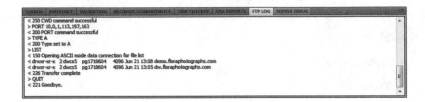

If you are behind a firewall or using a proxy server, you might have difficulties with FTP. Consult the network administrator about which settings you need to choose when setting up FTP. The most common change you need to make is to enable passive FTP, which helps with most simple firewall issues. To enable passive FTP, click the disclosure triangle next to More Options near the bottom of the window, and then click the check box beside Use Passive FTP, as shown in Figure 23.4.

FIGURE 23.4
Configure passive FTP to deal with the most common firewall issues.

For more complex setups, you might have to configure the firewall port and host in the Site category of the Dreamweaver Preferences dialog box. If you have a slow connection to the Internet, the default FTP timeout might be too short, causing your FTP connection to time out too often. You can increase this time also in the Site category of the Preferences dialog box.

Setting LAN Information

Select Local/Network in the Site Definition Wizard, as shown in Figure 23.5, if the server is on a computer that you can connect to directly by using a network. If you can access files on the server the same way you access your hard drive, moving files to and from it with ease, you have LAN access. You must know the correct web-accessible directory; your web administrator should be able to give you that information.

FIGURE 23.5
Select Local/Network when the remote directory resides within your LAN.

Set up LAN access to the remote server by entering the path to the remote directory. Click the Browse icon to browse to the directory or type in the path.

Setting RDS Access

You use the RDS setting only if your remote site is on a ColdFusion server. ColdFusion is one of the server-side scripting languages that Dreamweaver supports. As when you select FTP, you enter a hostname (the server address), a port, host directory, a username, and a password to connect to this type of remote site.

Setting WebDAV Access

WebDAV stands for "Web Distributed Authoring and Versioning." It is a popular extension to the standard HTTP protocol for reading and writing to remote file systems. It works through proxy servers and firewalls with relative ease—and is entirely cross-platform. Apple's MobileMe iDisk service, for example, uses this protocol to provide access on Mac OS X and Windows.

TIP

Version Control and Dreamweaver

WebDAV *can* be used as version control systems. A version control system monitors changes to files and ensures that a full history of activity is maintained. It can even help combine changes made by two developers to a single file. Dreamweaver's implementation of WebDAV only allows for reading and writing from/to the system—just like a normal file server. To gain access to *true* version control under Dreamweaver, you need access to a "Subversion" server. This is the only version control standard supported under Dreamweaver; it is discussed later in this hour.

Select WebDAV from the drop-down menu in the Site Definition Wizard, and then fill in the URL of your WebDAV file server (usually your website address) and the username and password assigned to you.

Moving a Site onto a Remote Server

If your server is located on a LAN, you normally connect to the server when you log on to your computer and you stay connected all day. If you access the remote server over the Internet by using FTP, you connect while getting and putting files onto the server and then you disconnect. Even if you don't disconnect on your end, your connection will most likely time out on the server if you have been inactive for a period and you will have to reconnect.

The Files panel contains buttons, as shown in Figure 23.6, that enables you to transfer files to and from the remote site. You can transfer files to your local site by clicking the Get button, and you can transfer files to the remote site by clicking the Put button. In Hour 24, "Maintaining a Website," you will learn about using the Synchronize command, which is a better way to transfer files. The Synchronize command detects whether a local file (or remote file) is newer and transfers it only if necessary, thus saving transfer time.

FIGURE 23.6
The buttons at the top of the Files panel help you transfer files between the local and remote sites.

The buttons at the top of the Files panel are as detailed here:

> ▶ **Connect/Disconnect**—This button establishes a connection to an FTP server. The button has a little green light that stays lit when you have

a connection to an FTP server. The light remains constantly lit when you have LAN access to your remote site.

▶ **Refresh**—This button manually refreshes the list of files in the Files panel.

▶ **Get**—This button retrieves files from the remote site and moves them to your local site.

▶ **Put**—This button places files from your local site onto the remote site.

▶ **Check In**—This button places files from your local site onto the remote site and marks them as "checked in" and accessible for other developers to edit.

▶ **Check Out**—This button retrieves files from the remote site, moves them to your local site, and marks them as "checked out" so that other Dreamweaver users can't modify them.

▶ **Synchronize**—This button triggers the Synchronize command that enables you to check which files are new and have to be uploaded to the remote site.

▶ **Expand/Collapse**—This button expands the Files panel into the Expanded Files panel.

Click the Expand/Collapse button on the far right of the Files panel to expand the panel, as shown in Figure 23.7. The expanded Files panel not only shows the local site, as does the collapsed Files panel, but also shows the remote site. A list of the files on the remote site appears when you are connected. When you want to collapse the expanded Files panel, click the Expand/Collapse button again.

FIGURE 23.7
Use the Expand/Collapse button to expand the Files panel.

Understanding Dreamweaver's Website Management Capabilities

Dreamweaver's file management system is useful if you are creating web pages with other people. Earlier, you defined the remote site in the Servers section of the Site Setup dialog box. You need to open that section again and edit settings for your server under the Advanced tab to enable additional settings related to remote files, as shown in Figure 23.8.

FIGURE 23.8
Enable features such as Check
In/Check Out so that you can
control collaboration with others.

Maintain Synchronization Information is checked by default, as it is needed for ensuring newer files aren't accidentally overwritten by whatever files are synched. If you uncheck it, Dreamweaver will warn you of the risks.

Check the box for Automatically Upload Files to the Server on Save to bypass manually synching your files. Note, however, that because you overwrite files when you transfer them from the local site to the remote site, you must be careful.

Enabling Check In/Check Out

You use the Check In/Check Out tools in Dreamweaver to make sure that only one person is working on a file at a time. When you have a file checked out, no one else can check out that file until you check it in, just like when you have a book checked out from the library.

When you turn on Enable File Check-Out, options that enable you to configure this feature appear (shown in Figure 23.8). Enter a name and an email address so that others accessing the remote site can see who has the file checked out. They'll be able to click your name and send you an email message about the file you have checked out.

When you check out a file from the remote site, Dreamweaver retrieves a copy of that file from the remote server to ensure that you have the most up-to-date version of the file in your local site. When Dreamweaver gets the file, it overwrites the file that exists on your local drive. The file has a green check mark beside it in your local site, as shown in Figure 23.9, showing that you currently have that file checked out. The checked-out file appears to Dreamweaver users with your name beside it on the remote server, signaling to your collaborators that you have the file checked out.

Transferring Files

When you check in a file to the remote site, Dreamweaver transfers the file back to the remote server to make it available for others to work on or view. Your name no longer appears beside the file's name.

Check In/Check Out is designed to help you manage a collaborative environment. The Check Out procedure forces you to download the most recent version of the file. While you have the file checked out, others cannot work on it. You can open the file after you check it in, but you cannot save any changes because Dreamweaver marks it as read-only.

Dreamweaver enables you to circumvent some of the Check In/Check Out safeguards. You can, for instance, override somebody else's checked-out file and check it out yourself. You can also turn off the read-only attribute of a file and edit it without checking it out. However, why would you want to do any of these things? Dreamweaver's Check In/Check Out process is fine for a small environment where you don't expect mischief. If you need tighter security and version control, you need to turn to Subversion, a more powerful version control system supported by Dreamweaver.

NOTE

Dreamweaver's Locking Mechanism

Dreamweaver creates a file on the remote server with the .1ck (for *lock*) file extension. This file contains the name of the person who has checked out the file. You don't need to worry about creating these .1ck files, but I mention them because you might get questions about these files from others who examine the remote site without Dreamweaver.

TIP

Don't Leave Without Checking Your Files In!

Remember to check in files when you are finished with them! Don't go on vacation with a bunch of files checked out if you want your co-workers to happily welcome you back when you return.

TIP

Everyone on the Team Needs to Use Check In/Check Out

Your project works more smoothly if everyone collaborating on the project turns on the Check In/Check Out functionality for the site. Otherwise, it's too easy to overwrite a file that someone else updated. Check In/Check Out works only if everyone on the team uses Dreamweaver and enables the Check In/Check Out functionality.

TIP

The Synchronize Command

To get only the files that are more recent than the files on the local site onto the remote site, you use the Synchronize command, which we discuss in Hour 24.

You can still use Get and Put when you have Check In/Check Out enabled. The Get command moves a file from the remote server and overwrites the local file. The file is read-only on your local machine because you won't have it checked out. If you try to put a file that someone has checked out onto the remote server, Dreamweaver warns you that changes to the remote copy of the file might be lost if you go ahead and transfer the file. You can choose to do the action anyway or cancel it.

To get or put files, first make sure that you select the correct site in the Site drop-down menu of the Files panel or the Site window. If you access your site via FTP, click the Connect button. If you have already connected or are accessing the files on a LAN, skip this step.

▼ TRY IT YOURSELF

Getting or Checking Out Files

TIP

Don't Transfer Dependent Files Multiple Times

Continually getting and putting dependent files slows down your transfers. Image files are usually much larger than HTML files and take longer to transfer. If the files haven't changed, you don't need to transfer them.

To get or check out files, follow these steps:

1. Select the files you want to transfer to your local site. You can also select an entire folder to transfer all of its contents.

2. Click the Get command, or click the Check Out command if you have Check In/Check Out enabled for this site.

3. Dreamweaver might display a dialog box, asking whether you would also like to download dependent files. **Dependent files** are images and other assets that are linked to the files you are transferring. You can disable this dialog box by checking the Don't Ask Me Again check box. I prefer to transfer the asset files manually instead of having Dreamweaver transfer them automatically.

▼ TRY IT YOURSELF

Putting or Checking In Files

To put or check in files, follow these steps:

1. Select the files you want to transfer to the remote site.

2. Click the Put command, or click the Check In command if you have Check In/Check Out enabled for this site and have checked out the selected file. If you transfer a file that is currently open, Dreamweaver prompts you to save the file before you put it on the remote site.

3. Dreamweaver might display a dialog box, asking whether you would also like to upload dependent files. You can disable this dialog box by checking the Don't Ask Me Again check box.

TIP

Dreamweaver and Content Management

Check In and Check Out are tools that were created for website developers. After a website is launched, maintaining the content is a task better suited for Adobe Contribute, which is a kind of content management option that works with Dreamweaver templates. You can find out more about these systems in Hour 14, "Using Site Assets, Library Items, and Templates."

Importing an Existing Website

When a website already exists at a remote site, you have to define the website in Dreamweaver, connect to the remote site, and download all the files in the site to work on it. Remember, you can edit only files that are located on your own machine. You can download and edit an existing site even if Dreamweaver wasn't involved in the site's creation.

Downloading a site for the first time might take some time, depending on how you are accessing the site and what your network connection speed is. After you initially download all the files, however, you should need only to download any files that change.

To import an existing website, all you have to do is mirror the existing site on your local drive. There is no conversion process, and the files remain unchanged in Dreamweaver.

> **TRY IT YOURSELF ▼**
>
> **Importing an Existing Website**

To import an existing website, follow these steps:

1. Set up both your local and remote info in the Site Definition dialog box. You should use a local directory that is empty.

2. Connect to the remote site using the Connect/Disconnect button in the Files panel.

3. Select the top entry in the remote site of the Files panel, selecting the entire site. If you select a file instead, you get only that file and not the entire site.

4. Click the Get button to transfer all the files on the remote site to your local site. You are asked whether or not you are sure you want to get the entire site. Answer "Yes," and the transfer completes.

You can also import and export a site definition, either to share with others or to back up your site definition. To do this, select Export from the Manage Sites dialog box (Site, Manage Sites). You can choose to either back up your site definition (saving your login, password, and local path information), or share the site definition with other users (without the personal information). Dreamweaver saves the file with the .ste extension. Select the Import command from the Manage Sites dialog box to import the site definition contained in the .ste file.

Subversion Version Control

As mentioned above, Subversion is more powerful version control that enables multiple users to work on a project, make changes, and safely combine those changes back together. It can also revert files to previous versions and display a full history of what has changed in a file over time. Unfortunately, Subversion is also a very complicated topic that requires a Subversion server, so we can only touch on the basics here.

Note that Subversion replaces the check in/checkout features enabled in Dreamweaver. You can't turn on a Subversion access without disabling check-in/check-out. Dreamweaver prompts you before making this change.

Understanding Subversion

Subversion works based on the idea that there is a central source code repository that all developers tie into. This repository exists on the Subversions server and is *not* located on your web server. Each developer downloads his or her own copy of the source code from the repository, called a *working copy*—this is your local copy of the site. As you make changes to the working copy, you *commit* them back to the Subversion repository, noting what has changed. Your fellow developers do the same. This builds a central location with all the latest changes and a full history of what everyone has done. You can easily retrieve and integrate your collaborators' changes into your own working copy automatically.

When you have a *working copy* that is ready for production, you transfer it to the remote server, just as you normally would.

Subversion is a unique system in that it allows developers to work on the same files at the same time, then attempts to combine the changes in a meaningful way when they are committed back to the Subversion repository. If this doesn't work for your group, you can even use a more traditional "check-in/check-out" method to prevent other users from making changes to files in the central repository. Unlike in Dreamweaver, you can't just override these settings because they're controlled by a central server.

Getting Started with Subversion

To get started with Subversion, you first need to establish a Subversion server and a repository for the project you are working on. You may want to check out "beanstalk"—which offers a low-cost Subversion repository and a simple interface for setting it up: http://beanstalkapp.com/. Another option is Dreamhost.com, which provides Dreamweaver compatible hosting and Subversion support for a reasonable monthly price.

After your server and repository are established, you need to open the Version Control category within the Advanced site settings, as shown in Figure 23.10.

FIGURE 23.10
Configure the Subversion repository for a project.

You need to check with your Subversion provider for all the correct protocol and path settings—these can vary greatly between implementations. After you have the information you need entered, click Test to verify that the repository can be found.

After you've connected to your repository, a Repository button becomes active. This button, when clicked, shows all the files in the central Subversion repository. You can select the files to move into your working copy, then use Get, Put, Check In, and Check Out to work with the files just as you would on any other server.

As you make changes to the files locally, you'll see symbols superimposed over the file icons in the Files panel. A plus symbol indicates that a new local file has been detected and should be transferred to the Subversion repository. A check mark shows that you've changed the file locally and need to commit it to the repository.

TIP

Version Control for Free!

Because the Subversion software itself is free (http://subversion.tigris.org/), there's nothing preventing even the smallest shops from using the technology. For a full picture of the software's capabilities, I urge you to read through the free online Subversion book at http://svnbook.red-bean.com/.

To send (commit) a file (or files) to the repository, just select it in the File panel, make sure the repository is also selected, and then click the Put button. You are prompted for a comment to post along with the files—this is tracked in the revision history.

To view the revision history, just right-click in the local files pane of the Files panel and choose Version Control, Show Revisions from the context menu. From this window you can even select a previous revision of your source code and click the Promote to Current button to revert to the state of the project at that time.

Summary

In this hour, you learned how to connect to a remote site and transfer files. You learned how to use the Server settings of the Site Setup dialog box and how to set up FTP, SFTP, local/network, WebDAV, and RDS connections. You also learned how to use Dreamweaver's internal file management feature, Check In/Check Out. You also learned about Subversion and how it can create a more managed and distributed development environment.

Q&A

Q. When is it appropriate to use Check In/Check Out?

A. There are two major uses for Check In/Check Out: for working in a small group and for working on a site from two computers. Check In/Check Out isn't designed for use by enterprise-type projects (those with many developers), but it is perfect for a small group of developers working on the same sites. I use it all the time when I work on a site with two computers (home and work computers, for instance). It helps me know whether I have uploaded my changes.

Q. I enabled Check-In/Check-Out, but the icon for Check In Files is inactive in the Files panel. What did I do wrong?

A. Dreamweaver tracks which files you have checked out. You can only check in a file that you have checked out. Make sure you have selected a file you have checked out, marked with a small check mark next to the file name.

Q. One of my co-workers left for a two-week vacation with a bunch of files checked out in his name. How can I work on these files while he is gone?

A. When you attempt to check out the files, Dreamweaver warns you that someone else has them checked out. It then asks you to override your co-worker's checkout. If you click the Yes button, Dreamweaver checks the files out to you. Just hope that your co-worker hasn't made any changes to the files and forgotten to move them onto the remote site.

Workshop

Quiz

1. When you're working in a collaborative environment and using FTP, it doesn't matter if everyone is using Dreamweaver's Check In/Check Out functionality. True or false?

2. Why do you have to define a remote site for a website?

3. What is Dreamweaver's most useful tool for troubleshooting a connection to a remote site via FTP?

Quiz Answers

1. False. It's too easy for one member of your group to overwrite the work of another member if not everyone is using the Check In/Check Out functionality. The only time you don't need to use this functionality when working with a group is when you are using a third-party program to manage version control.

2. To put website files on a public server or share files with a group, you have to define a remote site in Dreamweaver.

3. Dreamweaver's most useful tool in this situation is the FTP log. The FTP Log tab in the Results panel enables you to read the error messages sent back by the server. Alternatively, you can select the View Site FTP Log button in the Expanded Files panel.

Exercises

1. Define a remote site connection, using either the FTP setting or the Local/Network setting. If you don't have access to a remote computer, create a directory on your hard drive and name it **remote**. Pretend that this is a directory on a LAN and define it as a remote site. Try transferring files back and forth between the local and remote sites.

2. Turn on Check In/Check Out functionality for a defined site and connect to the remote site. What changes in Dreamweaver?

Maintaining a Website

Dreamweaver has various useful commands that can help you make sitewide changes and keep your site updated. In this hour, you use commands that are very powerful and can save you time. You should be careful when changing items sitewide in case you make a mistake. But, of course, you could just fix such a mistake sitewide, too!

Dreamweaver also has some built-in features for collaborating on web projects and communicating with your team members or clients. This hour looks at design notes and screen sharing built into Dreamweaver to help your project run smoothly.

Managing the Local and Remote Sites

Let's get started by exploring the features for managing the site files that are stored on your computer (local), as well as the files on your web server (remote).

The commands that you apply to an entire site (such as the commands to transfer files) are available from the menus in the expanded Files panel. The expanded Files panel showing both the local and the remote sites has File, Edit, View, and Site menus in the menu bar, as shown in Figure 24.1.

Synchronizing Your Files on the Local and Remote Sites

Synchronizing your files on the local and remote sites ensures that you have the most up-to-date files in both places. Dreamweaver has three commands that are useful in determining which site has the newer files: Select Newer Local, Select Newer on Remote Server, and Synchronize.

WHAT YOU'LL LEARN IN THIS HOUR:

- ▶ How to synchronize files on local and remote sites
- ▶ How to manage links
- ▶ How to use and save Dreamweaver searches
- ▶ How to add design notes to document your project and share ideas with others
- ▶ How to share your screen via a web browser through Dreamweaver's built-in Adobe ConnectNow feature
- ▶ How to generate reports about a website

If you want to check whether new files reside on the local site or the remote site, use the Select Newer Local and Select Newer Remote commands, respectively, from the Edit menu in the Files panel.

FIGURE 24.1
The Files panel menu gives you access to commands.

Finding Updated Files on a Remote Server

To see which files are newer on the remote site, follow these steps:

1. Connect to the remote site by clicking the Connect button at the top of the Files panel (F8) if you are using FTP to access the remote site.

2. Select either the root directory or a section of files in the local site.

3. Select Edit, Select Newer on Remote Server from the Edit menu.

Dreamweaver searches the files on the remote site to see whether any are newer than the same files on the local site. It then selects all the files that are newer on the remote site. If files that don't exist on the local site exist on the remote site, Dreamweaver selects those, too. With all the files selected, you simply get the files from the remote site to update your local files. To select files that are newer on the local site, you follow the same steps, except you use the Select Newer Local command in step 3.

You select the Synchronize command under the Site menu to automatically synchronize files between the local and the remote sites, bringing both sites up to date with the most recent files. When you synchronize files, Dreamweaver analyzes the files on both the local and the remote sites and gives you a report on which files it has to copy to synchronize the sites. You have total control over the process and can deselect any files you do not want transferred. Dreamweaver also tells you whether files are completely up to date and whether there is a need to synchronize.

To use the Synchronize command, you must have enabled Maintain Synchronization Information in the Advanced settings for the Servers section of each remote server you configure, as shown in Figure 24.2.

FIGURE 24.2
The Maintain Synchronization Information check box manages synchronization data for the site.

NOTE

The Option to Cloak

Use Dreamweaver's Cloaking feature to prevent files or directories not used by the live website from synchronizing or uploading when you are transferring files. You enable and disable cloaking in the Site Setup dialog under Advanced Settings. (You can also, as a matter of policy, cloak files with specific file extensions, such as layered graphics, documents from photoshop (.psd), or other working files. To cloak an individual folder or file, right-click on it in the Files panel and select Cloaking, Cloak. The folder or file icon appears in the site with a red line through it.

TRY IT YOURSELF ▼

Synchronizing Local and Remote Files

To synchronize the files in the local and remote sites, follow these steps:

1. Make sure that the site you want to synchronize is open in the Files panel. Select a different site from the Site drop-down menu if necessary.

2. If you want to synchronize only certain files or folders, select those files or folders.

3. Select Site, Synchronize from the Site menu. The Synchronize Files dialog box appears, as shown in Figure 24.3.

4. In the Synchronize drop-down menu, choose to synchronize the entire site or only the files you have selected.

Synchronizing Local and Remote Files
Continued

FIGURE 24.3
The Synchronize Files dialog box enables you to select which files to synchronize.

5. Select how you want to transfer the files in the Direction drop-down menu. You can transfer the newer files to the remote site, get the newer files from the remote site, or get and put newer files in both directions.

TIP

Synchronize When Collaborating

Because I often collaborate with groups of people on websites, I am usually interested in which files are newer on the remote site. Others on the team might have changed files and uploaded them while I was doing something else. I like to make sure that I'm looking at the most recent files in the project by synchronizing to get the newer files from the remote site.

6. Check the Delete Local Files Not on Remote Server check box if you want to get rid of any extraneous local files or the Delete Remote Files Not on Local Drive check box if there are extraneous files in the remote site. Careful! Someone else might have recently uploaded the files to the site.

7. Click the Preview button. If your files are up to date, you get a message saying no synchronization is necessary and asking whether you want to view a list of files to synchronize manually. Dreamweaver displays the Synchronize dialog box, shown in Figure 24.4, if files require synchronization. The Synchronize dialog box lists all the files that must be transferred for the local and remote sites to be in sync.

8. When you are ready to transfer the files, click OK.

CAUTION

Delete Files Carefully

Be very careful about checking the Delete Local Files Not on Remote Server check box because you don't want to delete files you need later. When you select this check box, you are deleting the files from your hard drive. If the files do not exist anywhere else, you can't restore them. Checking this box is a quick way to clean your local site of files that are not used.

FIGURE 24.4
The Synchronize dialog box lists the files to synchronize.

Several buttons at the bottom of the Synchronize dialog box enable you to modify the list of files to transfer. The following buttons help you fine-tune the synchronization process:

- ▶ **Get**—This command marks the file to be downloaded from the remote site to the local site.

- ▶ **Put**—This command marks the file to be uploaded from the local site to the remote site.

- ▶ **Delete**—This command marks the file to be deleted.

- ▶ **Ignore**—This command marks the file to be ignored by the synchronization process.

- ▶ **Mark Selected Files as Already Synchronized**—This command marks the file as already synchronized.

- ▶ **Compare**—This command opens the file in a file comparison utility. You specify a file comparison software program in the File Compare category of Preferences (Edit, Preferences).

While updating and editing files on a live website, you will probably use the Synchronize command many times. It's a quick and mechanical method of deciding which files have been updated and, therefore, you have to upload to the server. When you are collaborating with others, the Synchronize command is useful for helping you decide which files have been updated on the server and have to be updated on your local site. This saves you the trouble of downloading the entire site when only a few files have been updated.

Managing Your Links

Dreamweaver automatically updates links when you move or rename a file within the current website. When you define the website, make sure that you create a cache to speed up the update process. The cache is on by default, and it's best that you do not turn it off in your site definition. When you move or rename web files, Dreamweaver displays the Update Files dialog box. As shown in Figure 24.5, the dialog box displays a list of linked files. Click the Update button to update all the links or select individual files to update.

Use the Change Link Sitewide command located under the Site menu to change the URL of a certain link throughout the site. For instance, if you issued a new catalog for a new year, you might replace previous links with the new file name. The Change Link Sitewide dialog box, shown in

Figure 24.6, enables you to enter the old link and then select the path for the new link.

FIGURE 24.5
When you move or rename web pages, the Update Files dialog box appears, allowing you to update all the links to that file.

FIGURE 24.5
When you move or rename web pages, the Update Files dialog box appears, allowing you to update all the links to that file.

FIGURE 24.6
Use the Change Link Sitewide command to change all the links to a certain web page.

CAUTION

An Orphan Might Not Be an Orphan

Dreamweaver might say a file is an orphan even if your site uses that file. The file might be referenced in a behavior, for instance, such as an image file used with the Swap Image behavior. I recommend moving orphan files to a separate folder and making sure nothing "breaks" before deleting them.

TIP

Save the Link Checker Report

You can save the report after running the Link Checker by clicking the Save Report button—the small floppy disk icon on the left side of the Results panel. Then you can easily refer to it as you fix any problems with your site.

You can use the Link Checker, shown in Figure 24.7, to check all the links in your site. To open the Link Checker, select Site, Check Links Sitewide from the Files panel. The Link Checker displays three categories: broken links, external links, and orphaned files. **External links** are links that Dreamweaver cannot check. **Orphaned files** are those that do not have any files linking to them.

FIGURE 24.7
The Link Checker displays broken links, external links, and orphaned files.

Broken links need to be fixed. Fortunately, Dreamweaver makes that easy. You just select the broken link displayed in the Results panel group, click the Browse icon, and navigate to the correct file to fix the link.

The Link Checker opens in the Results panel group, located directly below the Property inspector. You can hide the panel group by clicking the arrow to the left of the panel title (Results), or you can close the panel group by selecting the Close Panel Group command from the panel menu, the menu in the upper-right corner of the panel.

Using, Saving, and Sharing Searches

So far, we've looked at changing links and file names, but Dreamweaver also has powerful find and replace capabilities to help with other sitewide changes. The Find and Replace command is under the Edit menu and it launches the Find and Replace dialog box, shown in Figure 24.8. You can run a search on the current document, all open documents, a certain folder, or an entire current website. You can search the source code, search the text, or search for a specific tag by using the selections in the Search drop-down menu.

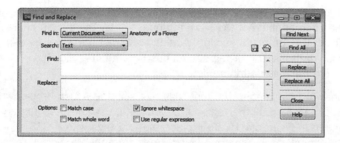

FIGURE 24.8
The Find and Replace dialog box enables you to search the source code, the text, or a specific tag and to focus on the current page, selected documents, specific folders, or the entire site.

To conduct searches, you enter a pattern of text or code into the Find text box. Click the Find button to find the next instance of the pattern or click the Find All button to display a list of all instances of the pattern, as shown in Figure 24.9. The Search panel of the Results panel group under the Property inspector displays the list.

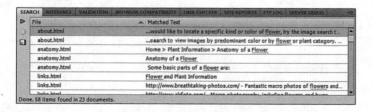

FIGURE 24.9
The Search panel displays the results of a Find All search.

The Text and Source Code search categories are self-explanatory: You search for text within the web page by using a Text search, and you search for code within Dreamweaver's Code view by using a Source Code search.

The Specific Tag search is a little more complicated, however. You use the Specific Tag search to find HTML tags in your code and modify the tag, modify an attribute of a tag, or strip the tag out of the code completely.

Using Search and Replace to Remove Font Tags

If you have old web pages, you might want to search your website for font tags because Cascading Style Sheets (CSS) styles, the more modern way of formatting page display, have replaced these tags and leaving them in place can create conflicting or inconsistent page designs. The following steps show how you can use a Specific Tag search to accomplish this task:

1. In the Find and Replace dialog box, set the scope of your search in the Find In drop-down menu.

2. Select Specific Tag from the Search drop-down menu.

3. Select Font from the list of tags directly to the right of the Search drop-down menu.

4. If you are looking for font tags with a specific attribute—for example, the face attribute or the size attribute—enter the search characteristics in the Attributes section. Add and subtract attributes by using the + and – buttons. If your tag search has no attribute, click the – button to delete the initial attribute listed.

5. Set what happens to the font tags by using the Action drop-down menu. To simply strip all the tags out of your site, use the Strip Tag action, as shown in Figure 24.10. To replace the font tags with a CSS style, use the Change Tag action and select Span from the drop-down menu to the right.

FIGURE 24.10
Select the replacement tag when doing a Specific Tag search.

Find Before You Replace

Never click the Replace or Replace All button before confirming that your search returns the correct findings by using the Find Next or Find All buttons.

6. Click the Find All button to display all the search findings.

7. Fine-tune your search by selecting the Find and Replace command again. Dreamweaver retains your search parameters. If your search returns the correct findings, select the Replace command or the Replace All command.

TRY IT YOURSELF ▼

Using Search and Replace to Remove Font Tags

Continued

8. In the Search panel, double-click each of the entries to apply a CSS style to the selection.

TIP

Search for Text Within Tags

Use the Text (Advanced) Find and Replace commands to search for text within specific HTML tags.

If you've created a complicated search that you want to reuse later or share with others, you can save the search as a Dreamweaver query file. To do this, click the Save Query button to save the current query in the Find and Replace dialog box. Dreamweaver prompts you to browse to a location and then save a file with the .dwr file extension. To load this query, click the Load Query button that looks like a file folder (refer to Figure 24.10). You can share these .dwr files with others so that they can run the query, too.

TIP

Recording Commands

Dreamweaver enables you to record a step or set of steps as Commands, which helps you to repeat a complicated process automatically. (Dreamweaver keeps you from recording steps that are not reproducible by Dreamweaver, such as selecting text on the page.) One method is to record a set of steps as you perform them by selecting Commands, Start Recording from the menu, continuing your actions as normal, and choosing Commands, Stop Recording when done. To apply the steps, select a suitable object and choose Commands, Play Recorded Command. Dreamweaver can record only a single set of steps in this way. When you record a new set of steps, it replaces the previous set.

If you want to save the recorded command to use after you shut down Dreamweaver, select Commands, Play Recorded Command. Right-click the final Run Command step in the History panel, and choose Save as Command. Saved commands appear at the bottom of the Commands menu so you can reuse them. Select Commands, Edit Command List to rename or delete an existing command.

Adding Design Notes to Pages

Design notes enable you to add notes to your web pages. You can use design notes to document your design process, share information with others, and keep any extra information that would be useful. Because design notes are not actually part of the web page, you can use them to record sensitive information you might not want people who view the web page to be able to read.

You can add a design note to any file in a website, including templates, images, and movies. You might want to add a design note to each image to list the name and location of the original image file. To add design notes to files in your site, you must enable design notes in the Design Notes category of the Advanced Settings section of the Site Setup dialog box, as shown in Figure 24.11. Edit the site definition by double-clicking the site name in the Site drop-down menu of the Files panel.

FIGURE 24.11
Enable design notes in the Design Notes category of the Site Definition dialog box.

▼ TRY IT YOURSELF

Adding a Design Note to a File

To attach a design note to a file, follow these steps:

1. When a file is open in the Document window, select File, Design Notes. Alternatively, you can right-click a file in the Files panel and select the Design Notes command.

2. The Design Notes dialog box appears, as shown in Figure 24.12. Select the type of design note you want from the Status drop-down menu.

3. Click the Date icon to insert today's date in the Notes field. Type a note in the field after the date.

4. Check the Show When File Is Opened check box if you want this design note to appear automatically the next time someone opens the file, as shown in Figure 24.13.

TRY IT YOURSELF ▼

Adding a Design Note to a File
Continued

FIGURE 24.12
You select the type of design note you want from the Status drop-down menu.

FIGURE 24.13
Design notes can be set to open automatically when a file is opened to prompt the viewer's action.

TIP

Record the Author

When you are in a collaborative environment, a useful name and value data pair to add to a design note is the name of the author of the note. To do this, you select the All Info tab in the Design Notes dialog box and click the + button. Name your new record **Name** and enter your name in the Value field.

FIGURE 24.14
You can add data to design notes by selecting the All Info tab.

5. Select the All Info tab in the Design Notes dialog box to see a list of the information in the current design note, as shown in Figure 24.14. Add a record to the list by clicking the + button, entering a name, and entering a value.

6. When you are done making changes in this dialog box, click OK.

Contribute Uses Design Notes

Adobe Contribute, a companion product to Dreamweaver, uses design notes to facilitate tracking revisions to a file. If you are working in an environment where some users are using Contribute, don't delete or modify any of the design notes Contribute has created.

A design note remains associated with a file even if it is copied, renamed, moved, or deleted. Dreamweaver saves your design notes in a directory called notes in your site root. This directory doesn't appear in the Site window. Notes are saved with the name of the file plus the .mno extension.

Sharing Your Screen with Adobe ConnectNow

When collaborating on projects, Dreamweaver offers the ability to share your screen with up to two other computers over the Web by using Adobe ConnectNow. Launch the feature by selecting File, Share My Screen from the menu. Your preferred web browser opens. You must login with an Adobe ID to continue.

When connected to Adobe ConnectNow, a special window opens (you may have to approve an add-in to enable this window). Click Share My Computer Screen and then choose whether to share your desktop or to check items from a list of specific windows or applications related to your web project (mostly Adobe products). After choosing settings, click Share, then Go to My Meeting Room. Onscreen instructions explain your options for sending invitations to participants.

The ConnectNow Screen Sharing panel, shown in figure 24.15, floats over your regular screen to give you (the presenter) access to tools to stop sharing, view attendee, chat with attendees, add share notes, use a webcam, or annotate the screen. Note that Stop Screen Sharing instantly ends the connection, without requiring a confirmation dialog box.

Participants who receive the invitation link can open a session in their web browsers, as shown in Figure 24.16. Like the presenter, they can chat, add shared notes, and view webcam video. Additionally, a control strip gives options to zoom, toggle full screen, follow the presenter's mouse, or request control of the user's computer. If the presenter grants permissions for a participant to control the presenter's computer, a note about who is controlling the screen appears and the remote attendee has full access to onscreen menus and panels to make changes.

FIGURE 24.15
Use the ConnectNow presenter controls to communicate with participants or to stop screen sharing.

FIGURE 24.16
The participant view includes a control strip for interacting with the screen as well as collaboration tools for communication with other participants.

Generating Reports About a Website

The reports that come with Dreamweaver enable you to compile information about your site, such as when files were created or what errors you've found in your site. These reports are useful for examining, troubleshooting, and documenting your website. You can also save and print the results of the reports. The following reports are available in Dreamweaver:

- ▶ Checked Out By
- ▶ Design Notes
- ▶ Recently Modified
- ▶ Combinable Nested Font Tags
- ▶ Missing Alt Text
- ▶ Redundant Nested Tags
- ▶ Removable Empty Tags
- ▶ Untitled Documents

Running a Website Report

FIGURE 24.17
Many reports are available to give you information about either your current document or an entire site.

To run a report, follow these steps:

1. Select Site, Reports (in either the Files panel or the menu bar). The Reports dialog box appears, as shown in Figure 24.17.

2. Select what you want to report on (the current document, the current site, the selected files, or a particular folder).

3. Select one or more of the reports. Some reports have additional settings you can make to refine the search. If the Report Settings button is active at the bottom of the dialog box, additional settings are available for that report.

4. Click the Run button to run the report.

5. A Results panel group appears with a list of files. You can save this report as well as open the individual files that it references.

Summary

In this hour, you learned how to synchronize files between local and remote sites and how to manage links in a website. You also learned how to create site maps that visually represent the relationship between the files in a website. You also learned how to use the Find and Replace command and how to save a custom query to reuse or share with others. You also learned how to add design notes to capture extra information about files in a website and how to share your screen with remote participants. Finally, you learned how to run reports on a website to monitor workflow in a project or to look for common file errors. These skills are important when you need to manage websites and all the files they contain.

Q&A

Q. Am I really going to goof up my files if I use the Synchronize command?

A. Using Synchronize can be a little scary. You might want to run the Select Newer Local and the Select Newer Remote commands first. Jot down the filenames that Dreamweaver selects. Then, when you run Synchronize, check to see whether that command comes up with the same filenames. This should reassure you that you can confidently use the Synchronize command in the future!

Q. Why does Dreamweaver list some of my files as orphaned files when they really aren't?

A. Dreamweaver checks whether files link to other files. However, behaviors might use the files that Dreamweaver lists as orphaned. For instance, you might have a web page loaded with the Open Browser Window behavior. Because the file is not actually linked to another file, Dreamweaver shows it as orphaned.

Q. Dreamweaver's Share My Screen feature only lets me invite two participants. What if I need to share my screen with more than two other people?

A. There are many commercial products and services for screen sharing, including a pro version of the tool included in Dreamweaver called Adobe Connect that you can purchase to do screen sharing. Visit http://www.adobe.com/products/acrobatconnectpro/ for details.

Workshop

Quiz

1. How can you tell which images in your entire site are missing alt text?

2. Dreamweaver can attach a design note to any file in a website, whether it's a web page or another type of file. True or false?

3. What are the four searches you can do in the Find and Replace dialog box?

Quiz Answers

1. Run the Missing Alt Text report on the entire site.

2. True. Dreamweaver can attach a design note to any file in a website.

3. You can do these searches in the Find and Replace dialog box: Source Code, Text, Text (Advanced), and Specific Tag.

Exercises

1. Run the Link Checker on a site you created or imported. Do you have any broken links? If so, fix them. Do you have any orphaned files? If you no longer need those files, delete them. If your site has external links, you should periodically check to verify that they are still valid.

2. Use the Find and Replace command to search for a specific tag in your website. Click the Find All button to view the Search panel. Save the query to your hard drive.

3. Create an Adobe ID and give the Share My Screen feature a try. Invite some friends to help you edit one of your Dreamweaver pages.

INDEX

FREE Online Edition

Your purchase of **Sams Teach Yourself Dreamweaver CS5 in 24 Hours** includes access to a free online edition for 45 days through the Safari Books Online subscription service. Nearly every Sams book is available online through Safari Books Online, along with more than 5,000 other technical books and videos from publishers such as Addison-Wesley Professional, Cisco Press, Exam Cram, IBM Press, O'Reilly, Prentice Hall, and Que.

SAFARI BOOKS ONLINE allows you to search for a specific answer, cut and paste code, download chapters, and stay current with emerging technologies.

Activate your FREE Online Edition at www.informit.com/safarifree

> **STEP 1:** Enter the coupon code: HYBVNCB.

> **STEP 2:** New Safari users, complete the brief registration form. Safari subscribers, just log in.

If you have difficulty registering on Safari or accessing the online edition, please e-mail customer-service@safaribooksonline.com